# Arguments and Agreement

# Arguments and Agreement

Edited by
PETER ACKEMA, PATRICK BRANDT,
MAAIKE SCHOORLEMMER, AND
FRED WEERMAN

OXFORD
UNIVERSITY PRESS

# OXFORD
UNIVERSITY PRESS

Great Clarendon Street, Oxford OX2 6DP

Oxford University Press is a department of the University of Oxford.
It furthers the University's objective of excellence in research, scholarship,
and education by publishing worldwide in

Oxford New York

Auckland Cape Town Dar es Salaam Hong Kong Karachi
Kuala Lumpur Madrid Melbourne Mexico City Nairobi
New Delhi Shanghai Taipei Toronto

With offices in

Argentina Austria Brazil Chile Czech Republic France Greece
Guatemala Hungary Italy Japan Poland Portugal Singapore
South Korea Switzerland Thailand Turkey Ukraine Vietnam

Oxford is a registered trade mark of Oxford University Press
in the UK and in certain other countries

Published in the United States
by Oxford University Press Inc., New York

British Library Cataloguing in Publication Data
Data available

Library of Congress Cataloguing in Publication Data
Data available

Typeset by SPI Publisher Services, Pondicherry, India
Printed in Great Britain
on acid-free paper by
Biddles Ltd. www.Biddles.co.uk

ISBN 019–928573–x   978–019–928573–0

1 3 5 7 9 10 8 6 4 2

# Contents

# Acknowledgements

This book is an offshoot of a workshop ('The Role of Agreement in Argument Structure') we organized at Utrecht University in August–September 2001. Although the present volume is only indirectly related to that event, we would still like to thank the following organizations, which helped make it possible: The Netherlands Organization for Scientific Research (NWO), The Royal Dutch Academy of Sciences, and the Utrecht Institute of Linguistics (OTS). We are grateful to all contributors to this volume for their enthusiastic cooperation and patience during the editing period. Many thanks as well to all our colleagues who helped us by reviewing the contributions, including the reviewers for OUP. Finally, a big thank you to Felipe Méndez Alvarado, Nina Schreiber, and Martin Urban for their help in the preparation of the manuscript and in compiling the index.

P.A.
P.B.
M.S.
F.W.

# 1

# The Role of Agreement in the Expression of Arguments

PETER ACKEMA, PATRICK BRANDT, MAAIKE
SCHOORLEMMER, AND FRED WEERMAN

## 1.1 Introduction

Agreement is the linguistic phenomenon in which particular features of one element in a clause (the 'controller') determine the morphological shape of another element (the 'target'). Agreement comes in many forms: there are many elements that can act as the controller and target in an agreement relation, and there is also considerable cross-linguistic variation in the amount and types of features for which agreement relations can be established (see Corbett 1994 for an overview).

There is a further dimension to cross-linguistic variation in agreement, which concerns the 'richness' of agreement morphology that languages employ to express a particular agreement relation. Agreement between the person and number features of the subject of a sentence (the controller) and the finite verb (the target) is one of the best-known instances of agreement. Many languages show this agreement relation. However, not all these languages show the same amount of variation in the form of the verb. Consider languages that distinguish three distinct persons and two distinct numbers for nouns. This gives six possible feature combinations for person and number. In some languages, every one of these different feature combinations in the subject results in a different form for the finite verb, as, for example, in Italian, illustrated by (1a) below. Other languages that show subject–verb agreement as such may not have distinct forms of the verb for each of the different person and number combinations in the subject. An example of this is English (see (2a) below). Italian can thus be said to have a rich inflectional paradigm for person and number agreement (or rich agreement morphology), while

English has poor agreement morphology, which abounds in syncretism (one form expressing multiple combinations of features).

It is a classic observation that languages with rich inflectional morphology for person and number allow certain arguments of the verb to remain unexpressed syntactically rather easily. Italian, which has a rich subject agreement paradigm, as illustrated for the verb *credere* 'to believe' in (1a), allows the subject to remain unexpressed syntactically, as in (1b). English, on the other hand, with its poor agreement paradigm, requires the subject to be present, as in (2b).

(1)  a. credere 'to believe'

|   | Sing. | Pl. |
|---|-------|-----|
| 1 | credo | crediamo |
| 2 | credi | credete |
| 3 | crede | credono |

  b. credo
   'I believe'

(2)  a.

|   | Sing. | Pl. |
|---|-------|-----|
| 1 | believe | believe |
| 2 | believe | believe |
| 3 | believes | believe |

  b. *(I) believe

A common term to refer to the phenomenon of not realizing an argument syntactically is 'pro-drop', the name given to it in Government and Binding (GB) Theory (Chomsky 1981). This name reflects the GB-analysis of the phenomenon. Since the Italian sentence in (1b) has the same meaning as the English one in (2b), it was argued that in cases of apparent subject drop there is in fact a syntactic subject present that realizes the argument in question, only this constituent does not have phonological content (it is 'dropped', as it were). In other words, an empty pronoun called 'pro' is supposed to be present in these cases.

So-called polysynthetic languages also show a relation between rich agreement and lack of (overt) syntactic expression of arguments, on an even larger scale. Verbs in these languages show rich inflectional morphology, expressing person and number features not only of subjects but also of objects. At the same time, the arguments of the verb need not be expressed by any syntactic constituent (compare Jelinek 1984). The polysynthetic languages are nevertheless usually seen as fundamentally different from pro-drop languages like Italian. Their syntax is considered completely 'non-configurational', in the sense that specific syntactic positions for specific syntactic constituents do not seem to exist. It seems that any noun phrase can be placed anywhere in the clause. It is even possible to split up a noun phrase and scatter its parts across the clause. Italian has much stricter restrictions on the placement of nominal constituents, its behaviour resembling a strictly configurational language like English in this respect.

Although the differences between pro-drop languages and polysynthetic languages are real, it would be rather unexpected if the ability to leave out an argument from syntax in the presence of rich inflection were not fundamentally the same phenomenon in both types of language. The question is then how this similarity can be captured, without obliterating the differences between the various types of language.

In generative syntactic theorizing, a popular way of accounting for language variation is in terms of so-called parameters. The idea is that there is a common scheme underlying all grammars of natural languages (Universal Grammar). Within this scheme, there are well-defined options for filling in a certain part of the scheme. These options are called parameters. The classical view on parameters is that they are all what one may call 'macroparameters': they have two values, and languages are divided into two classes according to the two possible values. Such a macroparameter has been proposed both for pro-drop and for polysynthesis. For instance, Mohawk and Navajo (two non-configurational languages) take the positive value of the parameter that concerns polysynthesis, whereas Italian and English take the negative value. Italian and English differ, however, with respect to the pro-drop parameter. Here, English takes the negative value and Italian the positive one.

In terms of parameter theory, accounting for the similarities and differences between pro-drop languages and polysynthetic languages involves establishing whether there is a macroparameter that sets polysynthetic languages apart from all other languages. If the non-syntactic expression of arguments in polysynthetic languages is determined by a positive setting of such a macroparameter, then the non-syntactic expression of a subject in a pro-drop language with the negative value for this parameter must be seen as a different process.

A similar question arises in connection with the pro-drop parameter. If there is a macroparameter that determines whether a language allows pro-drop or not, in a language that does not usually allow its subjects to be dropped we do not expect *any* pro-drop phenomena. Hence, any cases of non-syntactic expression of arguments in such a language must be regarded as fundamentally different from what happens in a pro-drop language.

The choice for one or the other value of a parameter is made by the language-learning child on the basis of particular cues in the input, so-called triggers. Given the apparent correlation between rich inflection and argument-drop, an important trigger for a positive setting of both the pro-drop parameter and the polysynthesis parameter would appear to be the presence of rich inflection. If this were indeed a crucial factor, and if we are in fact dealing with macroparameters, this means that we expect empty arguments to occur freely in languages with rich inflection and not to occur at all in languages without. The question is whether this expectation is borne out, and, if not, how to deal with these unexpected cases.

All contributions to this volume centre around the questions introduced above, which can be summarized as follows: what determines whether one or more arguments need not be expressed syntactically, and to what extent is this related to the inflectional make-up of the language?

Our intention in this first chapter is to identify the problems with what might be called the classical view on the relation between empty arguments and inflection, and to indicate how the connection between argument drop in typologically distinct languages might be approached. Various aspects of the central problem that are discussed in detail in the contributions to this volume will come up in this discussion. Where appropriate, we will explicate how particular contributions relate to the problem at hand, so that this chapter also serves as an introduction to the rest of the volume. (An overview of all contributions is provided in the concluding section of this chapter.)

## 1.2 The pro-drop parameter and its problems

In GB theory it was assumed that arguments are always expressed syntactically. In cases of pro-drop an empty pronoun pro occupies the relevant argument position (see section 1.1). Of course, not all languages allow pro-drop, so it cannot be assumed that pro is freely available. Conditions on the occurrence of pro must therefore be imposed, and it is here that the connection with the verbal agreement paradigm of the language is supposed to play a crucial role.

An influential proposal concerning the conditions on pro-drop was put forward by Luigi Rizzi (see Rizzi 1982; 1986a). Rizzi suggested that pro is subject to two distinct types of licensing condition: the occurrence of an empty pronoun must be *formally* licensed, and the *content* of the empty element must be licensed. Formal licensing restricts the occurrence of pro to a particular syntactic position, or particular positions, in a language. According to Rizzi, there is an arbitrary list of heads in a language (drawn from the inventory of heads such as C, I, V, P, ... ) that license the occurrence of pro within their government domain.

If pro is formally allowed to occur, its content must also be licensed, or recoverable, if it is to be usable. This can be achieved by rich inflection: person and number affixes on the verb can identify the person and number features of pro, but only if each affix is uniquely specified for a particular person/ number feature set—in other words, if the paradigm shows no syncretism.

Since formal licensing and licensing for content are kept distinct, this theory can account for the situation that a language has rich inflection but does not allow pro-drop (a situation that does indeed occur—see, for instance, Speas (Chapter 2 below) and Poletto (Chapter 6)). In such cases, the inflection of the language is rich enough to identify the content of pro, but there happens to be no head in the language that formally licenses this element. The classic theory also predicts the reverse situation to be possible: pro may be formally licensed in a language, while the agreement inflection in the language is not rich enough to identify its content. In that case, pro could occur as long as it does not have any referential content. This has been argued to account for the situation in a language like Dutch, where the expletive subject in an impersonal construction like (3a) can be dropped, whereas a referential pronominal subject cannot be dropped (3b).

(3) a. Gisteren    werd    (er)    de    hele    dag    geoefend
       yesterday    was    (there)    the    whole    day    practised
       'People practised the whole day long yesterday'
    b. Gisteren    werd *(zij)    de    hele    dag    geïnterviewd
       yesterday    was    she    the    whole    day    interviewed
       'She was interviewed the whole day long yesterday'

This theory therefore successfully captures the basic data. However, several problems arise.

### 1.2.1 *The role of inflection in licensing pro*

A first problem has to do with the supposed role that inflection plays in licensing pro: the inflection has to be rich in order for pro to be licensed. Soon after the classic theory was put forward it became clear that this correlation was not entirely correct. Because of Huang's influential work (1984; 1989), Chinese has become a famous example of a language that, despite a complete lack of agreement morphology on its verbs, allows arguments to remain unexpressed in both subject and object position:

(4) (Ta) kanijian (ta) le
    (he) see (he) ASP
    'he saw him'

Apparently, it is no coincidence that Chinese lacks agreement morphology entirely. Jaeggli and Safir (1989a) hypothesized, on the basis of the literature available then, that a language allows pro-drop if either all or no cells in its agreement paradigm contain an affix. This is expressed by their Morphological Uniformity Condition:

(5)  *Morphological Uniformity Condition* (Jaeggli and Safir 1989a)
     Null Subjects are permitted in all and only those languages that
     have morphologically uniform inflectional paradigms.

An inflectional paradigm is morphologically uniform if it contains either only underived or only morphologically complex (affixed) forms. If correct, the condition in (5) has important consequences for the theory on formal licensing of pro as well as for the theory on how the content of pro is licensed.

With respect to the latter, (5) obviously implies that, next to rich agreement, there is apparently a second way in which the content of pro can be recovered. According to Huang, the empty argument can be bound by a zero topic operator, which takes the topic of the previous discourse as antecedent. Zwitserlood and Van Gijn (Chapter 7 below) argue that a similar analysis can account for the interpretation of empty arguments in Nederlandse Gebarentaal (sign language of the Netherlands).

If languages with no agreement can resort to this linking-to-topic strategy to recover pro's content, there is no reason why languages with poor agreement could not do so as well. Hence, the absence of pro-drop from the latter type of languages cannot be due to an inability to license the content of the empty pronoun, as originally thought, but must somehow follow from the theory on how this element is formally licensed. The challenge posed by (5), then, is why languages with a great deal of agreement morphology or no agreement morphology at all seem to license the occurrence of pro, whereas languages with poor agreement morphology do not.

This challenge is taken up by Speas (Chapter 2 below). Speas proposes that (5) follows from a general economy condition on phrase structure that, roughly, states that a phrase may only be projected if its head or specifier contains overt material. In languages with agreement morphology, this morphology must be checked in a spec-head configuration against the subject, and a phrase must be projected in which this configuration is established, say an AgrP (cf. Chomsky 1995). Following Rohrbacher (1999), Speas assumes that, in languages with rich agreement, the agreement affix is an independent lexical item, which can be inserted directly in the head of AgrP, thereby licensing this projection. In languages with poor agreement this is impossible, and projection of AgrP is licensed only if this phrase contains an overt subject in its specifier position. Hence, pro-drop is ruled out in this type of language. In languages without any agreement, no AgrP needs to be projected to provide the correct checking configuration for agreement, so that questions of how to license this projection do not arise in the first place. Therefore, subjects may be empty in languages without agreement.

Speas's result is made possible by an interesting shift in perspective on the licensing relation between agreement and subjects. It seems fair to say that the conventional view is that having overt subjects is the norm, and that something special has to happen in terms of licensing to be allowed to use empty subjects. In contrast, in a theory like that of Speas the possibility of having an empty subject may be said to be the default—subjects are obligatorily overt only if so required by poor morphology in order to license an AgrP. In other words, it is not rich agreement that licenses an empty subject, but rather an overt subject that licenses having poor agreement. If there is no agreement at all, the need to license it does not arise. Such a shifted perspective on the agreement–subject licensing relationship may account for the connection between the form of the agreement paradigm and the possibility of pro-drop, as has also been noted by Weerman (1989) and Davis (2002).

Note that this proposal is based on the idea that an inflectional paradigm is a linguistically real item: Speas follows Rohrbacher (1999) in assuming that the distinction between rich agreement and poor agreement is based on a property of the paradigm as a whole. The question of whether or not properties of paradigms play a role in determining pro-drop is an important issue in the light of the phenomenon discussed in the next subsection.

### 1.2.2 *Partial pro-drop*

In section 1.1 we noted that a classic (macroparametric) pro-drop parameter implies that a language either allows empty subjects or does not. On closer inspection, however, it seems that more fine-grained distinctions are required. In particular, in some languages pro-drop can be limited to certain person/number combinations only. Partial pro-drop of this type occurs, for example, in Finnish and Hebrew (where it is further limited to the past and future tenses); see Borer (1989), Vainikka and Levy (1999), Alexiadou (Ch. 5 below), Koeneman (Chapter 3 below). Thus, as the data in (6) (from Vainikka and Levy 1999: 614) illustrate, pro-drop in Finnish is possible for first and second person pronouns but not for third person ones.

(6)    a.   \*Nousi    junaan
          step-PAST/3SG train-into
          '(He/she) boarded the train'
    b.   Nousin    junaan
          step-PAST-1SG train-into
          'I boarded the train'

The phenomenon of partial pro-drop raises questions about the role that the notion of paradigm plays in the grammar. One may wonder whether paradigms are linguistically significant units as such, or whether they are just the sum of a number of spell-out rules that determine how particular individual feature bundles are realized in the language. (This does not mean that these rules should operate entirely independently of one another; two rules can stand in an elsewhere relation, for example, so that the more specific one blocks application of the more general one.) The view that properties of paradigms as a whole can play a role in determining the morphosyntactic make-up of a language has recently been challenged, in particular by authors working in the Distributed Morphology framework (see Halle and Marantz 1993; Bobaljik 2002; 2003). If the possibility of identifying the content of empty pro in general turns out to be a property of individual affixes (or, rather, individual feature bundles) rather than of paradigms as a whole, the case for the paradigm as a linguistically significant unit is weakened.

Interestingly, however, Koeneman (Chapter 3 below) actually argues that the possibility of partial pro-drop is directly connected to the form of some of the paradigms in the language. It is not an idiosyncratic property of some individual affixes that they happen to be able to identify pro, but, Koeneman argues, it is their connection to the pronominal paradigm of the language that licenses this. The inflectional paradigm in a partial pro-drop language is not rich enough to identify the content of pro. However, for certain persons the forms that realize the inflectional features are (more or less) identical to forms of the pronominal paradigm; see also Alexiadou (Chapter 5 below). The affixes that are linked to the pronominal paradigm in this way thereby acquire pronominal status themselves, and it is this that makes them eligible licensers of pro-drop. Toivonen (2001) provides a comparable account of DP-internal pro-drop of possessors in Finnish.

The question of how to account for the possibility of partial pro-drop is also addressed by Alexiadou. In general, Alexiadou relates the variation in pro-drop to alternative ways of satisfying the Extended Projection principle (EPP). The EPP is implemented by Chomsky (1995) as follows: there is a particular head in the functional structure of the clause that carries an uninterpretable nominal feature, which must be checked by a noun phrase. Alexiadou proposes that an alternative way to check this feature is to move a verb with special person marking to the head in question (see also Alexiadou and Anagnostopoulou 1998). In that case, the presence of a noun phrase checking this feature is superfluous, resulting in pro-drop. Depending on the occurrence of marked person morphology, argument-drop may be possible or not. If not, an overt subject must appear, satisfying the EPP. In support of the relevance of person morphology, Alexiadou shows that, in Hebrew and Finnish, pro-drop correlates with person marking on V, accounting for partial pro-drop. There are also cases from Italian supporting the hypothesis that person marking is crucial for pro-drop: in the present subjunctive, where the verb is not marked for person, it is necessary to have a second person singular pronoun expressing the subject.

### 1.2.3 *Asymmetric pro-drop*

Another phenomenon that shows that pro-drop cannot easily be accounted for in terms of a binary parameter is its restricted syntactic distribution in some languages. It is possible for pro to occur in a language only in certain syntactic positions. A position that seems to be particularly favoured in this respect is directly after a fronted finite verb. Thus, in standard Arabic, which allows both VSO and SVO orders, pro-drop is possible only in the former order (see Mohammad 1990; Plunkett 1993b; Ackema and Neeleman 2003). Similarly, Old French, which was a verb-second language, allows pro-drop only in V2 clauses with a sentence-initial constituent other than the subject (see (7a)), i.e. in clauses where an overt subject would occur immediately after the fronted verb (see Adams 1987b; Vance 1999). Sentence-initial subjects must not be dropped, as illustrated in (7b).

(7)    a.  Einsi corurent—par mer
           thus ran-3PLR by sea
           'Thus they ran by the sea'
       b.  *—corurent einsi par mer

This kind of 'asymmetric' pro-drop seems to involve a restriction on the formal licensing of pro rather than on content licensing. Indeed, Adams (1987) gives an account in terms of formal licensing. Nevertheless, Poletto (Chapter 6 below) shows that here, too, there can be differences between individual person/number combinations with respect to where they license a pro in the clause. Also, Poletto shows that even closely related languages can vary in this respect, by discussing the different diachronic developments in some Northern Italian dialects. Poletto's findings cast doubt on the possibility that asymmetric pro-drop of this sort can be handled by the same macroparameter that, according to the classical view, is supposed to distinguish languages that allow (subject) pro-drop across the board (like standard Italian) from languages that do not allow it at all (like English). Indeed, it renders doubtful the idea that asymmetric pro-drop can be handled by a macroparameter of this sort at all.

### 1.2.4 *Pro-drop and mood*

In languages with poor agreement, which according to Jaeggli and Safir's Morphological Uniformity Condition in (5) should not allow pro at all, empty subjects can nevertheless be allowed in specific syntactic constructions. Imperatives are a typical case. As discussed by Bennis (Chapter 4 below), in languages like Dutch and English, which do not allow pro-drop in indicative clauses even if they express an order (see (8a)), the subject of an imperative can or must nevertheless be left out. In this case the verb appears in an uninflected form (see (8b)). Interestingly, as discussed by Bennis, there are inflected imperative verb forms in Dutch as well, namely in plural or polite contexts—but in these cases the subject must be overt again (see (8c) and (8d)).

(8)  a. *(Jij) ruimt   nu   je   kamer op!
        you clean-2SG now your room PRT
        Go clean your room!
     b. Ruim (jij)   je   kamer op!
        clean (you) your room PRT
        Go clean your room!
     c. Ruimen   *(jullie)  nu   je   kamer eens op!
        clean-PLUR you-PLUR now your room once PRT
        Go and finally clean your room!
     d. Geeft   *(u)              mij   nu    m'n  geld      terug!
        Give    you (POLITE)   me    now   my   money    back
        You give me my money back now!

Bennis argues that the possibility of having an empty subject in an imperative is due to a unique property of these clauses, namely that their subject can only be second person. He assumes there is a functional head connected to Force located in the C-domain of the clause (cf. Rizzi 1997). In imperatives, in contrast to indicatives, this head must be specified as second person. Agreement with this uniquely specified head licenses pro's content. Bennis further argues that the absence of overt inflection on the verb follows from this analysis. Inflected imperative verbs are too overspecified to co-occur with pro: they are not only second person, but also polite (8c) or plural (8d). The general [2] feature in the Force head can still license a pro in these cases, but the verb cannot check off its [polite] or [plurality] feature by agreeing with pro, which is just [2]. Such checking is required, however, as the relevant features are uninterpretable on the verb (see Chomsky 1995).

The possibility of allowing pro in imperatives only might seem to challenge accounts of formal licensing of pro based on Morphological Uniformity (see

(5)), like that of Speas (Chapter 2 below). Note, however, that if we may regard the inflectional paradigms for indicative and 'core' imperatives as in (8b) as two distinct ones, rather than as one big verbal paradigm, the data appear to fit, and may even provide some evidence for (5). If there is no agreement at all in imperatives like (8b), this makes their paradigm of the 'Chinese' type, which, as we have seen above, licenses pro.

An interesting parallel with the distinction between indicatives and imperatives in Dutch and English can be found within the class of indicative clauses in Swahili. Apart from clauses with an overt subject and subject agreement on the verb, there are cases where the subject agreement on the verb is left out and the subject is empty (Ud Deen 2003). This is illustrated in (9).

(9)  a. *(Juma)   a    -li    -mw   -on   -a        Mariam
        *Juma*    $SA_{3s}$ *-past* *-OA_{3s}* *-see* *-indicative*   Mariam
        Juma saw Mariam.
     b. Ø   -ta   -ku   -pig   -a
        *fut* *-OA_{2s}* *-hit* *-IND*
        (I) will hit you.

According to Ud Deen, the subject is a null constant that is linked to the topic of the discourse in cases like (9b). His analysis of how the empty subject is content-licensed in these cases thus is similar to Huang's hypothesis about how pro can be interpreted in Chinese and to Zwitserlood and Van Gijn's analysis of dropped arguments in Nederlandse Gebarentaal (Chapter 7 below). The striking property of Swahili is that the use of agreement on finite (indicative) verbs seems to be optional. Hence, we might say, as in the case of imperatives versus indicatives in Dutch, that we must distinguish two paradigms that can be used with verbs in Swahili: one with various subject agreement affixes, and one without any. That the latter licenses pro-drop would then be in accordance with (5).

The proposals of Poletto and Bennis both avoid generalizations about what makes languages as a whole 'pro-drop' or 'non-pro-drop'. They talk about particular cases of zero argument licensing within languages, accounting for the fact that in particular sentence types only zero subjects are allowed. Thus, there seems to be little room for a classic 'pro-drop parameter' in these approaches.

### 1.2.5 *Pro-drop and the interpretation of pro*

As noted above, the classical theory of pro-drop predicts that there should be an implicational relationship between the possibility of referential pro-drop in a language (as in (1b), repeated in (10a)) and the possibility of expletive pro-drop (as in (3a), repeated here as (10b)). If a language allows referential pro-drop, it formally licenses pro, and its inflection is rich enough to identify the content of pro. In that case, it should also license expletive pro-drop, where only formal licensing of pro is required.

(10)    a.  credo
            I believe.
        b.  Gisteren werd (er) de hele dag geoefend
            yesterday was (there) the whole day practised
            People practised the whole day long yesterday.

The implicational relation between different types of pro-drop can be extended to include pro-drop of the subject of so-called weather predicates. Such subjects have been argued to fall between fully referential subjects (which receive a theta role of the verb) and expletives (which receive no theta role) in that they receive a so-called quasi-theta role. An example of such a subject is the non-referential pronoun that appears with English *rain*:

(11)    *(It) rains

In English, such a subject cannot be empty. There are, however, languages that make a distinction between referential subjects and subjects with a quasi-theta role with respect to the possibility of pro-drop. Thus, the subject of a Finnish weather predicate can be empty, whereas a third person referential pronoun such as *he* or *she* cannot be dropped (see section 1.2.2).

(12)    a.  Sataa.
            rains
            It is raining.
        b.  *(Hän) puhuu suomea
            she/he speaks Finnish

Rizzi (1986a) argued that, whereas a referential pronoun is fully specified for person and number features, quasi-argumental pronouns carry only a number feature. This means that when such pronouns are empty the agreement morphology on the verb needs to content-identify only a number feature rather than both number and person features. The following types of pro-drop result:

(1.13)   a.  referential pro-drop (pro has a full theta role)
         b.  quasi-argumental pro-drop (pro has a quasi-theta role)
         c.  expletive pro-drop (pro has no theta role)

Rizzi's theory of content licensing, coupled with the assumption that a quasi-argumental pronoun has fewer features than a pronoun with a full theta role, results in an implicational hierarchy of the three types of pro-drop in (13). If a language has (13a) it must have (13b, c) as well, and if it has (13b) it must have (13c), but, crucially, not the other way around: a language cannot have (13a), for instance, but disallow (13b) and (13c).

This implicational hierarchy is supported by a number of languages. However, as shown by Cabredo Hofherr (Chapter 8 below), it cannot be maintained. A closer look at the empirical evidence reveals that, within the class of subjects that receive a full theta role, a distinction must be made between subjects that have an antecedent in the discourse (anaphoric pronouns) and those that have so-called arbitrary reference. With respect to pro-drop, the latter appear to pattern with the class of pronouns of (13b) rather than with the other pronouns of (13a). In other words, a referential pronoun with arbitrary interpretation is dropped more easily than an anaphoric referential pronoun.

The two different types of interpretation of subject pronouns can be illustrated with lexical pronouns, for which the same distinction holds. Consider, for example, the different interpretations of the pronoun *they* in (14). In (14a) *they* is anaphoric; it refers to the same persons that *John and Mary* refers to. In contrast, *they* in (14b, c) does not refer to persons introduced in the discourse before, but receives arbitrary reference. In (14b) the reference is quasi-universal, as the sentence expresses the view that people in general drink a lot of wine in France. In (14c) it is existential. The sentence expresses the view that some person or persons have stolen my bicycle.

(14)  a. John and Mary came in. They sat down.
      b. In France they drink a lot of wine.
      c. They stole my bicycle.

Cabredo Hofherr shows that in languages like Finnish and Russian an arbitrary pronoun can be empty, while an anaphoric pronoun cannot. Recall that Finnish allows for quasi-argumental pro but does not allow pro-drop of a subject like *she* with a theta role assigning predicate (see (12)). However, it turns out that, if the subject of such a predicate is arbitrary, pro-drop is possible:

(15)  Metsästä löytää    helposti mustikoita
      forest  find.3SG easily   blueberries
      One finds blueberries easily in the forest.

If all languages that allow quasi-argumental pro-drop also allow this type of arbitrary pro-drop, as seems to be the case, the implicational hierarchy of different types of pro-drop should be reformulated as follows:

(16)  Anaphoric pro-drop → Arbitrary pro-drop and quasi-argumental
pro-drop → Expletive pro-drop

Cabredo Hofherrr argues that the hierarchy in (16) can be accounted for in terms of content licensing as well. The crucial idea is that arbitrary pro and quasi-argumental pro share the property of having some deficiency in their person and number marking. Anaphoric pro, on the other hand, has full person and number features, and therefore fully specified agreement morphology is necessary to identify its content. Expletive pro, finally, does not require any licensing at all, since it does not exist, according to Cabredo Hofherr: the relevant sentences do not have a subject at all.

Arbitrary pro and quasi-argumental pro are not equal in all respects. Cabredo Hofherr argues that their deficiency in person and number marking is different. From this she derives some differences between the two with respect to the interpretation of the subject (always [+human] for arbitrary pro, never [+human] for quasi-argumental pro) and some differences between the types of agreement on the verb with which the two go together (quasi-argumental pro always coinciding with default third person singular agreement, whereas arbitrary pro can coincide with plural agreement).

### 1.2.6  *Person/number—or other features*

The idea that person and number features of pro are identified by agreement on the verb needs some refinement, as there are cases (witness the data discussed in 1.2.5) in which these features are deficient. However, the basic idea that the properties of person and number features are crucial in determining when pro-drop is allowed or not has not been challenged. A more radical departure from this idea might be in order, however. The focus on person and number features could be the result of focusing on a particular set of languages. An indication for this is provided by the data from Nederlandse Gebarentaal (sign language of the Netherlands, henceforth NGT) discussed by Zwitserlood and Van Gijn (Chapter 7 below). They argue that the features for which verbs in NGT agree are not person and number, but rather gender and location features. In particular, NGT employs location and shape marking as a grammatical means to convey what sort of object is referred to. Moreover, verbs in NGT differ with respect to whether they show such agreement with all arguments, agreement with some arguments only, or no agreement at all. All the same, arguments of all these types of verb can be dropped, given the proper pragmatic context. As Zwitserlood and Van Gijn note, such data imply that agreement (let alone person and number agreement) need not be pivotal in licensing pro-drop.

Zwitserlood and Van Gijn's results show that, in order to arrive at a more general theory of zero argument licensing in relation to agreement, the set of features considered must perhaps be enlarged. For example, the question arises as to whether location agreement behaves in parallel to person agreement generally, and what the relevant distinctions are in this domain.

In fact, we have already seen that person features may not be the only means to license the content of pro. Languages like Chinese, without any inflection on the verb, allow empty arguments as well. In these cases the empty argument is assumed to receive its content via identification with the topic of the discourse. This raises the more principled question of whether morphological features on the verb ever play a role in licensing pro, or whether, in fact, all cases of pro-drop are really cases of topic-drop.

It is not easy to distinguish zero argument-drop from topic-drop, since pronouns are most often topics, in the sense that their referents are given (anaphorically or deictically). Nevertheless, a distinction between topic-drop and pro-drop is necessary in order to account for the distribution of empty arguments in languages like Dutch. Dutch does not allow empty arguments in general, hence it is not a pro-drop language. However, it is possible to drop a topic from the initial position of a main (not a subordinate) clause:

(17)  Question:   Wat is er   met Jan aan de hand?
                  what is there with John on the hand
                  What's the matter with John?
      a. Answer:  Heeft een been gebroken
                  has  a   leg  broken
                  He has broken a leg.
      a′. Answer: *Ik geloof dat een been heeft gebroken
                  I believe that a   leg   has  broken

Thus, Dutch topic-drop is more restrictive than pro-drop in that it can apply only when the topic occupies a main clause initial position (compare the impossibility of topic-drop in the embedded clause in (17a′)). At the same time, it is less restrictive than pro-drop because it can apply not only to topic subjects but to any topic appearing in main clause initial position, even to non-argumental adverbs like *gisteren* 'yesterday', as shown by (18). (Note that, given the verb-second constraint operative in Dutch main clauses, we must assume that the initial position in the answer in (18) indeed contains an empty topic.)

(18)  Question: Wat heb je   gisteren   gedaan?
                what have you yesterday done
                What have you done yesterday?

Answer:     Ben ik naar de film geweest
            am I to   the film been
            I went to the movies then.

In fact, we have already seen some data that are problematic for the idea that
pro-drop and topic-drop can be collapsed entirely. The cases of arbitrary pro-
drop discussed in 1.2.5 illustrate this—arbitrary pronouns typically do not
function as topics in the discourse.

These data do not imply that the content of pro in languages like Italian,
Chinese, and NGT cannot be identified via a link with the topic (see e.g.
Samek-Lodovici (1996) on Italian in this respect), but it does indicate that
pro-drop cannot be equated with topic-drop.

## 1.3 Pro-drop and non-configurationality

The classical theory of pro-drop is based on the assumption that the only
difference between pro-drop languages and non-pro-drop languages is that
pronominal subjects can remain empty in the former but not in the latter. The
position of pro is identified via formal licensing, but the positions in which
subjects show up in pro-drop languages are not assumed to be different from
those in which obligatorily overt subjects show up. On closer inspection, it
turns out that the syntax of subjects in pro-drop languages deviates from that
of subjects in non-pro-drop languages in a number of respects. As we will see
in this section, one may even wonder whether pro-drop languages do in fact
have a structural subject position, or whether in such languages apparent
subjects are really optional additions to the clause in a dislocated position. If
so, this would be reminiscent of the behaviour of all syntactic noun phrases in
non-configurational languages. The question is, then, to what extent pro-
drop languages are non-configurational.

### 1.3.1 *The syntax of subjects in pro-drop versus non-pro-drop languages*

Overt subjects in pro-drop languages do not seem to show the same behaviour as overt subjects in non-pro-drop languages. For example, Rizzi (1982)
already connected the possibility of having subjects invert with the VP and
(presumably as a consequence of this) allowing subject extraction out of
clauses introduced by a complementizer (circumventing the *that*-trace filter)
with the pro-drop nature of a language. As illustrated in (19) and (20), overt
subjects in Italian can occur after the VP just as well as preverbally, whereas in
English, subject inversion of this type is impossible. That Italian is not
sensitive to the *that*-trace filter, whereas English is, is shown in (21).

(19)  a.  Gianni ha parlato
          John   has spoken
      b.  Ha parlato Gianni

(20)  a.  John has spoken
      b.  *Has spoken John

(21)  a.  Chi$_i$ credi   che ha   parlato Italiano t$_i$?
          who think-2SG that has-3SG spoken Italian
          Who do you think has spoken Italian?
      b.  *Who$_i$ do you believe that t$_i$ has spoken Italian?

Contrary to first appearances, even a preverbal subject in a pro-drop language does not behave as though it is in the same type of position as a subject in a non-pro-drop language. In the classic conception of pro-drop it was assumed that overt pronominal subjects occupy a structural A-position, say spec-IP, specifically connected with the subject argument (in particular, with nominative case) in pro-drop languages just as in non-pro-drop languages. Pro-drop, then, also involves such a structural subject, the only difference being that the pronominal subject is not phonologically realized. But, in recent years, various pieces of evidence have been advanced to show that overt subjects in pro-drop languages, in contrast to subjects in non-pro-drop languages, are in an A'-position, rather than an A-position. On various counts, subjects in pro-drop languages behave on a par with clitic-left-dislocated elements (when the subject is a topic) or with elements that are A'-moved to the left periphery (when the subject is focused) (Barbosa 1996; 2000; Alexiadou and Anagnostopoulou 1998; Ordóñez and Treviño 1999; Alexiadou, ch. 5 below, and references mentioned there). (Alexiadou (Chapter 5) shows that there are subtle differences between pro-drop languages with respect to the properties of their subjects (cf. also Costa and Galvez 2002).) Let us briefly illustrate the A'-status of subjects in a pro-drop language with two of the arguments advanced in this literature.[1]

First, as is well known, an English sentence like (22a) (see below), with both a quantified subject and a quantified object, is ambiguous. The subject can take scope over the object, but the reverse scopal relation is possible as well. Thus, (22a) can mean that there is one student who filed every article, but it can also mean that for every article there is a student (not necessarily the same one) who filed it. This ambiguity is often accounted for in terms of Quantifier

---

[1] We simplify matters here by restricting ourselves to preverbal subjects. However, as Alexiadou (Chapter 5 below) argues in detail, in VSO orders in (the relevant class of) pro-drop languages the subject is not in a designated structural subject position either (spec-IP), but remains in VP (or vP) (see also Costa 1996).

Raising at LF. This rule raises the quantified object to a position that is equal in height to the subject (see May 1985). If scope is determined by c-command and if QR derives a representation in which the subject and the object mutually c-command each other, the two readings are accounted for.

As Alexiadou and Anagnostopoulou (1998) show, parallel sentences in a pro-drop language like Greek fail to show this ambiguity. Here the subject necessarily takes wide scope, as illustrated by (22b). This sentence can mean only that one and the same student filed every article. This is accounted for if the position of the subject is out of reach for QR of the object, which might indicate that the subject is in a dislocated position. Interestingly, the same lack of ambiguity is found in Chinese, a pro-drop language without any agreement morphology, as shown by Aoun and Li (1993) (who provide a different account of these data); see (22c).

(22) a. Some      student    filed          every      article.        $\forall > \exists$  $\exists > \forall$
     b. Kapios    fititis    stihiothetise  kathe      arthro          $^*\forall > \exists$  $\exists > \forall$
        some      student    filed          every      article
     c. (Yaoshi)  yige       ren            piping     meigeren...     $^*\forall > \exists$  $\exists > \forall$
        if        someone    criticized     everyone

Secondly, Barbosa (2000) shows that the syntax of preverbal subjects in European Portuguese is exactly like the syntax of other constituents when these occur preverbally, indicating that there is no preverbal position that is specifically privileged in hosting subjects only (i.e. there is no spec-IP position). Her argument is based on the direction of cliticization in European Portuguese. When we look at objects, for instance, we see that dislocated objects functioning as topics require that any clitics in the following clause follow the verb (there is enclisis). Quantified objects that are fronted by operator movement, on the other hand, require that any clitics in the following clause precede the verb (there is proclisis); see (23).

(23) a. Esse     livro,     dou-lhe /    *lhe-dou
        that     book       give-him /   him-give
        'That book I will give him'
     b. [Nenhuma resposta]$_i$  me-deram /   *deram-me t$_i$   até hoje
        no       answer     me-gave /    gave-me          until today
        'They gave me no answer until today'

Barbosa notes that this is presumably a 'second position clitic' effect. Such effects are widely attested cross-linguistically. They involve clitics that impose a prosodic constraint on their context; in particular, they require that they occur in the second position within their intonational phrase (IntP).

Dislocated elements are not parsed within the same IntP as the rest of the clause—they are typically followed by a break, indicated by the comma in (23a). As a result, the clitic must follow the verb in (23a), or it would end up in initial position in its IntP, causing ungrammaticality. The A'- moved quantifiers in (23b), on the other hand, are in the same IntP as the rest of the clause, as a result of which it is proclisis rather than enclisis that ensures the clitic is in second position in its IntP.

Crucially, preverbal subjects impose exactly the same pattern of cliticization on the clause that follows them: when they are topicalized we find enclisis; when they are quantified there is proclisis:

(24)   a.   O Pedro viu-o /   *o-viu
            the Pedro saw-him / him-saw
       b.   Alguém *viu-o /   o-viu
            someone saw-him / him-saw

In Barbosa's words, 'this casts doubt on the idea that there is an extra position for subjects that is unavailable to objects, namely A-movement to spec-IP. If there were such an option, we would expect subjects to have a different behaviour from other fronted DPs' (2000: 62). In particular, we might expect preverbal non-quantified subjects to co-occur with proclitics, since, if such a subject were in spec-IP and the verb (plus clitics) in I, these two would surely be in the same IntP, so that the clitics should directly follow the subject to be in second position, rather than invert with the verb.

Data like these indicate that, in pro-drop languages, subjects—at least overt ones—do not occupy a structural position that is reserved for subjects only, like spec-IP. They appear not in an A-position, but rather in an A'-position. Which particular position this is may differ from language to language, and perhaps even from construction to construction (see Alexiadou, Chapter 5, and Poletto, Chapter 6 below).

### 1.3.2 *Pro vadis?*

The properties of overt subjects in pro-drop languages just discussed call into question not only the existence of a structural subject position (an 'EPP' position) in these languages but, because of this, also the very existence of pro itself. The reason to assume that a pro is present in apparently subjectless clauses in pro-drop languages is that the subject argument of the verb in such sentences is just as syntactically active as it is when overt. It can, for example, act as an antecedent for an anaphor, or as the controller for the understood subject of an infinitival complement:

(25)  a. Cura se stesso
      cures himself
      'He cures himself'
   b. Ritengo    [di essere   simpatico]   (Rizzi 1986a: 541)
      believe-1SG  to be      nice
      'I believe that I am nice'

Apparently, the subject argument of the verb is somehow realized even when it is not a visible DP. According to some hypotheses about argument realization, an argument can be realized only in one particular syntactic structural position (compare Baker's (1988) Uniformity of Theta Assignment Hypothesis (UTAH)). If this is a universal principle, then the fact that we see subject arguments being realized in a specific syntactic subject position in non-pro-drop languages like English implies that the subject argument in (25), which is realized somehow, must be realized in this same position as well. In other words, there must be a pro, in the syntactic subject position.

Note that this also implies that, if the arguments for the dislocated status of overt subjects in (some constructions in some) pro-drop languages are correct, these sentences too must contain pro in the structural subject position. After all, things in dislocated positions are not supposed to be in the theta-assignment domain of the verb, even in theories not adopting UTAH. (In other words, *Lui parla* would be similar to an English sentence like *He, he speaks*, with the second *he* phonologically empty.)

However, the assumption that pro-drop languages have a structural syntactic subject argument position begs the question of why the subject that fills this position *must* be empty. Why, if this position exists, is it impossible to place a subject with phonological content there, just as in non-pro-drop languages? After all, overt subjects in pro-drop languages do not show any alternation between having A and A'-properties. Faced with this question, two lines of inquiry are open. Either an account must be found of the obligatory emptiness of DPs in structural subject position in pro-drop languages, or the theory must be set up in such a way that subject arguments need not always be realized in a specific syntactic position.

With respect to the first option, we can consider extending a proposal by Baker (1996), which deals with the question of why the elements in syntactic argument positions in polysynthetic languages are necessarily empty. In such languages, overt NPs (not only subjects but also objects) occur in dislocated positions (see Jelinek, Chapter 9 below, and Baker, Chapter 10). Baker argues that in these languages all syntactic A-positions can only contain pro, not an overt nominal argument. According to Baker, this is because the agreement morphology in these languages, perhaps because it is very rich, has the property of absorbing Case. If we interpret the classic GB Case filter in its strictest sense, only NPs with phonological content require Case (cf. Chomsky 1981). That would mean pro does not require Case. Therefore, if agreement in a language is such that it absorbs a verb's Case, only empty pro can appear as nominal argument and no overt NPs are allowed as such.

This proposal establishes the connection between rich agreement and pro-drop in yet another way, with the bonus that it explains why we can use *only* pro in syntactic A-position. The question is now whether the proposal can be extended from polysynthetic languages to 'classic' pro-drop languages like Italian. This would require a type of agreement that absorbs subject case (nominative) but not object case—which is not unlikely, in view of the fact that polysynthetic languages typically have both subject and object agreement (cf. Jelinek, Chapter 9 below), while in a language like Italian finite verbs show only subject agreement.

There is a possible alternative account. Perhaps the reason why there can be no overt subjects in a specific 'EPP' position (spec-IP) in pro-drop languages is not so much that the subject agreement absorbs the nominative Case, but that this agreement can itself be the realization of the subject argument (see also Koeneman, Chapter 3 below). This is an instance of the second option mentioned above, in that it allows for realization of subject arguments (and perhaps other arguments) in other ways than by a constituent in a particular syntactic A-position. The 'other way' would be that the subject argument in a pro-drop language can be realized morphologically instead of syntactically, by the agreement on the verb. In that case, we cannot have a DP subject realizing the same argument in a syntactic A-position, although we can have a DP in a syntactic A'-position that doubles this argument, just as in cases of clitic left dislocation. This is the intended result.

Under this second alternative the element pro would be superfluous, as no specifier of IP occupied by this element would ever be projected in pro-drop languages. Or at least, if there were a spec-IP, it would not be the same type of A-position as it is in non-pro-drop languages. (It is possible in principle that it is not the presence or absence but the status of spec-IP that differs between these languages, where it is an A'-position in pro-drop languages—see Borer (1995) for a proposal along such lines. Given this, pro-drop languages might even differ with respect to the position of overt subjects, in the CP domain or in the IP domain, as long as the overt subject is in an A'-position; cf. Alexiadou (Chapter 5 below) and Poletto (Chapter 6).)

The idea that the relation between agreement and pro-drop results from the agreement itself realizing an argument, with the concomitant demise of the element pro, has been formally worked out in various ways; for some concrete proposals see Weerman (1989), Manzini and Savoia (1997), Ordóñez and Treviño (1999), and Manzini and Roussou (2000). (Alexiadou and Anagnostopoulou (1998) and Tóth (2000) ultimately reject the idea, mainly because of the fact that pro-drop languages do not behave entirely like non-configurational languages.)

This latter view tallies well with the perspective on the licensing relationship between subjects and agreement according to which (overt) subjects license (poor) agreement, rather than (rich) agreement licensing (empty) subjects (see section 1.2.1). We could even assume that agreement *always* realizes the subject argument (which would also make the theory more in line with some version of UTAH), even in non-pro-drop languages. If the referential properties of an argumental agreement affix are indeterminate because there is syncretism in the paradigm, the affix is anaphoric and must be bound by an overt subject in syntactic A-position. If there is no syncretism, or if there can be no confusion with other affixes because there is no paradigm at all but rather just a single affix (compare the 'no-agreement but pro-drop' languages of section 1.2), such binding is not required, and the language will allow pro-drop.

Such a proposal has various implications. For instance, a language like Chinese must have an empty agreement affix. Interestingly, not all languages without an agreement paradigm seem to allow pro-drop (although Speas (Chapter 2 below) argues that at least some examples of this are only apparent). Perhaps a distinction can be made between languages in which there is a single empty agreement affix and languages that genuinely do not have any agreement at all. In the latter, the subject argument must be realized syntactically after all, disallowing pro-drop (cf. Ackema 2002). The difference between syntactically present agreement affixes that fail to be phonologically spelt out and genuine absence of agreement affixes is discussed in detail by Baker (Chapter 10 below), albeit in a different connection.

A further implication of the idea that the agreement affix realizes the verb's subject argument is that the phenomena showing the syntactic activity of the subject argument in pro-drop languages (see (25)) cannot be dependent on the presence of a DP in syntactic subject position. For independent reasons, it has indeed been argued that anaphors are bound by a higher thematic function of the predicate that they are linked to, rather than being directly bound by the DP that satisfies that thematic function (see Williams 1989; Grimshaw 1990; Reinhart and Reuland 1993; Neeleman and Van de Koot 2002). Similarly, in control relations the choice of controller has been argued to be determined by semantic/thematic properties of the matrix predicate, rather than by syntactic c-command and locality (see Chierchia 1984; Farkas 1988; Culicover and Jackendoff 2003; Landau 2003).

### 1.3.3 *Polysynthesis*

The idea that inflectional morphology can represent a verb's arguments has been influential for another class of languages than the pro-drop languages discussed so far—namely, for polysynthetic languages. An important property of such languages is that all NPs in the clause are optional, are ordered freely, and sometimes can even appear as a split constituent—these languages are non-configurational.

This behaviour of NPs has been taken as evidence that they are not the true arguments of the verb. Rather, the rich inflection on predicates in these languages, which expresses the phi-features of both subjects and objects, is taken to be the realization of the verb's arguments (cf. Jelinek 1984). Jelinek proposes that there is a parameter distinguishing non-configurational, polysynthetic languages from configurational ones—namely, the Pronominal Argument parameter. If this parameter is set positively, only morphologically attached person-marking elements (affixes or clitics) can serve as arguments. Consequently, there are no syntactic phrases in argument position in these languages; all NPs are in an A′-position. Indeed, Jelinek (1984; Chapter 9 below) and Baker (1996; Chapter 10 below) show that all overt nominal constituents in polysynthetic languages have properties that are reminiscent of clitic-left-dislocated constituents.

In particular, in addition to the characteristics mentioned at the beginning of this section, non-configurational languages show the following properties. First, NPs in such languages must be referential; no DP quantification occurs, but only adverbial quantification. Second, NPs can show a different case distribution compared to the pattern shown by the agreement morphology—while the agreement morphology shows a nominative–accusative pattern, the NPs may occur in an ergative–absolutive pattern. Moreover, Jelinek shows that these languages lack the equivalent of the English dative shift construction, by which an oblique argument becomes one that is structurally case marked. In general, Jelinek argues that NPs in polysynthetic languages never receive structural case. Third, the optionality of syntactic NPs contrasts with the obligatory presence of agreement morphology for both subject and object features. Fourth, NPs in polysynthetic languages are islands for extraction (cf. Baker, Chapter 10 below). This, too, may indicate that they are adjuncts (cf. Huang 1982). If the NPs are indeed optional adjuncts to the clause and there is obligatory rich agreement morphology, then it is tempting to consider the agreement affixes to be the realization of the verb's arguments.

If arguments must be realized by morphologically attached elements in a polysynthetic language, it follows that such elements must be present in the morphosyntactic representation. However, this requirement does not say anything about how these elements are phonologically realized. Strictly speaking, the elements in question are not required to be phonologically realized at all. If there is no visible inflectional morphology on a verb, this can mean either of two things. Either there is no such inflectional morphology present, or the inflectional morphemes do not have phonological content (they are 'zero' affixes). There is no reason why zero affixes would be disallowed in polysynthetic languages.

Baker (Chapter 10 below) shows how this 'null agreement or no agreement' issue can be decided for particular languages, by studying the properties of overt NPs in a language and comparing them with the properties that NPs have in polysynthetic languages with full agreement paradigms (i.e. the properties just mentioned above). It turns out that in Mapudungun, NPs cannot be quantificational and are islands for extraction even where there is no overt object agreement on the verb. In Kinande, on the other hand, the syntactic behaviour of NPs crucially depends on whether or not there is visible agreement: when there is, the NP behaves like a dislocated constituent, but when there is not, the NP behaves like a constituent in an A-position. As Baker concludes, this indicates that Mapudungun is a polysynthetic language with empty object agreement, whereas Kinande does not have empty agreement, but can leave out agreement altogether (like other Bantu languages such as Swahili; cf. section 1.2.4).

### 1.3.4 *Unifying macrovariation and microvariation*

Jelinek's Pronominal Argument parameter is based on the idea that arguments can be realized by inflectional morphology on the verb. Baker's (1996) Polysynthesis parameter expresses a similar idea, but Baker still assumes that arguments are realized syntactically in polysynthetic languages too, the difference with configurational languages being that they must be realized by empty pros. The inflectional morphology on the verb serves as a licenser of pro and, via its Case-absorbing properties, accounts for the absence of overt NPs in syntactic A-positions.

There is a conspicuous parallel with the discussion about the status of subject arguments in pro-drop languages. Here, too, the question is whether there is a pro in a syntactic A-position that is licensed by inflection on the verb, or whether there is no such syntactic subject position and it is the inflection itself that realizes the syntactic argument. It is no coincidence that this parallel discussion arises for both types of language, as the behaviour of subjects in pro-drop languages shows some similarities to the behaviour of all arguments in polysynthetic languages.

This brings us to the question of how to account for language variation in syntactic argument drop. Two types of approach can be distinguished, which we may call the macroparametric and the microparametric approach. Both Jelinek's Pronominal Argument parameter and Baker's Polysynthesis parameter are macroparameters. According to the Pronominal Argument parameter, for instance, languages either realize all arguments by morphologically attached elements or realize none at all. However, the problems with the classic pro-drop parameter discussed in section 1.2 have led some researchers to proposals that divide languages not into pro-drop and non-pro-drop languages, but into languages that may allow pro-drop in some constructions, or for some persons, but not in others.

Such approaches do not have to mean that the pro-drop parameter is replaced by totally language-specific rules that determine whether or not a subject may be empty—which would allow an entirely arbitrary (potential) range of variation among languages. Rather, as we will argue now, it is possible to make a connection between the microparametric and the macroparametric views in a way that can also account for the partial parallel between pro-drop languages and polysynthetic languages.

Suppose there is a pro-drop parameter of the following type:

(26)  An affix with the phi features $< \alpha, \beta >$ can realize an argument of the predicate (yes/no).

The paradigms for inflectional morphology expressing phi-features are hierarchically organized. Patterns of syncretism do not seem to be arbitrary, but show that some feature dimensions are subordinate to others. For example, some languages show paradigms in which the person dimension is neutralized in the plural. So, no person distinctions are made in the plural morphology, whereas there are morphological person distinctions in the singular. Now, given that the person feature may neutralize, the same might be true for the number feature, which would yield a paradigm with the same forms for the singular and plural of a particular person feature—for example, second person—but with different forms for different persons. However, number neutralization accompanied by person distinctions seems to be more rare at best.[2] In terms of the hierarchical make-up of the paradigm,

---

[2] Of course, any two cells in a paradigm can contain the same overt affix, given the possibility of accidental homonymy. This situation must be distinguished from instances of neutralization of some dimension in another dimension of the paradigm, however; see Blevins (1995) for a detailed discussion of this issue.

this means that the person dimension is usually subordinate to the number dimension.

Let us suppose that an agreement paradigm is organized in general in accordance with (27), although this could be worked out in several ways and without making very specific claims about the exact nature of the features that must be distinguished. (Note that, in principle, there can be language variation with respect to this also; see below.) The top node (Agreement) indicates that we are dealing with affixes that are specified for phi-features, rather than, say, case. In a language without any apparent agreement, the paradigm is not split any further. The dimension labelled 'external' is meant to distinguish subject agreement from object agreement affixes. The dimensions 'sing(ular)', 'deic(tic)', and 'speak(er)' make a distinction between singular and plural, between first/second person and third person, and between first and second person respectively.

(27)

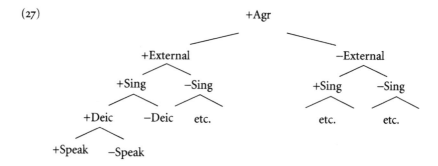

Patterns of syncretism are accounted for by the assumption that at any point in this hierarchy a paradigm can stop splitting.

Suppose now that, by analogy to this, a parameter that refers to agreement features, such as the pro-drop parameter in (26), need not be set for the paradigm in its entirety, but that it can be set at different hierarchical points in the paradigm. If we set it at the highest point of the paradigm, its effects are those of a macroparameter. If it is set at one of the lowest points, it resembles a microparameter. However, it can also be set at intermediate points. Crucially, in all these cases we are dealing with precisely the same parameter, meaning that whenever it is set positively we are dealing with the same process of argument drop. Consider how this would work.

If the parameter is set at the highest point in (27), we are, in effect, dealing with a parameter resembling Jelinek's Pronominal Argument parameter or Baker's Polysynthesis parameter. In this case the instantiation of the parameter in (26) is (28).

(28)   An affix with the phi-features <+Agr> can realize an argument of the predicate.

If the 'yes' value is chosen for the parameter in (28), a polysynthetic language results in which all the predicate's arguments are realized morphologically (since all affixes expressing phi-features will at least have the specification [+ Agr]).

Suppose now that the parameter is set one dimension lower in (27). It can then read as follows:

(29)   An affix with the phi-features <+Ext> can realize an argument of the predicate.

This will result in the pattern shown by classic pro-drop languages. The partial parallel between pro-drop languages and polysynthetic languages is accounted for, because pro-drop languages have a positive setting for the same parameter that is set positively for polysynthetic languages, although it affects only their subjects.

Setting the parameter in (26) at a still lower point in the feature hierarchy— namely, at the deictic dimension—yields (30), which results in a partial pro-drop pattern of the Finnish type in which first and second person arguments may be dropped, but third person arguments may not.

(30)   An affix with the phi-features <+Deic> can realize an argument of the predicate.

Finally, setting the parameter positively at the lowest level of (27) can result in a pattern of pro-drop in which first person singular arguments are the only ones that can be dropped. Diary-drop might be a case in point (cf. Haegeman and Ihsane 2001).

Obviously, this speculation raises several questions. First, at each dimension in the feature hierarchy there is an asymmetry between the two values of the feature in question, in the sense that, cross-linguistically speaking, the parameter is more likely to be set positively for one value than for the other. In particular, there are languages in which both subjects and objects can be dropped and languages in which only subjects can be dropped, but we do not know of languages in which only objects, but not subjects, can remain empty. In our terms, this means that the parameter can be set positively on the <+External> value but not on the <−External> value. This problem may be solved by invoking the idea of unmarked, default values for features. The feature <+External> is the likely default, since on an observational level object agreement co-occurs with subject agreement but not necessarily vice versa (cf. Moravcsik 1978). The desired result then follows if parameters like (26) can refer only to default values. In that case, object drop is possible only if the parameter is set at a higher point in (27) than at the <Ext> dimension, thereby automatically affecting subjects as well. (This hypothesis makes a number of specific predictions. For example, it should be possible for languages to drop singular arguments without dropping plural ones but not the other way around, and it should be possible to drop deictic arguments without dropping non-deictic ones but not the other way around—i.e 'anti-Finnish' should not exist. These predictions will not be tested here.)

The second, related issue concerns the exact nature of the features. For instance, the distinction at the hierarchically lowest dimension is given in terms of <Speaker> in (27). An alternative would be to use the feature <Addressee> instead. This feature would, of course, result in second person being the default, rather than first person. To us, it is not so clear which person is to be considered the default at the relevant dimension. Purely on the basis of the evidence, we have to assume that the parameter can also refer to <+Addressee>, because there are languages that allow for pro-drop of second person arguments only (e.g. some northern Dutch dialects). It may be that there is variation in the feature make-up used in agreement. The same point can be made with respect to the number of dimensions that must be distinguished in various languages. (For recent discussion of such issues, see Harley and Ritter (2002) and Bejar (2003).) We will leave this matter open here.

In this way, the microparametric and the macroparametric view are not mutually exclusive, but may actually be manifestations of a single parameter that can be set at different points in the feature hierarchy.

In principle, the different views on the scope of the pro-drop parameter can be tested by testing the predictions they make with respect to the acquisition of the relevant phenomena. On the macroparametric view, the language-learning child is predicted to start out with one value for the parameter, say non-pro-drop (given the subset principle),[3] and then at a particular point in

---

[3] The subset principle states that if the set of sentences that is allowed under value A of a parameter is a subset of the set of sentences that is allowed under value B of that parameter, then the L1 learner should start out by assuming value A. If the parameter has value B in the target language, the child will encounter positive evidence that will induce him to set the parameter to this value (namely, when it encounters a sentence that is not permitted under value A). If the child were to start out by assuming value B, he would require negative evidence to learn a grammar with value A, since he would have to know that certain sentences that are permitted under value B are not permitted in the target language. It is usually assumed, however, that learners do not have access to negative evidence. No positive evidence will induce a learner to set the parameter to value A, since all sentences permitted by this value are also permitted under value B.

time may opt for pro-drop across the board. The microparametric view, by contrast, requires construction-specific learning—it makes no particular prediction about the developmental path that children follow.

The view just outlined leads to yet another expectation: the pattern of pro-drop shown in acquisition may follow the development of the agreement paradigm. As long as the child assumes that no feature distinctions are made for agreement on finite verbs, it can set the parameter in (26) only at the highest point in (27). In that case, in any language any sentence with an empty argument will be taken as positive evidence for pro-drop across the board, as in the macroparametric view. However, once the child acquires the notion of paradigm splitting, he or she must determine whether or not (26) must instead be set at the level of the new feature dimension that he or she distinguishes. If the subset principle is correct, the child has to assume that the parameter is set at the newly developed lower dimension rather than the higher one. As a result, at this stage the child stops dropping objects, and allows only subject drop. Positive evidence for object drop is then required to return to the higher-dimension parameter setting. A similar development will occur at any point at which a new dimension in the agreement paradigm is assumed by the learner.

This offers a new perspective on the empirical problem for the subset principle in the acquisition of pro-drop, which concerns 'unlearning'. Children seem to unlearn dropping arguments in many languages, thus apparently being sensitive to negative evidence (see e.g. the papers in Roeper and Williams (1987)). Under the view just presented, children actually learn the new grammar by invoking positive evidence only. Morphological evidence leads them to split the agreement paradigm, and the subset principle consequently determines that the parameter in (26) refers to the newly distinguished (lower) feature dimension rather than to the higher dimension. Thus, although the child starts out by not allowing pro-drop at all, he or she may subsequently show a development from full pro-drop to pro-drop in more and more restricted contexts until the adult level of pro-drop is reached. In this way, the result is achieved without invoking negative evidence.

## 1.4  Overview

The classic idea of pro-drop was that if a language has rich agreement it may leave the associated arguments empty. This idea soon proved to be problematic in view of the amount of variation that languages show in pro-drop and agreement patterns. As a response to this, the connection between agreement morphology and empty arguments might be abandoned altogether, which would predict a random distribution of agreement properties and empty argument possibilities across languages. This is not what the observed data show either, however.

The contributions to this volume show that the classic idea is not entirely wrong, but is too coarse-grained. It turns out that, at a deeper level of analysis, many more refined and interesting connections between agreement morphology and the absence of one or more syntactic arguments can be found. We will conclude by briefly repeating which of these connections are discussed in the contributions to this volume.

The first set of papers (Speas, Koeneman, Bennis) are concerned with the nature of the connection between properties of agreement (paradigms) in particular languages or contexts and the ease with which arguments can be left unexpressed syntactically in these languages or contexts.

Speas argues that Jaeggli and Safir's (1989a) Morphological Uniformity Condition (see (5) above) derives from a general economy condition according to which a phrase is projected only if it has content, where content is defined as dominance of a distinct phonological or semantic matrix by its head or its specifier. According to this proposal, overt subjects are required if and only if a language has non-distinct ('lexical' or 'weak') agreement. Since weak agreement leaves the projected AgrP without content (in this sense), a phonologically expressed subject must project to provide content.

Koeneman addresses the issue of 'partial pro-drop', i.e. the option of dropping arguments with a particular person/number specification but not others. His proposal is that the agreement is pronominal (and thereby licenses pro-drop) if and only if the relevant paradigm does not have syncretic forms that collapse two or more cells. Koeneman's findings are in accordance with the idea that the organization of paradigms is crucial for the possibility of leaving arguments syntactically unexpressed.

Bennis similarly narrows the domain in which something like a pro-drop parameter might apply, showing that properties of particular constructions can license pro-drop in languages that do not generally allow arguments to be left syntactically unexpressed. Bennis's empirical focus is on Dutch imperatives, which, according to his proposal, carry a second person feature on a projection within the CP domain of the clause. This feature can license a pro argument in subject position. Interpreting imperatives generally involves reference to the addressed person, someone present in the utterance situation. Bennis's account thus seems to support the hypothesis that a feature like [+/− deictic] is important for the non-expression of arguments.

The papers by Alexiadou and Poletto also argue against the hypothesis that a single parameter distinguishes languages that generally allow pro-drop from those that do not. More fine-grained distinctions appear to be necessary to account for differences within as well as among languages at the 'micro-level'. Demonstrating that the possibility of pro-drop correlates with the marking of person features on verbs in Greek, Hebrew and Finnish, Alexiadou argues that languages are parametrized by strategies they have available to satisfy the Extended Projection principle. A verbal head may check the EPP in particular languages if it is marked for person and raises to the INFL/Tense projection.

Connecting the insight that (i) morphologically realized person and number features (cf. Koeneman, Alexiadou) and (ii) certain types of (marking of) sentence mood (cf. Bennis) may be decisive in licensing subject drop, Poletto accounts for small-scale differences among French and certain Northern Italian dialects at different historical stages by assuming that pro may be formally licensed by a C(omplementizer) containing a marked feature (such as 'imperative'). Consequently, pro needs to be identified by morphologically realized person and number features (cf. Rizzi's distinction (1982; 1986a) between formal licensing and identification).

The contributions by Zwitserlood and Van Gijn and Cabredo Hofherr focus on the interpretation of empty arguments. In their study of agreement and argument-drop in Nederlandse Gebarentaal (sign language of the Netherlands), Zwitserlood and Van Gijn show that person and number are not the only features that are relevant for argument-drop. Instead, argument-drop is systematically licensed in NGT; also in constructions with location and/or shape agreement. Zwitserlood and Van Gijn further investigate the tension between the 'classical' pro-drop parameter and a 'topic-drop' parameter as proposed initially for Chinese (Huang 1984). In NGT, argument-drop is possible also in the absence of any agreement in appropriate discourse contexts, suggesting that topic-drop is an option in NGT.

Observing that pronouns with arbitrary reference are more easily droppable than anaphoric pronouns, Cabredo Hofherr argues that Rizzi's theory (1986a) of subject drop should be modified so that more weight is given to the referential properties of the argument expressions in question. The ease with which arguments can be dropped is mirrored in an implicational hierarchy with anaphoric pronouns at the top (hence hardest to drop), arbitrarily referring/quasi-argumental pronouns in the middle, and expletive pronouns at the bottom.

In their contributions, Jelinek and Baker argue that there is a macroparameter that decides whether arguments need not—or rather must not—be expressed by phrasal nominal expressions. The domain they investigate is not that of 'classical' pro-drop languages, though, but that of polysynthetic (or non-configurational) languages.

Jelinek links the positive setting of what she terms the Pronominal Argument parameter (determining the choice to realize arguments exclusively as pronominal affixes or clitics) to general properties of information structure encoding. She argues that, in Pronominal Argument languages, occupation of an A-position goes along with givenness/referentiality (which corresponds to the fact that clitics and agreement affixes generally cannot be stressed). If argument positions must be filled by clitics or agreement elements, then various properties of the languages in question follow, such as the fact that they do not feature A-quantification (since expressions in A-positions must be referential) or the fact that focused elements have to be expressed as overt nominal expressions in A-bar positions.

According to Baker, it is these syntactic properties of polysynthetic languages that help the child to set the value of his proposed Polysynthesis parameter, which determines whether every argument of a head should be related to a morpheme (agreement) in the word containing that head. At first sight, a language like Madupungun appears to be a problem for Baker's theory: there is no visible object agreement in Madupungun, but overt object expressions in this language still behave as if in dislocated (A-bar) positions (as in polysynthetic languages). Accordingly, Baker argues, it must be the case that empty morphemes can function as agreement expressions in polysynthetic languages.

# Part I
# The Agreement–Pro-Drop Connection

# 2

# Economy, Agreement, and the Representation of Null Arguments

MARGARET SPEAS

## 2.1 Introduction

This chapter takes a new look at the way in which null arguments are licensed. I propose that there is no licensing condition *per se*, and hence no 'pro-drop' parameter *per se*. Rather, null arguments occur wherever general principles of economy permit them to occur. I will argue that this proposal captures the cross-linguistic distribution of null arguments more accurately than theories with licensing and identification conditions; it encodes the long-standing intuition that there is a relationship between 'rich' agreement and the licensing of null arguments, which has been abandoned in licensing and identification theories; and it lends insight into how Economy principles work to constrain phrase structures which are generated in the absence of any specific X-bar component, as in the theories of Speas (1990), Kayne (1994), and Chomsky (1994).

I will begin by laying the proposal out in general terms, and will follow this with a discussion of the implications of the proposal for the projection of phrase structures. In section 2.4 I will show how this proposal offers both empirical and theoretical advantages over theories that have licensing and identification conditions. In section 2.5 I will address a question which is central to the enterprise of explaining the distribution of null arguments—namely, the problem of isolating a specific morphological correlate to 'rich'

This paper was originally written in the early 1990s. It has not been published before, and since it has nonetheless been influential, it was decided that it should be published here with minimal updating.

For initial inspiration and ongoing encouragement on this paper, I am grateful to Chisato Kitagawa. I would also like to thank the UMass. students who have heard this in various forms and have offered valuable comments, as well as audiences at ESCOL 1994, LSA 1994, the University of Oviedo, CUNY, Indiana University, and the University of Illinois. For specific comments and/or very valuable discussion, I am grateful to Bernhard Rohrbacher, Tom Roeper, Andrew Radford, Kyle Johnson, Hagit Borer, Lyn Frazier, Betsy Ritter, Anne Lobeck, Beatrice Santorini, Molly Diesing, Greg Carlson, Jon Nissenbaum, Jose Escribano, and Ana Ojea Lopez.

agreement. I will deal with some potential counter-examples to the proposal in section 2.6.

For the most part, I will be focusing on null subjects, since most of the so-called pro-drop languages that have been extensively studied have Subject agreement but no overt Object agreement. In section 2.7 I will discuss how my theory may be extended to null objects. In general, I will use the term 'null argument' when I mean to make a general point, although the illustrations prior to the final section will all pertain to null subjects.

## 2.2 Projecting agreement and its specifier

Early generative theories of pro drop, such as that of Taraldsen (1980), encoded the intuition that there is a relationship between 'rich' agreement and the licensing of null arguments. This intuition has been notoriously difficult to justify empirically, yet, as I will argue in detail in section 2.4, there are compelling reasons to continue to believe that such a relationship exists.

As a starting point, then, I will be assuming that there exist two types of agreement, for which I will adopt Chomsky's (1989) terms, 'strong' and 'weak', although I will diverge from Chomsky in my characterization of the two types. I will be further assuming that there is a relationship between strong agreement and the possibility of having a null subject, and I will assume that the generalization in (1) is an accurate description of the relationship between strong agreement and null subjects cross-linguistically. Once I have presented my proposal in general terms, I will examine these assumptions in detail, will argue that they are fundamentally correct, but will propose modifications where they are not correct.

(1)  *Jaeggli and Safir's generalization* (Jaeggli and Safir 1989a)
     Null subjects occur in the context of either very rich agreement or no agreement at all.

What Jaeggli and Safir observed is that null subjects are found in languages like Italian, Spanish, Navajo, and Hindi,[1] where the agreement morphology seems in some intuitive sense to be sufficient without the overt subject, and they are also found in languages like Japanese, Chinese, and Thai, which have

---

[1] One possibility that will not be discussed here is that overt agreement morphemes in some languages are incorporated pronouns. This possibility seems to exist independently of the strength of AGR, although to my knowledge there are no languages which have incorporated pronouns coexisting with agreement morphology within a word, and no current theory of incorporated pronouns explains this fact.

no person–number agreement at all. The condition under which null subjects are excluded is that found in languages like English: there is some residual agreement, but it is not 'rich'. The theory that I will propose will explain Jaeggli and Safir's generalization.

As a preliminary to the proposal, consider the syntactic status of the morpheme that expresses agreement. As has been pointed out by various people, including Kinyalolo (1991), Carstens (1991), Bouchard (1992), Fukui (1993b), and Kayne (1994), agreement, unlike other morphemes like Tense or Aspect, does not receive an independent interpretation, and hence it ought to be absent at LF. The question, then, is whether it occupies an independent syntactic head prior to LF.

Belletti (1990) claims that in Italian inflectional affixes do occupy Functional head positions, and the verb moves in order to support the affix(es). English lacks verb movement (at least, verb movement to AGRS), so perhaps inflectional affixes are not base-generated in Functional head positions in English. In Chomsky (1989) it was suggested that English has affix lowering rather than verb raising, but more recent work dispenses with lowering in favour of the view that the actual affix is base-generated on the verbal stem. Chomsky doesn't discuss whether languages like Italian also have verbs which are base-generated with inflectional affixes attached or whether instead Italian differs from English in this regard.

The view that I will adopt here is one proposed by Rohrbacher (1992; 1994), who claims that in languages which have strong agreement, each agreement morpheme has its own lexical entry, while in languages with weak agreement, the morphemes do not have independent lexical entries. Rather, verbs in weak agreement languages are listed in the lexicon in verbal paradigms, and hence agreement has no independent lexical entry in such languages.

(2)   *Rohrbacher's generalization*
      Strong morphemes have individual lexical entries. Weak morphemes
      do not have individual lexical entries.

Rohrbacher points out that this typological difference correlates in an interesting way with the long-standing debate in the field of morphology about the nature of inflectional morphemes. According to one approach, inflectional morphemes are listed individually in the lexicon and affixed to their host by syntax-like principles (Lieber 1992; Jensen and Strong-Jensen 1984; LaPointe 1980; Fabb 1984). According to the other approach (Anderson 1992; Beard 1991), inflectional paradigms are created by special rules of morphology, and are mapped onto abstractly specified syntactic structures. Rohrbacher points out that each approach runs into problems, but that such problems can be resolved if we take the view that both theories are correct. In particular, languages with strong morphology are languages in which each inflectional affix has its own individual listing in the lexicon.[2] Since these affixes have lexical entries, they are available to the computational component and hence may head their own projections.

Languages with weak morphology are languages in which inflectional affixes do not have independent lexical entries. Rather, they are listed in the lexicon in paradigms and are inserted into syntactic representations already attached to their host. A large portion of Rohrbacher's work is devoted to trying to determine what morphological properties correlate with the existence of an individual lexical entry for a given affix. I will address this issue in section 2.5. In languages with strong agreement, then, a morpheme AGR heads the AGR projection. In languages with weak agreement, the AGR morphology is just part of an inflectional paradigm.

(3)  a. Strong AGR                    b. Weak AGR

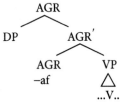    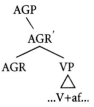

The descriptive generalization that emerges is the following:

(4)  a. A language has null subjects if AGR is base-generated with a morpheme in it.
b. A language cannot have null subjects if AGR is base-generated on the verb.
c. A language has null subjects if it has no AGR.

Previous works that have noticed a generalization resembling this one have accounted for it by claiming that an occupied AGR is rich/strong enough to license *pro* in subject position. As I will discuss in section 2.4, such theories do not explain the fact that null subjects occur in languages which lack agreement altogether.

---

[2] Rohrbacher did not mean to say, nor do I, that a language must have strong or weak morphology throughout its lexicon. As the debate among morphologists suggests, many language have aspects of their lexicon that involve strong morphology and others that involve weak morphology.

I claim instead that the generalizations in (4) follow directly from a principle of Economy which can be stated as in (5).

(5)    Project XP only if XP has content.

In strong AGR languages, the affix is base-generated in the AGR head position, and so AGRP has content. In weak AGR languages, however, the affix is base-generated on the verb, and so something else must give content to the AGRP projection. Therefore, either a pleonastic must be inserted in spec, AGRP, or an NP must move to that position. If the spec,AGRP remains empty in a weak AGR language, AGRP cannot be projected without a violation of the Economy principles.

I have expressed the Economy principle in (5) as a sub-case of the general principles of Economy of Derivation. At this point, we might also express the relevant constraint as a constraint on representation, expressed perhaps as in (6), prohibiting a representation in which both the head and the specifier of XP are radically empty. A proposal along these lines, involving a PF licensing condition, has been made by Tait and Cann (1990). In section 2.3, I will show why I believe that the relevant constraint must be a constraint on derivation, not representation, and hence applicable prior to spell-out rather than at PF. For now it is sufficient to note that the relevant Economy principle has the effect of making representations like (6) impossible.

(6)    XP

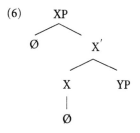

Before we proceed with the analysis of null argument licensing, it remains to specify what counts as 'content' for the purposes of the Economy principles. The intuition that should be captured is that, if you take YP in (6) and add nothing to it, you cannot treat it as though there were a newly projected phrase. You must add something with content in order to project a new phrase. Since all structures must be interpreted at both the interface levels, PF and LF, I take the relevant notion of content to be as follows:

(7)    A node X has content if and only if X dominates a distinct
       phonological matrix or a distinct semantic matrix.

If XP in (6) dominates no phonological material except that which is in the complement YP, then XP dominates no *distinct* phonological matrix. Similarly, if XP dominates no semantic material except that which is in the complement YP, then XP dominates no *distinct* semantic matrix. Note that traces will in effect count as contentful, since they mark a place which has at some point in the derivation been *filled* by a contentful item.

This view of how Economy principles constrain the projection of structures disallows the projection of structure prior to spell-out which will not be filled until after spell-out, since projection takes place only in the presence of some distinct content.

Thus, in a language in which AGR is base-generated on the verb, there is no head with content available to head the AGRP. The only way that AGRP can be projected without violating the Economy principles is if AGRP has a specifier with content before spell-out. Therefore, either an NP must move to spec,IP, or a pleonastic must be inserted.

If AGR is base-generated with a morpheme in it, AGR has content and hence AGRP can be projected. There is no necessity for the specifier of AGR to be *filled*. The null subject, which I assume is base-generated in a VP-internal position, may stay in its VP-internal position, and the specifier of AGRP remains truly empty.

To summarize: a language with weak AGR must have a filled spec,AGRP prior to spell-out, while a language with strong AGR may leave spec,AGRP empty. Before I go on to discuss languages that lack AGR altogether, let us clarify the relationship between spec,AGRP and the VP-internal subject position. In a language like Italian, pro remains in its VP-internal position until spell-out. I assume that at LF, pro moves to the spec of AGRP in order to satisfy the requirement that AGR be checked in a spec–head relation. In a language like English, spec,AGRP must be filled prior to spell-out. This proposal implies that in such a language, pro is possible in the spec of VP in principle, but that some overt element must nonetheless occupy the spec of AGRP. Hence, we must be sure we can rule out sentences which have a null subject in spec,VP and a pleonastic inserted into spec,AGRP. That is, we must rule out sentences like (8).

(8)   *There [pro saw Mary]

The problem posed by (8) is a general one that arises in any theory in which spec,IP is disassociated from spec,VP: why can't a pleonastic co-occur with pro? I suggest that this is due to the fact that pro does not have its own phi features, and it must receive phi features in a spec–head relation with AGR at LF. I follow Chomsky (1989) in assuming that, at LF, the associate of an expletive adjoins to the expletive. If this associate is an NP with its own phi features, those features may percolate to the dominating node, and thus are in a spec–head relation with AGR. If the associate is pro, there are no features to percolate, and pro is only adjoined to the spec of AGR, it is not itself the spec; hence pro is unable to receive features and the derivation crashes at LF.

(9) a.

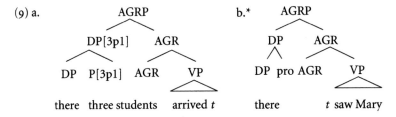

Thus, pro is permitted in principle within VP in a language like English, but sentences like (8) are ruled out by independent principles. The null subject parameter has to do specifically with a requirement on the spec of AGRP.

Turning now to languages that lack AGR altogether, my claim is that there is no need for an AGR projection at any level. Hence, the requirements on licensing that projection never arise. Thus, I am suggesting that the AGRP projection is necessary only in languages which have some sort of agreement, no matter how residual. I would maintain, with Tateishi (1989), that languages like Japanese and Chinese do have functional heads such as Tense and Aspect, but they lack the head AGR. My claim is thus similar to that of Kuroda (1988), who claims that some languages lack the agreement relation; but I believe that what is lacking is the AGR head, not the agreement relation. I adopt the theory of Chomsky (1992) whereby structural Case must be represented at LF in terms of a spec–head relation in which the spec and head are coindexed and hence abstractly agree. However, I take the position that in languages which have AGR features, the relevant head is AGR, while in languages which lack AGR, the relevant head may be Tense, Aspect, or perhaps the verb. (Cf. Carstens and Kinyalolo (1989), who outline a theory of agreement in which what is necessary is a spec–head relation, but this need not involve a head labelled AGR.)

In Japanese, then, there is no AGR head at all. In a language like Japanese, the subject may be null because nothing forces movement into the spec of AGR, since there is no projection to be made legitimate. The reason that an AGRP projection is necessary in languages with residual agreement is that AGR features, if they exist in a language, must be checked in a spec–head relation by LF. Since spell-out is the point at which the derivation has no further access to the lexicon, no new heads can be added to a phrase marker after spell-out. Thus, if AGR is to be needed at LF, the AGRP projection must exist prior to spell-out. Therefore, in a language which has AGR features, there must be an AGR projection with content before spell-out.[3]

(10)  Type (a)  Morpheme heads AGRP, spec may be empty

Type (b)  Morpheme is attached to V, spec must be filled

Type (c)  No AGR projection

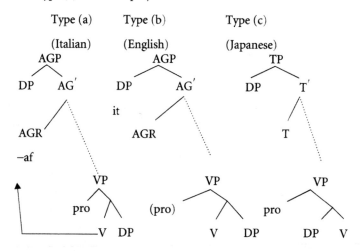

I have proposed that the contexts in which null subjects are possible follow from an independently needed principle of Economy of Projection, along with a parameter regarding whether AGR affixes have independent lexical entries. A maximal projection must have content in order to be projected, and so null subjects are possible either in languages in which the head of AGRP has content or in languages in which there is no necessity to project AGRP at all.

One very nice consequence of the view that AGRP projects only if it has content is that the fact that languages like English must have overt subjects need not be stated as a substantive principle. That is, the effects of the Extended Projection principle now follow naturally: languages with weak agreement must have a specifier of AGRP which has content; hence they will always have a surface subject, even if no theta role is assigned to an

---

[3] In the diagrams in (10) there seems to be a relationship between verb movement and strong morphology, since the verb in a Spanish-type language moves to pick up the stranded AGR morpheme. However, my theory in principle allows for two other types of language. First, agreement morphemes could have independent lexical entries but not be verbal affixes, so they would stand alone and not trigger verb movement. Such a language, possibly exemplified by Warlpiri, would be predicted to allow null subjects. Second, affixes could be base-generated on the verb but verb movement could then take place for some other reason. Such a language would be predicted not to allow null subjects, for reasons discussed in section 2.3. I will claim that Yiddish and German exemplify this possibility.

external argument. We do not have to stipulate the Extended Projection principle in any form.[4]

A second consequence of the proposal outlined here is that there is now no need for a special licensing condition on pro. The languages that allow *pro* will be those that can fulfil the economy principles without having a filled spec,AGRP. As I will discuss in more detail in section 2.4, the licensing condition on pro runs into empirical difficulties when faced with languages like Japanese which have pro but lack agreement entirely, and such a condition has the conceptual problem that it requires syntactic conditions that refer to the phonological nature of the licensee. In the theory I have proposed, both of these problems are solved. Languages like Japanese can have pro because no principles require the projection of a legitimate AGR projection, and so nothing will require an overt specifier. The apparently special properties of null arguments follow from the fact that they lack independent content, and hence cannot suffice to license the projection of an AGR phrase. Thus, their status as phonetically null is incorporated into the theory without special stipulation.

## 2.3 Implications for the theory of phrase structure projection

In the proposal outlined above, general principles of Economy constrain the projection of syntactic phrases. In this section, I will consider in more detail the means by which phrases are projected and the way in which the Economy principles constrain phrase structures. I will focus on two central implications of the proposal: first, the status of AGR as a head which may either lack content or be altogether missing and, second, the status of the operative Economy principle as a principle of derivation.

### 2.3.1 *AGR as a contentless category*

Central to my theory is the idea that, in a language like English, the head of SAGRP has no content prior to spell-out. Further, I am assuming, following Speas (1990), Hoekstra (1991), Kayne (1994), and Chomsky (1994), that X-bar theory is not a primitive component of the grammar, but is rather an artefact of more general principles which constrain the output of free phrase-building. We need to make sure, then, that the general principles we are assuming are capable of projecting phrases whose specifiers have content but whose heads

---

[4] I will show in section 2.5 how this result also extends to languages that allow null pleonastics but not null referential subjects.

do not. First, I will justify the assumption that AGR has no content in languages like English, and will elaborate on what sort of category it is.

As mentioned above, various people have observed that AGR lacks independent semantic content. This view contrasts with the one in Chomsky (1994), where AGR is considered to contain a bundle of features which are matched with a raised verb and with the NP in specifier position.

The assumption that AGR lacks content and that principles of economy constrain projections allows us to eliminate certain redundancies in Chomsky's theory. In Chomsky's checking theory, the features involved in agreement (N features) appear in three places: on the affixes themselves (which are attached to the verb in English-type languages); in an unpronounced lexical entry AGR, which is the head of the AGR phrase; and on the NP to be agreed with. The unpronounced features of AGR must eventually be matched with both the NP and the verbal affix, and then they disappear. Chomsky supposes that, if these unpronounced features do not disappear by the interface level, the derivation crashes because there are features with no interpretation. 'Strong' features must be gone by PF, and 'weak' features must be gone by LF. In the theory presented here, these features appear only on the verbal affix (which may either be on the verb or may project its own phrase) and on the NP to be agreed with.

Beyond this possibly minor redundancy in Chomsky's system, there are three more serious problems with this version of the checking theory that lead me to reject the hypothesis that AGR is an unpronounced bundle of features. First, why should unpronounced features have to disappear by PF? PF allows other null feature bundles, so why not unpronounced features in AGR? Second, there is something amiss in the fact that the features of AGR never get to reach an interface level. This requires that we allow the grammar to contain lexical entries whose content is never visible at either interface level. They are both unpronounced and uninterpreted. Third, stating the distinction between strong and weak agreement in terms of whether the features must disappear before PF reduces the distinction between strong and weak agreement to a mere stipulation, bearing no correlation to the type of morphology, and hence leaving Jaeggli and Safir's generalization unexplained.

For these reasons, I reject the idea that the lexicon contains bundles of unpronounced features of the category AGR. Rather, I assume that phi features are semantic features associated with particular morphemes, either pronouns/NPs, or affixes. These features must be checked by being in a spec–head relation with an NP bearing such features by LF. This means that, in a language in which inflectional morphemes are base-generated on the verb, AGR is 'truly empty'. In fact, there seems no compelling reason to label the relevant head specifically 'AGR'. Rather, as Kayne (1994: 30) suggests: 'In cases where movement is called for, but where no contentful head is available, the moved phrase must become the specifier of a head lacking intrinsic content. It may be that this is what one means by Agr° ...'.

### 2.3.2 On the derivation of phrase markers

It turns out that making the assumption that AGR has no content in an English-type language allows us to restrict the possible ways in which phrases in general can be projected, resolving an open question in the systems of both Chomsky and Kayne. The open question has to do with whether phrases are projected one node at a time, or whether larger pieces of a phrase marker can be created by a single operation. Chomsky (1994) claims that phrase markers are built up by the operation MERGE, which takes as input two phrase markers and yields a new phrase marker, whereas in Kayne's (1994) system, entire phrases are projected freely, subject to the constraints such as the Linear Correspondence axiom.[5] Below I will show that only the system in which entire phrases project is viable, once we adopt the view that AGR may be contentless. This means that the Economy condition relevant to my proposal must be a condition on derivation rather than a condition on representation.

In the case of a head with no intrinsic content, MERGE would have to take this head (assuming that the lexicon can include dummy heads) plus its complement and yield a new phrase marker. This is in violation of the principle of economy that we have suggested. In a system like Chomsky's, either there can be no contentless heads, or the principles of Economy apply to representations at spell-out but not to derivations. Above I have defended the view that AGR is a contentless head. Can we adopt the position that the Economy conditions apply to representations at spell-out rather than to derivations?

This view would predict that in cases where AGR lacks content initially but then verb movement has provided the head of AGR with content by spell-out, null subjects should be permitted. As mentioned briefly above, my system allows for languages which have the AGR affixes base-generated on the verb, but then have verb movement for some independent reason. It turns out that such languages do not allow null subjects. French is the most straightforward example—it is standardly taken to have weak agreement, but it has verb

---

[5] Projecting more than one node at a time becomes necessary in Kayne's system in order to explain why heads cannot adjoin to maximal projections. If the phrase has another phrase above it, the representation is ruled out by the LCA. However, if a head adjoins to the top of the phrase marker, the only way to rule it out by the LCA is to force the head to have a specifier position.

movement. However, it does not have null subjects under standard accounts.[6] Another example is auxiliaries in English. I assume that these are base-generated in some verbal projection, but move to AGR prior to spell-out. Thus, verb movement by itself is not sufficient to provide content to AGR for the purposes of the principles of Economy under consideration here. This means that the relevant principle must apply prior to verb movement, i.e. to the derivation. When verb movement takes place, there must be a contentless head for it to adjoin to, otherwise the conditions for checking of agreement features will not be satisfied. Thus, we must reject Chomsky's proposal that all phrase markers are created by the binary operation MERGE.

Instead, I advocate a view that is more in keeping with the proposal of Kayne (1994), Hoekstra (1991), or Speas (1990), where phrase markers are freely constructed, subject to constraints, whose *effects include* that phrase markers will be only binary branching. In Kayne's work, this effect is a by-product of the Linear Correspondence axiom, and in the work of Speas and Hoekstra it is a by-product of the fact that other relations of grammar are strictly local and bi-unique. My view, then, is that the phrase-building operation is not MERGE, but the operation PROJECT ALPHA (Speas 1990), which says nothing more than that any head may project any number of dominating nodes. Minimal and maximal projections are defined on specific representations, so X-bar theory is eliminated in that the labels on nodes and the internal structure of the categories follow from the interaction of other principles. However, the fact that syntactic phrases exist independent of the items within them remains as a primitive.[7]

Under this view, an entire phrase can be projected, but only if either a head or a specifier with content is available. In principle, Project Alpha applies freely. In practice, however, it is constrained by principles of Economy of Derivation.[8]

---

[6] In section 2.5, I will discuss the proposal of Rohrbacher (1994) that French does in fact have null subjects.

[7] This is essentially what remains in the theory of Kayne and Chomsky too. For Kayne, the problem is that, in order to rule out adjunction of a head to a non-head, it is necessary to stipulate that the topmost head in a chain of heads must have a specifier. Having to make this stipulation undermines the project of doing away with X-bar principles, since there is a principle that stipulates the requirement of a specifier in the topmost projection. For Chomsky, the problem is to distinguish correctly between projections and segments, and the solution amounts to a stipulation that MERGE may yield either segments or projections.

[8] This leaves open the possibility that there might be cases where some other considerations outweigh the cost of violating the Economy principles. Grimshaw (1997) proposes an Optimality-theoretic account of functional projections which includes a ranked constraint requiring that heads be filled. This has clear similarities to what I am proposing here, but since ranking has not been crucial to the analysis of any of the facts relevant to my proposal, I have not been able to make a fruitful comparison of the two.

A proposal with many similarities to this one has been made by Tait and Cann (1990), who give an account of null subjects in Italian using the following constraint on PF representations:

(11)    *PF-licensing principle* (Tait and Cann 1990)
Lexical $\alpha$ must be PF-licensed.
$\alpha$ is PF licensed iff
a. $\alpha$ is headed by $\beta$ which contains phonological material, or
b. $\alpha$, or the head of $\alpha$, is bound by a PF-licensed position.

This is similar to my proposal in that a phrase is licensed iff it is headed by something with content (for Tait and Cann, phonological content) or bound, where spec–head indexing counts as binding of the head of $\alpha$. It differs from my proposal primarily in being a condition on PF representation rather than on derivation. Above I mentioned the problem of languages in which fully inflected verbs move to AGR prior to spell-out (e.g. French) as a reason for thinking that the condition should be derivational. There are a few other reasons.

One problem with Tait and Cann's condition is that it is not clear how PRO can be licensed, particularly when it has no controller.[9] In my theory, there are several possible approaches to PRO. Perhaps the most obvious is to say that infinitives have no AGR at all. PRO would then occupy either the specifier of VP (PredP) or possibly the specifier of the TP whose head is occupied by 'to'. Related to this is the problem of empty operators. These are empty categories which may occupy the specifier of a CP that does not have a phonetically realized head, and the relationship between an empty operator and its identifying antecedent is generally taken not to involve binding *per se*. In my theory, the operator would be a category with semantic content, as it has scope-bearing features. Thus a phrase containing it plus a null head could be projected. For these reasons, I consider the condition that constrains phrase structures containing empty elements to be a condition on derivation rather than a condition on representation.[10]

---

[9] They mention that strictly semantic coindexing is not sufficient to count as binding, and that this has consequences for PRO, but they do not elaborate.

[10] One other proposal similar to mine is that of Contreras (1994), who proposes that spec,IP is not projected in Spanish. He does not discuss the Japanese-type languages, and he states his condition as a type of licensing condition; but the spirit of his proposal is to limit projection of unfilled positions by means of general principles.

## 2.4 Empirical and theoretical challenges to licensing and identification theories of null arguments

In this section, I will point out some problems with current theories of null arguments. These problems fall into three types. First, there is a relationship between agreement and the licensing of null arguments which is not captured in current theories. Second, the licensing condition relies on an arbitrary designation of what will be a licensing head in a given language. Third, the licensing and identification conditions both call for a relationship between levels of the grammar that I will argue is too strong.

Before proceeding to discuss these issues, we should address a much more fundamental question: on what basis have we decided that the null argument parameter is in fact anchored in some deeper principle of the grammar? The alternative would be to say that children simply learn through positive evidence which arguments may be null. Why do we not say that the children of Italian or Japanese speakers hear sentences lacking subjects, and hence know that subjects may fail to be pronounced, while children of English speakers do not hear such sentences, and hence know that subjects must be pronounced?

First of all, such a simple picture cannot be right because English-speaking children do in fact hear sentences lacking subjects: imperatives, non-finite clauses, and matrix sentences in the 'diary-drop' register all may lack subjects in English. Somehow, the child must learn to differentiate these contexts from those in which subjects may not be dropped, and hence at the very least the child is learning a rule more complex than the simple picture outlined above would suggest.

Second, the evidence from language acquisition is not consistent with the hypothesis that children learn whether their language omits subjects simply through positive evidence. Such a hypothesis would require that we assume that children start out by assuming that subjects cannot be dropped, until they have heard some evidence containing omitted subjects. But child language universally allows subjects to be null, indicating that children begin by assuming that subjects can always be omitted, and then must learn to *stop* omitting subjects if they are acquiring a language like English.

Finally, the possibility of omitting the subject of a finite clause does not exist as an isolated property in those languages which allow it. Rather, the existence of this property implies various other properties in the language, such as the possibility of postposing the subject, the lack of overt pleonastics, and the lack of that-t effects. This clustering of properties is compelling evidence that the relevant parameter is linked to a principle of UG, and is not a simple surface phenomenon.

### 2.4.1 *Agreement and null argument licensing*

Early accounts of the conditions on null arguments, such as Taraldsen (1980), drew a direct relationship between 'rich' agreement and the licensing of null subjects. In more recent work, it has become clear that the role of rich agreement is less direct. On the one hand there exist languages like German, which seems to have relatively rich agreement yet does not allow referential null subjects. On the other hand there are languages like Japanese, which lack person and number agreement altogether, yet allow referential null subjects. Thus, there is not a direct implicational relationship between rich agreement and the licensing of null subjects.

To capture the fact that Agreement seems to be correlated with the presence of null arguments yet is not a necessary or sufficient condition on them, Rizzi (1986a) proposed the following principles, in which agreement participates in the *identification* of pro, but not in the licensing of pro:

(12)   a. Pro is formally licensed through Case assignment by a designated head.

   b. Pro has the grammatical specification of the features of its licensing head coindexed with it.

The licensing class of heads in a given language may include INFL, and rich features of INFL will be shared by pro through the coindexation specified in (12b). However heads other than rich INFL can also serve as licensers, as long as there is a way for pro to get phi features. For example, Rizzi (1986a) argued that Italian has pro in object position, and suggested that there is an independent rule that can assign arb interpretation to a direct argument, and that this rule applies in the syntax in Italian but only in the lexicon in English. Thus, null objects can get (arb) features in Italian but this is not possible in English, so pro would wind up featureless and hence is not permitted. Under Rizzi's conditions in (12), rich agreement is not directly correlated with the licensing of pro. Pro is licensed by a designated head, and agreement is implicated only in the identification condition. Given the existence of languages like Japanese, we might consider divorcing AGR entirely from the theory of null arguments. Yet there are some compelling reasons to believe that there is in fact a relationship between agreement and the licensing of null arguments, and this relationship seriously weakens the plausibility of theories in which the licensing of pro is not linked to any property of agreement.

The first of these reasons is the intriguing generalization of Jaeggli and Safir (1989a), mentioned above and repeated here.[11]

(13)    *Jaeggli and Safir's generalization*
        Null subjects occur in the context of either very rich agreement or no agreement at all.

Jaeggli and Safir observed that null subjects are in general found in languages like Italian, Spanish, Navajo, and Hindi, where the agreement morphology seems in some intuitive sense to be sufficient without the overt subject, and they are also found in languages like Japanese, Chinese, and Thai, which have no person/number agreement at all.[12]

The condition under which null subjects are excluded is that found in languages like English: there is some residual agreement, but it is not 'rich'.

Jaeggli and Safir's generalization makes it apparent that null subjects are *unlicensed* in impoverished agreement languages. A licensing condition such as Rizzi's does not predict this correlation, since in principle any head could be a designated licensing head. Further, we cannot appeal to the identification condition to explain this generalization, because languages with no agreement at all have alternative ways of identifying null arguments, which for some reason languages with weak agreement are not permitted to use. Thus, there is a relation between agreement and null argument licensing which is not captured in current theories of the distribution of null arguments.[13]

The second reason to believe that there is a relation between agreement and null argument licensing has to do with a correlation between the two which is found in language acquisition. It is well known that children set the null argument parameter (in whatever form it may take) at around the time that they acquire inflection (see Hyams 1986; Hyams and Jaeggli 1988; Deprez and Pierce 1993; Lebeaux 1988). Roeper and Rohrbacher (1993; 2000) have found that in fact English-speaking children who have not yet set the parameter

[11] The issue of the empirical validity of this generalization will be addressed in section 2.5. I will argue that it is valid in essence, but that there are some languages with strong agreement which nonetheless do not allow null subjects. This kind of counter-example to the generalization will be shown to be consistent with the proposal I am making.

[12] Tateishi (1989) and Noguchi (1992) have argued that honorification in Japanese involves some sort of agreement. Since this agreement does not involve the standard sort of person and number features, I will assume that it does not involve an AGR projection.

[13] The theories of Huang (1984; 1989) and Borer (1989) are theories which do not have licensing and identification conditions *per se*. A detailed comparison of these two theories with the present one is beyond the scope of this chapter, although aspects of Huang's theory do figure in my discussion of null objects in section 2.7. Future work could find ways of combining their insights about control with my view of the nature of strong agreement, since the head projected by strong agreement will c-command other nodes in the tree in a way which an affix attached to the verb will not.

systematically allow null subjects *only* in the absence of agreement. Their sentences which lack subjects also lack agreement, and those which have agreement never lack subjects. Thus, we find examples like (14a, b) but never examples like (14c).

(14)　a. Where go?
　　　 b. Where dis goes?
　　　 c. *Where goes?

Roeper and Rohrbacher's data cannot be explained in terms of an identification condition, because children have some means of identifying the null subject in (14a), so they should be able to use that same means to identify a null subject in a sentence like (14c). Instead, these data indicate that null arguments fail to be *licensed* in the presence of weak agreement, yet are licensed when there is no agreement. See Roeper and Rohrbacher (2000) for extensive data and further discussion.

This problem of the correlation between agreement and null argument licensing becomes magnified when we consider how it bears on the nature of the Extended Projection principle. The EPP states that all clauses must have a subject, and a question has always arisen as to whether the EPP holds in languages which allow null subjects. When there is no thematic external argument, various researchers have pointed out that it would impose redundancy to insert a null pleonastic, which receives no interpretation at LF, for the sole purpose of satisfying the EPP. Some, such as Safir (1985) and Borer (1986), have proposed that (their formulation of) the EPP holds only in languages which do not allow null arguments. Safir, for example, suggests that nominative case must be phonetically realized in non-null subject languages, but not in null subject languages. But now it is a mystery why this realization condition is correlated with impoverished agreement. Why is it that nominative case need not be phonetically realized in languages with either rich agreement or no agreement at all? Why does the EPP hold only in languages with impoverished agreement? The relationship between the manifestation of EPP in such theories is still in need of explanation.

### 2.4.2 Theoretical problems with the licensing condition

There are further problems with an approach that specifies a licensing condition for null arguments. The most obvious of these is that the class of 'designated heads' which license pro is completely arbitrary. The licensing class of heads in a given language may include INFL, and strong features of INFL will be shared by pro through the coindexation specified in the identification condition. However heads other than rich INFL can also serve as licensers, as long as there is a way for pro to get phi features. For example, Rizzi argues that Italian has pro in object position, licensed by the designated verbal head, which assigns the null object an arbitrary interpretation. Because of this arbitrariness, it is not clear that saying that a child learns which are the classes of designated heads is any theoretical improvement over saying that a child learns the class of positions that can be null.

A further problem with the licensing condition approach is that this condition has two unusual properties, both having to do with the special phonological status of pro. First, the condition necessitates that the grammar allow some heads to be designated as licensers of a category with particular phonological properties (namely, the property of being unpronounced). There are no equivalent designations in other components of syntax involving other phonological properties. For example, there do not exist specific heads that license stressed NPs, specific heads that assign theta roles only to overt NPs, or specific heads that subcategorize for NPs with nasal consonants in them. Second, it necessitates that a particular lexical entry, pro, is subject to a special requirement in virtue of its phonological status. Such a condition is especially surprising in that the intuitive content of the need for a special requirement on an unpronounced constituent is satisfied by the identification requirement, independent of an additional licensing condition: if a constituent is not pronounced, it must be recoverable. Intuition aside, there are no other lexical items whose phonological properties cause them to be subject to some special syntactic requirement. Even the Case filter, which states that all NPs must bear Case to be visible, applies to any NP chain, and in the view of some (e.g. Chomsky 1992) also to pro, and hence need not include reference to the phonological properties of the NP. The Empty Category principle actually does not apply to all empty categories, but only to the non-pronominal ones, i.e. to traces. Traces occupy positions which were filled at some point in the derivation, and so Economy principles obviously allow the position they occupy to be generated at the time they are filled. Hence, the ECP is not a condition on categories in virtue of their status as phonologically null, but rather on categories in virtue of their status as launching sites for movement. Thus, neither the Case filter nor the ECP are actually principles which apply to a given entity because it is phonologically unpronounced. If, as is generally assumed, pro is simply a pronoun which lacks phonetic realization, there is no reason to expect its phonetic properties to call for a special licensing requirement.

A theory in which no special licensing condition on null arguments is needed will be more in keeping with the working hypothesis of Principles and

Parameters theory, that the modules of grammar are separate and distinct. The theory that I have outlined here accomplishes this goal.

## 2.5 Morphological properties and agreement strength

### 2.5.1 *Is there a morphological correlate to strong AGR?*

In the theory outlined above, I have adopted the view that there are two types of agreement, which we may term strong and weak agreement. I have proposed that strong agreement has an individual lexical entry, while weak agreement is listed in a paradigm and base-generated attached to the verb. A well-known problem in research into the relationship between agreement and null arguments is the difficulty in finding a systematic cross-linguistic correspondence between some particular morphological properties and the syntactic property of being strong enough to license null arguments or rich enough to identify them. The conclusion of most researchers, with which I will concur, is that there is no absolute cross-linguistic morphological correlate of 'strong' agreement.

However, whereas other researchers have drawn the further conclusion from this lack of absolute correlation that no property of AGR can be implicated in the licensing of empty categories, I do not draw this conclusion. Rather, I maintain that there is a correlation between weak agreement and the impossibility of leaving the specifier of AGRP null. In other words, if the agreement morphology shows the relevant property (which, I will claim, is the Full Paradigm property of Rohrbacher (1994)), then the individual affixes may have individual lexical entries and hence project an AGRP with no specifier. However, there can be languages which have the Full Paradigm property but still do not list the affixes individually. What we cannot have is languages which have some agreement but do not have the Full Paradigm property and which allow the specifier of AGRP to be null. Throughout this discussion, it is crucial to keep in mind that my proposal does not contain any specific *licensing condition* on pro; rather, the possibility of any null specifier follows from general principles of economy of projection. Thus, the lexical idiosyncrasy in my proposal involves whether a given set of morphemes in a language that has a Full Paradigm have independent lexical entries or are instead listed in the lexicon as part of a verbal paradigm. This idiosyncrasy is equivalent to a difference like that between object pronouns in English versus those in French, where the French pronouns simply have the morphosyntactic property of being clitics, while the English ones have the morphosyntactic property of being independent words.

The first step in this discussion will be to review the first influential attempts to find a morphological correlate of 'strong' agreement: Jaeggli and Safir's (1989a) Morphological Uniformity condition. I will claim, following Rohrbacher, that the Morphological Uniformity condition has clear and fatal counter-examples. I will then introduce Rohrbacher's Full Paradigm condition, and show that it is promising but, as it stands, makes undesirable predictions about the correlation between verb movement and pro-drop. Finally, I will argue that Rohrbacher's condition can in fact be taken to be a description of the morphological conditions under which agreement affixes might be given independent lexical entries, as long as we do not consider it to be obligatory that they do so.

### 2.5.2 *The Morphological Uniformity condition*

In their discussion of the relationship between morphological properties and the licensing of null subjects, Jaeggli and Safir (1989a) surveyed agreement paradigms in diverse languages and suggested the following descriptive generalization.

(15)   a. *The null subject parameter*
       Null subjects are permitted in all and only languages with
       morphologically uniform inflectional paradigms.
       b. Morphological Uniformity
       An inflectional paradigm P in a language L is morphologically
       uniform iff P has either only underived inflectional forms or only
       derived inflectional forms.

Languages like Spanish are morphologically uniform in that each form in the paradigm includes forms homophonous with the bare stem. Languages like Chinese and Japanese are morphologically uniform in that all verbal forms lack agreement morphology.

This hypothesis is intriguing, since it seems to capture why both Chinese and Italian allow null subjects while English does not. It characterizes 'weak agreement' as agreement that does not involve a uniform paradigm, and predicts, as my theory does, that null subjects should be allowed in all languages which do not have weak agreement.

Unfortunately, there are clear empirical problems with Morphological Uniformity. First, we find languages like Swedish, which have uniform paradigms with no apparent agreement morphology, yet do not allow null subjects.

(16)   a. 'throw'    present indic.
       kasta-r   kasta-r kasta-r kasta-r kasta-r kasta-r

    b. I dag    har    det    kommit    manga    linvister    hit.
       today    have    there    come      many      linguists    here.
    c. Reganade    det i  gar?
      rained       it      yesterday   (Platzack 1987)

Swedish meets Jaeggli and Safir's definition of Morphological Uniformity in that there is no agreement morphology at all (and this is the case in all tenses), only a suffix marking tense. Jaeggli and Safir's hypothesis predicts that Swedish will behave like Japanese in allowing null subjects. Instead, it behaves like English: null subjects are not allowed.

    Actually, if we look at some other aspects of the grammar of Swedish, we find evidence that Swedish is a language that has *weak* agreement, although Jaeggli and Safir's description of weak (i.e. non-uniform) fails to capture it. Swedish is distinguished from Japanese in having a residue of agreement in at least two different parts of the grammar. First, Swedish has gender and number agreement between nouns and determiners and adjectives. Second, the past participle, which 'functions, in effect, as an adjective' (Aulette 1975: xxvii) shows the same agreement as other adjectives.

(17)   Det-Adj-N agreement
      a. en          fin         lägenhet
         a           fine        flat (common gender)
      b. ett        fint        museum
         a           fine        museum (neuter gender)
      c. tva        museer
         two        museums
(18)   Past participles
      a. Brevit      var      skrivet
        letter-the   was    written
        'The letter  was    written'
      b. Breven     var      skrivna
        letters      was    written-pl
        'The letters  were   written'

The Swedish facts are a counter-example to Jaeggli and Safir's hypothesis about the relationship between overt morphology and null subjects. However, they seem to support their more general observation that null subjects are impossible in languages with weak agreement.[14]

---

[14] Under the theory being defended here, we are led to claim that Swedish requires an AGR projection at LF because the presence of residual agreement signals that it is an agreement-type

A second counter-example to Jaeggli and Safir's hypothesis is pointed out by Rohrbacher (1994). He shows that there are languages like Brazilian Portuguese, which have uniform paradigms with at least some marking for agreement, yet which also disallow null subjects. In fact, Rohrbacher draws attention to the fact that both European Portuguese and Brazilian Portuguese have uniform paradigms, yet European Portuguese allows null subjects while Brazilian Portuguese does not (examples from Rohrbacher 1994: 262):

(19)   European Portuguese        Brazilian Portuguese
       compr-ar 'to sell'         fal-ar 'to speak'
       1st compr-o compr-amos     1st fal-o fal-a
       2nd compr-as compr-am      2nd fal-a fal-am
       3rd compr-a compr-am       3rd fal-a fal-am

(20)   a. (*pro*)  Vi        seu      pai      quando    passei.
                   saw-1sg   your     father   when      passed-1sg
          'I saw your father when I passed by'   (European Portuguese)
       b. *(Eu)    vi        seu      pai      quando   *(eu)    passei.
          I        saw-1sg   your     father   when     I        passed-1sg
          'I saw your father when I passed by'   (Brazilian Portuguese)

Finally, as Rohrbacher points out, problems arise when we try to apply the uniformity criterion to languages that permit null expletives but do not permit null referential subjects. For example, German paradigms are uniform and Yiddish paradigms are not, lacking an affix for the first-person singular. Yet both languages allow null pleonastics in some contexts, and in fact the range of null pleonastics allowed in Yiddish seems to be greater than that in German.

(21)   German: *arbeiten* 'to work'
       Sing.      Pl.
       1 arbeit-e    arbeit-en
       2 arbeit-est  arbeit-et
       3 arbeit-et   arbeit-en

---

language. Since there is no overt verbal morphology to license that AGR projection, an overt subject is needed. I do not know how the presence of residual agreement would lead to the postulation of an AGR projection. The fact that past participles show agreement, however, is interesting. Perhaps the presence of the constructions with past participles signals the presence of AGR projections in the language, and once the language learner learns that such projections exist, they are assumed to be required in general. How this works will need to be explored carefully in future work.

(22)  Yiddish: *lib-n* 'to love'

| Sing. | Pl. |
|-------|-----|
| 1 lib | lib-n |
| 2 lib-st | lib-t |
| 3 lib-t | lib-n (Rohrbacher 1992) |

(23)  a. *Heute    arbeitet
          today     work-3sg
          'Today (he/she) works'
      b. *Leyenen  ot   di    bikher   (Yiddish)
          read-3pl  prt  those books
          '(They) read those books'

(24)  Null pleonastics in German
      a. Heute wird     getanzt
          today becomes  danced
          'Today there was dancing'
      b. Heute ist *?(es) klar   dass die Frau    das Buch gekauft hat
          today is         clear  that the woman  the book bought  has
          'Today it is clear that the woman has bought the book'
      c. Heute regnet *(es)
          today rains              (adapted from Travis 1984: 162)

(25)  Null pleonastics in Yiddish
      a. Ikh    meyn    az   in der krom kumt 0 a kind
          I       think   that in the store comes  a child
      b. Haynt geyt 0 a regn
          today goes    rain
          'Today it's raining'   (Travis 1984: 164)

The specifics of my own analysis of these various facts will be discussed further below. For now, we can conclude with Rohrbacher that the Morphological Uniformity condition cannot be correct.

### 2.5.3 *The Full Paradigm condition*

In this chapter I have adopted the proposal of Rohrbacher that some affixes have independent lexical entries while others are base-generated on their host. Rohrbacher's work was principally concerned with characterizing the morphological trigger for V-to-I movement, and only secondarily concerned with null subjects. However, he concluded that the conditions under which INFL is 'strong enough' to trigger V-to-I movement are the same ones as those in which INFL is 'strong enough' to license referential null subjects. He proposed that INFL has its own lexical entry, and hence both triggers V-to-I movement and can in principle license null subjects if and only if it has what he calls a Full Paradigm, which he defines as follows:

(26)    INFL is a referential category with lexically listed affixes in exactly those languages where regular subject-verb agreement minimally distinctively marks all referential INFL-features such that a. and b.:
a. In at least one number and one tense, the person features [1st] and [2nd] are distinctively marked.
b. In at least one person of one tense, the number feature [singular] is distinctively marked. (Rohrbacher 1994: 118)

In this system, it doesn't matter whether every cell in the paradigm has an overt affix, as long as the marking is distinctive in the way described in (26). A paradigm meeting the description in (26) is what Rohrbacher calls a Full Paradigm. The affixes of such a paradigm each have individual lexical entries. Rohrbacher adopts the theory of Speas (1994) whereby if an AGR affix heads its own projection, then null subjects are licensed. Thus, in Rohrbacher's theory, languages with Full Paradigms have both V-to-I movement and the possibility of null subjects. Although I adopt Rohrbacher's distinction between lexically projected affixes and affixes which do not have an independent lexical entry, there are two problems with his theory of the morphological correlate to strong agreement. The first problem is that his theory collapses the conditions for licensing null subjects with those for triggering V-to-I movement. The second is that he claims that all languages with a Full Paradigm have individually listed or 'referential' agreement affixes.

His prediction regarding the relationship between V-to-I movement and null subjects is that a language should allow null subjects iff it has V-to-I movement. Interestingly, I do not know of any languages which allow null subjects yet do not have V-to-I movement.[15] However, there do seem to be languages which have V-to-I movement yet do not allow null subjects. I will limit my attention here to the main cases that Rohrbacher discusses: French, which is not normally described as allowing null subjects but which clearly has V-to-I movement, and Yiddish and German, which allow only pleonastics to be null.

---

[15] Rohrbacher adopts my theory of the Chinese-type languages, which allow null subjects because they have no AGR at all. Therefore, in such languages it should not matter whether there is V-to-I movement. Insofar as Rohrbacher adopts my theory of AGR-less languages, he has the same problem with Swedish that I do, as described in the previous footnote.

French verbal morphology does not meet Rohrbacher's criterion for a Full Paradigm, yet French is the language used by Pollock (1989) to argue for his theory of verb movement. Rohrbacher's suggestion is that although the *suffixes* on French verbs do not have independent lexical entries, the subject clitics in French are actually AGR morphemes, to which the verb cliticizes. Since these clitics head the AGR projection, the specifier of AGR is null in sentences like (27).

(27)   Je   parle Anglais = *pro* je + parle Anglais
       1 sg speak English

This suggestion is supported by facts about colloquial French, for which I refer the reader to Rohrbacher's chapter 5. One problem with this suggestion is that it is now unclear where the affixes on the verb itself come from. French seems to have both independent AGR morphemes and also AGR morphemes on the verb. A more serious problem is that if these clitics are AGR, it is not clear why the clitic is not obligatory in the third person:[16]

(28)   Marie   parle    Anglais
       M       speaks   English

Thus, it seems to me that French remains as a counter-example to the claim that strong inflectional morphology is the trigger for V-to-I movement. Rather, I would claim that the trigger for verb movement differs from the criteria by which affixes are determined to have lexical entries and hence to project their own phrases. In a language like French, the *affixes* are base-generated on the verb, and the inflected verb moves to AGR.

The problems with the claim that all languages with a Full Paradigm have lexically listed agreement affixes arises when we look at languages like German and Yiddish, which seem to have strong agreement but allow only (certain) pleonastics to be null. Both German and Yiddish have referential INFL by Rohrbacher's definition, and so ought to have both V-to-I movement and null subjects.[17] In both of these languages, however, referential subjects cannot be null, although certain pleonastics may be null, as shown in (21–25) above. Because of this contrast between referential and pleonastic subjects, it has

---

[16] Rohrbacher does cite very interesting statistics about the frequency with which the clitics occur in spoken French. Still, among the studies he cites, clitics are absent in between 20% and 35% of sentences with NP subjects, so it seems clear that the clitic is not obligatory.

[17] Yiddish quite clearly has V-to-I movement, as demonstrated by Diesing (1990). With German it is hard to tell whether there is V-to-I movement: in matrix sentences the inflected verb occupies C, so may or may not have moved through I, and in (V-final) embedded sentences the inflected verb is final and so may or may not have undergone string-vacuous movement.

often been suggested that German AGR is strong enough to license null subjects, but not rich enough to identify them, and so null subjects are only possible if they need not be identified, i.e. if they are pleonastic. This is the approach that Rohrbacher follows, although he notes some interesting empirical problems with it. However, this sort of solution to the problem posed by German and Yiddish begs the question of whether there is a morphological correlate to strong/rich agreement: if the conditions on pro are supposed to be correlated with some morphological property, then how come the agreement in Yiddish and German is not rich enough to identify null subjects?

Furthermore, two additional sets of facts make this explanation insufficient. First, German and Yiddish differ in the contexts in which they allow null pleonastics. Specifically, in German certain constructions which might otherwise have a null pleonastic require an overt pleonastic if no other phrase is filling the specifier of CP; in Yiddish the specifier of IP (AGRP) must be filled, but not the specifier of CP. Therefore, some additional condition must be added over and above the identification condition. We will see below that this additional condition can be stated in terms of the Economy of Projection principle on which our analysis of null subjects is based, and that when it is so stated, the identification condition becomes unnecessary.

Second, German and Yiddish differ in the range of pleonastics which may be null. In Yiddish, any pleonastic which is not in first position (spec,IP/ AGRP) may be null, while in German only pleonastics which are not associated with any type of external argument or quasi-argument may be null. This means that the identification condition would have to be fairly complicated, and ad hoc. I will suggest instead that the facts follow from the nature of default agreement, which is found when the external argument bears no thematic role.

### 2.5.4 Null pleonastics: against the identification condition

2.5.4.1 *Yiddish null pleonastics* Yiddish does not allow null referential pronouns. Therefore, in my theory it should be classified as a language with weak AGR, needing a filled specifier in order for the AGR phrase to be projected. This requirement ought to hold whether the subject is referential or not. Interestingly, the facts of Yiddish as described by Diesing (1990) confirm this view, in that null pleonastics can never occupy the specifier of IP. Diesing's claim is that in general the verb in Yiddish moves to INFL (rather than to CONP as in other Germanic languages), and that the specifier of IP may be occupied either by the subject or by a topic. What is interesting from our point of view is that the specifier of IP must be filled. Null pleonastics may occur only if some other phrase occupies the specifier of IP.

(29)  *Haynt  leyenen  ot    di     bikher
      today   read-3pl  prt   those  books
      'Today (they) read those books'

(30)  a. Es       kumt   a       kind  in     krom
         comes    a      child   in    store
         'A child comes into the store'

      b. Ikh   meyn   az es   kumt   a    kind   in    der   krom
         I     think  that    comes  a    child  in    the   store
         'I think that a child comes into the store'

      c. In   krom    kumt 0   a     kind
         in   store   comes    a     child

      d. Ikh   meyn   az    in   der   krom    kumt 0   a     kind
         I     think  that  in   the   store   comes    a     child

      e. Es             geyt a    regn
         goes           rain
         'It's raining'

      f. Haynt          geyt 0 a        regn
         today          goes            rain
         'Today it's raining'   (Travis 1984: 164)

Thus, following Diesing, the adverb or PP in clause-initial position in (30c,d,f) is in the specifier of IP. (30a,b,e) would be ungrammatical without the pleonastic because the specifier of IP would be unoccupied. Since Yiddish is a language in which AGR affixes are base-generated on the verb, not having their own lexical entries, the specifier of AGRP must be occupied. Unlike in English, this specifier position is not necessarily an A-position, therefore the occupant need not be the subject.[18]

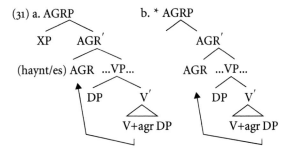

(31) a. AGRP                    b. * AGRP

         XP      AGR′                    AGR′

     (haynt/es) AGR  ...VP...       AGR  ...VP...

                    DP    V′              DP   V′

                       V+agr DP              V+agr DP

---

[18] The question of whether the A/A′ distinction is primitive or derives from some other subsystem of the grammar such as Case Theory is beyond the scope of this chapter.

When the subject is referential, it must be overt if it is to be the specifier which allows AGRP to be projected. Just as with pleonastic constructions in English, we need to rule out structures in which a null subject occupies the specifier of VP while some other overt element occupies the specifier of AGRP. We can adopt essentially the same analysis that we adopted in section 2.2: the subject in spec,VP must raise at LF for Feature Checking. The landing site of this movement is a position adjoined to the XP in the specifier of AGRP. If the raised subject is pro, which lacks its own phi features, it will not be possible for Feature Checking to take place, since no phi features will percolate to the XP which is in the appropriate spec,head relation.

(32)   *AGRP

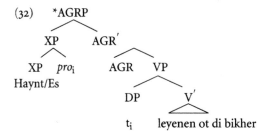

Thus, both Yiddish and English are languages in which agreement affixes are base-generated on the verb. The languages differ in two ways: in Yiddish, the verb must move to AGR in the syntax, and in Yiddish the specifier of AGRP need not be an A-position. Because the specifier need not be an A-position, pleonastics need not be overt if some other phrase occupies this position.

2.5.4.2 *German null pleonastics*   The standard view of the Verb Second effect in German is that it involves movement of the inflected verb to C, along with movement of some XP to the specifier of CP. Thus, the obligatorily overt pleonastics in sentences like (33) and (34) are fulfilling a requirement that the specifier of CP be filled (see Safir (1985) for an analysis along these lines).

(33)   a. Es        wird        getanzt
           pl.         becomes    danced
           'There was danced'
       b. *Wird      getanzt
           becomes   danced
(34)   a. Es   sind   drei   Kinder     gekommen
           pl.   are    three   children   come
           'There have come three children'
       b. *Sind   drei   Kinder     gekommen
           are     three   children   come

Thus, some condition must be added to the licensing and identification principle stipulating that the first position cannot contain a null pleonastic, even though these are in principle permitted, as we see in (35b,d).

(35)    a. Es     wurde   gestern    auf   dem   Schiff   getanzt
           EXPL   was     yesterday   on    the     ship     danced
           'There was dancing on the ship yesterday'
     b. Gestern    wurde (*es)   auf   dem   Schiff   getanzt
           yesterday   was           on    the     ship     danced
           'There was dancing on the ship yesterday'
     c. Sie    sagte,   es       wurde   getanzt
           she    said    EXPL     was     danced
     d. ... wenn   getanzt   wurde
           since       danced    was

These facts follow directly from the principles of Economy of Projection if we assume that the relevant condition is that CP must be projected in German. If the head of CP is filled by an overt complementizer, as in (35d), then nothing needs to be in the specifier of CP. If no overt complementizer occupies the head of CP in the initial structure, then CP must have a filled specifier, either a pleonastic or some other XP. As we saw in Yiddish, the head must be filled *before V-movement* in order for the specifier to be empty. The pleonastic arises only if neither spec,CP nor the head of CP has any content prior to V-movement.

In section 2.5.3, we saw that German overt pleonastics show up in spec,CP, but do not appear in spec,IP(AGRP). The spec,AGRP seems to be allowed to be null when the subject is non-thematic. However, the facts now become more complex, since some types of pleonastics cannot be null. Following Safir (1985), we may characterize those contexts in which pleonastics must be overt as those in which the predicate assigns some sort of thematic role to its external argument, in contrast to the cases above, where there is no external argument whatsoever. The predicates which assign some sort of thematic role to an external argument include weather predicates and predicates which take a sentential subject.

(36)    a. Es   ist   klar,   dass   die   Frau     das   Buch   gekauft   hat
              is    clear   that   the   woman   the   book   bought   has
           'It is clear that the woman has bought the book'
     b. Heute   ist es   klar   dass   die   Frau     das   Buch   gekauft   hat
           today   is     clear   that   the   woman   the   book   bought   has
           'Today it is clear that the woman has bought the book'

c. *Heute ist klar dass die Frau das Buch gekauft hat
today is clear that the woman the book bought has
'Today it is clear that the woman has bought the book'

(37) a. Es regnet
it rains
'It is raining'
b. Heute regnet es
today rains
c. *Heute regnet.
today rains    (Travis 1984: 162)

These facts suggest that the specifier of AGRP cannot be empty, unless the predicate is one which assigns no theta role at all, as in (37a). Aside from the cases in (36), then, German behaves exactly as English does: the inflectional morphology is base-generated on the verb and hence, in order for AGRP to be projected, the specifier of AGRP must be filled, either by a pleonastic or by a referential NP.

As for the sentences in (36) where the pleonastic does not occur, for some reason the specifier of AGRP need not be filled when the predicate assigns no role at all to an external argument. I would like to suggest that in this case, the agreement on the verb is default agreement, which does not need to be checked at LF. The suggestion that the agreement found with this sort of predicate is a default agreement is not new; Burzio (1986) characterizes similar cases in English as involving a failure of agreement:

(38)    There's three cats on the porch

So suppose German differs minimally from English in that default agreement need not be checked at LF. If agreement need not be checked, then there is no reason that AGRP would have to be projected. In embedded clauses, the verb could remain *in situ,* and in matrix clauses it could move directly to C. In either case, no AGRP would be projected, and so there is no expletive.

### 2.5.5 Discussion: licensing, identification, and morphology

In this section we have reviewed two of the most promising attempts to find a specific morphological property which correlates with syntactically 'strong' agreement. The problem of whether there is a morphological correlate to strong AGR is independent of whether the theory of null subjects involves licensing and identification, Feature Checking, or Economy of Projection. In my theory, strong agreement is defined as agreement which has an independent lexical entry for each affix. If there should turn out to be no morphological correlate of strong agreement, then whether affixes have independent entries will have to be stipulated, as other theories will have to stipulate that given heads are Licensers or that N or V features are strong. The advantage that my theory has over these others is that I will only have to stipulate something that must be determined for any item in a language anyway: what sort of representation it has in the lexicon. I do not need to add any other features or conditions.

We saw that Jaeggli and Safir's (1989a) Morphological Uniformity condition suffers from fatal empirical weaknesses. I argued further that Rohrbacher's (1994) Full Paradigm condition on the referentiality of INFL is problematic in that it predicts that all languages with V-to-I movement allow null subjects, and it requires us to add an ad hoc and empirically insufficient identification condition to capture the facts of German and Yiddish, which have V-to-I movement but allow only null pleonastics, and these only in certain contexts. Thus it seems that we must conclude, at least at present, that there is no absolute morphological property which correlates with strong AGR.

What, then, of the descriptive generalization made by Jaeggli and Safir upon which my theory is based: that null subjects occur in the context of either strong AGR or no AGR at all? If this generalization is abstract rather than directly related to some morphological property, then why did Jaeggli and Safir make the original observation based upon surface properties of the languages that they had looked at? Do we expect now to find a language which has a morphological paradigm like that of English but which allows null subjects?

We can answer this question by observing more closely the cases which constitute counter-examples to the proposed morphological correlates. We find languages like Swedish, which show that Morphological Uniformity is not the correct characterization of strong vs. weak agreement, but which confirm the observation that languages with weak agreement do not allow null subjects. We also find languages like Brazilian Portuguese, Yiddish, and German, which meet Rohrbacher's criterion for strong agreement, yet still do not allow the specifier of AGRP to be null. What we do not find is languages with paradigms like English but which allow the specifier of AGRP to be null. In other words, if a language has a Full Paradigm, the agreement affixes may be listed as independent lexical entries, but they are not necessarily so listed. Whether they are so listed is a language-specific idiosyncrasy. However, if the language has some agreement but does not have a Full Paradigm, the affixes *cannot* be listed independently; the paradigm must be stored as such and the affixes must then be base-generated on the verb. Thus, when we look across languages, we will find that languages with weak agreement, which we are now defining as languages with some agreement but without a Full Paradigm, cannot allow the specifier of AGRP to be null, and some languages with strong agreement (i.e. with a Full Paradigm) will allow the specifier of AGRP to be null (although others will not).

## 2.6  Checking the typological predictions

Our theory so far is that general economy principles dictate that in languages with weak agreement, the specifier of AGRP must be overt, whereas in languages with no agreement at all, there is no such requirement, because there is no AGRP at any level. In languages with strong agreement we will find some which allow the specifier of AGRP to be null and others which do not, depending upon whether the agreement affixes have independent lexical entries. The predictions of this theory so far are clear: a language should forbid null subjects if and only if it has weak agreement, and should allow null subjects if it has no agreement at all.

| (39) | Predicted language types | | |
|---|---|---|---|
| | Agreement type | spec,AGRP may be null | spec,AGRP must be filled |
| | Strong | Spanish | Yiddish |
| | Weak | * | English |
| | None | Japanese | * |

In a recent article claiming that there is no systematic relationship between richness of agreement and the licensing of null subjects, Hermon and Yoon (1990) cite examples that they believe instantiate the two types above[19] which the present theory predicts should be impossible. They cite Irish as a language that has weak agreement yet allows null subjects, and cite Papiamentu, Duka, Guaymi, and Tagalog as languages that have no agreement at all yet do not allow null subjects. I will outline in this section what my theory would have to say about these languages. The suggestions made in this section will be of necessity sketchy. There is clearly a good deal of work to be done toward a complete analysis of the phenomena in question; my goal here is to demonstrate a plausible response to the apparent counter-examples that I have encountered so far.

---

[19] They also discuss languages like German, which has strong agreement but disallows referential null subjects; but as outlined above, my theory does not predict that such a language would have to have null subjects.

## 2.6.1 *Weak agreement and null subjects: Irish?*

Hermon and Yoon consider Irish to have weak agreement because many but not all Irish inflected verbs are in the so-called 'analytic' forms, which have no person/number marking. This can be illustrated by the paradigm for the conditional of the verb *cuir*, 'put', as given in McCloskey and Hale (1984: 489).

(40) Sing. chuirfinn      Pl. chuirfimis
          chuirfea            chuirfeadh sibh
     (m.)  chuirfeadh se      chuirfeadh siad
     (f.)  chuirfeadh si

In this paradigm, the third-person singular and plural and the second-person plural are in the analytic form. The verb itself shows tense and mood, but no person or number. The first-person singular and plural and the second-person singular are in the synthetic form, which encodes person and number as well as tense and mood. Hermon and Yoon consider this a weak paradigm, since four out of seven forms fail to show person/number agreement features.

However, Irish differs from a language like English in that when the verb is marked for person and number (i.e. is in the form known as the 'synthetic' form), null subjects are possible. Null subjects are not possible with the analytic forms.[20] This means that null subjects will often be possible with some members of the paradigm but not with others. I would treat this not as a weak agreement system but rather as a strong agreement system with lexical gaps. Using the paradigm above as an example, I would claim that the analytic forms of each verb are listed, in their gapped paradigm. In addition, the lexicon includes listings of each of the agreement affixes. In keeping with general principles of economy, a representation in which there is *both* an independent AGR affix and an analytic form verb is redundant, since each analytic form verb is drawn from a cell in the paradigm.

(41) Stem= *chuir* 'put (conditional)'
     1 sing.              1 pl.
     2 sing.              2 pl. chuirfeadh
     3 sing. (m.) chuirfeadh 3 pl. chuirfeadh
     3 sing. (f.)  chuirfeadh

(42) AGR affixes
     -finn   (1 sing.)
     -fimis  (1 pl.)
     -fea    (2 sing.)

---

[20] McCloskey and Hale note that null pleonastics are possible in certain circumstances with the analytic forms.

Under this analysis, Irish is similar to Hebrew, which has been described as having partial pro-drop. A thorough analysis of such languages is beyond the scope of this article. See Speas (1994) for a few comments on Hebrew, and Benedicto (1993) for a more thorough discussion, and an analysis that is not related to the present theory. At any rate, it seems clear that Irish is not a weak agreement language in the sense that English is. Thus, it does not falsify the predictions outlined above.

### 2.6.2 *No agreement and no null subjects: Haitian and Tagalog*

Hermon and Yoon (1990) mention four languages as having no agreement at all but still not allowing null subjects: Papiamentu, Duka, Guaymi, and Tagalog. The information available to me on the first three of these is rather sketchy, and so I will look at another language, Haitian Creole, which seems to have properties similar to those cited by Hermon and Yoon.

Ultimately, of course, a more thorough analysis of these possible counter-examples should be done; here I hope just to sketch out what my analysis of such cases would have to involve. As for Tagalog, both Kroeber (1991) and Hung et al. (1992) analyse it as *having* a form of agreement (although the agreement morphemes themselves indicate features other than person and number), and so I will set it aside. Haitian Creole has also been described as a language lacking agreement but disallowing null subjects. However, for reasons independent of the present theory, DeGraff (1993) argues that the morphemes that other people have analysed as pronouns are in fact agreement markers, which are clitics rather than affixes. Thus, in a sentence like (43), the obligatory person/number morpheme is not a pronoun; rather it occupies the head of AGR, and differs from a language like Italian only in that it cliticizes but does not completely affix to the verb.

(43)  *(mwen/ou/f/nou/yo)    achte    yon    chemiz
     1sg/2sg,pl/3sg/1pl/3pl)    buy    DET    shirt
     'I bought a shirt'    Haitian (from DeGraff 1993)

These AGR morphemes are lacking in constructions where no thematic role is assigned to the subject, as in (44). This resembles the situation in German, where I suggested that such constructions actually have no agreement, and hence no AGR projection. As in German, Haitian does have agreement in constructions where an external theta role is assigned to a sentential argument, as in (45).

(44)  a. te    fe    fret
     ANT    make    cold
     'It was cold'

b. Gen    jwet    sou    tab    la
    have    toys    on    table    DET
    'There are toys on the table' (DeGraff 1993: 72)

(45) *(li)    difisil    pou    nou    jwenn    travay
     3 sg    hard    for    1 pl    find    job
     'it is hard for us to find a job' (DeGraff 1993: 85)

If an analysis along these lines can be extended to those languages which have been said to lack agreement but have obligatorily overt subjects, then the predictions of my theory will be met: all languages which lack agreement also allow null arguments.[21]

## 2.7 On null objects

I have claimed that null subjects are licensed whenever they are not needed as a specifier to license the presence of a projection. In Speas (1994; 1996), I attempt to extend this theory to null objects. Here I would like simply to sketch the issues that arise and suggest a line of research.

The problem is clear: I have claimed that null arguments are possible whenever a given category has a filled head. This appears to predict that all languages ought to allow null objects, since the verb will license the projection of VP with or without an overt object.

The idea that I would like to pursue in future research is that objects are in fact in specifier positions, and null objects are licensed if they are not needed in order to allow the projection of a VP shell in the sense of Hale and Keyser (1991) and Larson (1988).[22]

Larson and Hale and Keyser propose that the internal structure of VP includes more than one maximal projection of the predicate. That is, they suggest that in addition to the immediate projection of the lexical head, there is an upper VP shell into which the verb moves. The direct object, in their theory, occupies the specifier of the internal VP, and the verb moves over it to reach its surface position.

---

[21] In analysing a language that appears to have obligatory subjects, it is important to consider whether the relevant obligatory position is really the specifier of AGRP. If the language has some reason necessarily to project some other functional projection that has no contentful head (eg. CP), then we may find some other specifier position to be obligatory, as in German matrix sentences where the specifier of CP is obligatory.

[22] I am grateful to Jon Nissenbaum for extensive discussion of the possibility that all direct objects are specifiers. He has pursued this idea in an analysis of French participle agreement.

(46)   VP 'shells'

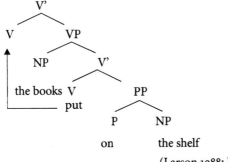

(Larson 1988; Hale and Keyser 1991)

Actually, it is unclear whether the verb moves to its surface position or is base-generated in the upper VP and controls the lower V position. Hale and Keyser use the movement account because they want to claim that a phrase like *shelve the books* is derived through movement from an underlying structure which is just like (46), and in which the N *shelf* moves through an empty P, an empty V, on up to the higher V. The problem with this is that for many such derivations there is evidence that the resulting verb must be formed in the lexicon rather than in the syntax. These problems might be avoided if a fully derived verb were inserted into the higher position, and controlled lower positions. For the simple verb phrase in (46), this results in a structure like (47).

(47)

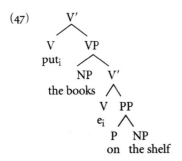

We may note that the operation of a general principle of economy such as the one that I made explicit above in (5) is implicit in the work of Hale and Keyser and of Larson. In their theories, VP shells are allowed to be projected above the VP which projects from the verbal lexical entry. Presumably this process is restricted so that only XPs which will receive some sort of interpretation can be projected. It is interesting, then, if we find empirical consequences supporting the presence of such a principle.

Suppose that (47) is the underlying structure for a ditransitive VP in English. The lower verbal head is empty. By the Economy principles discussed above, we would expect that the specifier of this projection could then not be empty. If it were, both the head and the specifier would be empty and the lower VP projection would not be licensed. (Recall that pro does not count as a specifier with content, because it does not have phi features until they are filled in by agreement or control.)

(48)  \* VP

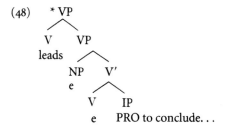

```
        * VP
        /  \
       V    VP
     leads  /  \
          NP    V'
          e    /  \
              V    IP
              e    PRO to conclude. . .
```

I would like to tentatively suggest that languages which lack null object pronominals use a control-type structure like (47) as the underlying structure for transitive and ditransitive VPs, and that languages like Italian which allow null objects use a raising-type structure like (46), as illustrated in (49).

(49)

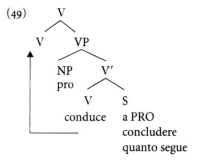

```
            V
           /  \
          V    VP
          ↑   /  \
            NP    V'
            pro  /  \
               V    S
          conduce  a PRO
                   concludere
                   quanto segue
```

In Speas (1994; 1996) I pursue this idea further, trying to find some independent evidence for this proposed difference between Italian and English. The results were not conclusive in any way, and so I will not review those suggestions here. Future research must seek such independent evidence to support the tentative suggestions made here.

I will close this section with some brief comments on previous accounts of the licensing of null objects. Two tacks have been taken in the literature to attempt to explain the distribution of null objects. Both wind up amounting essentially to a stipulation that null objects are or are not permitted in a given language.

As was discussed above, Rizzi (1986a) proposed that pro is formally licensed through Case assignment by a designated head, and that languages vary with respect to which heads are designated. In Italian, both INFL and V are designated heads, while neither is in English. Under this theory, there should be no correlation whatever between richness of agreement and the licensing of null arguments (although there could be a correlation between rich agreement and the identification of null arguments). A given head either is or is not a designated head.

Huang (1984; 1991) outlines a theory which, like mine, does away with a specific licensing condition on null arguments. Rather, pro is in principle licensed in any position in every language, but its actual distribution is constrained by the operation of a Generalized Control Rule. The way in which Huang accounts for the various familiar cases is summarized in (51).

(50)    *Generalized Control Rule* (Huang 1984)
An empty pronominal is controlled in its Control Domain.
Control Domain: The lowest NP or S that contains the pronominal and a SUBJECT accessible to the pronominal.

(51)    a.  English subject of finite clause
GCR forces pro to be coindexed with AGR, and then AGR fails to be rich enough to identify pro.
b.  Italian subject of finite clause
GCR forces pro to be coindexed with AGR, and then AGR is rich enough to identify pro.
c.  Chinese subjects
GCR forces pro to be coindexed with higher subject.
d.  Chinese objects
GCR forces object to be coindexed with subject, in violation of principle B. Null objects in Chinese are variables, not pro.
e.  Null object in language with rich object AGR [Pashto] GCR forces pro to be coindexed with Object AGR, which is rich enough to identify pro.

Unfortunately, some problems with Huang's approach have been uncovered by researchers who have applied his criteria to other languages which lack agreement. Huang's theory makes the prediction that null objects can be pro only in a language which has rich object agreement. In a language like Chinese with no agreement, null objects must be variables. However, several authors who have applied Huang's tests to other languages lacking agreement have found that, by Huang's tests, these languages have pro in object position. Two such languages are Korean, investigated by Yoon (1985), and Thai, investigated by Hoonchamlong (1991). A summary and discussion of these types of data can be found in Cole (1987) and in Speas (1996). Cole proposed that the GCR is parameterized: languages like Thai do not apply the GCR to small pro. The problem with this is that Huang's GCR was designed to be a simple extension of the principles of control, and was intended to be subject to internal parameterization with respect to the possible minimal domain and possible controllers. However, it was not intended to apply only to one type of null pronominal, or only in some languages. Further, there is no clear independent evidence of the operation or lack of operation of the GCR in the relevant languages. If we have to stipulate whether a given language uses/ does not use the GCR for small pro, as Cole suggested, then we might as well simply stipulate that the language does/does not allow null pronominal objects. Thus, as with the designated head theory, we are left with a stipulation that a given language either does or does not allow null pronominal objects.

What I have presented in this section is an attempt to apply a general principle of Economy of Projection to account for the distribution of null objects. The account is very sketchy, but I hope to have demonstrated an alternative to either stipulating a class of licensing heads or allowing the Generalized Control rule to apply only in certain languages.

## 2.8 Conclusion

I have proposed that a very general principle of Economy of Derivation constrains how phrases are projected, in a way that explains the distribution of null subjects, and possibly all null arguments. My suggestion is that, adapting the proposal of Rohrbacher (1992; 1994), strong AGR is listed in the lexicon with each affix having an individual lexical entry, while weak AGR is listed attached to its verbal host in a paradigm. This proposal, combined with general Economy principles that have the effect that XP is projected only if X or spec,XP have content, yields the result that null subjects are not allowed in languages with weak AGR, since in such a language the head of AGRP will have no content. Languages which lack agreement altogether, such as Japanese and Thai, do not project an agreement phrase at all, and so the question of the content of such a phrase does not arise.

The Extended Projection principle follows very naturally under this theory. We expect to find overt pleonastics in just those environments where the head of a necessary phrase does not have the content required to license the projection. Evidence from German and Yiddish suggests that this explanation of the distribution of pleonastics is superior to previous explanations that were linked to some version of the Extended Projection principle—along with an identification condition on empty categories.

Crucial to my proposal is the claim that AGR can be radically empty in weak agreement languages. I defended this view, and showed how it leads us to conclude that the principles that govern the generation of phrase structure project entire phrases, rather than just one node at a time.

Since my proposal makes use of the distinction between strong and weak agreement, I addressed the question of the relationship between strong/weak agreement and specific properties of morphological paradigms. I argued that locating the weak/strong distinction in whether a language does/does not assign individual lexical entries to its agreement affixes allows the learned idiosyncrasy to be located in properties of the mapping from lexicon to syntax which must be learned in any case. With this proposal there is no need to add an additional condition regarding whether a given head is a member of the class of licensing heads.

I suggested that the Full Paradigm condition of Rohrbacher (1994) seems to characterize correctly the morphological property correlated with strong agreement, if we consider a Full Paradigm to be a necessary condition on the language treating agreement affixes as individual lexical items, but not as a sufficient condition. If a language has a Full Paradigm, it may list each affix separately, but it need not. On the other hand, if a language does not have a Full Paradigm, then all affixes must be base-generated on the verb. One important thing that differentiates this proposal from similar ones which contain licensing and identification conditions on pro is that the possibility of any null specifier follows from general principles of economy of projection. Thus, the lexical idiosyncrasy in my proposal involves whether a given set of morphemes in a language that has a Full Paradigm have independent lexical entries or are instead listed in the lexicon as part of a verbal paradigm. This idiosyncrasy is one which must be learned in any case; it is equivalent to (for example) a difference like that between object pronouns in English and those in French, where the French pronouns simply have the morphosyntactic property of being clitics, while the English ones have the morphosyntactic property of being independent words.

I also made some tentative suggestions about the application of the Economy principles to the projection of VP shells, and hypothesized that null objects are possible only in languages in which V raising is possible within a VP shell.

If the proposals outlined here are on the right track, then the licensing condition on null arguments will no longer need to be stipulated. If they are on the wrong track, then it would seem that the project of looking for an explanatory theory of the licensing of pro is itself on the wrong track. The present proposal turns out to have interesting implications for the theory of how children can go from thinking that their language allows null subjects to learning that it does not. Rather than taking the position that the child begins by believing that the null subject parameter has a positive setting and then learns that this was incorrect, the child would begin by not being aware that the language had agreement, and thus would treat the language as being like Japanese. Null subjects are permitted because no AGRP is assumed to exist. When the child learns that his/her language has AGRP, s/he must at the same time learn whether AGR is strong or weak. If the language lacks a Full Paradigm, then s/he knows that affixes must be base-generated on the verb, and hence knows that null subjects are not permitted. If the language has a Full Paradigm, s/he must still learn whether affixes are individually listed, but once this is learned, the possibility or lack thereof of null subjects will follow. Under this view, there is no null subject parameter, only an AGR strength parameter, coupled with the general principles of Economy of Representation.

# 3

# Deriving the Difference between Full and Partial Pro-Drop

OLAF KOENEMAN

## 3.1 Introduction

A much-studied phenomenon in linguistics is the possibility of leaving out a subject from a tensed clause. In Spanish, for instance, a declarative tensed clause can consist of a tensed verb only (see (1a)). The English equivalent of the Spanish sentence is ungrammatical (see (1b)), showing that this possibility is parametrized across languages.

(1)  a.  Habla                                   (Spanish)
         speak-3sg
         '(S)he speaks'
     b.  *Talks                                  (English)
         talk-3sg
         '(S)he talks'

The parameter postulated to capture this contrast is usually referred to as the pro-drop, or null-subject, parameter. It seems to be the case that the choice between the two values that this parameter can take is not arbitrary. The option of dropping an argumental, or thematic, subject (i.e. subjects that receive a fully-fledged theta role from the predicate) seems related to an identification requirement: an overt subject can be left out from a tensed clause if the language in question has rich agreement inflection. In the present-tense paradigm, Spanish has six distinct endings following the verbal stem, whereas English has only one, the third-person singular -s, which

I would like to thank Peter Ackema, Fred Weerman, and four anonymous reviewers for commenting on an earlier and inferior version of this chapter. Naturally, I take full responsibility for the final outcome.

alternates with a zero ending. It is therefore intuitive to claim that subjects can remain absent in the former because inflection provides enough information to recover the missing argument (e.g. Taraldsen 1980; Rizzi 1982). This view is captured by (2):

(2)  *Identification condition (loosely stated)*
     An overt subject can be left out from a declarative clause if verbal
     agreement is rich enough to identify it.

Although the idea that the values of the null-subject parameter are derivable from a condition like the one in (2) has received widespread acceptance and seems empirically successful, it has not remained unchallenged. There are roughly three problems.

First of all, languages like Chinese and Japanese do not show subject agreement on verbs at all and yet they have the possibility of leaving out the subject in a tensed clause. These languages, then, are a direct problem for an hypothesis claiming that a positive setting of the null-subject parameter is related to rich inflection.

Second, there are languages that do not allow argumental subjects to be dropped but do have specific constructions without an overt subject, such as expletive constructions (e.g. in Russian), impersonal passives (e.g. in German), or generic impersonal constructions (e.g. in Icelandic). Under the assumption that subject-drop is determined by a binary-valued parameter, these languages cannot be described by adopting either setting, suggesting that the hypothesis in (2) at least needs refinement.

Third, there are languages that do have argumental subject drop but only partially so. Hebrew and Standard Finnish have six distinctions in their agreement paradigm, like Spanish. However, thematic subjects can be dropped only in first- and second- and not in third-person contexts. In Hebrew, this is even further restricted to the past and future tense. Data are from Vainikka and Levy (1999) (hereafter V&L).

(3)  a. Nousin        junaan                              (Finnish)
        step-past-1sg  train-into
        'I boarded the train'
     b. *Nousi        junaan
        step-past-3sg  train-into
        'He boarded the  train'
(4)  a. Aliti         al ha-rakevet                       (Hebrew)
        step-past-1sg  on the-train
        'I boarded the  train'

b. *Ala al        ha-rakevet
stepped-past-3sg   on the-train
'He boarded the    train'

Again, these languages cannot be accounted for by adopting a simple binary parameter: Hebrew and Finnish provide evidence for two settings at the same time. Interestingly, however, subject-drop in Hebrew is blocked altogether in the present tense, which differs from the past and future tenses in that person and number marking on the verb is absent. This means that, despite constituting a problem for a binary parameter approach, Hebrew still provides evidence for a correlation between pro-drop and agreement inflection, just as (2) claims.

Given the intuitive plausibility and empirical success of the condition in (2), I believe that it is still fruitful to maintain it and to find solutions for the problems mentioned. The success of the 'identification approach' then hinges on the success with which potential counterexamples are tackled. This chapter will focus on the third one, the existence of the partial pro-drop languages Hebrew and Standard Finnish.[1] V&L have proposed complementing (2) with a particular licensing condition, a strategy superficially reminiscent of Rizzi (1982).[2] This enables them to integrate languages with partial pro-drop into one and the same theory. I will argue that there is no need for such an additional licensing condition, and that (partial) pro-drop of argumental subjects can be accounted for basically by referring to properties of the agreement paradigms.

The central hypothesis will be that in the partial pro-drop languages under discussion the paradigm of agreement forms and the paradigm of subject pronouns are connected in the lexicon: first/second-person affixes in Finnish and Hebrew form the bridge between two paradigms, the agreement paradigm and the paradigm of pronouns, and are as such part of both. The first- and second-person agreement markers share with the third-person marker

---

[1] See Jaeggli and Safir (1989a), Speas (1994), and Koeneman (2000: 60, n. 7) for discussion of the problem raised by languages like Chinese and Japanese. The second problem, i.e. subject-drop in specific constructions, can be immediately dismissed by stating that (2) is intended to make predictions for the possibility of dropping *argumental* subjects only. See Rizzi (1982), Vikner (1995), and Cabredo Hofherr (Chapter 8 below) for approaches that try to incorporate expletive constructions into the theory of pro-drop.

[2] Rizzi's (1982) motivation for a licensing condition is different from the motivation in V&L— namely, the attempt also to capture languages that have constructions with empty expletives. Since this chapter deals only with argumental pro-drop, the critique of the introduction of a licensing condition is directed against a condition of the type introduced by V&L and not against Rizzi's approach. Whether expletive-drop has to be accounted for with the use of a licensing condition is a different issue.

the fact that they are affixal and must be generated on the verb. At the same time they share with pronouns the fact that they can function as a subject of the clause on their own. The third-person affixes, on the other hand, are not directly connected to the pronoun system. In short, the representation is the one given in (5).

(5)                                   {1st/2nd person affixes}

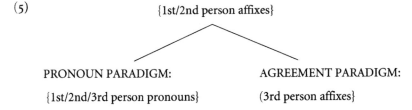

PRONOUN PARADIGM:                          AGREEMENT PARADIGM:

{1st/2nd/3rd person pronouns}              (3rd person affixes}

When the verb is generated in the syntax, the presence of a first/second-person affix on it allows the absence of an overt DP subject in Hebrew and Standard Finnish, just as in Spanish. The third-person affixes, however, stand in direct opposition to the pronouns and are consequently treated as elements without pronominal behaviour. They are, therefore, not able to license argumental subject drop in syntax. I will make this proposal more concrete later on, but let me mention at this point that the rather unique representation in (5) is related to the fact that, unlike third-person affixes, first/second-person affixes have a strong morphological connection, either synchronically or diachronically, with first/second-person pronouns. Since such a connection is not attested in, for instance, the Romance null-subject languages, the agreement and pronoun paradigms are not connected as in (5) in, for instance, Spanish. Hence, the contrast between full and partial pro-drop is derived.

This chapter is organized as follows. First, I will present the relevant data in section 3.2 and show that there is actually a cluster of facts that an analysis ideally should account for. In sections 3.3 and 3.4, the proposal introduced above will be outlined in more detail. After that, I will argue in section 3.5 that other analyses run into problems that are not encountered by the current proposal. Section 3.6 contains a general conclusion.

## 3.2 Finnish and Hebrew: some syntactic and morphological background

The central fact to be explained is that in Standard Finnish and Hebrew an overt DP subject does not have to appear in the presence of a first/second-person agreement marker, whereas it is obligatory to have one in third-person contexts.[3] V&L mention some additional facts that seem to cluster together with the partial pro-drop paradigm, one syntactic and one morphological. Despite these similarities, there is an important word-order difference between Hebrew and Standard Finnish that I would like to discuss as well. Let us look at each in turn.

Although no overt subject has to appear in first/second-person contexts, it is not forbidden to have one. This is not surprising, because in a full pro-drop language like Spanish nominative pronouns can show up as well. However, whereas in Spanish this overt pronoun always receives an emphatic interpretation, pronouns in Hebrew do not seem to be stylistically marked in the same way (V&L 635, n. 13), at least not obligatorily. For Standard Finnish the judgements are mixed, but apparently overt pronouns do not have to be emphatic for all speakers. Hence, we find the contrast in (6):

(6)  a. %Me lähdimme kotiin                                    (Finnish)
        we went-1pl home
     b. Ani   ohev bananot                                      (Hebrew)
        I     like-1sg bananas
     c. Yo hablo                                                (Spanish)
        speak-1sg
        #'I speak'
        '*I* (emphatic) speak'

---

[3] This turns out to be a simplification. In both Hebrew and Standard Finnish, it is possible to leave out a third-person DP in embedded clauses if and only if the matrix clause contains a c-commanding antecedent (cf. Vainikka 1989; Borer 1989). The nature of the relationship between the main-clause antecedent and embedded affix is unclear to me. A syntactic binding account (see Borer 1989) is not completely obvious, as syntactically binding an anaphor from outside the tensed clause it is in is generally prohibited. V&L suggest a more pragmatic solution. In main clauses, first- and second-person subject pronouns do not have to be generated because their referential properties are determined on the basis of 'immediate conversational context'. In contrast, a third-person referent (in the matrix clause) is determined on the basis of a broader discourse context (1999: 649), requiring the presence of an overt subject pronoun or lexical DP. In embedded clauses, the situation is different because the referent can now be determined indirectly via the matrix clause, so that in that event no third-person pronoun has to be generated. This analysis has two problems. First, it leaves unexplained why inserting a third-person pronoun in main clauses would help at all in determining the intended referent. After all, a pronoun does not add any features to the ones introduced by the verbal agreement, thereby narrowing down the possible referents. One could hypothesize that pronouns add gender, a feature that agreement does not spell out. This, however, would work only for Standard Finnish but not for Hebrew, where the verb is also marked for gender. Second, it is not at all obvious that a pragmatic mechanism applying to the 'immediate conversational discourse' should be able to look over an embedded clause boundary but not over a main clause boundary. After all, third-person pronouns are perfectly able to do both. Since I have no alternative to offer, I only mention the intricacies here and leave the issue for further research.

The second property that Hebrew and Finnish have in common is morphological in nature. Hakulinen (1979) and V&L note that first/second-person agreement affixes are special in that they show a morphological relationship with first/second-person subject pronouns. This is shown for Standard Finnish in Table 3.1 (from V&L). The correlation is most striking in the plural, where *-mme* and *-tte* correspond to *me* and *te* respectively. Although the correlation is less clear in the singular, it is to be noted that this is due to historical changes. *Sinä* is reconstructed from *tinä* as a result of a *si → ti* rule, which, not unimportantly, is still active in present-day phonology. The first-person singular affix *-n* is reconstructed from *-m*. In the third person such a correlation is absent, also diachronically.

Interestingly, a similar correlation exists in Hebrew (see also Berman 1990). Take a look at Table 3.2. The correspondence is clear in the past, where the second-person affixes *-ta*, *-t*, and *-tem* correlate with *ata*, *at*, and *atem*, respectively. Likewise, the first-person plural affix *-nu* corresponds to *anaxnu*. The similarity is less clear in the first-person singular, although both *-ti* and *ani* both end in *-i* (preceded by an alveolar stop). In contrast, the third-person affixes show no correspondence with the pronouns whatsoever ( *hu* vs. no affix, *hi* vs. *-a* and *hem* vs. *-u*). Although V&L treat the agreement endings in the future tense on a par with those of the past tense, the morphological correspondence is significantly less clear here. Note that the first-person singular prefix *e-* can no longer be straightforwardly linked to *ani*, and that the second-person singular affixes no longer show the same gender distinction that the past-tense affixes and pronouns do. In the plural, the similarity

TABLE 3.1. Subject–verb agreement and personal pronouns in Standard Finnish

|  | 1s | 2s | 3s | 1pl | 2pl | 3pl |
|---|---|---|---|---|---|---|
| Agreement | -n | -t | -V | -mme | -tte | -vAt |
| Pronouns | minä | sinä | hän | me | te | he |

TABLE 3.2. Subject–verb agreement and personal pronouns in Hebrew

|  | 1s | 2s.m | 2s.f | 3s.m | 3s.f | 1pl | 2pl | 3pl |
|---|---|---|---|---|---|---|---|---|
| AGR past | -ti | -ta | -t | o | -a | -nu | -tem | -u |
| AGR fut. | e- | te- | te- -i | ye- | te- | ne- | te- -u | ye- -u |
| Pronouns | ani | ata | at | hu | hi | anaxnu | atem | hem |

has eroded as well, as first-person plural has changed-*u* for -*e* and second-person plural has lost the final -*m*. In fact, Ariel (2000) observes that the future agreement endings are hardly felt as referential any more by Hebrew speakers. Colloquial speech shows that in the future tense overt first- and second-person pronouns have almost become the rule, and that null subjects occur only in fixed expressions. This again provides an argument for the thesis that pro-drop possibilities and morphological richness correlate.

Although the morphological correspondences in Hebrew (past tense) and Standard Finnish are admittedly not perfect, an inspection of some Romance agreement and pronoun paradigms reveals that here correspondences are accidental at most. Examples are the similarity between the Greek first-person singular marker -*o* and the pronoun *ego*, or between the Spanish third-person singular -*a* and the corresponding feminine pronoun *ella* (Table 3.3).

One can therefore conclude that there is something systematic, or robust, about the correspondences in Standard Finnish and Hebrew that these Romance paradigms lack. What is significant, I believe, is that in Standard Finnish and Hebrew morphological correspondences cross the number as well as the person dimension of the paradigms, whereas this is not the case in Romance.

Despite these two similarities (non-emphatic personal pronouns and robust morphological correspondence), there is an important syntactic difference between the two languages with partial pro-drop. In Standard Finnish, pro-drop correlates significantly with possible word orders, whereas a similar effect is absent from the Hebrew grammar. The observation is that topicalization of a nominal constituent appears to be blocked in first/second-person contexts (cf. (7a) vs. (7b)), whereas this operation is obligatory in third-person contexts when the subject and verb invert (cf. 8a,b vs. 8c) (cf. Vilkuna 1989; Holmberg and Nikanne 1993).

TABLE 3.3. Romance agreement and nominative pronoun paradigms

|  | 1s | 2 | 3s.m | 3s.f | 1pl | 2pl | 3pl.m | 3pl.f |
|---|---|---|---|---|---|---|---|---|
| *Spanish* | | | | | | | | |
| Agreement | -o | -as | -a | -a- | amos | -áis | -an | -an |
| Pronouns | yo | tú | él | ella | nosotros | vosotros | ellos | ellas |
| *Greek* | | | | | | | | |
| Agreement | -o | -is | -i | -i | -ume | -ete | -un | -un |
| Strong pronouns | ego | esu | autós | autè | emeis | eseis | autoi | autés |
| Weak pronouns | – | – | tos | tè | – | – | toi | tes |

(7)  a. Pyysin        heti          palkankorotusta              (Finnish)
         ask-past-1sg  immediately   raise
         'I asked for a raise immediately'

     b. *?Palkankorotusta  pyysin        heti
         raise              ask-past-1sg  immediately
         'I asked for a raise immediately'

(8)  a. Liisa  pyysi        heti          palkankorotusta
         Lisa   ask-past-3sg immediately   raise
         'Lisa asked for a raise immediately'

     b. Palkankorotusta  pyysi         heti          Liisa
         raise            ask-past-3sg  immediately   Lisa
         'Lisa asked for a raise immediately'

     c. *Pyysi        heti          Liisa  palkankorotusta
         ask-past-3sg  immediately   Lisa   raise
         'Lisa asked for a raise immediately'

These patterns cannot be repeated for Hebrew. As (9a) shows, for instance, topicalization in first/second-person contexts is possible (Hagit Borer, p.c.).

(9)  Bananot 'axalti 'etmol                                     (Hebrew)
     Bananas ate-1sg yesterday
     'Bananas, I ate yesterday'

To conclude, Standard Finnish and Hebrew have three properties in common (partial pro-drop, the non-emphatic use of pronouns, and the morphological correlation between pronouns and agreement) but differ significantly on another point, word order. What I will argue in the next section is that the cluster of three can be related to the hypothesis presented briefly in 3.1. As I will show in 3.4, the word-order differences between the two languages fall out from an independent property—namely, the fact that Standard Finnish is, at least to a significant extent, a topic-prominent language. If one takes this into account, the proposed analysis is able to account for the Finnish word-order facts in a straightforward manner.

## 3.3 The status of subject agreement

The assumption that the pro-drop parameter refers to an identification requirement accounts for Spanish and Greek in a very plausible way. The agreement paradigms of these languages contain six distinctions, and every person–number combination is spelled out by a unique affix:

(10)  a.   Spanish        b.   Greek

| | Sing. | Pl. | | Sing. | Pl. |
|---|---|---|---|---|---|
| 1st | -o | -amos | 1st | -o | -ume |
| 2nd | -as | -áis | 2nd | -is | -ete |
| 3rd | -a | -an | 3rd | -i | -un |

Hence, the number/person features of the dropped subject are fully recon-
structable from morphology. This view, however, does not immediately
explain why languages like German and Icelandic do not have argumental
pro-drop. As can be observed in (11), some person–number combinations are
expressed by a unique affix as well:

(11)  a.   German        b.   Icelandic

| | Sing. | Pl. | | Sing. | Pl. |
|---|---|---|---|---|---|
| 1st | -e | -en | 1st | -i | -jum |
| 2nd | -st | -t | 2nd | -ir | -ið |
| 3rd | -t | -en | 3rd | -ir | -ja |

Therefore, one would expect pro-drop to be an option in, for instance, the
first/second-person singular in German and first/second-person plural in
Icelandic, contrary to fact. In fact, even English is predicted to have pro-
drop in third-person singular contexts, where the verb carries the unique
morpheme -*s*. An obvious solution to this problem is to assume that the
possibility of leaving out a thematic subject hinges not on individual affixes
but on the paradigm as a whole (cf. e.g. Jaeggli and Safir 1989a; Rohrbacher
1994; Koeneman 2000). Although German and Icelandic can be characterized
as having rich agreement, in the impressionistic sense of having a considerable
number of distinct forms, both paradigms have two slots in the paradigm
representation containing the same form, -*en* and -*ir* respectively: they show
syncretism. Suppose now that we make the following hypothesis:

(12)  *Identification condition (replacing (2))*
      If the paradigm contains no syncretic forms collapsing two or more
      cells, i.e. if there are not two or more person–number combinations
      expressed by one and the same affix, agreement is characterized
      as [+pronominal].

The condition in (12) is basically what constitutes the parameter for argumental
pro-drop: it looks at the agreement paradigm of a language and determines
whether the affixes contained in it are [+pronominal] or [−pronominal].
The consequence of having [+pronominal] agreement, which is the case in
Spanish and Greek, is that the agreement morphemes can at LF be interpreted

as pronominal and are consequently able to receive a theta role from the predicate. Therefore, no DP subject needs to be generated. This means, in other words, that agreement can satisfy the Extended Projection principle (the requirement that every clause has a subject), essentially the view expressed in Alexiadou and Anagnostopoulou (1998) and others. In German and Icelandic, on the other hand, the presence of the affixes -*en* and -*ir* is enough to block such a characterization. Agreement in this language is [−pronominal] and perhaps best called anaphoric: it requires the presence of an overt DP subject. The difference between Spanish and German is given in (13).

| (13) | Type of agreement? | Pronominal | Anaphoric |
|------|--------------------|-----------|-----------|
|      | Pro-drop?          | Yes        | No        |

Before turning to the case of partial pro-drop, I would like to compare the formulation of the pro-drop parameter in (12) with Speas's proposal in this volume. She argues, following Rohrbacher (1994), that in languages with a so-called full paradigm affixes are lexical entries that are generated in an agreement projection, whereas affixes are generated on the finite verb in languages that lack such a paradigm. Only in the first case can an affix sufficiently license an agreement projection and leave its specifier unfilled, giving rise to the pro-drop phenomenon. The definition of a full paradigm is given in (14).

(14)   INFL is a referential category with lexically listed affixes in exactly those languages where regular subject–verb agreement minimally distinctively marks all referential INFL-features such that (a) and (b):

    a. In at least one number and one tense, the person [1st] and [2nd] are distinctively marked.

    b. In at least one person of one tense, the number feature [singular] is distinctively marked.

In order to obey (14), there should be enough distinct affixes to uniquely mark first person, second person (hence by implication third person), and number. Given a paradigm with six cells (three persons and a number distinction), a language can have a full paradigm if it has four distinct affixes in the right place (for example, one for every person in the singular and the fourth affix for the plural) or if it has five or more distinct affixes. In those cases, Speas argues, the language *may* have (or may 'license') an agreement projection without an overtly filled specifier—that is, show pro-drop. Unfortunately, it is not true that all languages with four, five, or six distinct affixes show argumental pro-drop.[4] Take German, which has five distinct affixes (under the reasonable assumption that the -*t* we find in third-person singular and second-person plural is not a case of real syncretism) but no argumental pro-drop. This means that it is impossible to predict which of the languages obeying (14) actually have pro-drop. Whether a language with a full paradigm has lexically listed affixes, then, boils down to 'a language-specific idiosyncrasy'.

It is striking, however, that the chance of pro-drop increases significantly once the number of distinct affixes increases. Middle English (four distinct affixes), as well as German and Yiddish (five distinct affixes), do not have argumental pro-drop, but Spanish, Greek, and Italian (six distinct affixes) do, exactly as (12) predicts. Since (12) makes predictions where (14) fails to do so, it is also capable of identifying less prototypical pro-drop languages. Standard European Portuguese, for instance, has six distinctions in its paradigm. In Brazilian Portuguese, however, the second-person and third-person distinction in the plural has been lost. Similarly, in the colloquial version of European Portuguese, the second-person plural pronoun, *vos*, has become more or less obsolete and has been replaced by *vocês*, followed by a verb with third-person plural agreement (Hundertmark-Santos Martins 1998). This means that, just as in Brazilian Portuguese, the distinction between second- and third-person agreement disappears in the plural (see (15b)).

(15)  a. Standard Portuguese     b. Brazilian/Colloquial Portuguese

| | Sing. | Pl. | | Sing. | Pl. |
|---|---|---|---|---|---|
| 1st | -o | -amos | 1st | -o | -amos |
| 2nd | -as | -ais | 2nd | -as | -am |
| 3rd | -a | -am | 3rd | -a | -am |

Since Brazilian and Colloquial Portuguese have a syncretic form in their paradigm, the prediction is loss of argumental pro-drop. Brazilian Portuguese has indeed lost this property, but Colloquial Portuguese has retained it in its grammar and thus behaves unexpectedly. Although I do not understand this fact, I believe that more progress is to be expected if we adopt (12) and deal with the consequences (i.e. look for factors that allow Colloquial Portuguese to retain argumental pro-drop) than if we adopt (14) and lose all relevant predictive power.

---

[4] Although it may be true that all languages with 4, 5, or 6 affixes have *some* form of pro-drop, either argumental or expletive, (14) cannot be the correct prerequisite for that. Dutch is a language with only 3 distinct affixes but it still allows null pleonastics—namely, in impersonal passives:

(i)  In de straat werd gedanst   Dutch
     in the street was danced

Let us, equipped with (12), now turn to the partial pro-drop languages. It is still not obvious why Hebrew and Standard Finnish would not allow for full pro-drop, like Spanish. After all, their agreement paradigms have six distinctions and contain no syncretic form. What I would like to propose is that where most languages (whether pro-drop or not) have two independent paradigm representations in the lexicon, one for agreement affixes and one for pronouns, these two paradigms are connected in the Hebrew and Standard Finnish lexicon. The morphological correspondence between agreement and pronoun forms in these languages is not merely a superficial property but triggers this encoding in the lexicon. More concretely, the first/second-person affixes share one property with the third-person agreement affixes—the fact that they are bound morphemes—and one property with the pronouns—their morphological similarity. The fact that first/second-person affixes have these two properties combined in them has as a consequence that the paradigms of personal pronouns and agreement affixes are intertwined, as indicated in (16). The result of this is that the third-person affixes and the pronouns get to stand in direct opposition. As indicated in the representation, I hypothesize that the feature that distinguishes them is [αpronominal]:

(16)                              [αpronominal]

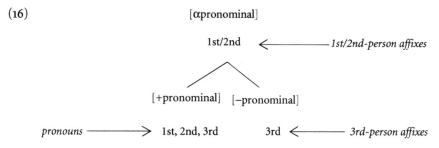

Given the representation in (16), third-person affixes are marked as [−pronominal], pronouns as [+pronominal], and first/second-person affixes are underspecified for this feature.

There are two properties in the output of Hebrew and Standard Finnish that lead the child to the representation in (16): the morphological similarity of first- and second-person affixes and pronouns and the partial pro-drop paradigm itself. The fact that argumental pro-drop is not possible for all persons reinforces the child's hypothesis that the agreement paradigm cannot be independent from the pronoun paradigm. A more fundamental question, of course, is why a representation like (16) is constructed by the grammar at all. I will come back to this issue at the end of this section. Let us first look at the consequences of the hypothesis.

Four results follow from (16). First of all, the analysis captures the partial pro-drop phenomenon itself. A consequence of (12), which is basically the evaluation procedure that determines whether agreement affixes are marked [+pronominal] or [−pronominal], is that overt DP subjects can remain absent in the presence of [+pronominal] agreement. Now, applying (12) blindly to the Hebrew and Standard Finnish agreement affixes would provide the qualification [+pronominal] for all these affixes, because both languages have six distinct agreement morphemes. However, assignment of the feature [+pronominal] is not unproblematic. As was hypothesized, the six affixes do not form an independent paradigm in Hebrew and Standard Finnish, but are intertwined with the pronoun paradigm. Hence, the procedure in (12) applies to the representation in (16). As can be observed, third-person affixes are already marked [−pronominal]. Therefore, they cannot be assigned the feature [+pronominal] any more, because that would lead to a conflicting feature makeup. Since third-person agreement markers therefore remain [−pronominal], overt DPs are obligatory in those contexts. On the other hand, first/second-person affixes are marked [+pronominal] and overt DP subjects are not obligatory.[5]

A second result is that the analysis is able to explain why overt pronoun subjects do not need to have an emphatic interpretation, as in Spanish. As noted, the first/second-person affixes are underspecified for the relevant feature, i.e. they are [αpronominal]. This means that their interpretation can go either way, depending on what is in the numeration, the initial selection of items from the lexicon used for structure building. If a nominative pronominal subject is part of the numeration, a first/second-person agreement affix will automatically be interpreted as [−pronominal]. It is interpreted [+pronominal] otherwise. Hence, when a pronoun is selected from the lexicon, it does not only emphasize the agreement affix on the verb. Since its presence causes the agreement affix to be interpreted as [−pronominal], the pronoun crucially satisfies one of the predicate's thematic functions. In Spanish, on the other hand, agreement is always [+pronominal]. After all, its agreement paradigm does not contain any syncretic form, so that (12) applies. At the same time, there is no systematic correspondence between

---

[5] Possessive constructions in Standard Finnish also show the partial pro-drop phenomenon, where an overt possessor can be left out only if the noun carries a first/second-person affix (Vainikka 1989). Vainikka proposes that third-person affixes are anaphors subject to the binding theory. Toivonen (2001a) offers an LFG analysis for these possessive constructions, arguing that first/second-person possessive markers optionally have a PRED feature. The effect of this is that they have a dual function, a pronoun function, or an agreement function. It will be clear that this view is very close to the one presented here.

affixes and pronouns, so that no representation as in (16) is built. Therefore, agreement affixes are always interpreted as [+pronominal] and always receive the verb's external theta role. Hence, pronouns in Spanish are licensed only if they add information—namely, emphasis—to the structure.[6]

A third result is that the analysis captures the difference between full and partial pro-drop, since the difference has been related to an independent property of the agreement paradigms—namely, the presence or absence of a systematic correspondence between agreement affixes and pronouns. Hence, the difference between a Spanish-type language and a Hebrew-type language is explained.

A fourth result is that the analysis correctly captures the difference between Standard and Colloquial Finnish. The spoken variant differs from the standard version in two respects, as can be concluded from comparing Table 3.4 with Table 3.1. (Data are from V&L.)

The first-person plural affix -*mme* has been replaced by -*tAAn* and no longer shows a correspondence with the first-person plural pronoun *me*. The general morphological correspondence is thereby fatally weakened, as it was noted earlier that the evidence for this correspondence was particularly clear

TABLE 3.4. Subject–verb agreement and personal pronouns in Colloquial Finnish

|  | 1s | 2s | 3s | 1pl | 2pl | 3pl |
|---|---|---|---|---|---|---|
| Agreement | -n | -t | -V | -vAAt | -tte | -V |
| Pronouns | mä | sä | se | me | te | ne |

---

[6] Italian is different from Spanish and Greek in that it has a full paradigm of weak pronouns coexisting next to a paradigm of emphatic pronouns. Greek has weak nominative forms only for the third person (see Table 3.3). These, however, are not normally used as subjects of a clause (see Holton et al. 1997). Now, weak Italian pronouns can appear in a clause-internal position preceding the verb without obligatorily bearing stress, as Alexiadou (Chapter 5 below) notes. She argues that Italian is an in-between case, more pro-drop than German but less than Spanish and Greek, and proposes that Italian has two ways of satisfying the EPP (the requirement that every clause have a subject): either agreement or weak pronouns can do so. Although it is possible to reformulate this idea within the present proposal (for instance, by saying that verbal agreement in Italian only optionally receives the external theta role), it seems likely to me that Italian is going through a development towards what French is nowadays. Colloquial French also has two pronominal forms for each person–number combination:
(i) *Moi    ĵ*        embrasse   souvent   Marie                                          (French)
     I-emph. I-non-emph. kiss         often       Marie
For French it has been claimed that weak pronouns function as agreement markers, so that in fact French has double agreement. Similar claims have been made for certain Italian dialects (see further note 7). If true, Italian might reflect a process that reanalyses preverbal weak pronouns from subjects to agreement markers. In that case, it is not surprising that these pronouns appear without an emphatic interpretation, as agreement markers always do.

in the plural. A second difference is that Colloquial Finnish has neutralized the morphological distinction between third-person singular and plural. Consequently, the ingredients necessary for building the representation in (16) are lost and the input to (12) is an independent agreement paradigm consisting of only five distinct affixes. Since this paradigm contains one syncretic form, the affixes in it do not count as pronominal. The prediction is therefore that Colloquial Finnish should pattern with German and Icelandic in not allowing argumental pro-drop. This prediction is correct, as can be concluded from the discussion in V&L. This provides strong confirmation for the claim that one syncretic form in the paradigm can destroy the option of dropping argumental subjects altogether.

Having pointed out the results of the present analysis, let me now turn to an issue as yet unresolved. Note that nothing in the analysis really dictates that in the Hebrew and Standard Finnish lexicon there must be a connection between the agreement and pronoun paradigm. Even if there is a morpho-logical correspondence between first/second-person agreement affixes and pronouns, that in itself does not exclude the possibility of there being two distinct paradigm representations, just as in Spanish. Although I do not have a fully-fledged analysis on this point, I would speculate that slightly different historical developments must be responsible for the difference.

It seems to be generally agreed upon that there exists a process by which lexical items can become morphological entities, bound by a lexical item. Subject agreement is then seen as the end result of a 'cline' (a series of gradual transitions) that takes pronouns as input, produces clitics at an intermediate stage, and stops when the items have become morphological entities (see Givón 1975; Hopper and Traugott 1993; Ariel 2000; and references cited in these works).[7] Synchronically, we can observe that in the Indo-European

---

[7] Synchronic evidence for the reality of this process of categorial reanalysis in the realm of agreement is that there are quite a few cases in which the categorial status of the elements observed is actually being debated. Mostly the choice is between (subject) clitic or (subject) agreement affix, in other words between D or AGR. One might think of complementizer 'agreement' in Frisian (see several papers in Hoekstra and Smits (1997)) or possessive 'agreement' on nouns in Finnish (see Kanerva 1987). What complicates matters further is that, besides the debate about categorial status (D or AGR), there is a question about the grammatical *function* of the elements under discussion, where the choice is usually between subject or agreement marker. The literature on Romance languages shows that this last choice is particularly hard to settle for weak pronouns and clitics. Take the Northern Italian dialects (see Brandi and Cordin 1989) and Colloquial French. Although French elements like *je*, *tu*, and *il* are traditionally analysed as (weak) pronominal or clitical *subjects*, there is a growing body of evidence suggesting that they function as *agreement markers* (see the development of research in Muller 1984; Roberge 1986; Hulk 1986; Auger 1992; Zribi-Hertz 1993; De Wind 1995; Ferdinand 1996). Note that this is not the same as saying that they are agreement *morphemes*: agreement markers can simply come in different shapes cross-linguistically (as a morpheme or a particle, for instance). If correct, this line of research shows that categorial status and grammatical

languages the forms of the affixes are clearly distinct from those of the pronouns. This seems to indicate that historically the reanalysis process goes hand in hand with the development of the new generation of pronouns. We can thus distinguish three stages: one in which a particular item X is listed as a pronoun or clitic, one transitional stage in which X functions either as pronoun or affix, and the final stage, in which X has been reanalysed as an affix. Now, at the intermediate stage, where X is ambiguous between a pronoun and an affix, it makes little sense to assume two lexical listings: one X that is [+pronoun] and one X' that is [−pronoun]. Rather, one could list just one form and assign an underspecified feature to it. In a language with six forms, one would then economize on six listings in the lexicon. Schematically, this development is represented in (17), where the trigger for a transition from Stage 2 to Stage 3 is the development of new pronouns:

(17)   Stage 1 $\longrightarrow$       Stage 2 $\longrightarrow$       Stage 3

     X = [+pronoun]   X = [αpronoun]   X = [−pronoun]

       < n e w p r o n o u n s >

What makes Hebrew and Finnish different, I believe, is that at Stage 2 not all pronouns started appearing as affixes, only the first- and second-person pronouns did so. This entails that third-person endings must have a different origin. For Standard Finnish, this can be argued for fairly straightforwardly. The third-person plural, *-vАt,* is etymologically the plural of the present participle and is not related to a pronoun (Comrie 1981: 217; Bátori 1982). The third-person singular consists of a lengthening of the stem vowel, so that it is hard to see how these forms could be related to personal pronouns. In Hebrew, the third-person singular in the past tense is zero, with *-a* as a gender marker for female. The third-person plural in the past tense, *-u,* is etymologically related to a plural nominal case ending *-uu,* and not to an

---

function do not necessarily show a 1:1 mapping (with pronominal Ds standardly analysed as subjects and agreement affixes as agreement markers), but that the relation is an empirical issue. Now, if D-elements can function as agreement markers, there is no reason why (rich) agreement affixes could not function as subjects, the claim adopted here.

Agreement markers (weak pronouns, clitics, or morphemes) can precede or follow the verb. Which option is realized probably depends on another factor—the position of the verb at the time at which subject elements are reanalysed as agreement markers. In fact, Alexiadou and Fanselow (2000) argue that the observed correlation between rich subject agreement and verb movement in Germanic (see Holmberg and Platzack 1991; Rohrbacher 1994) should be viewed as the outcome of an interplay of precisely these two factors, verb movement and reanalysis. On the basis of the current data one would be inclined to conclude that preverbal agreement markers are always weak pronouns or clitics, whereas postverbal markers are morphemes: categorial status correlates with the position of the verb. This is hardly surprising. After all, morphological inflection is and was predominantly suffixal in all languages under discussion. Hence, a categorial reanalysis from D(P) to AGR is easiest if the verb happens to precede it.

independent pronoun (Bauer and Leander 1922: 309–11). Bauer and Leander suggest that the third-person singular prefix in the future tense, *y(e)*-, should be reconstructed as a Proto-Semitic third-person singular masculine pronoun *yaa*-. (According to Tamar Zewi (p.c.), *ye*- is probably not a Proto-Semitic property, as Akkadian does not show consonants of semi-vowels at the beginning of its prefix forms.) Martin Baasten (p.c.), however, informs me that this may be questioned, as the form never appears in isolation.[8]

What I conclude from this is that a stage in which only first- and second-person but not third-person pronouns optionally appeared as affixes on the verb is very plausible. I suggest that the representation that captures all forms most economically at such a stage is the one in (18), where the first- and second-person forms are underspecified for the feature [pronoun]:

(18)

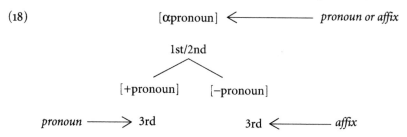

Since the agreement paradigm and the pronoun paradigm share four forms, these four will now not have to be represented twice. The advantage of the overlapping representation in (18) is thus clear: it is economical. By constructing (18), the overall number of items listed in the lexicon is reduced by four.

Note that the prediction is that at this stage Standard Finnish and Hebrew should have full pro-drop. The third-person affixes are marked [−pronoun], but the only consequence is that they are not syntactic elements. The feature that determines pro-drop possibilities, however, is [αpronominal], and this feature can be assigned to determiners and affixes alike. Which feature value is assigned to an affix depends on characteristics of the agreement paradigm itself. Since both languages have six distinct affixes, all agreement affixes will be marked as [+pronominal] by (12), and there is no affix already marked [−pronominal], as in the modern varieties of these languages. Hence, full pro-drop is expected, just as in Spanish.

After some time, the forms of the first/second-person affixes and pronouns start gradually to look different, either because of phonological processes or because new pronouns are invented, and eventually separate forms have to be

---

[8] Thanks to Martin Baasten (Leiden University) for discussing this issue with me and for pointing out Bauer and Leander (1922).

distinguished. The determiner forms will have to be stored under the left branch of the representation, directly dominated by the label [+pronoun], as illustrated in (19). At the same time, however, the other first- and second-person forms at the top of the representation become pure affixes and can no longer be used as determiners. This entails that the feature [αpronoun] becomes inadequate as a characterization of the first- and second-person forms at the top of the representation, which is therefore ill formed:

(19)   *

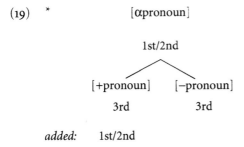

In order to solve the problem, I suggest that the language learner's initial strategy will be not to break the representation into two independent paradigms. Before doing that, he or she will make sure that there is no other feature that correctly captures the relevant contrast. The search for this feature, however, will be successful, and rather than break the representation in two, the language learner replaces the feature [αpronoun] by [αpronominal]—that is, he or she switches to the representation in (16), repeated here as (20).

(20)

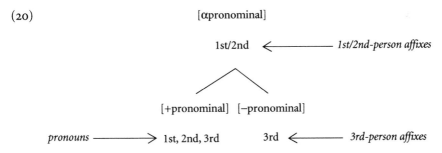

Now the representation no longer determines whether particular forms are morphemes or syntactic items, but it determines the interpretability of them at LF. This gives the correct outcome for Standard Finnish and Hebrew, as we saw: third-person affixes become marked [−pronominal], even though they are part of a paradigm with six distinctions, and they trigger generation of an overt subject from now on. On the other hand, first- and second-person affixes are marked [αpronominal], and antecedents are optional at most. The partial pro-drop paradigm has come into being.

## 3.4 Word order in Standard Finnish and Hebrew

Recall from Section 3.2 that Standard Finnish shows a word-order asymmetry correlating with pro-drop possibilities (see (7) and (8)): in first/second-person contexts topicalization is blocked, whereas this operation is obligatory in third-person contexts if the verb would otherwise appear in sentence-initial position (i.e. if subject–verb inversion occurs). Such an asymmetry is absent in Hebrew, where topicalization is possible in any context.

I would like to argue that the facts follow from the present analysis in combination with an independent property of Standard Finnish—namely, the fact that it is a topic-prominent language (cf. Vilkuna 1989). The language requires a topic in preverbal position much as a language such as English requires a preverbal subject.[9] What argues for this particular property? Note first of all that, if we hypothesize some requirement in Standard Finnish for the clause to start with a topic, we immediately obtain a trigger for the fronting operation that obligatorily takes place in third-person contexts where the subject and the verb have inverted. Moreover, it appears that the nature of the fronted category is not arbitrary, as, for instance, in a verb-second language. If an adverb is fronted in a third-person context, the sentence remains ungrammatical. The fronted constituent must be nominal, shown by the following contrast (from Holmberg and Nikanne 1993):

(21)  a. *Ilmeisesti  on    tämän  kirjan  kirjoittanut  Graham  Greene
          evidently   has   this   book    written       Graham  Greene
          'Graham Greene has evidently written this book'
      b. Ilmeisesti  tämän  kirjan  on    kirjoittanut  Graham Greene
         evidently   this   book    has   written       Graham Greene
         'Graham Greene has evidently written this book'

This contrast constitutes independent evidence for the topic-prominent character of Standard Finnish. Under the assumption that Standard Finnish requires an element in first position that introduces what the proposition is

---

[9] This means that the distribution of topics in Standard Finnish is larger than in English, which prohibits topics in many non-root environments. The same is not true for left-peripheral focus constituents in Finnish, which appear in root clauses, as well as in root-like embedded clauses. See Vilkuna (1989) for further discussion.

about, the contrast in (21) is a consequence of the fact that adverbs are not very suitable elements for introducing what the following proposition is about. Note that topic-prominent languages are thus fundamentally different from the Germanic verb-second languages. The latter require exactly one XP to precede the fronted verb, where the categorial status of this XP, and by implication the degree of topic-hood, is irrelevant: adverbs and focus constituents can equally satisfy the verb-second constraint, whereas they are unable to satisfy the Finnish topic constraint. Whatever the trigger is for XP-movement in verb-second languages, it cannot be equated with the requirement to start off a sentence with an XP introducing what the sentence is about, i.e. a topic.[10]

Topic-prominent languages come in several kinds. In some languages, such as Hungarian, you can topicalize more than one constituent. In Standard Finnish, however, there can be only one topic. If more than one nominal constituent precedes the verb, the first one is interpreted as a focus, the second one as a topic (Vilkuna 1989). This is illustrated in (22) and (23):

(22)  a. János    Marit      tavaly      vitte       Párizs-ba    (Hungarian)
         Janos    Mari-acc.  last year   took away   Paris-to
      b. Marit     János      tavaly      vitte       Párizs-ba
         Mari-acc.  Janos     last year   took away   Paris-to
      'As for János and Mari, last year he took her to Paris'

---

[10] One anonymous reviewer wonders what the syntactic consequences are of the difference between topic prominence in Finnish and Verb Second. This is a very difficult question to answer. The fact that topic prominence should be distinguished from the V2-type of XP-movement could imply that the syntactic representations underlying these clauses should be distinct. Alternatively, it could be that the topic condition in the Finnish grammar refers to the same syntactic position that hosts fronted XPs in verb-second constructions, whether this is spec-CP or one of the projections in a split-CP structure in Rizzi's proposal (1997). In general, we can observe that, cross-linguistically, movements to the left periphery of the clause are (at least) parametrized with respect to (i) whether particular movements are obligatory or not, (ii) whether there are clause-type or co-occurrence restrictions, and (iii) what order multiple XP-fronting results in. It is far from settled whether the cross-linguistic differences observed should be handled by parametrizing the underlying functional structure (the availability of projections and/or their order) or by keeping the structure constant and parametrizing the movement rules (the availability of them and/or their targets). I believe it is fair to conclude that embedding Finnish topicalization within a broader picture of left-peripheral movements is beyond the scope of the present concern. In order to derive the attested word orders in Standard Finnish, my own analysis is combined with the reasonably theory-independent statements in (24), reflecting that having exactly one topic is obligatory in Finnish, in contrast to the other languages considered in this chapter. This property can be cast in a range of possible syntactic representations, but, in the light of the theoretical possibilities, I have no concrete arguments for singling out any particular formalization at this point.

(23)  Marjan        Jussi otti mukaan Pariisiin viime  vuonna  (Finnish)
      Marja-acc.    Jussi took along  Paris-to  last    year
      'It was Marja whom Jussi took to Paris last year'
      #'As for Marja, Jussi took her to  Paris last year'

All in all, it seems that the grammar of Finnish minimally contains the following two conditions:

(24)  a. A non-imperative sentence should have a T[opic] when possible
         (Vilkuna 1989).[11]
      b. The topic condition is subject to economy: (24a) must be
         satisfied as economically as possible.

The word-order facts can now be derived by combining (24) with the hypothesis that first/second-person affixes are [αpronominal] and third-person affixes [−pronominal]. To see how this works, one should recognize that pronouns are, at least by default, interpreted as topics. They do not themselves introduce new information but refer back to information already given: they are semantic variables that are either semantically bound or have a contextually specified value (see Chierchia (1995) for details). For this reason, it is in most cases infelicitous to start a conversation with 'he', for instance (unless for stylistic purposes, such as in a novel). Note that it is very natural to start a conversation with 'I' or 'you'. This, however, is not incompatible with the claim that pronouns are topics. In any discourse situation, a speaker and hearer are presupposed, in contrast to a third-person referent. It is this knowledge that first/second-person pronouns refer back to when they are introduced at the beginning of a discourse.

With this in mind, let us now turn to the word-order facts. In third-person contexts, a clause can start with a subject DP or nominative pronoun that is interpreted as the topic. If in a clause the subject and the verb are inverted, the condition in (24a) is violated, since no topic appears in sentence-initial position. As the verb carries agreement that is marked [−pronominal], this

---

[11] Note that Vilkuna's topic rule (cf. 24a) holds in non-imperative sentences only. It is not *a priori* guaranteed that every clause has a suitable topic. In some cases, e.g. in impersonal constructions and imperatives, (24a) does not have to be satisfied. One anonymous reviewer wonders why (24a) fails to hold in imperatives, considering that topics can appear without any problem in e.g. French:
(i)  Ce  texte là,    ne  le lis  plus
     that text there  neg. it read no more
A way of accounting for the absence of structures like (i) in Finnish is to assume that (24a) is not entirely correct and that it *does* hold in imperatives. Under the assumption that the implicit second person in these constructions counts as the topic of the sentence, (24a) is satisfied, and having another topic is blocked by (24b) (cf. Vilkuna 1989: 62).

element cannot be interpreted as the topic of the clause. For that reason, some nominal constituent must be fronted. In first/second-person contexts the situation is different. The reason for this is that, if no overt pronoun is part of the numeration (i.e. among the words selected from the lexicon to build a structure with), the first/second-person agreement marker will automatically be interpreted as [+pronominal]. Hence, the most economical way of satisfying the condition in (24a) is to interpret the agreement marker on the verb in clause-initial position as the topic of the clause. Therefore, fronting of another nominal constituent is effectively blocked by economy, since the operation is not motivated. Hence, the different word orders are derived.

Recall that in Hebrew pro-drop does not correlate with different word-order possibilities in a similar way. The reason for this is straightforward: Hebrew is not topic-prominent, so that its grammar does not contain the conditions in (24). Hence the difference between Hebrew and Standard Finnish falls out from independently motivated properties of the Finnish grammar.

## 3.5 Discussion

In this section I would like to point out the advantages of the present analysis by mainly (but not exclusively) comparing it to the one proposed by V&L. They propose to enrich the theory of pro-drop with the licensing condition stated in (25):

(25)   *Principle of Obligatory Occupant Licensing (POOL)*
       In order to be licensed, both the head and the specifier of a syntactic
       position must be filled by syntactic material at some level of
       representation.

They assume that all languages have an abstract bundle of φ-features (basically pro) which counts as syntactically visible material. These φ-features are located in spec,VP if identified by rich features on V, as in Spanish, or in AGR, as in English or German. The position in which these features are generated is thus parametrized and determined by the agreement properties of the language. In the former case, you can move these features from spec,VP to spec,AGRP (cf. 26a), so that spec,AGRP is licensed. The result is a sentence without an overt subject. When the φ-features are generated in AGR, they cannot be moved to spec,AGRP in order to license this position. Hence, an overt DP is moved from spec,VP to spec,AGRP (cf. 26b), thereby licensing this position. The result is a clause with an overt subject.

(26)   a.   AGRP                           b.      AGRP

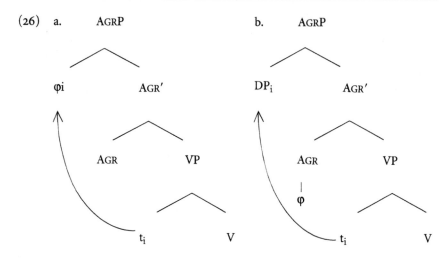

What makes partial pro-drop languages different is that in Hebrew and Standard Finnish, V&L argue, the strategy in (26a) is used in first- and second-person contexts and the strategy in (26b) is used in third-person contexts. In Standard Finnish, moreover, there is an additional way of licensing spec,AGRP in third-person contexts—namely, by leaving the DP subject in spec,VP and moving another nominal constituent in spec,AGRP. This accounts for the data in (8) and (21): subject–verb inversion leads to obligatory topicalization.

There are a couple of problems for this analysis which the alternative offered in this chapter does not run into.

First, V&L's proposal enriches the theory of argumental subject-drop with a licensing condition on top of the identification condition. In the present analysis this complication is unnecessary.

Second, the possibility of having non-emphatic pronominal DPs in Standard Finnish and Hebrew is not related to the mechanism that leads to partial pro-drop, so that the contrast with, for instance, Spanish is not derived.

Third, V&L's analysis does not account for all the word-order facts in Standard Finnish, it seems. Note that in third-person contexts there is the possibility of leaving the DP subject in spec,VP. In that case spec,AGRP can be licensed by moving another nominal constituent to spec,AGRP. If so, why would it not be possible in first/second-person contexts to leave the abstract $\varphi$-feature bundle in spec,VP and move another constituent to spec,AGRP? This would give rise to topicalization in first/second-person contexts, a possibility that must be excluded (cf. 7b); but, as far as I can see, it is not. In my analysis, all grammatical options are derived and the ungrammatical ones blocked by a combination of the topic-prominent character of the language and the now independently motivated [±pronominal] distinction within the agreement paradigm. As a trigger for movement, the notions of topicalization and licensing of a specifier can obviously be related to one another: the first can be seen as an instantiation of the second. Topic prominence can therefore easily be incorporated into V&L's analysis, and this would make their analysis of third-person contexts a notational variant. However, that would not be enough to block topicalization in first/second-person contexts.

Fourth, V&L's licensing condition crucially relies on the presence of pre-fabricated, empty specifier positions that have to be licensed, as well as on the availability of an abstract bundle of φ-features, reminiscent of pro. Without the presence of these empty elements, their licensing condition would collapse. In this sense, their analysis is not minimal, or minimalist. Note that, for instance, in a bare phrase structure approach (see Chomsky 1995) maximal constituents *create* specifiers by merge or move to the root structure, meaning that the structural position is radically absent before one of these operations has applied. The alternative analysis offered here is compatible with this view, since nothing in it hinges on the presence of empty specifiers or pro-like elements in the structure.

The fifth and most important problem is that their analysis does not reach the goal of deriving the difference between full and partial pro-drop. What V&L essentially propose is that Hebrew and Standard Finnish use two parameter settings, one for first- and second-person and another for third-person contexts. Alexiadou's proposal (Chapter 5 below) is similar in this respect. She argues that third-person affixes are different from first- and second-person affixes in that they lack person marking. Consequently, they cannot check the EPP feature, and a DP subject must do the job instead. Speas (Chapter 2 above) suggests that Hebrew might fall under her analysis of Irish, for which she claims that first- and second-person affixes are lexically listed, in contrast to third-person affixes. Hence, only first- and second-person affixes are able to license an agreement phrase in the absence of an overt subject. The common feature in all these accounts is that a distinction is made for the syntax of first and second person on the one hand and third person on the other.

The point, however, is that none of the authors offers an explanation for why this difference exists in the first place, other than that it derives the partial pro-drop paradigm. Put differently, their conclusion is similar to mine, but it remains unclear what they base their on. The result is that, as an explanation for partial pro-drop, these accounts are circular as they stand. Admittedly,

V&L and Alexiadou observe the morphological correspondence that is present only between first- and second-person pronouns and affixes but, as V&L (p. 645) themselves admit, this in itself does not derive the fact that subject-drop is possible in precisely those contexts where we find this morphological correlation between pronouns and agreement markers. One does not follow from the other: in no sense does morphological correspondence *determine* insertion in spec,VP in V&L's analysis, a characterization of [+person] in Alexiadou's account, or lexical listing in Speas's proposal. After all, that would make a wrong prediction for Spanish, where morphological correspondences are lacking but pro-drop nevertheless exists. I therefore conclude that these analyses are in need of some hypothesis that derives the paradigm-internal differentiation in Hebrew and Standard Finnish leading to partial pro-drop. The main purpose of this chapter is to do just that. In my analysis, the morphological correspondence *causes* the partial pro-drop paradigm through the specific encoding in the lexicon, so that the difference from full pro-drop receives an explanation.

## 3.6 Conclusion

Standard Finnish and Hebrew differ from a language like English in that argumental pro-drop is possible, and differ from Spanish in that the phenomenon is limited to first/second-person contexts. Two further properties distinguish the partial pro-drop languages from a full pro-drop language like Spanish: (i) overt nominative pronouns are not obligatorily emphatic; (ii) there is a morphological correlation between first/second agreement affixes and first/second pronouns. The hypothesis put forward here makes use of the morphological correspondence to account for the other two facts, thereby explaining the difference between full and partial pro-drop. The main achievement is that the proposal overcomes the need to complicate the theory of pro-drop by adding a licensing condition. Argumental subject-drop basically reduces to an identification requirement, at least for a subset of the world's languages. Needless to say, further research must reveal whether the facts discussed here for Hebrew and Standard Finnish really form a cluster. More generally, it remains to be seen if and how the identification strategy must be fitted into a broader theory of pro-drop that includes languages like Japanese and Korean (in which clause-level identification does not play any role) as well as non-argumental pro-drop.

# 4

# Agreement, Pro, and Imperatives

HANS BENNIS

## 4.1 Introduction: the pro-drop parameter

In the literature the occurrence of an empty subject in finite clauses is generally related to a parametric choice in the grammar of the language in question. The well-known and much debated pro-drop parameter is taken to be the relevant principle that determines whether a language does or does not allow for empty subjects in non-infinitival clauses. These empty subjects are called pro subjects or simply pro. The occurrence of pro is often related to the nature of the verbal inflectional paradigm of the language, in such a way that a 'rich' inflectional paradigm allows pro to appear, whereas languages with 'poor' inflectional systems do not allow for pro subjects. The pro-drop parameter is thus related to the morphosyntactic specificity of the inflectional system in a particular language. For instance, in a language such as Italian the verbal inflectional paradigm is fully specified for pronominal properties. It is specified for the features person and number (the so-called φ-features), and the specification of this feature set gives rise to a unique morphosyntactic realization. It makes sense intuitively that Italian allows a lexical subject pronoun to be absent, because of the fact that the subject properties can be recovered through the verbal inflection. In languages such as English and Dutch the inflectional paradigm is much less specific. It is impossible to recover the pronominal features of an empty subject through the morpho-syntactic properties of the inflection alone. There is no morphosyntactic gender distinction and the person distinction is far from optimal (e.g. in the plural the person distinction is absent). A lexical subject thus has to be

This chapter is closely related to Bennis (forthcoming). The general idea, however, differs. I thank Sjef Barbiers, Marjo van Koppen, Johan Rooryck, Wim van der Wurff, four anonymous reviewers, and the audiences of the Workshop on Agreement (Utrecht, August 2001) and the Linguistics Colloquium Groningen (January 2002) for comments.

present. In this way, the occurrence of subject pro is directly related to the nature of subject–verb agreement in finite clauses.

On the other hand, it has been observed that pro-drop phenomena show up not only in languages with rich inflectional systems such as Spanish and Italian, but also in languages with no verbal inflection, such as Chinese (see Jaeggli and Safir 1989a; Huang 1989). So it appears to be the case that both rich inflectional verbal paradigms and the poorest inflectional systems (i.e. no verbal inflection) generally allow pro-drop, whereas poor paradigms with an underspecified inflectional system require the subject to be lexical (see Speas, Chapter 2 above). It is not immediately evident that a pro-drop parameter can account for such a distribution of pro other than by stipulating that a particular language is either pro-drop or non-pro-drop.

In the early days of the pro-drop parameter (cf. Chomsky 1981; Rizzi 1982) it was argued that the occurrence of pro correlates with other systematic syntactic properties of the subject. If correct, it corroborates the parametric approach to the occurrence of pro. If a number of specific properties in a language can be reduced to one by the postulation of a general parameter that is supposed to be part of Universal Grammar, the parameter provides insight in the systematic correlations within the grammar and, as a consequence, it strengthens the UG approach. It has been argued that the presence of pro subjects is related to two other properties of the grammar: the occurrence of complementizer-trace phenomena and the availability of subject inversion. Although the idea that one parameter may account for a number of different but related properties has been very inspiring, the empirical justification for the pro-drop parameter proves to be weak. For instance, the complementizer-trace phenomenon—that is, the extraction of a subject from a finite subordinate clause that is introduced by a lexical complementizer—can easily be found in a non-pro-drop language such as Dutch, whereas subject extraction from a position right adjacent to the complementizer has been shown to be impossible in a pro-drop language such as Italian. This has weakened the pro-drop parameter approach. If there is no uniform correlation between the occurrence of empty subjects and the specificity of the inflectional paradigm, and there is no correlation between the occurrence of pro and other subject properties such as complementizer-trace phenomena and subject inversion, it seems to be the case that the pro-drop parameter is a descriptive statement, rather than a grammatical principle.

In the chapter by Speas (this volume) the pro-drop parameter is rephrased as a parameter that determines whether the AGR position in a particular language is weak (no pro-drop) or strong/absent (pro-drop). The strength of AGR is related to properties of the inflectional paradigm, in such a way that a language with a fully specified paradigm ('full paradigm') may have strong AGR and pro-drop, whereas a language with an incomplete paradigm has weak AGR and no pro-drop. This analysis can be considered to be the minimalist version of the pro-drop parameter.

In this chapter I will adopt another approach to the occurrence of empty subjects in non-infinitival clauses. First I will show, as others have done before, that the availability of pro is not language-specific, but rather construction-specific. The presence of empty subjects depends to a large extent on the type of construction. In this chapter I will concentrate on the imperative construction. This construction clearly allows pro subjects in 'non-pro-drop' languages such as Dutch and English.

We could adopt an approach in which for each construction type in each language the pro-drop parameter is implemented—for instance, as a pro-drop feature [ ± pro-drop]. Such an approach might be empirically correct; it would, however, increase the purely descriptive, ad hoc status of the pro-drop parameter. In order to understand the occurrence of empty subjects as a grammatical property, we have to look more closely at the properties that determine the occurrence of pro. I will argue that there are two factors involved in the determination of pro subjects: the nature of subject–verb agreement and pronominal properties in terms of φ-features.

The basic idea is quite simple. The hypothesis that I will try to substantiate in this chapter is given in (1).[1]

(1)   Pro subjects in non-infinitival clauses may appear if:
    (i)  the relevant φ-features of the empty subject can be recovered through agreement;
    (ii) the uninterpretable φ-features on the non-infinitival verb can be deleted through agreement.

In line with the Minimalist Program (Chomsky 1995), I shall assume that features can be either interpretable or uninterpretable. For instance, the feature for plurality can be expressed either on nouns or on verbs. Given that plurality (and φ-features in general) is typically interpreted as a property of nominal phrases, we assume that [plu] is *interpretable* on nouns but *uninterpretable* on verbs. Intuitively speaking, the hypothesis in (1) claims that empty subjects are possible only if we are able to recover the interpretation of the empty subject by other means,[2] and, secondly, that the verb may

---

[1] The hypothesis in (1) will be reformulated below.
[2] The analysis given in this chapter is in several ways reminiscent of the analysis of pro-drop given in Bennis and Haegeman (1984). In that paper we discussed pro-drop phenomena in West Flemish, a

not carry additional pronominal information, i.e. information that is not or cannot be interpreted as part of the interpretation of the (empty) subject.

## 4.2  Pro in imperatives

### 4.2.1  *The imperative verb*

In this chapter I will concentrate on simple imperatives in Dutch.[3] What I call 'simple imperatives' are those imperatives that have a more or less specialized verb form which shows up in the first position of the clause, in a position that is normally restricted to finite verbs, i.e. the landing site for finite verb movement in root clauses (Verb Second).[4] These imperative verbs are generally considered to be verbs that are inflected for second person. Standard

language in which pro-drop is possible owing to the fact that complementizer inflection makes it possible to recover the pronominal properties of an empty subject.

[3] There are various other construction types that may acquire imperative force. There are (i) imperative V2 clauses, (ii) imperative infinitival constructions (see Den Dikken 1992), and (iii) imperative participial constructions (see Rooryck and Postma 2001). Examples are given in (i)–(iii).

(i)  Jij      gaat    nu      maar    eens    naar    huis!
     you     go      now     PRTs            to      home
     'You should go home now!'

(ii) Ophoepelen     jij/jullie!
     away-go[INF]   you [±plu]
     'You go away!'

(iii) Opgehoepeld    jij/jullie!
     away-gone[PART]  you [±plu]
     'You go away!'

[4] It is not the case that the phenomenon of V1, i.e. a finite verb in first position of a root clause, can unambiguously be related to imperative constructions. A variety of functionally marked constructions are characterized by Verb First, involving construction types such as joke introduction, narrative V1, yes/no questions, and topic-drop. Examples are given below.

(i)   Zitten   twee    mannen  in      de      kroeg   (joke introduction)
      sit      two     man     in      the     pub
      'There are two men in the pub'

(ii)  Zegt     die     een     tegen   de      ander:  (narrative V1)
      says     that    one     to      the     other
      'The one says to the other:'

(iii) Ga       je      met     mij     mee?    (yes/no question)
      go       you     with    me      PRT
      'Are you coming with me?'

(iv)  Wil      ik      wel     doen    (topic-drop)
      want     I       PRT     do
      'That is OK with me'

We thus observe that there is no unique relationship between imperative force and the syntactic implementation of imperatives. On the one hand, imperative force can be expressed by various constructions, as we saw in n.3; on the other hand, the typical imperative construction (simple imperatives) is characterized by V1, which also characterizes various other construction types such as yes/no questions and narrative V1. The often-expressed idea that there is a one-to-one relation between pragmatic function and syntactic construction should obviously be abandoned as far as V1 and imperatives are concerned.

Dutch has different realizations of the imperative inflection: the usual form corresponds to the stem of the verb, but in special cases we find an inflected form in which -*t* (polite ) or -*en* (plural) is added to the stem. Examples are given in (2) and (3).[5]

(2) a. Hoepel(-ø)   nu   maar   op!
     go        now   PRT   away
     'Go away!'
   b. Loop(-ø)   naar   de   maan   jij/jullie!
     walk      to     the   moon   you[±pl]
     'You, go away!'
   c. Wees(-ø)   (jij)        maar   niet   bang!
     be       (you[−pl])   PRT   not   afraid
     'Don't be afraid!'

(3) a. Kom-*t*   allen   tezamen!
     come   all   together!
     'Come together!'
   b. Wees-*t*   U        maar   niet   bang!
     be      you[+polite]   PRT   not   afraid
     'Don't be afraid!'
   c. Wez-*en*   jullie     maar   niet   bang!
     be      you[+pl]   PRT   not   afraid
     'Don't be afraid!'

### 4.2.2 *Subject pronouns in imperatives*

In imperative constructions the subject is generally absent. However, it can be added as a second-person pronoun, as in (4).

---

[5] The occurrence of the verb form *wees(t)/wezen* in (2c) and (3b, c) indicates unambiguously that these sentences are imperatives, since these forms of the verb *zijn* ('to be') show up in imperatives only. In yes/no questions, for instance, we find different verb forms: *ben, bent,* or *zijn,* as in (i).

(i) a. Ben/*Wees   je      bang   voor   slangen?
     are     you[−pl]   afraid   for   snakes
   b. Bent/*Weest   U        bang   voor   slangen?
     are     you[+polite]   afraid   for   snakes
   c. Zijn/*Wezen   jullie     bang   voor   slangen?
     are     you[+pl]   afraid   for   snakes

The stem *wees* also appears in other forms of the irregular verb *zijn* 'to be', such as the infinitival form *wezen* 'to be'—which in most environments is an alternative to the infinitive *zijn*—the participle *geweest* 'been', and the past tense *was* 'was'. However, the verb forms *wees* and *weest* are exclusively reserved for imperative use in Standard Dutch, and thus constitute an interesting test as to whether a particular construction can be taken to be imperative.

(4)  a. Ga      jij               maar  weg!
        go       you[−pl]          PRT   away
        'You, go away!'
     b. Gaat    U                 maar  weg!
        go       you[+polite]      PRT   away
     c. Gaan    jullie            maar  weg!
        go       you[+pl]          PRT   away

In (4) the imperative inflection agrees with the lexical subject. It is interesting to observe that the non-inflected (or ø-inflected) imperative may co-occur with a singular or a plural second-person subject pronoun when this pronoun occupies a right-peripheral position, as in (5a). This is not the case for *t*-inflected or *en*-inflected imperatives in Standard Dutch, as is clear from (5b, c).

(5)  a. Ga      maar  weg   *jij,*   *jullie!*
        go       PRT   away  you     [±pl]
     b. *Gaat   maar  weg   *jij,*   *jullie!*
        go       PRT   away  you     [±pl]
     c. *Gaan   maar  weg   *jij,*   *jullie!*
        go       PRT   away  you     [±pl]

A more detailed discussion of pronouns in subject position and subjects in right-peripheral position in imperatives will be presented below.

### 4.2.3  *The occurrence of pro in imperatives*

It is possible to leave out the subject if the imperative verb is uninflected. If the imperative verb has *t*-inflection or *en*-inflection, the subject *U* or *jullie*, has to be present (6b, c). In older varieties of Dutch (7a) and in regional varieties (7b) we find the *t*-inflected verb without a lexical subject, but in modern Standard Dutch this is no longer acceptable.

(6)  a. Kom     (jij)     eens   hier!
        come     (you)    PRT    here
        'Come here!'
     b. Kom-*t*   *(U)            eens   hier!
     c. Kom-*en*  *(jullie)       eens   hier!

(7)  a. Kom-*t*   allen    tezamen!
        come-*t*  all      together
        'Come together!'
     b. Kom-*t*   (gij)                  eens   hier!
        come-*t*  (you[regional])        PRT    here

It is well known that the absence of a lexical subject in imperatives does not imply that the subject is absent (e.g. Beukema and Coopmans 1989; Potsdam 1998; Rupp 1999). First of all, the non-lexical subject in imperatives is necessarily interpreted as the addressee. It seems to be most efficient to relate the interpretation of the subject to the non-lexical subject position. Moreover, the non-lexical subject can generally be replaced by a lexical pronominal subject (*jij*) without substantial differences in interpretation. The major interpretive difference is that a lexical subject in imperatives is stressed. We thus may assume the non-lexical subject to be the weak variant of the lexical subject. Confirmation for an analysis along these lines comes from the fact that weak subject pronouns do not occur in imperatives. Whereas strong and weak subject pronouns generally show an identical distribution, in imperatives *jij* cannot be replaced by its weak counterpart *je*, as is shown in (8).

(8) a. *Ga  *je*      maar  weg!        (cf. Ga *je* nu al weg?)
       go   you[weak]  PRT   away
       'Go away!'
    b. *Wees  *je*      eens  niet  zo  stoer!   (cf. Ben *je* altijd zo stoer?)
       be      you[weak]  PRT   not   so  brave
       'Don't be so brave!'

In this respect the imperative subject behaves like a subject in a pro-drop language, such as Italian or Spanish, where the strong lexical pronoun has the empty pronoun pro as its weak correlate.[6] The only difference between imperatives with a lexical subject (*jij*) and imperatives without (pro) is the emphatic nature of the lexical pronoun.

Another argument to claim that an empty subject has to be present in imperatives comes from the fact that the empty subject is syntactically active in binding and control. This is shown in (9).

(9) a. Geef jij$_i$/pro$_i$ jezelf$_i$ nu eens     wat rust!      (reflexive)
       give you        yourself PRTs some  rest
       'Give yourself some rest!'
    b. Herinner jij$_i$ / pro$_i$ $_i$  dit gesprek     nog maar eens!  (inherent reflexive)
       remember you      you this conversation PRTs
       'Remember this conversation!'
    c. Beloof    jij$_i$/pro$_i$ mij nou maar [om PRO$_i$ op tijd thuis te zijn]! (control)
       promise you       me PRTs     for on time home to be
       'Promise me to be home on time!'

---

[6] Italian has weak subject pronouns, but they appear to occupy positions different from the structural position of pro (see Cardinaletti 1997; Alexiadou, Chapter 5 below).

We conclude that Standard Dutch shows pro-drop phenomena in uninflected imperatives. The questions arise why pro is allowed in imperatives in Dutch, and why it occurs in uninflected imperatives only.

### 4.2.4 *The interpretation of pro in imperatives*

As is clear from the preceding sections, the pro subject in imperative constructions can be interpreted as second-person singular. This interpretation corresponds to the interpretation of the lexical pronoun *jij*. However, pro can also be interpreted as a plural element corresponding to the pronoun *jullie*. We can force a plural interpretation of the empty subject by introducing a plural anaphor or quantifier that has pro as its antecedent. This is illustrated in the examples in (10).

(10)  a.  Geef *pro*$_i$ elkaar$_i$    de  hand!
          give        each other  the  hand
          'Give each other a hand!'
      b.  Herinner pro$_i$  jullie$_i$    het  gesprek      van  vorige  week!
          remember      yourselves  the  conversation  of   last    week
          'Remember last week's conversation!'
      c.  Beloof pro$_i$  mij  om PRO$_i$  het  probleem  samen$_i$ op  te lossen!
          promise    me   for      the  problem   together    to solve
          'Promise me to solve this problem together!'
      d.  Ga pro$_i$  allemaal$_i$  in  de   rij     staan!
          go       all       in  the  line   stand
          'Stand in line!'

The pro subjects in (10) must be plural, owing to the fact that the anaphor (*elkaar* or *jullie*) or the quantifier (*samen* or *allemaal*) requires a plural antecedent.

Pro in uninflected imperatives can also be interpreted as the polite pronoun U, as is demonstrated in (11).

(11)  a.  Let $_i$  goed  op Uzelf$_i$!    (reflexive)
          watch  good  on yourself[+polite]
          'Watch yourself carefully!'
      b.  Vergis pro$_i$  U$_i$              niet!      (inherent reflexive)
          mistake      yourself[+polite]  not
          'Don't make mistakes!'
      c.  Probeer pro$_i$ [PRO$_i$ U$_i$    die  gebeurtenis te herinneren]! (control+inh.refl)
          try           you[+polite] that event      to remember
          'Try to remember that event!'

As was shown above, *t*-inflected and *en*-inflected imperative verbs do not occur with a pro subject in modern Standard Dutch; the polite pronoun *U/jullie* must be present. Pro appears in uninflected imperatives only. Interpretatively it may occur as the non-lexical counterpart to *jij, jullie*, and *U*.

### 4.2.5 *Lexical subjects in right-peripheral position*

A somewhat unexpected fact is that we find postverbal subjects in Dutch imperatives. In other sentence types in Dutch, the subject has to appear left- or right-adjacent to the finite verb in root clauses. In imperatives it appears to be the case that adjacency to the verb is not required. In simple imperatives this can be observed in clauses in which the nominative subject follows a verbal particle (such as *weg* in (12a)). In perfect imperatives we may find the subject following the participle.[7] This is demonstrated in (12b).[8]

(12)  a.  Ga  maar  weg  jij!
       go  PRT  away  you
       'You, go away!'
   b.  Was  maar  niet  weggegaan  jij!
       was  PRT  not  away-gone  you
       'You shouldn't have left!'

[7] As has been observed in the literature, imperatives do not occur with past-tense marking. Relevant examples from Dutch are given in (i).

(i)  a.  *Ging dan maar weg!
      went  PRTs  away
   b.  *Was maar niet bang!
      was  PRT  not  afraid

I will assume that this implies that there is no formal expression of Tense in imperative clauses. However, there is a set of perfective imperatives, or rather optative constructions, that occur with a past-tense auxiliary. Examples are given in (ii).

(ii)  a.  Had  dat  nou  toch gedaan
      had  that  PRTs  done
      'You should have done that.'
   b.  Was maar niet zo haastig geweest
      Was PRT not so fast  been
      'You should not have been in such a hurry.'

These clauses have most of the properties of simple imperatives, such as V1 and the non-lexical second-person subject. In this case, the past auxiliary seems to implicate irrealis instead of past (the participle indicates perfect aspect). Wolf (2003) argues that past imperatives are marginally possible. Insofar as the cases mentioned there are acceptable, they differ both in interpretation and in syntactic properties from the simple imperatives discussed here.

[8] At first sight, these sentences constitute genuine cases of postverbal subjects, since the intonational pattern is neutral and appears to differ from that of clauses with a right-dislocated constituent. If the sentences in (12) were indeed legitimate cases of postverbal subjects, we would have a striking similarity between Dutch imperatives and a language such as Italian: (1) the occurrence of pro subjects; (2) the non-occurrence of weak lexical pro-drop in nouns in subject position (cf. (8)); and (3) the occurrence of postverbal subjects (cf. 4, 1).

A careful study of the data indicates that the pronouns in (12) should not be analysed as right-peripheral subjects, but rather as instances of right disloca- tion. First of all, we find full DPs in the same position as *jij* in (12).

(13)  a.  Wees maar gerust    *mijn kind!*
          be    PRT  unafraid  my    child
          'My child, don't be afraid!'
      b.  Was   maar  niet   weggelopen    *sukkel!*
          was   PRT   not    away-walked   fool
          'Fool, you shouldn't have walked away!'

The clause-final DP cannot be the syntactic subject, given that the subject in imperatives must be second person.[9] Putting these DPs in the canonical subject position indeed results in strong ungrammaticality, as is demon- strated in (14).

(14)  a.  *Wees mijn   kind   maar gerust!
      b.  *Was  sukkel maar niet   weggelopen!

In contrast with (14), the addition of a second-person pronoun to the sentences in (13) is possible:

(15)  a.  Wees *jij* maar gerust mijn      kind!
      b.  Was  *jij* maar niet   weggelopen sukkel!

This shows that the postverbal DP subject in imperatives is right-dislocated and coindexed with pro (13) or the pronoun *jij* (15) in subject position. The same conclusion can be derived from the observation that the second-person pronoun *jullie* can appear in clause-final position, although it does not occur in subject position, as we see in (16).

(16)  a.  Ga pro$_i$ maar weg  jullie$_i$!
          go      PRT  away you[+pl]
          'You, go away!'
      b.  *Ga jullie    maar  weg!
          go  you[+pl]  PRT   away

The fact that there is no strict agreement between the grammatical subject and a right-dislocated constituent that is coreferential with the grammatical

---

[9] These postverbal DPs are like vocatives in several respects. This is, of course, to be expected, given that these DPs have to be interpreted as addressees. For our purposes it does not really matter whether we take them as vocatives or as genuine right-dislocated DPs, as long as they are not taken to be syntactic subjects.

subject is by no means typical for imperatives. In other sentence types (with an overt grammatical subject) we find the same 'sloppy' agreement between subject and sentence final DP, as is shown in (17).

(17)  a. Gaat [jullie elftal]$_i$ / Gaan [wij]$_i$ de wedstrijd winnen, [mannen]$_i$?
        goes your team [−pl] / go we[1plu] the match win, men[3pl]
        'Is your team / Are we going to win the match, men?'
      b. Gisteren hebben [zij]$_i$ weer eens gewonnen, [het eerste elftal van Ajax]$_i$
        yesterday have they [+pl] again won, the first team of Ajax[−pl]
        'Yesterday they finally won again, the Ajax first team'
      c. [Jij]$_i$ hebt het nog steeds niet door hè, [makker]$_i$
        you[2sg] understand it PRTs not, friend[3sg]
        'You still don't understand it, friend'

We observe that the agreement relation between the verb and the grammatical subject is much stricter in observing the identity of φ-features than the coreference relation between the grammatical subject and a right-dislocated constituent. I will refer to this difference as a difference between *syntactic agreement* (verb–subject agreement) and *interpretive agreement* (see note 24 below for further elaboration on this issue).

We thus conclude that clause-final subjects in Dutch do not occur. Although imperatives may give the impression of allowing right-peripheral subjects, closer scrutiny has demonstrated that these clause-final, nominal phrases cannot be analysed as syntactic subjects. Rather, in these cases the pro subject is accompanied by a coindexed right-dislocated nominal phrase, which is connected to the pro subject through interpretive agreement.

## 4.3 On the nature of agreement

In the preceding paragraph we have established the occurrence of pro in Dutch imperatives. We have seen that various arguments corroborate the assumption that an empty pronominal subject is present in uninflected imperatives. This immediately brings us to the question of what exactly determines the presence of pro. It is hard to see how a parameter would enlighten us here. In order to find an answer to this question we shall look into the specific properties of the imperative construction, since this construction appears to be the only construction in Dutch in which a clear instance of subject pro is found productively.[10]

---

[10] It has been argued that Dutch allows empty expletive subjects, and that these subjects should be analysed as pro subjects. It is indeed the case that in sentences without a thematic DP subject the subject position can remain empty in Dutch. This phenomenon can be observed in impersonal

In Chomsky's minimalist framework (1995; 2001a) the operation Agree plays a central role in the core system ('narrow syntax'). In order to derive a well-formed LF structure, uninterpretable features have to be deleted in the course of the derivation. Agree is the operation that establishes a relation through which uninterpretable features can be deleted under identity with interpretable features. In what follows, I take these ideas as a useful point of departure for a formal implementation of the agreement process in Dutch imperatives.

For subject–verb agreement this system implies that the uninterpretable φ-features of the finite verb must be deleted under identity with the interpretable features of the subject in an Agree relation. Movement of the finite verb to a functional head position in the verbal domain (e.g. Tense) results in a configuration that allows the features of the inflected verb to be deleted.

In this theory the presence of an empty pro subject is surprising at first sight. The theory appears to force us to assume that pro has interpretable features, but it is hard to see how an empty category can have interpretable φ-features of itself—the assumption being that the interpretation of empty elements is contextually determined. In line with many proposals in the literature, we may assume that in pro-drop languages it is the verbal inflection that provides the interpretable features for pro (see below). In languages such as Italian and Spanish, the verbal paradigm is fully specified with respect to the (uninterpretable) φ-features for person and number. We now may expect

---

passives (as in (i) below), among others. However, in Bennis (1986) I have argued extensively that there is no expletive pro subject in these cases.

Another relevant set of examples is found in the so-called diary style, in which first-person-subject pronouns can be dropped (as in (ii) below). Although these sentences may contain a pro subject, they differ from imperatives in at least two important aspects: the pronoun can be dropped from first position only, and the sentences are stylistically marked. I leave this construction out of consideration here.

A third set of subjectless sentences can be found in clauses with topic-drop. If the subject is third-person, non-human, the subject can be dropped from first position. The phenomenon in which non-human topics can be dropped from sentence-initial position is well known and often discussed in the literature. A subset of these cases involves subject drop (as in (iii) below). Because this involves a marked subset of cases of pronoun-drop, restricted to sentence-initial position, I will not discuss this phenomenon here either.

(i) In de Arena  wordt  gevoetbald      door Ajax
    In the Arena  is       played-football by    Ajax
    'Ajax plays football in the Arena.'

(ii) Ben  naar de film   geweest
     Am   to    the movie been
     'I went to the movies.'

(iii) Interesseert me  niks
      Interests    me  nothing
      'It doesn't interest me at all.'

pro to appear if the φ-features of pro can be interpreted as a consequence of Agree with the specified inflected verb. In these cases Agree thus establishes two things: it determines the feature value of *pro*—i.e. pro has an interpretable and specified set of features due to Agree with the inflected verb[11]—and Agree allows the uninterpretable features of the inflected verb to be deleted as soon as the feature value of pro has been fixed. No parameter is involved, since the possibility of a pro subject is completely determined by the presence of specified φ-features on the inflected verb.

We thus have two different oppositions that are relevant. Features can be interpretable or uninterpretable; in the domain of subject–verb agreement this opposition is related to a categorial difference: φ-features receive an interpretation in the case of nouns but not of verbs. The other opposition is between specified and underspecified inflection. Lexical pronouns in Dutch, for instance, are lexically specified for the features person, number, and gender. Inflected verbs have a specified inflection if the language in question has a verbal paradigm in which each set of φ-features gives rise to a unique morphosyntactic realization. In a language such as Dutch, the verbal paradigm is poor in the sense that the verbal inflection is underspecified. For instance, the uninflected (or zero-inflected) verb may be used in agreement with first- and second-person-singular pronouns. Given the fact that verbal inflection in Dutch is underspecified, pro is impossible, owing to the fact that the feature specification of pro cannot be established on the basis of inconclusive evidence.

If this line of argumentation is correct and if it is correct that pro may appear in Dutch imperatives (cf. section 4.2), the question arises as to what makes the verbal inflection in uninflected imperative verbs specified.

### 4.3.1 *The imperative feature*

A first relevant observation is that the subject in imperatives always refers to an addressee. The notion of addressee is syntactically implemented as the feature for second person.[12] In line with tradition, we thus assume that imperatives are second person. The verbal inflection for second person is relatively complex, especially in comparison to first- and third-person inflection in Dutch. The table in (18) gives a schematic representation of the patterns of second-person inflection and the corresponding second-person pronouns.

---

[11] I will assume here that the features of pro are assigned to pro under Agree. As an alternative, we may assume that pro is maximally underspecified for φ-features—i.e. it has a complete set of possible feature specifications. Of this set the feature specification(s) that can be checked through Agree is taken to be the relevant set for interpretation.

[12] Similar ideas have been put forward in Barbiers (forthcoming) and Platzack (forthcoming).

The pronominal formal addressee *U* (feature [polite]) requires *t*-inflection, independent of whether the subject is interpreted as plural or not, and

(18)    Verbal inflection (I) and subject pronouns (II) for second person

| [polite] | + | | − | |
|---|---|---|---|---|
| [plural] | | + | − | |
| Subj ... Vfin | | | + | − |
| I | -*t* | -*en* | -*t* | -*ø* |
| II | *U* | *jullie* | *jij / je* | *jij / je* |

independent of word order (19a). The (non-formal) plural addressee *jullie* always requires *en*-inflection (19b). The non-formal, non-plural addressee *jij* (and its weak counterpart *je*) requires *t*-inflection if the subject precedes the finite verb and zero inflection if the subject follows. This is demonstrated in (19).

(19)    a. U          heb-*t*   altijd    gelijk
           You[polite]  have    always    right
        a'. Altijd heb-*t* U gelijk
        b. Jullie      hebb-*en*  altijd     gelijk
           You[pl]    have     always
        b'. Altijd                hebb-*en*  jullie    gelijk
        c. Jij                   heb-*t*  altijd    gelijk
           You[−pl,  −polite]have    always    right
        c'. Altijd heb-ø jij gelijk

In imperatives we find the same three inflected verbs: *t*-inflected verbs co-occurring with the polite pronoun *U*, *en*-inflected verbs co-occurring with the plural pronoun *jullie*, and zero-inflected verbs co-occurring with the non-polite, non-plural pronoun *jij* or with *pro*. This is shown in (20).

(20)    a. Wees-*t*    U                niet  bang!
           Be[imp]    you[polite]      not   afraid
        b. Wez-*en*    jullie           niet  bang!
           Be[imp]    you[pl]          not   afraid
        c. Wees-*ø*    jij/pro          niet  bang!
           Be[imp]    you[−pl,−polite]  not   afraid

As is clear from (20) (see also the examples in (6)) a pro subject is possible only if the imperative verb has zero inflection, as in (20c).

In (18/19c) we observe that o inflection in non-imperative second-person constructions appears only in clauses in which the subject *jij* follows the verb.

In the literature (see Travis 1984; Zwart 1993) it has been argued that the distribution of the inflectional marking of second-person-singular verbs supports the view that the finite verb in Dutch root clauses does not uniformly target the same structural position.[13] In line with the analysis of Zwart (1993), we may assume that the finite verb in verb-second contexts moves to the C-position in subject-non-initial main clauses and to a lower functional head—i.e. AgrS or T—in subject-initial main clauses. For second-person [−polite, −pl] contexts in Standard Dutch this implies that the C-position is the target for zero-inflected verbs and the lower head the target for *t*-inflected verbs.

In much recent work (see e.g. Rizzi 1997) it is assumed that the complementizer domain (the C-domain) is the locus of Force. The distinctive property of marked sentence types such as interrogation, topicalization, and exclamation can syntactically be realized as a syntactic feature in the C-domain, which leads to the introduction of (root) phrases such as TopP. This view allows us to explain why imperative verbs with a [−polite, −pl] subject show up in the uninflected form, and not with a *t*-inflection. Imperatives belong to the class of marked sentence types. The relevant imperative feature is located in the C-domain.[14] In order to provide the imperative feature with a lexical base, the verb moves to C.[15] Given that verbs that are second person singular have a zero inflection in C, it follows that the ungrammaticality of (21b) is a consequence of the fact that the imperative force is located in C.

(21)  a. Wees        maar  niet  bang!     [-0: Vf in C]
         Be[imp] you  PRT   not   afraid
      b. *Wees-*t*     maar  niet  bang!     [-*t*: Vf not in C]
         You be[imp]  PRT   not   afraid
         'Don't be afraid'

---

[13] Another argument to support this claim is that weak subject pronouns may occur in first position, in contrast to weak object pronouns. If the first position in the clause is a topic position, we expect strong pronouns only. This indicates that clause-initial subject pronouns may occupy a lower position in the clause, which is different from the topic position. This in turn implies that the position of the finite verb may be either above the subject position (the C-position) or below (AgrS or T).

Arguments from Dutch dialects (see Zwart 1993) further support this analysis. In various Dutch dialects the inflection of the verb in subject-non-initial root clauses is identical to the inflection of the complementizer in finite subordinate clauses (the C-position), whereas the verbal inflection in subject-initial root clauses and in subordinate clauses is clearly distinct (lower functional head).

[14] There are various arguments to support the view that in Dutch the C-domain consists of various functional projections (see Bennis 2000). This is irrelevant for the present discussion. Therefore I present the C-domain as simplex below.

[15] An issue which is not addressed here is the fact that Dutch imperatives do not allow the [Spec,CP] position to be filled. In other languages (e.g. English, German, French) this appears possible to some extent. I will leave the question why there is such a difference for future research.

In this section I have claimed two things: (1) imperatives have a syntactic feature for second person, owing to the fact that the subject always refers to an addressee and illustrated by the fact that imperative verbs show second-person inflection; and (2) the imperative feature is located in the C-domain of root clauses. We now may combine these two observations by assuming that the imperative construction is characterized by the presence of the feature for second person in the C-position.[16] This hypothesis is formulated in (22).

(22)    Imperative Force is instantiated as a syntactic feature [2] in the C-domain of root clauses.

This assumption straightforwardly accounts for several properties of the imperative construction:

- First, it follows that only verbs that are inflected for second person can occur in the imperative construction. Verbs that have [1] or [3] in their feature makeup will give rise to a clash between the C-feature and the V-feature.
- Another consequence is that the uninflected verb (and not the *t*-inflected verb) shows up if the subject is singular, non-polite, since the [2]-feature is located in C, and not in AgrS/T (see (19c)).
- A third consequence is that only second-person pronouns may appear as a lexical subject in imperatives. As will be shown in the next section, this is not as trivial as it seems.
- It follows that there are no embedded imperatives.
- And, finally, as I will show below, the distribution of pro in imperatives can be made to follow from (22) as well.

### 4.3.2 *Person properties of polite pronouns*

A rather strange property of the polite pronoun *U* is that it can be either second or third person. This property can be observed in two contexts. First, it shows up in cases of agreement with the finite verb. In (18) we saw that the polite pronoun gives rise to *t*-inflection, independent of its position relative to the inflected verb. In this respect, the inflection of the polite verb is generally identical to the inflection of third-person verbs. However, there are cases of irregular verbs in which there is a difference between *t*-inflected second-person verbs and *t*-inflected third-person verbs. The most salient case is the verb *hebben* ('to have'). Third-person-singular subjects require the verb form

---

[16] Other marked sentence types, such as questions, do not have a person feature in C, given that their subject is not uniform with respect to person.

*heeft*, whereas the second-person pronoun *jij* requires the verb form *hebt*. This is illustrated in (23a, b). Interestingly, both verb forms co-occur with the polite subject pronoun *U*, as is shown in (23c).[17]

(23)  a.  Hij          heeft / *hebt  betaald
          He           has            paid
      b.  Jij          *heeft / hebt  betaald
          You          have           paid
      c.  U            heeft / hebt   betaald[18]
          You[polite]  has/have        paid

A second manifestation of the person ambiguity of polite pronouns is found in binding contexts. If the antecedent of a reflexive pronoun is third person, the form of the reflexive is *zich(zelf)* ('himself'). In the case of second-person pronouns, the reflexive is *je(zelf)* ('yourself'). With the polite pronoun we find an ambiguity between *zich(zelf)* and *U(zelf)*. This is demonstrated in the inherent reflexive construction in (24).

(24)  a.  Hij  vergist        zich
          He   make-mistake   REFL
      b.  Jij  vergist        je / *zich
          You  make-mistake   REFL
      c.  U    vergist        U / zich
          You  make-mistake   REFL

We may even combine the properties discussed with respect to (23) and (24). The sentences in (25) are equally acceptable and semantically identical.[19]

(25)  a.  U *hebt* U vergist              infl = 2   refl = 2
      b.  U *heeft* zich vergist          infl = 3   refl = 3
      c.  U *hebt* zich vergist           infl = 2   refl = 3
      d.  U *heeft* U vergist             infl = 3   refl = 2
          You have REFL made-mistake

---

[17] The form *heeft* is considered to be the most formal variant. In line with this, the sentence *U heeft betaald* ('You have paid') is probably one of the most frequent sentences in written Dutch, given that it is automatically produced after a successful electronic payment by card.

[18] The traditional reason given for the inflectional ambiguity in this case is that the second-person subject pronoun *U* is a rather late development (nineteenth century) and is considered to be derived from *U Edele* ('You honourable') which was a third-person noun phrase (*WNT* 1984; Paardekooper 1948; Bennis 2004) and which is now used as a second-person pronoun.

[19] These sentences suggest that there is a principled distinction between subject–verb agreement and agreement in binding relations. Some people have argued that binding can be reduced to agreement (Pica, Postma, Reuland). It appears to be the case that the sentences in (25c, d) are problematic for such an analysis.

Although an analysis of this construction is beyond the scope of this chapter, I will assume that the polite pronoun is ambiguous between second person and third person, and that *U* can be second person and third person at the same time with respect to different agreement relations.

The interesting case for us here is that the ambiguity of polite constructions in subject–verb agreement disappears in imperatives. This is shown in (26).[20]

(26)  a. Hebt / ??Heeft  U           mij   nu    maar  lief!
         Have / Has      you[polite]  me    PRTs        dear
         'Love me!'
      b. Hebt / ??Heeft  U           de moed   eens om dat te zeggen!
         Have / Has      you[polite]  the courage PRT for that to say
         'Don't you dare say that'

Even more interesting is the very strong contrast between (27) and (28).

(27)  a. Vergist        U     U     niet!
         Make-mistake   you   2REFL  not
      b. Vergist        U     zich  niet!
         Make-mistake   you   3REFL  not

(28)  a. Vergis   *pro*  U    niet!
      b. *Vergis  *pro*  zich  niet!

In (27) we observe that a lexical polite subject *U* can occur as an antecedent of either *zich* or *U* in imperatives. This is similar to what we have seen in (24c). However, if pro is the subject, it may be interpreted as a polite pronominal (28a), but it does not allow third-person agreement in binding (28b).

These data can be explained right away if we assume that the C-feature [2] is the formal, morphosyntactic instantiation of imperative force, as was claimed in (22). The unacceptability of *heeft* in (26) follows from the fact that *heeft* has an inflectional feature [3] that cannot be combined with the imperative feature [2]. In (28) we go one step further: owing to the fact that imperatives are specified for [2], pro must also carry the feature [2], and consequently binding agreement requires the anaphor to be specified for [2] as well. The difference between (27b) and (28b) comes from the fact that the

---

[20] In (26) we expect the sentences with *heeft* to be fully ungrammatical. The fact that they appear to be marginally possible may reside in the fact that these V1-clauses can also be taken to be yes/no questions (cf. note 4 above). Although the particles strongly suggest an imperative interpretation, an interrogative interpretation cannot be excluded completely. In the interrogative clause the agreement ambiguity shows up, just as in declarative clauses.

lexical subject pronoun *U* is ambiguous between [2] and [3] in (27b), whereas pro is unambiguously [2] in (28b), since the person feature of pro is determined by Agree with the feature [2] in C.

### 4.3.3 *The legitimation of pro in imperatives*

Above it was argued that Dutch imperatives are characterized by the presence of the force feature [2] in the C-domain of root clauses. I will now come back to the topic of this chapter: the occurrence of pro. Given that pro has no inherent lexical interpretation, the basic idea is that pro is legitimate only if its interpretation can be established by other means.

Let us look at a more formal account of the appearance of pro in terms of recent ideas on agreement and the role of features. The paradigm of Standard Dutch subject pronouns consists of nine members.[21] These are given in (29).

(29)  ik     [1]        wij      [1, pl]
      jij    [2]        jullie   [2, pl]
      U      [2, pol]   zij      [3, pl]
      het    [3]
      hij    [3, m]
      zij    [3, f]

As is indicated in (29), I shall consider singular to be absence of plurality, which encodes the fact that plurality is generally more complex both in form and in meaning. In the same way non-polite is the absence of a feature for politeness. Compared to (29) the verbal inflectional system is heavily underspecified, as is clear from (30).

(30)  V–ø     ( [1] / [2] )
      V–t     ( [2, pol] / [3] / [3, m] / [3, f] )[22]
      V–en    ( [1, pl], [2, pl], [3, pl])

The first step in the analysis is that the inflected verb moves to C. This movement is driven by the same considerations that trigger V-movement in other root clauses in Dutch. There is and has been a lot of discussion on what exactly determines Verb Second in languages such as Dutch (e.g. Zwart 2001). I will not dwell on the issue here. A minimal condition on the movement of the inflected verb to C is that the verb agrees with the features that are generated in C.

---

[21] I will not take into account weak pronouns and lexical variants.

[22] I will leave out of consideration here the *t*-inflected verbs in sentences in which the second-person pronoun *jij* precedes the finite verb. Given that imperatives always have a C-domain in which the C-position is filled with the inflected verb, the zero-inflected verb is the relevant verb form here (cf. 4.3.1).

Above I hypothesized that simple imperatives are characterized by a force feature [2] in C. We now have to refine this formulation somewhat. All verbs that are second person can be moved to C in imperatives—i.e. V[2], V[2, pol] and V[2, pl]. The C-feature thus indicates non-distinctness. In order to distinguish the referential, pronominal feature [2], i.e. second person singular (cf. 29), from the imperative feature, I will refer to such a feature with {2}. All finite verbs that have a feature for second person in their feature specification are in accordance with the non-distinctness feature {2}, whereas [2] corresponds to the singular, non-polite second person only.

Note that it is not the case that the imperative feature will be deleted as a consequence of verb movement. The feature(s) on the inflected verb and the feature {2} on C are both uninterpretable features, since they represent nominal features on the head of a projection in the verbal domain. The only way to get rid of an uninterpretable feature is in an Agree relation with an interpretable feature.[23] The deletion process of uninterpretable nominal features on a finite verb can thus take place only through Agree with a nominal projection, in this case the subject. It is clear that an overtly expressed pronoun is able to delete the φ-features of V. In order to do so, the specified feature value of the pronoun has to agree with the feature specification of the inflected verb. If that is the case, the uninterpretable verbal φ-features can be deleted under Agree.

It has been argued above that pro does not co-occur with an underspecified verbal paradigm (see Speas, Chapter 2 above). Pro does not have inherent φ-features, and its interpretation cannot be established through Agree with the underspecified inflected verb. As a consequence, the uninterpretable features on V cannot be deleted. It follows that languages such as Dutch are not 'pro-drop languages'. This was hypothesized in (1), which is given below in a slightly different way.

(1′)   Pro subjects in non-infinitival clauses may appear if:
  (i) the relevant (interpretable) φ-features of the empty subject can be recovered through Agree;
  (ii) the (uninterpretable) φ-features on the non-infinitival verb can be deleted through Agree.

---

[23] A different situation would arise if the C-feature had been interpretable, e.g. [Tense]. In that case movement of the inflected verb to C does result in the deletion of the Tense feature. The intuitive logic behind the idea that uninterpretable features can be deleted in an Agree relation with interpretable features only is that features have to receive an interpretation. If uninterpretable features could be deleted in a relation with other uninterpretable features, we would have a situation in which features could be deleted without having received an interpretation.

Only if the verbal paradigm is fully specified, as it is in languages such as Italian, can pro be interpreted, since the inflected verb carries a specific feature set. If pro is thus interpreted, it is in turn able to remove the uninterpretable φ-features of the inflected verb through Agree.

For languages without inflected verbs, such as Chinese, the situation is different. In those languages the verb has no morphosyntactic φ-features, and consequently the requirement that the uninterpretable φ-features on V should be deleted (1′ ii) is vacuously met. Given that the empty category may receive its interpretation through other means, e.g. pragmatically, it follows that pro may appear in these languages without formal restrictions on its interpretation. This perspective allows us to simplify the hypothesis in (1′) to (1″).

(1″)    Pro subjects in non-infinitival clauses may appear only if the (uninterpretable) φ-features on the non-infinitival verb can be deleted through Agree.

In (1″) we have removed (1′i). The natural assumption that pro subjects must receive a specific interpretation is not directly related to Agree. The interpretation of pro can be established through Agree with the (fully specified) inflected verb, but also through non-syntactic operations as long as (1″) is not violated, i.e. if the verbal paradigm has no uninterpretable features, as in Chinese. If the inflected verb is underspecified, pro does not occur, owing to a violation of (1″).

Let us now see what happens in simple imperatives in Dutch. After movement of the verb to C, we have a configuration as in (31).

(31)          C          —          SUBJECT
         ╱        ╲                    |
    {2}          V–0 (-[1]-/-[2]-)   pronoun / pro

The inflected verb is underspecified with respect to its φ-features. As in non-imperatives, it will not license pro. Instead of Agree with the inflected verb, Agree may also involve {2}. Let us see what happens if this is the case.

First we predict that the pro subject with the non-distinct feature {2} can have an interpretation that is either second singular, second plural, or second polite. This is precisely what we have found in section 4.2.4: interpretively pro may occur as the non-lexical counterpart to *jij*, *jullie*, and *U*.

The second consequence is that pro co-occurs with the ø-inflected verb only. The feature {2} on pro is able to delete the feature [2] on the verb in C. Given that second-person-singular pronouns and inflection are both characterized by [2] (cf. 29 and 30), the zero-inflected verb is able to get rid of its uninterpretable φ-feature in accordance with 1″.

If the verb has *t-* or *en-*inflection, the situation changes. The inflected verb in C does not have the feature specification [2] in its representation, but rather [2, pol] or [2, pl] (see 30). If the non-distinctness feature {2} is present on the subject as a consequence of Agree, deletion of the uninterpretable V-features is not possible: the feature {2} on pro is not able to cause deletion of the more specified sets [2, pol] resp. [2, pl]. In those cases an overt pronoun corresponding to {2} has to be inserted. This causes *U* ([2, pol]) resp. *jullie* ([2, pl]) to show up.[24]

## 4.4 Conclusion

I have argued that the appearance of a pro subject in non-infinitival clauses depends on the possibility to delete the uninterpretable φ-features on the verb without having to insert an overt subject. I argued that (1″) is the condition that determines the occurrence of pro. This condition is repeated below.

(1″)   Pro subjects in non-infinitival clauses may appear only if the (uninterpretable) φ-features on the non-infinitival verb can be deleted through Agree.

We have discussed three different situations:

- In languages with a fully specified inflection pro is generally possible, and its interpretation is determined by the features that the inflectional element demonstrates.[25] The uninterpretable features on the verb can be deleted as a consequence of Agree.
- In languages without inflection pro is possible as well, and its interpretation is morphosyntactically unrestricted.[26] The interpretation will be determined by other means, e.g. by pragmatic processes. The verb has no uninterpretable φ-features and (1″) is thus satisfied.

---

[24] It is interesting to observe that the empty subject with the feature {2} can be the antecedent for plural or polite anaphors (cf. 10 and 11). It indicates that Agree is crucially different from binding. I discussed a similar issue before in relation to right-dislocated subjects (see section 4.2.5). I conclude that subject–verb agreement requires feature identity, whereas binding or coindexation requires interpretive identity. This view is corroborated by the fact that a singular DP with a plural interpretation (e.g. *het elftal* 'the team') can be the antecedent for the plural anaphor *elkaar* (*het elftal speelt elkaar de bal toe* 'the team plays the ball towards each other') but does not show up as a subject with a plural verb (*\*het elftal wilLEN winnen* 'the team wants to win').

[25] What exactly constitutes full specification is to some extent language-specific. As argued in Speas (Chapter 2 above), languages such as Brazilian Portuguese seem to have a fully specified inflectional paradigm and do not allow pro.

[26] What exactly constitutes absence of inflection has to be investigated in more detail, given that a language such as Swedish appears to have no inflectional paradigm for φ-features. Still, Swedish does not allow pro subjects (see Speas, Chapter 2 above).

• Finally, in languages with an underspecified inflection pro is generally impossible owing to the fact that the underspecified inflection provides insufficient information in order to delete the uninterpretable V-features as a consequence of Agree. An overt pronoun has to do the job.

However, in special circumstances a construction feature may provide additional information in such a way that a pro subject is allowed. We find this situation in imperatives in Standard Dutch, in which case the presence of the feature {2} in the C-domain allows pro to occur, but only if the verb shows zero inflection.[27]

The final conclusion is that there is no pro-drop parameter and that the occurrence of pro is to a large extent determined by independent properties such as the nature of the verbal inflection and the operation Agree. Moreover, I argued that the occurrence of pro is not a language-specific property. In languages with an underspecified verbal inflection pro shows up only on the condition that the inflectional paradigm can be specified through other means. In Dutch imperatives the construction feature {2} arguably provides the means to specify the verbal paradigm in such a way that a pro subject will become available.

---

[27] Of course this analysis of Standard Dutch does not imply that in other languages with underspecified inflection the imperative allows a pro subject in the case of zero-inflection only. Older or regional varieties of Dutch and other 'non-pro-drop languages' such as French allow pro in imperatives in other contexts. A detailed analysis of the inflectional system of these languages is required in order to determine what properties are relevant and which properties make it possible to delete the uninterpretable V-features.

# Part II

## Microvariation in Pro-Drop Languages

# 5

# Uniform and Non-Uniform Aspects of Pro-Drop Languages

ARTEMIS ALEXIADOU

## 5.1 Introduction: pro-drop languages lack a specifier position for 'subjects'

In a recent paper, Alexiadou and Anagnostopoulou (1998) put forth an approach to the pro-drop parameter and the Extended Projection principle (EPP), according to which (1) EPP is universal and is understood as a D feature on I (Chomsky 1995) and (2) pro-drop languages satisfy this feature via V-movement to I owing to the pronominal nature of their verbal agreement. In these languages A-movement to spec,IP is not needed, and all movement to the preverbal position is A'-movement. Non-pro-drop languages, however, necessarily move or merge a DP in spec,IP to check EPP. The approach made the prediction that pro-drop languages have no expletives, overt or covert. The empirical support for this proposal came from a discussion of Spanish and Greek data.

The question that immediately arises is whether all pro-drop languages behave alike. As has been pointed out in the literature, languages such as Italian or partial pro-drop languages such as Hebrew and Finnish lack the properties that characterize the Greek/Spanish system. It is thus the aim of this chapter to address the similarities and the differences between Greek/Spanish on the one hand, and Italian and Hebrew/Finnish on the other, in terms of the general framework introduced in Alexiadou and Anagnostopoulou (1998).[1] Before I proceed to my factual discussion of the cross-linguistic

I am grateful to the participants of the workshop on Agreement in Argument Structure in Utrecht in Aug. 2001, to two anonymous reviewers, and to the editors of this volume for helpful comments and suggestions. The work presented here was partially financed by the DFG grant AL554/1-1, which is hereby acknowledged.

[1] Languages of the Chinese type of pro-drop will not be discussed here, as I adopt the view that these are actually topic-drop languages.

variation, I summarize the approach and the predictions made in Alexiadou and Anagnostopoulou (1998).

### 5.1.1 *The EPP as a parameter*

The EPP is understood as the requirement that every sentence must have a subject. Within the framework of Government and Binding theory, EPP was intended to capture the necessity of expletives in languages such as English. The presence of *there* or *it* in spec,IP was obligatory in cases where no overt DP appeared in that position. The way this principle is understood and implemented in syntactic theory has changed over the years. Specifically, in recent syntactic theory subject properties are associated with phrase structural heads and positions in a local relation with those heads. With the introduction of checking theory, EPP is reduced to a (nominal) feature on AgrS and subsequently T (Chomsky 1995; 2001a). In both the previous and the recent stages of the theory, however, EPP is understood as a universal property that all languages must obey.

Within this set of assumptions, it is taken for granted that there is an EPP feature located on a designated functional head that is satisfied by the presence of an XP in the spec position of this head. There are two possibilities for the checking of this feature: either a DP moves to the specifier of the head containing this feature (1), or an expletive is merged in that position (2).

(1)    a. A man arrived
       b. [$_{EPP}$ DP A man [vP arrived t ]]
(2)    a. There arrived a man/*the man
       b. [$_{EPP}$ there [$_{vP}$ arrived a man]]

In the configuration (2b) definiteness restriction (DR) effects are observed. The configurations in (1b, 2b) are assumed to be universal. Hence the standard view has been that in pro-drop languages such as Italian, Greek, and Spanish pro (expl/referential) takes over the role of this XP, alternating with an overt DP (see Rizzi 1982):

(3)    a. Gianni/pro è  arrivato                                      (Italian)
          Gianni/he  is arrived
       b. pro$_{expl}$ è arrivato Gianni

Moreover, recent work has shown that languages may differ as to whether they make another, non EPP-related, vP-external specifier available for the subject DP, independently of the pro-drop nature of the language, and this correlates with the availability of transitive constructions in subject inversion—that is, (expl) VSO orders. On the one hand, languages such as Icelandic license such a position and permit Transitive Expletive Constructions (TECs); on the other hand, English does not license such a position and lacks TECs (Bobaljik and Jonas 1996; McCloskey (1999) shows that such a specifier is licensed in Irish as well; see section 5.1.2).

(4)  a.  There arrived a man/* There bought a man the book     (English)
     b.  A man arrived/A man bought the book

(5)  a.  að     lasu  einhverjir stúdentar bókina              (Icelandic)
         there  read  some       students  the book
         'Some students read the book'
     b.  Einhverjir stúdentar lasu      bókina
         'Some       students  read the book'

However, the universality of EPP, or rather the uniformity according to which it is satisfied across languages, has been questioned. There are two recent views on how EPP can be understood as a parameter. According to one view, there are languages in which EPP is inactive, e.g. Irish (McCloskey 1996; 1999). According to a second view, EPP is universal; what is parameterized is the mode of EPP checking (Alexiadou and Anagnostopoulou 1998).

In particular, as we argued for in detail in Alexiadou and Anagnostopoulou (1998), languages split into two groups on the basis of the mode of EPP checking. Languages such as English, Icelandic, Mainland Scandinavian, and French move or merge an XP to the specifier of the EPP-related projection, while pro-drop languages move or merge an X°. This latter group satisfies the EPP via V-raising (or merging of a clitic). The two options are schematically represented in (6):

(6)  1.  a.  [$_{EPP}$ A man [$_{FP}$ came t ]]             (English/Icelandic)
         b.  [$_{EPP}$ there [$_{FP}$ came a man ]]
     2.      [$_{EPP}$ irthe [$_{FP}$ o Janis ]]           (Greek/Spanish/Irish)
             came-3sg   the John-nom

Since all pro-drop languages have V-raising to the relevant head in INFL, as has been established independently in the literature, this is sufficient to check EPP as their verbal agreement morphology is *pronominal*, i.e. it includes the D feature required (see Taraldsen 1980; Rizzi 1982), adopting the view that pronouns are D-type elements (Postal 1969 and much subsequent work). And indeed, in both Spanish and Greek, verbs make distinctions for all persons. The relevant paradigms are given in Tables 5.1 and 5.2. Note that the morphology of these two languages is not 'pronominal' in the same way. In Spanish the person/number forms are related and are independent of tense/aspect,

TABLE 5.1.  Spanish *hablar* 'speak', first conjugation

| Present | | Imperfect | |
|---|---|---|---|
| habl-o | habl-a-m-o-s | habla-b-a | hablá-b-a-m-o-s |
| habl-a-s | habl-áis | habla-b-as | habla-b-ais |
| habl-a | habl-an | habla-b-a | habla-b-an |

TABLE 5.2.  Greek *grafo* 'write'

| Aspect | Imperfective | | Perfective | |
|---|---|---|---|---|
| | Active | Non-active | Active | Non-active |
| Non-past | graf-o | graf-ome | grap-s-o | graf-t-o |
| | graf-is | graf-ese | grap-s-is | graf-t-is |
| | graf-i | graf-ete | grap-s-i | graf-t-i |
| | graf-ume | graf-omaste | grap-s-ume | graf-t-ume |
| | graf-ete | graf-osaste | grap-s-ete | graf-t-ite |
| | graf-un | graf-onte | grap-s-un | graf-t-un |
| Past | e-graf-a | graf-omun | e-grap-s-a | graf-tik-a |
| | e-graf-es | graf-osun | e-grap-s-es | graf-tik-es |
| | e-graf-e | graf-otan | e-grap-s-e | graf-tik-e |
| | graf-ame | graf-omastan | grap-s-ame | graf-tik-ame |
| | graf-ate | graf-osastan | grap-s-ate | graf-tik-ate |
| | e-graf-an | graf-ontan | e-grap-s-an | graf-tik-an |

while in Greek it is difficult to separate Tense from Agreement morphology (Rivero 1994).

For Spanish, Ordóñez (1997) suggests that parts of the verbal agreement system of the language contain person morphemes of the type found in the pronominal system. As shown in (7), the verb form of the first person plural distinguishes between the stem, -*m*-, which is a person morpheme, -*s*-, which is the plural morpheme, and -*o*-, which is identical to the so-called word markers of the Spanish nominal system (Harris 1991) (see (7b)).

(7)  a.  habla-*m*-o-s    *m* = person morpheme, s = plural morpheme
         speak-1st.pl. past   -o- word marker
     b.  hij-o-s
         son-word marker-plural marker

For Greek, a correlation has been made between pronominal forms and non-active (past and non-past) imperfective, as the first- and second-person forms seem to contain similar person forms to those of the pronoun (Drachman 1997). Moreover, historically the second-person past non-active form was built on analogy with the first person by replacing -*m*- with -*s*-. Indeed, -*m*-/-*s*- are the same morpheme we find in first- and second-person pronominal clitics (8):

(8)   emis       me         mou        mas        se         sou        sas
      1st:pl:nom  1st:sg:acc  1st:sg:gen  1st:pl:acc  2nd:sg:acc  2nd:sg:gen  2nd:pl:acc

Still, both languages have distinct forms for the different persons/numbers. The above paradigms lead to a formulation of the EPP as in (9); see e.g. Alexiadou and Anagnostopoulou (1998: 519, n. 29), Chomsky (1999), Davis (1998):

(9)   There is a designated functional head in INFL containing an EPP feature where EPP = a D(ef)/person feature.

On this view, an XP or an X° containing person/definiteness features is responsible for the checking of the EPP feature. Naturally, the question that immediately arises is why person/D should be the crucial feature. We could establish a link between Person and the EPP, if we identified the projection relevant for EPP checking with TP. This is so for the following reason. In the recent literature, EPP is taken to be a property of Tense (see Chomsky 1999). Davis (1998) and others have shown that a link exists between Person and Tense in the sense that both Person and Tense are deictic (and hence definite) categories involving anchoring to speaker/speech time (see e.g. Guéron and Hoekstra (1988) for an early such proposal). Hence if we identify the FP related to EPP with Tense, we have an explanation as to why Person is the crucial feature for the purposes of EPP checking.[2]

A related question concerns the link between person and D(ef). I assume that the formulation in (9) is to be understood in terms of Ritter's (1995) observations on the structure of noun phrases. That is, the presence of a definiteness feature does not necessarily imply the presence of a person feature. The presence of person, however, necessarily implies the presence of

---

[2] Thanks to an anonymous reviewer for pointing this out to me. This line of argumentation is in fact pursued in Alexiadou (2003a). Note also that this view departs from Alexiadou and Anagnostopoulou (1998), who argued that AgrSP is the EPP-related projection, though one could assume that Person is 'identified' in AgrSP. Irrespective of the labels attributed to the EPP projection, however, recent work, most notably Cardinaletti (2004), has shown that there are several subject positions in clause structure with distinct properties (see also Alexiadou 2003a). What is crucial for my discussion here is that there is an FP for EPP purposes. The presence of other projections, which are not relevant for the purposes of EPP checking, does not undermine the main point.

definiteness. This means that a DP or a verbal head/clitic not marked for person, but marked for definiteness—as is the case in, for example, English expletive constructions and perhaps Irish VSO—can check the EPP.

Though the approaches developed in Alexiadou and Anagnostopoulou (1998) and McCloskey (1996) differ in how they view the EPP as a parameter, for both of them there are languages which truly lack a specifier position designated for the EPP. Under Alexiadou and Anagnostopoulou's analysis, these languages have certain properties in common, which I summarize in the next section. For ease of reference I refer to the EPP position as spec,EPP.

### 5.1.2 *Properties of the languages lacking spec,EPP*

In the SVO orders of languages that lack a spec,EPP the subject behaves as a clitic left-dislocated (CLLD-ed) element (see the references and the discussion in Alexiadou and Anagnostopoulou (1998), and also Barbosa (1995; 2000)).[3] For instance, preverbal indefinite subjects have obligatorily wide scope in Greek as opposed to their English counterparts. In (10a) the indefinite 'some student' in a preverbal position has necessarily wide scope over the universally quantified NP in object position, while in the postverbal position (10b) the subject can have narrow or wide scope.

(10)   a. Kapios fititis    stihiothetise kathe arthro
          some    student filed         every article
       b. stihiothetise kapios fititis kathe arthro

If preverbal subjects in Greek were raised to an A-position, they would preserve their narrow scope interpretation. In English, on the other hand, preverbal subjects are ambiguous. This is expected if they undergo A-movement. The subject in (10a) behaves like the CLLD-ed object in (11).

(11)   kapjo pedi to       eksetase   kathe   kathigitis
       some child cl-acc. examined   every   professor

Moreover, indefinite preverbal subjects obligatorily take wide scope over negation in Greek. In (12a) the subject takes wide scope over negation, while in (12b) both readings, i.e. 'many-not' and 'not-many' are possible:

---

[3] The term CLLD refers to the phenomenon in which a phrasal element, usually a DP, appears in sentence-initial position, to the left of the material contained within the clause, and is connected with the clause through the intermediary of the pronominal element, namely a clitic. Evidence from acquisition supports the conclusion that in SVO orders in languages without spec,EPP the subject behaves as a CLLD-ed element (see Grinstead 1998).

(12)  a.  Poli     andres  dhen  eroteftikan ti  Maria
Many men    not    fell-in love    Mary
'Many men are such that they have not fallen in love with Mary'
   b.  Den      eroteftikan  poli   andres ti    Maria
Not      fell-in      love   many men    Mary
'Many  men are      such   that they     have not fallen in love with Mary'
'Few men fell in love with Mary'

Assuming the split CP system introduced in Rizzi (1997), I take CLLD-ed elements to occupy a designated position in the left periphery (13).

(13)  [$_{TopicP}$ O Janis [$_{IP}$    pandrefitke ti  Maria]]
John-nom  married      Mary-acc

A second property shared by the languages that lack spec,EPP is that VS(O) orders never involve a covert expletive pro.[4] VS(O) orders are in fact never associated with DR effects.[5]

(14)  a.  ke ksafnika    beni o  Janis      apo  to   parathiro
and suddenly  enters  John-nom  from  the  window
   b.  ka    ksafnika  beni   o   fititis
and  suddenly  enters  the  student

Languages that lack spec,EPP may differ as to whether they make another, non EPP-related vP external specifier available for the subject DP, like non-pro-drop languages. This is present in Irish (McCloskey 1999) but not in Greek. Evidence for this conclusion related to the placement of subjects with respect to adverbs that are generally taken to be VP adjoined. As the examples below show, in Irish the subject must precede the adverb, while in Greek the subject follows this adverb.

(15)  a.  an ehi idhi    diavasi$_j$ [$_{vP}$ kala[$_{vP}$ **o Petros** t$_j$ to   mathima]]
if has already read      well    Peter      the lesson
'If Peter has already read the lesson well'
   b.  *an ehi idhi o Petros$_i$ diavasi$_j$ [$_{VP}$ kala[$_{VP}$ t$_i$ t$_j$ to mathima]]

(16)  Nì chluinfeadh **aon duine** [$_{XP}$ chóiche arís Ciarán ag      gabháilcheoil]
neg hear-cond  any person      ever again      making music
'No one would ever hear Ciarán making music again'

---

[4] There is some disagreement concerning referential pro, but Manzini and Roussou (2000) argue that it can be dispensed with.

[5] See Jelinek (1984) for Spanish, Alexiadou and Anagnostopoulou (1998) for Greek, and McCloskey (1996) for Irish. The argument made in Alexiadou and Anagnostopoulou (1998) linking the presence of an expletive to the presence of DR effects can be summarized as follows: the expletive is analysed as a determiner taking an NP as its complement. Hence DR effects are expected if a D-type element occupies the EPP position.

(17) represents the different positions available to Irish and Greek subjects: subjects are located in spec,FP2 in Irish, but in spec,vP in Greek. In both languages verb movement to F°1 is sufficient to check the EPP feature:

(17)    FP1 (EPP)

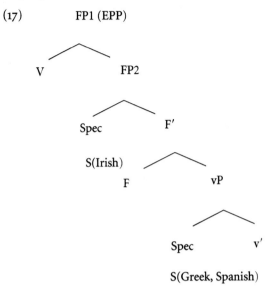

S(Greek, Spanish)

Crucially, under the above analysis the pro-drop character of a language is related to the availability of the VS(O) order, as discussed in detail in Rizzi (1982).

A further property found in languages in which subjects remain in the vP is that VS(O) orders can function as thetic judgements, i.e. as answers to the question 'What happened?', where all information contained is new or the constituents receive 'wide focus'.

(18)    What happened?
    a. molis    espase    o Janis        tin    kristalini    lamba
       just     broke     the-John-nom   the    crystal       lamp
       'John just broke the crystal lamp'
    b. *molis o Janis espase tin kristalini lamba

A final point of Alexiadou and Anagnostopoulou's analysis is that the presence of an overt subject within the vP in VSO orders is nothing else but a clitic-doubling configuration, where pronominal agreement doubles the S which is located in the vP. The availability of V [$_{vp}$ SO] and the availability of clitic doubling are linked together. Greek has extensive clitic doubling of objects (see Anagnostopoulou 1994; 2003; Greek does not respect Kayne's generalization, the clitic agrees in all features with the doubled object):

(19)  tin      ide i    Maria              ti gata    Greek
      cl-ACC   saw-3S   the-Mary-NOM       the-cat-ACC
      'Mary saw the cat'

Verbal agreement actually 'spells' out the features of the subject much as the clitic spells out the features of the object. Doubling, in both cases, is nothing else but an instance of feature movement. This configuration permits checking of the Case of the subject without DP movement. For the languages where the subject is located outside the vP, movement of the subject to spec,FP2 is Case related (see McCloskey 1996).

Table 5.3 summarizes the cross-linguistic variation with respect to spec,EPP and the other properties that correlate with its presence or absence (the reader is referred to Alexiadou and Anagnostopoulou 1998 for details). According to this analysis, being pro-drop means that a language has pronominal agreement and hence lacks overt subjects; its SVO orders involve CLLD of the subject; it permits VS(O) orders without DR effects and hence lacks overt or covert expletives.

Although Greek (and Spanish) seem to be well behaved with respect to the properties identified in Table 5.3,[6] languages such as Italian or partial

TABLE 5.3. Cross-linguistic variation in spec,EPP and related properties

| Language | Spec,EPP | Spec,FP2 | Overt Expletive | DR | (expl) VSO |
|----------|----------|----------|-----------------|----|-----------| 
| Icelandic | + | + | + | + | + |
| English | + | − | + | + | − |
| Greek | − | − | − | − | + |
| Irish | − | + | − | − | + |

[6] There are some differences between Spanish and Greek, which, however, do not pertain to the licensing of the spec,EPP position. These are discussed in detail in Alexiadou (2000) and can be summarized as follows. While, in Greek and Spanish, preverbal subjects can be shown to occupy an A'-position, the preverbal position in Spanish can contain phrases other than the subject, i.e. the subject competes with other elements for the preverbal position. Moreover, the verb is adjacent to the XP that precedes it (see Zubizarreta 1998):
  (i) a. María  presentó  su  renuncia  ayer
         Mary   presented  her resignation yesterday
      b. ayer        presentó María su renuncia
         yesterday presented Mary her resignation
      c. *Temprano Julia salia de casa
         early       Julia left home
  (ii) a. *LAS ESPINACAS Pedro trajo
          the spinach       Pedro brought
      b. *algo  donde encontraste?
         something where you found
         'Where did you find something?'

pro-drop languages such as Hebrew or Finnish depart to a varying degree.[7] Here I am mainly concerned with these differences. Concentrating on Italian and Greek first, I demonstrate that these two pro-drop languages are not uniform, as they show several differences with respect to the properties discussed in section 5.1.2, e.g. lack of VSO, presence of expletives, and presence of DR effects in Italian, as opposed to Greek. I show that this correlates with the syntactic evidence provided by Italian for an active spec,EPP. Turning to languages such as Hebrew and Finnish, which are pro-drop only in certain tenses (Hebrew) and certain persons (Hebrew and Finnish), I show that the distribution of pro-drop correlates with the distribution of person morphology.

In my approach I build on the assumption that EPP is a D/person feature located in a functional head in Infl, T, that must be checked either by an $X°$ or by an XP. To see whether a language makes use of the one or the other option, I use the properties discussed in section 5.1.2, and the correlation between these and the presence or absence of spec,EPP illustrated in Table 5.3, as a diagnostic for whether this position is active in a language or not. I further examine the consequences this has for subject interpretation and the licensing of pro-drop in general. The possibility will be explored here that the reason why languages show pro-drop properties to a varying degree is due to the fact that their structure is not uniform, either because it can be interpreted ambiguously (Italian) or because different persons and different tenses have a different syntax (Hebrew and Finnish). When a language is 'mixed' in this sense, then the properties of Table 5.3 will be present to a varying degree. Hence the overall conclusion is in agreement with Poletto (Chapter 6 below) and Koeneman (Chapter 3 above) that syntactic properties are crucial in the determination of pro-drop.

As shown in (ic) and (ii), the preverbal subject in Spanish competes with focus, emphatic, topic, and wh-phrases for this fronted position. In this respect, Spanish resembles the Germanic languages, especially Icelandic and Yiddish. Thus the preverbal position in Spanish is not uniquely for CLLD-ed material. In Greek, there is no such competition in the sense that the language permits multiple dislocations.

While Zubizarreta argues that the preverbal subject is indeed interpreted as a topic, Suñer (2002) and Goodall (2001) present arguments that the EPP is active in Spanish. Suñer, in particular, offers an analyis of preverbal subjects in terms of Cardinaletti's cartography of subject positions: while full NP subjects do not occupy the same position as pro and weak pronouns, they occupy a higher A-position in clause structure. Here I follow Zubizarreta's analysis (1994; 1998; 1999).

[7] Another issue concerns the similarities between pro-drop languages and non-configurational languages of the type discussed in Jelinek (1984) and Baker (1996), since on the view expressed above their verbal agreement seems to take over the function of the subject. I will not discuss this here (see Alexiadou and Anagnostopoulou 2000).

The chapter is structured as follows. In section 5.2 I discuss certain differences between Italian and Greek; in section 5.3 I offer an explanation of these differences; and in section 5.4 I discuss Hebrew and Finnish as instances of partial pro-drop languages.

## 5.2 On some differences between Italian and Greek

In this section I consider in detail differences in word order as well as in the interpretation of subjects between Italian and Greek. The main characteristics that I am concerned with are the availability of SVO, where S is interpreted as being in a dislocated position, the availability of VS(O), and its relationship to the presence of DR effects. From an interpretive point of view, attention will be concentrated on the availability of a wide-focus interpretation of the inverted orders, as this correlates with their syntax.

### 5.2.1 *SVO*

Both Greek and Italian permit SVO orders. As is the case in Greek, DP subjects in Italian can be left-dislocated, preceding CLLD-ed objects and wh-phrases (20a, b) (Cardinaletti 1997: 43; Poletto 2000). Note that quantifiers which cannot be CLLD-ed cannot precede wh-elements (20c):[8]

(20)  a.  Piero a Gianni non gli ha parlato ancora
          Peter to John   not to-him has spoken yet
          'Peter has not spoken to John yet'
      b.  Gianni quando      vienlo
          John    when comes-scl
      c.  *Nessuno quando viene
          nobody when comes?
          'When does nobody come?'

However, both Cardinaletti (1997; 2004) and Poletto (2000) point out that preverbal subjects in Italian need not be left-dislocated. Evidence for this comes from the following observations. First, a DP subject can be found in positions 'internal' to the sentence, as in Aux to Comp contexts. In these cases a quantifier such as *nessuno* that cannot be left-dislocated is also grammatical. But truly CLLD-ed elements are ungrammatical; see Cardinaletti (1997: 43). This suggests that the preverbal subject cannot be truly CLLD-ed:

---

[8] Italian like Greek has a split CP. There are differences as far as the dislocation properties of QPs in the two languages are concerned, which merit further investigation. In addition, Giannakidou (1997) and Ordóñez (1997) report that negative QPs in preverbal position are CLLD-ed in Greek and Spanish.

(21)    Avendo Gianni/non avendo nessuno telefonato a Maria
        having John/not having anybody called Mary
        'John having/nobody having called Mary'

(22)    *Avendo a Roma vissuto per venti anni
        having in Rome  lived    for twenty years

Second, some dialects of Italian make a distinction as to the type of subject that can be doubled by a clitic: dialects such as those from the area of the central Veneto do not permit clitic doubling of the preverbal subject when this is a quantifier, but they allow it when the subject is a DP: see Poletto (2000: 141f.).

(23)    a.  Nane el          magna
            John subject clitic eats
        b.  Nisun   (*el)     magna
            Nobody subject clitic eats

Third, and more importantly, (most) Italian speakers cannot reproduce the scope effects reported in section 5.1.2 for Greek. Wide scope effects readily obtain when the subject is clearly in a dislocated position (Zubizarreta (1998), citing Guasti (1996)):

(24)    Molti studenti cosa non hanno letto?
        many students what not have read
        'many students are such that they have not read something'/*'few students have read something'

Finally, SV(O) orders in Italian can function as answers to the question 'What happened?' as opposed to their Greek counterparts: see Calabrese (1992), Pinto (1997), and Cardinaletti (2004):

(25)    What happened?
        Carlo ha  presentato          Sandro a  Maria
        Carlo has presented/introduced Sandro to Mary
        'Carlo introduced Sandro to Mary'

If the preverbal subject was interpreted unambiguously as a clitic left-dislocated element, hence having properties of a topic, i.e. 'old information', SVO orders could not be licit answers in environments which require that all information provided be new.

   To conclude, in this section evidence was presented that preverbal subjects in Italian are not necessarily interpreted as CLLD-ed DPs. As we will see in the next section, this behaviour correlates with the behaviour of inverted orders.

## 5.2.2 Subject inversion

**5.2.2.1 VS(O)** Italian does not permit the VSO order at all, while this is possible in Greek, as discussed in section 5.1.2:[9]

(26)  *Ieri      ha     dato    Gianni   un   libro   a    Maria
       yesterday has    given   John     a    book    to   Mary
       'Yesterday John gave a book to Mary'

Benincà (1988) and Pinto (1997) point out that Italian permits VS orders, but with restrictions. In particular, it permits VS orders with certain unaccusatives, but not with all (see also Belletti 1999; Cardinaletti 2004):

(27)  a.  Che cosa è successo?
          what        happened
      b.  è entrata  Beatrice
          is entered Beatrice
          'Beatrice (has) entered'
      c.  è morto Fellini
          is died Fellini
          'Fellini (has) died'
      d.  #è impallidito  Berlusconi
          is  turned pale  Berlusconi
          'Berlusconi (has) turned pale'
      e.  #si è stufata      Penelope
          refl-is got fed up Penelope
          'Penelope (has) got fed up'

According to Pinto (1997: 21), the examples in (27d–e) are not felicitous under a wide-focus interpretation: they only allow a narrow reading on the subject.

VS orders under the wide-focus interpretation with unergatives are impossible with most verbs, with the exception of *telefonare* 'call' (see Benincà 1988; Pinto 1997: 22):

(28)      What happened?
      a.  #hanno urlato   due terroristi
          have     shouted two terrorists
          'Two terrorists (have) shouted'

---

[9] According to Cardinaletti (2004), Italian permits VSO when the subject is focused. Here I do not consider in any detail the focus interpretation(s) available to VSO and VOS orders (see Alexiadou, forthcoming).

    b.  ha    telefonato    Dante
        has    called        Dante
        'Dante (has) called'

On the other hand, in Greek no such restrictions are observed with the VS order.[10]

(29)  gelase      i      Sofia
      laughed    the    Sofia
      Sofia laughed

Moreover, Italian exhibits DR effects to a certain extent (see Belletti 1988; 1999; Pinto 1997). Again, this is not the case in Greek (cf. 16):

(30)  a.  è arrivato Gianni
          is arrived Gianni
      b.  *all' improvviso è    entrato    l'uomo      dalla finestra
          suddenly              entered    the man     from-the window
      c.  #è    arrivato    lo    studente
          is    arrived     the   student

Both Pinto and Belletti seem to agree that the distribution of definite post-verbal subjects in Italian is regulated by (31):

(31)  Definite subjects can appear postverbally in Italian, if they satisfy the following two conditions:
      a. the definite description identifies its referent in a unique way;
      b. the definite description must bear new information (as the postverbal subject position is normally identified with focus).

Pinto (1997), Tortora (1997), and Cardinaletti (2004) argue that verbs that permit inversion with definite subjects in Italian differ in their lexical structure from those that do not permit inversion. In particular, the former contain a locative or temporal argument, which can be overtly or covertly realized. The aforementioned authors agree that when the locative remains implicit, it is interpreted deictically. Thus a sentence like (28b) means that Dante called here. Thus in those cases what occupies the preverbal position is a null locational goal argument of the unaccusative verb (Cardinaletti 2004: 62). That inversion is closely related to deixis is supported by the data in (32, 33), from Pinto (1997: 130):

---

[10] Roussou and Tsimpli (2002) offer a more detailed study of the differences between Italian and Greek VS(O), which also seems to suggest that the Italian VS orders are indeed very restricted.

(32)   Da      questo   porto è partito   Marco Polo
       from    this     harbour left      Marco Polo

(33)   *Dal    porto        è partita    la   nave
       from    the harbour  left   the ship

According to Pinto, the reason for the ungrammaticality of (33) is related to the difference between the demonstrative *questo* 'this' and the determiner *il* 'the'.

In addition, the overt presence of a locative is obligatory in the case of verbs like *live*. Pinto explains this by suggesting that unaccusative verbs are inherently telic, while this does not hold for the other cases of inversion verbs in Italian, which necessarily need to express their locative argument.

Interestingly, as pointed out by Pinto (1997) and Alexiadou (2000), the restrictions found with the Italian VS pattern are similar to the ones we find with locative inversion in English (see the discussion in Levin and Rappaport 1995). Assuming an analysis of locative inversion in terms of EPP checking (Collins 1997), this supports an analysis of these partterns as being closely related to their English counterparts, i.e. as licensing a spec,EPP, where the locative is situated (see also Tortora 1997 and Cardinaletti 2004 for similar conclusions).

To summarize, VS orders in Italian are restricted, while VSO ones are not allowed. We have seen that partial evidence for the presence of a spec,EPP can be formulated for this language for certain inverted orders, since this position is occupied by an overt or covert locative with the verbs that permit inversion with definite subjects. In addition, DR effects arise to a certain extent. These two observations, following the reasoning of section 5.1.2, lead to the conclusion that in Italian in certain cases an XP checks the EPP. This is in agreement with the conclusions in Cardinaletti (1997) and Poletto (2000) concerning the status of the preverbal subject in Italian, which can in fact be located in spec,EPP. This is also supported by the fact that SVO orders can function as thetic statements, i.e. lack topic-like properties.

5.2.2.2 *VOS*   To complete the picture, though a detailed investigation of this pattern is beyond the scope of this chapter, note that VOS in Italian is possible, though often judged marginal (Rizzi 1991), while it is not marginal in Greek. It is often pointed out that Italian VOS is subject to a number of restrictions.[11] These disappear under the following conditions: if the object is

---

[11] Apparently, the VOS order also ameliorates if the subject is an indefinite or if the progressive aspect is used.

removed, via cliticization, dislocation, or relativization, or if the subject carries heavy stress:

(34)  a.  ??ha mangiato la   mela Gianni
          has eaten       the apple Gianni
      b.  la   mela, l'ha   mangiata Gianni
          the apple it has eaten       Gianni
      c.  l'ha    mangiata Gianni
          it has  eaten    Gianni
      d.  la   mela  che   ha   mangiata Gianni
          the apple that has eaten       Gianni
      e.  ha   mangiata la   mela *Gianni*
          has eaten     the apple *Gianni*

Pinto (1997), Belletti (1999), and Zubizarreta (1998) observe that VOS orders in Italian are infelicitous as answers to the question 'What happened?' This is shown by the contrast in (35a, b) and (35c, d):

(35)  a.  Che cosa è successo?
          What happened?
      b.  #ha scritto   una   lettera d'amore   Beatrice
          has written   a     love    letter    Beatrice
      c.  chi  ha    scritto   lettere d'amore?
          who has   written   love    letters
      d.  ha scritto una lettera d'amore   Beatrice

The restrictions in (35) are consistent with the judgements in (34), since movement of the object necessarily results in a focalization of the subject.[12]

   To summarize, Italian preverbal subjects, unlike their Spanish/Greek counterparts, need not be left dislocated. Moreover, Italian inverted orders are far more restricted than those of Greek. Italian provides partial evidence for expletives. The differences between the two languages are summarized in Table 5.4.

## 5.3 Deriving the differences

### 5.3.1 Morphological patterns

A first hypothesis is to try and locate the differences between Italian and Greek concerning the nature of their verbal agreement. The only difference that can

---

[12] Belletti (1999) further observes that the marginality of (34a) disappears if the subject bears contrastive focus. Anna Cardinaletti (p.c.) notes that in VOS the subject does not necessarily bear contrastive focus.

TABLE 5.4. Overview of differences between Greek and Italian

| Language | Spec,EPP | Spec,FP2 | Expletive | DR | VSO |
|---|---|---|---|---|---|
| Greek | – | – | – | – | + |
| Italian | ?–/?+ | – | –/+ | –/+ | – |

be detected between the two languages is in the present subjunctive, where the Italian verbal paradigm does not make a person distinction for the singular. As can be seen from Table 5.5, in the singular of the subjunctive, all persons bear the same form. In fact in that case the presence of the second-person pronoun is obligatory (36), from Cardinaletti (1997: 52). Without the pronoun, the example is ambiguous between first and third person:

(36)   Non sapevo *tu* fossi malato
       not knew you were-subj sick

According to Cardinaletti (1997; 2004), *tu* in (36) is a weak subject pronoun (Cardinaletti and Starke 1999), i.e. a kind of deficient XP occupying a specifier position. Its weak status can be seen in that it cannot be modified (37) or bear emphatic stress:

(37)   *pensa    solo tu   sia in    grado   di   aiutarlo
       he thinks  only     are-subj  able    to   help him
                                              (Cardinaletti 1997: 52)

Although Cardinaletti herself does not view this position as the projection where EPP is checked, I assume that it is (see also the discussion in the next section).

TABLE 5.5. First conjugation *parlare* 'speak'

| Italian | | | Greek | | |
|---|---|---|---|---|---|
| Present | Imperfect | Present subjunctive | Present | Imperfect | Present subjunctive |
| parlo | parlavo | **parli** | milao | milusa | milo |
| parli | parlavi | **parli** | milas | miluses | milas |
| parla | parlava | **parli** | mila | miluse | mila |
| parliamo | parlavamo | parliamo | milame | milusame | milame |
| parlate | parlavate | parliate | milate | milusate | milate |
| parlano | parlavano | parlino | milun | milusan | milun |

In embedded interrogatives when the verb inflects for subjunctive, the preverbal subject is tolerated more easily. This is observed in dialects of Italian, but also for some speakers in Standard Italian as well, from Poletto (2000: 157–8):

(38)  Me  domandavo  cossa  che  Nane  fasesse  casa      (Paduan)
      me  ask          what  that  John  do-subj  at home
      'I wondered what John was doing at home'

(39)  ?mi chiedo  cosa  Gianni  faccia   adesso     (Standard Italian)
      me ask      what  John    do-subj  now
      'I wonder what Gianni is doing now'

Does this lack of distinctions in the paradigm lead to bleeding of pro-drop? This hypothesis seems attractive. For instance, Cameron (1992) presents evidence from dialects of Spanish in which the loss of null pronouns compensates for the loss of verbal morphology. In those dialects the presence of overt subject pronouns goes together with morphophonological changes in the verbal morphology.

There are other cases which suggest that morphology cannot be the only factor (cf. Speas 1994), but structural properties play a very important role. On the one hand, there are cases showing that syncretism in paradigms is not enough. An example is the syncretism observed in French verbal morphology from the thirteenth century on. According to Roberts (1993), French remained a pro-drop language three centuries after the restructuring of the verbal paradigm took place (see section 5.3.2).

On the other hand, there are languages with more or less explicit paradigms which are non-pro-drop. An interesting case in point is Surselvan (a Swiss dialect of Rhaeto-Romance, data from Sprouse and Vance (1999: 265 f.)):

(40)  *cumprar* 'buy' present tense
      jeu cumprel    nus cumprein
      ti cumpras     vus cumpreis
      el cumpra      els cumpran

The verbal paradigm is rich enough, but null pronouns are regular with second person only (41):

(41)  Ier        has ti/e    cumprau  ina  tastga
      yesterday  have you     bought   a    bag

(42)  Ier        ha el/*e     cumprau  ina  tastga
      yesterday  has he       bought   a    bag

Another case is the contrast between European and Brazilian Portuguese (BP). The paradigms for both dialects of Portuguese are given in (43):

(43) European Portuguese                      Brazilian Portuguese

| *Present* | | *Subjunctive* | | *Present* | | *Subjunctive* | |
|---|---|---|---|---|---|---|---|
| canto | cantamos | cante | cantemos | canto | cantamos | cante | cantemos |
| cantas | (cantáis) | cantes | (canteis) | – | – | – | – |
| canta | cantam | cante | cantem | canta | cantam | cante | cantem |

The only difference in the paradigm is the lack of second person in BP. However, BP is a non-pro-drop language, as can be seen in (45), where the presence of an overt subject is necessary, although it has been already mentioned in the discourse (see Britto 2000 for data).

(44)  O João   vai   trazer   a    salada?
      João    will   bring   the   salad
      'Will João bring the salad?'

(45)  O João, *o vinho* *pro/ele vai trazer
      'João will bring *the wine*'

To conclude, the verbal paradigm of Italian does not radically differ from that of Greek, and hence lack of morphological properties cannot be the source for the differences discussed in section 5.2. In that section we saw that Italian seems to have access to an EPP-designated position both in SVO and in inverted orders. The evidence to be presented in 5.3.2 further supports this conclusion. Certain types of subject in Italian obligatorily occupy spec, EPP. As a result Italian subjects in general are not obligatorily interpreted as being left-dislocated.

### 5.3.2 *The availability of weak subject pronouns in Italian: further evidence for spec,EPP*

As already mentioned in the previous section, according to Cardinaletti (1997; 2004) and Cardinaletti and Starke (1999), Italian, like French, has weak subject pronouns, which alternate with overt DP subjects and null variants.[13] Although these are found in literal registers, native speakers of Italian seem to have clear intuitions about them (A. Belletti and A. Cardinaletti, p.c.).

---

[13] According to Cardinaletti (2002), DPs, weak pronouns, *tu*, and pro occupy different positions in clause structure. DPs and some weak pronouns, but not *tu*, are in a higher position, while pro and *tu* are in a lower position. Between these two positions, a further position, EPP-related, is recognized, in which locatives and subjects in SVO orders, which have a thetic interpretation, are located. For my purposes it suffices to agree with Cardinaletti that expletives must indeed be merged in spec,EPP; the crucial point here is that the lexical subject does not appear in an A'-position in Italian necessarily.

These subjects are full phrases, but deficient with respect to a number of properties (see also (36, 37) above), patterning with their French counterparts. Assuming that in French the DP subject and the weak pronoun occupy the same structural position, namely spec,EPP, we can suggest the same for their Italian counterparts.

(46)  a.  Il est parti
          he is left
      b.  Jean est parti

As can be seen in (47), these subjects appear in preverbal position, competing with subject-less structures and structures containing a 'strong' pronoun or a full DP. The pattern in (47c, d) suggests that while in (d) the EPP is checked by the weak pronoun, in (47c) V-movement is sufficient for the purposes of EPP checking:

(47)  a.  lui/lei              egli/essa
          he/she strong =XP  he/she weak =XP
      b.  Essa/Maria  l'ha    fatto
          she/Maria   it has  done
      c.  Gianni partira   quando  avrà finito          il lavoro
          Gianni will leave  when    will have finished  the work
      d.  Gianni$_i$ partira  quando  *lui/✓egli$_i$  avrà  finito          il lavoro
          Gianni will leave when     he            will  have finished  the work

In addition, they are not emphatic and cannot be modified or coordinated:

(48)  ✓Anche  lui/*anche  egli  ha   dichiarato  la propria disponibilità
          also   he /also    he   has  declared    the own availability

As shown in (49), they occur always in preverbal position, they cannot occur in their base position (49b), and they cannot precede CLLD-ed objects (49c):

(49)  a.  (Egli)  ha   aderito
          he     has  adhered
      b.  ha aderito *egli/✓lui/✓Gianni
      c.  ✓lui/✓Gianni /*Egli  Maria  non l'ha     appoggiata
          he/Gianni /he        Maria  not her has  supported
          'He/Gianni has not supported Maria'

Cardinaletti (1997) convincingly argues that such pronouns occupy a position similar to that of weak subject pronouns in French (46). As already mentioned, I take this to be spec,EPP.

The hypothesis I pursue here is that the presence of overt weak subject pronouns provides further substantial evidence for the presence of spec,EPP, and hence for ambiguous structures in Italian.[14] Support for this view comes from other cases where overt weak subject pronouns compete with structures where spec,EPP is not occupied that have been discussed in the literature—i.e. the counterpart of (47c, d) or (49a) existed in other languages as well. These cases are very similar to what we find in Italian, suggesting that the language has certain structures which are ambiguous.

A case in point is the loss of pro-drop in the history of French. As is well known, Old French (OF) and Middle French were pro-drop, but Modern French is not. Roberts (1993) notes a difference between the subject pronouns of OF and those found in Modern French. In particular, although OF had subject pronouns, these were not 'weak', as is the case in Modern French. This is manifested by the fact that in OF subject pronouns could be coordinated (50a), while this is no longer possible in the modern language (50b):

(50)  a. e        jo e  vos   i       irum
         and I   and  you  there  will go
      b. *je      et tu    irons    à Paris
         and I   and you  will go  to Paris

Assuming Cardinaletti and Starke's analysis of weak pronouns, this means that in (50b) the pronoun is in spec,EPP; on the other hand, the strong pronoun of (50a) behaves like any other preverbal subject in a 'real' pro-drop language, i.e. it is in an A'-position.

Consider now the change in the French pronominal system as described in Roberts (1993). By the sixteenth century the situation was very similar to that of Modern French. There are two series of pronouns: weak and strong. The *moi* series replace the *je* series in being the strong variant. In late Middle French overt weak pronouns co-occur with empty subjects (from Sprouse and Vance 1999: 263):

(51)  a. si   publiee    que   ne    se    puet    retourner
         so   published  that  neg   refl  can     return
         'So well publicized that (it) cannot be taken back'
      b. par   la    ville   qu'ell   ne    se    pourroit   compter
         around the   town    that it  neg   refl  could      count
         '(the joy concerning which was so great) around the town that it
         could not be counted'

---

[14] Note here that, if referential pro exists, then it behaves like a weak pronoun (see Cardinaletti 1997). See also note 13.

Moreover, overt expletives appear and they are in competition with 'null' ones (data from Sprouse and Vance 1999: 278–9):

(52)  a.  Par  celle  raison  il fault          que  je  soye  le   plus  saige
          by   this   reason  it is necessary  that  I   be    the  most  wise
      b.  Or   nous  fault          yci   laissier  le nom    du pays
          now  to us  is necessary  here  to leave  the name  of the country

The complete loss of the null variant occurs in the middle of the seventeenth century after the development of the series of the weak pronouns. This suggests that the presence of XP elements in spec,EPP co-occurs with the loss of pro-drop after a period where both systems are active side by side. As Roberts argues, this is not related to the changes in the verbal morphology of French (which took place earlier), though one could argue that the development of the weak series for the pronouns was initiated to compensate for the loss of morphology.[15]

A second case in point is Surselvan (data from Sprouse and Vance 1999: 265f.). As mentioned in the previous section, in this Romance dialect second-person weak subjects co-occur with pro-drop structures:

(53)  Ier         has   ti/e  cumprau  ina  tastga
      yesterday   have  you   bought   a    bag

In addition, the dialect has overt expletives in alternation with null ones:

(54)  ozildi     eis'i scumandau  da  fimar  depertut
      nowadays   is it forbidden  to  smoke  everywhere

Since overt weak subjects occupy the canonical subject position, speakers have evidence that the spec,EPP position is active, and that EPP is 'checked' by an XP. Structures containing an overt subject alternate with subject-less structures, suggesting that the SV(O) is ambiguous between two variants, one that satisfies the EPP via XP-merging and one that does so via V-raising (55).

(55)  a.  [$_{TopicP}$ S [$_{EPP}$ V] ]
      b.  [$_{EPP}$ S V]

The situation in Italian seems to be like the one in Middle French and Surselvan as these have been analysed by Sprouse and Vance, i.e. containing

---

[15] As pointed out to me by an anonymous reviewer, it is often argued that Modern French is about to become pro-drop again. To the extent that this holds, I believe this is related to the reanalysis of the weak subject pronouns as clitics, along the lines of what is suggested in section 5.3.2 for the dialect of Veneto. For further discussion on the role of subject pronouns in French, see Auger (1993; 1996) and Zribi-Hertz (1994).

two grammars in competition (Kroch 1989). This means that the syntactic structure is ambiguous between two variants: one in which the EPP specifier is filled and one in which it is not. Thus preverbal subjects are ambiguous with respect to A and A'-properties and can be interpreted as thetic sentences, and in VS orders an expletive or a locative appears in spec,EPP. Such a mixed system is not found in Greek, which lacks overt weak subject pronouns and seems to provide the Italian type of evidence for locatives. Thus Greek is well behaved with respect to the parameter, as this is interpreted in section 5.1.2.

If Italian is analysed along these lines, the following observations are in order. The EPP-XP grammar could survive as in French—either because it is somehow easier to parse (cf. Sprouse and Vance 1999) or because the structural properties are those of a language which is an EPP-XP language, i.e. restrictions in inversion etc. Alternatively, the pro-drop grammar could become the main active one. This can happen, for instance, when weak subject pronouns become clitics, i.e. X° elements, a development/partition which is natural in Cardinaletti and Starke's system. One could imagine that dialects of Italian behave (or would behave) differently with respect to this— i.e. they could exhibit different values of the parameter. Interestingly enough, the historical development of at least one Italian dialect supports this view, also strengthening the approach to the Italian system as involving ambiguous structures. The case in point is the Veneto dialect (see Poletto 1996 for data and analysis).

In the fifteenth century, Veneto had weak subject pronouns for all persons (56):

(56)  a/e    te/ti   el/la   a/e   a/e   i/le   expl: l
      1sg    2sg     3sg     1pl   2pl   3pl

These show a behaviour similar to that of Modern French weak subject pronouns, as they are omitted in coordination (57), and hence can be analysed on a par:

(57)  El m'      ha    lagò   le    cavale   e     si    andò
      he to me   has   left   the   mares    and   so    went

Moreover, (58) shows that null and overt expletives alternate, as we have also seen for Middle French and Surselvan:

(58)  a.  manco mal   savara a    dir ...
          luckily     (it) means  that ...
      b.  El    me      par    che'   l    sarare     cossa   giusta
          it    to me   seems  that   it   would be   right   thing

In the seventeenth century, these subject pronouns are obligatory when there is no overt DP. At this stage clitics cannot appear with QPs (59).

(59)  a. la    mormolla  de  ti
          she  murmurs   of  you
      b. I     toroere   vale pì         che no valse qui   de Hisperite
         your oak woods are more precious that not    those of Hesperide
      c. Agno  pomaro    fea  pumi  indorè
         Every apple tree made golden apples

At this stage, Poletto claims, the subject pronouns are syntactic heads and are in complementary distribution with overt DPs.

In the modern variety, the clitics are not complete for all persons: compare (56) to (60). Exactly those clitics missing in the modern variety are the ones that had the same form in the older variety.

(60)  *parlo* 'speak'
      parlo      parlem
      te parli   parle
      el parla   i parla
      la parla   le parla

At this stage, clitics can co-occur with DPs.

The paradigms in (56) and (60) are very interesting. As Renzi and Vanelli (1983) have observed, person and number must be realized at least once, either via a clitic or on the verbal form, in all the dialects they have investigated. This is confirmed by Poletto (1996). Hence the change in the paradigm is one towards a system which head-marks person once.

Consider now the stages once again. There is a first stage where weak subjects in Veneto are like those of Middle French and of Modern Standard Italian. Hence we have evidence that the language contains ambiguous structures. In the second stage, weak subjects become clitics. Clitics and the DPs are in complementary distribution, and the choice of a DP or of a clitic reflects the actual structure and the ambiguity of the system, one containing overt DPs in spec,EPP and one having clitics in EPP°. Finally, subject clitics are maintained only in those forms where person morphology is non-distinct. In this case EPP is satisfied via V-raising + clitic merge in cases where the verb is not marked for person. Crucially, once weak subject pronouns become heads, evidence for the spec,EPP position becomes obsolete.[16]

---

[16] As Cardinaletti and Starke (1999) note, when two deficient forms compete, weak forms and clitics, the latter take precedence over the former. Note here that at least in the Central Veneto dialect subject clitics cannot co-occur with QPs (Poletto 2000), suggesting that the clitic is present only where the subject is CLLD-ed.

Note here that the description of the Veneto dialect suggests that the actual features responsible for EPP checking are those related to person. It also suggests that person/definiteness must be marked at least once in the structure. This will become relevant in section 5.4, where I turn to Hebrew and Finnish.[17]

### 5.3.3 *Deriving further differences*

We have seen so far that Italian VS orders are similar to those found in English or French to a certain extent due to the mixed character of spec,EPP in Italian. What about the lack of VSO orders and the apparent restrictions on VOS orders? Below I attempt an answer to the first problem; I leave a full investigation of both issues for further research (Alexiadou, forthcoming).

Alexiadou and Anagnostopoulou (2001) argued that languages such as English or French are subject to an intransitivity constraint on inverted orders of the type in (61).

(61)   At spell-out the vP-VP should not contain more than one argument, at least one DP argument must check Case overtly.

(61) can be violated in languages that permit clitic doubling, such as Greek and Spanish. Languages such as Icelandic always escape (61) as they make use of spec,FP2 for subjects. Such a position is not available in French, Italian, or Greek. In Greek (and Spanish), VSO orders with both arguments vP internal are possible, since (as mentioned in section 5.1.2) verbal agreement is sufficient to check the features of the subject. Italian and French do not belong to the group of clitic-doubling languages. As a result, verbal agreement never 'spells out' features of the subject DP in Italian; it never checks its Case, enabling it to escape the intransitivity constraint. For this reason, neither French nor Italian permits VSO orders (see Belletti 2001 and Roussou and Tsimpli 2002 for alternatives).[18] Support for this analysis comes from the observation that while VSO orders are impossible, VSPP orders are acceptable. Consider (62), from Belletti (1999: 11):

---

[17] There is evidence for overt expletives in Italian involving clitic-expletives; see (i) from Zubizarreta (1998):

(i) u    ie    mwera y galinne
expl loc dies  chickens
'Chickens die'

If one analysed the expletive in (i) as a clitic, then this dialect of Italian would be satisfying the EPP via clitic merge, i.e. head-merge. Now in this case the merging of the expletive clitic has an effect: it leads to DR effects. Considering the other properties introduced in section 5.1.2, this dialect would pattern more like English than like Greek.

[18] Note here that Italian dialects that have subject clitics use non-agreeing forms in subject inversion, suggesting that the clitic clearly does not spell out the features of the subject.

(62)  a.  (?) ha telefonato  Maria   al        giornale
          has phoned           Mary    to the    newspaper
      b.  (?) ha parlato  uno   studente  col        direttore
          has spoken       a     student   with the   director

In (62) the object is introduced by a preposition, which 'assigns' Case to it. Hence the only DP that must check Case in T is the subject, and (61) is respected.

With respect to VOS, I refer the reader to Cardinaletti (2001), Belletti (1999; 2001), and Zubizarreta (1998). Further research is necessary in order to determine whether or not the conditions behind Italian VOS are similar to the ones found in e.g. Greek/Spanish VOS (Alexiadou, forthcoming).

Table 5.6 summarizes the results so far, showing that Italian is midway between Greek and French in this respect.

## 5.4  Partial pro-drop languages: person splits in Hebrew and Finnish[19]

According to the hypothesis that is being developed here, a language will lack spec,EPP if it lacks the syntactic evidence for such a projection. The syntactic evidence involves the behaviour of preverbal subjects, the presence of weak subject pronouns, the availability of free inversion, the presence of expletives, V-raising to the relevant head in INFL, and the status of V-agreement as pronominal.

The question that arises next is: how do partial pro-drop languages like Hebrew or Finnish fit into the general picture? Common to both these languages is that they are pro-drop in the first and second but not in the third person. I examine these in turn (see also Koeneman, Chapter 3 above).

TABLE 5.6. Differences and similarities between Greek, Italian, and French

| Language | Spec,EPP | Spec,FP2 | Expletive | DR | VSO | Doubling |
|----------|----------|----------|-----------|------|-----|----------|
| Greek    | –        | –        | –         | –    | +   | +        |
| Italian  | –/+      | –        | – /+      | –/+  | –   | –        |
| French   | +        | –        | +         | +    | –   | –        |

---

[19] It has been argued that spec,FP2 is active in both languages: for Finnish see Holmberg and Nikanne (2002); for Hebrew see Shlonsky (1997).

### 5.4.1. *Partial pro-drop in Hebrew: different structures for different tenses*

As Shlonsky (1997), Borer (1986) and others have pointed out, Hebrew is an SVO language with V-raising, which allows pro-drop only with first and second person in future and past tense. According to Doron (1999), the VSO order is ungrammatical in Hebrew:

(63)  a.  tixtevi        sipur
          2fs write-fut  story
      b.  (*hem)    yixtevu    sipur
          they 3pl  write-fut  story

As Shlonsky (1997) observes, morphology is not the main factor for this split, as e.g. Palestinian Arabic has referential null subjects in conjunction with third person:

(64)  katbat      riwaaye
      write-3fs  story
      she    wrote  story
      'She   wrote  a story'

The verbal paradigm of Hebrew and Palestinian Arabic is similar; if anything the latter is less explicit.

(65)  Hebrew root: *ktb* 'write'

|  | *Future* | | *Past* | |
|---|---|---|---|---|
|  | *Singular* | *Plural* | *Singular* | *Plural* |
| 1 | ?e-xtov | ni-xtov | katav-ti | katav-nu |
| 2m | ti-xtov | ti-xtəv-u | katav-ta | katav-tem |
| 2f | ti-xtə'v-i' | ti-xtəv-u | katav-t | katav-tem |
| 3m | yi-xtov | yi- xtəv-u | katav | katv-u |
| 3f | ti-xtov | yi- xtəv-u | katv-a | katv-u |

(66)  Palestinian Arabic imperfect

| 1 | ?a-tkub | m-nu-ktub |
|---|---|---|
| 2m | tu-ktub | tu-kutb-u |
| 2f | tu-kutbi-i | tu-kutb-u |
| 3m | yu-ktub | yu-kutb-u |
| 3f | tu-ktub | yu-kutb-u |

I propose that the reason for this behaviour is related to the ways the verbal system marks person. Let us then consider the relation between agreement suffixes/prefixes and pronouns for past and future in Hebrew in some detail (from Ritter 1995, Vainikka and Levy 1999; see also Koeneman, Chapter 3).

In Hebrew, verbal forms bear no person morphology in the present tense, and they do not allow null subjects:

(67)   Present
       *Singular*          *Plural*
       Masc.    Fem.       Masc.    Fem.
       kotev    kotevet    kotvim   kotvot

As (68) shows, the first- and second-person affixes in the past tense are related to the pronoun forms. A similar relationship can be observed in the future tense. However, no such relation can be observed for the third person.

| (68) | | 1sg | 2sgm | 2sgf | 3sgm | 3sgf | 1pl | 2pl | 3pl |
|---|---|---|---|---|---|---|---|---|---|
| | Past | -ti | -ta- | -t | 0 | -a | -nu | te-u | -u |
| | Future | e- | te- | -te-i | ye- | te- | ne- | te-u | ye-u |
| | Pronoun | ani | ata | at | hu | hi | anaxnu | atem | hem |

Building on Vainikka and Levy's observations, but without adopting the specifics of their analysis, we arrive at the following proposal: in Hebrew the verbal morphology does not contain any person specification for the third person in the future and past tense, and has no person specification at all for the present tense. As a result, the syntax of the present tense and that of the third person past and future must be different (in agreement with Shlonsky 1997 and Ritter 1995). As Shlonsky argues, the present tense is a participial structure, i.e. the verb is actually a participle. In the third person future and past, since the verb itself is not pronominal, in order for the EPP feature to be satisfied the insertion of a pronoun is necessary. This pronoun lacks person specification but carries definiteness features (Ritter 1995), which suffice to check the EPP (see section 5.1.1).

In support of this, note that in colloquial Hebrew, where the first person singular form has been suppleted by the third person, null subjects are impossible (cited in Artstein 1999):

(69)   ?oxal  et    ha-banana    Standard
       (I) will eat   the banana

(70)   ani yoxal  et    ha-banana    Colloquial
       I will         eat    the banana

(71)   hu yoxal et ha-banana       Standard third person
       he will   eat the banana

This behaviour correlates with the observation that Hebrew has certain expletives, and shows DR effects in free inversion, as discussed in Borer

(1986) and Shlonsky (1997) (see (72–74); free inversion in Hebrew is in fact very much restricted.

(72)  ze nira            she-Nurit    amda              lenaceax
      it seems-past-3sgm  that Nurti   stand-past-3sgf   to win
      'It seemed that Nurit was about to win'

(73)  neʕelmu      harbe   sfarim   mə ha sifrigu
      disappeared  many    books    from the library

(74)  * neʕelmu      ha-sfarim   mə ha sifrigu
      disappeared   the books   from the library

Moreover, preverbal subjects in Hebrew are not unambiguously interpreted as being clitic left-dislocated; see Borer (1995) and Doron and Heycock (1999) for extensive argumentation.

### 5.4.2  Finnish: XP versus X° depending on person

Finnish is a V-raising language which, like Hebrew, is pro-drop in the first and second person, but not in the third (from Vainikka and Levy (1999); see also Koeneman, Chapter 3).

(75)  *Nousi     junaan
      step-3sg   train-into
      'He/she boarded the train'

(76)  Nousin     junaan
      step-1sg   train-into
      'I boarded the train'

Unlike Hebrew, the lack of pro-drop in Finnish is not conditioned by Tense. As was the case in Hebrew, we find a link between person marking on the verb and the availability of pro-drop. As Vainikka and Levy point out, the verbal inflection in the first and second person relates to the form of the first- and second-person pronouns. However, no such relation exists between the third-person verbal morphology and third-person pronouns:

(77)

|  | 1sg | 2sg | 3sg | 1pl | 2pl | 3pl |
|---|---|---|---|---|---|---|
| Agreement | -n | -t | -V | -mne | -tte | -vAt |
| Pronoun | minä | sinä | hän | me | te | he |

As (77) suggests, the third-person verbal morphology belongs to a different paradigm, one lacking person/pronominal specification. In agreement with what was said earlier with respect to Hebrew, we can conclude that in this case verbal morphology is not sufficient to check EPP. If I am correct in

interpreting EPP as a person feature on a functional projection, then whenever V does not contain the relevant feature,[20] an XP must be merged.
Interestingly, as Vainikka and Levy point out, Colloquial Finnish is non-pro-drop, and in that variety one cannot establish a link between pronouns and verbal agreement. This suggests that no form of the Colloquial Finnish verbal paradigm classifies as pronominal, and hence it is unable to check the EPP.

This mixed character of Standard Finnish correlates with the fact that the language possesses overt expletives (*sitä* and *se*); see (78a, b) from Vainikka and Levy (1999: 652), (78c) from Holmberg and Nikanne (2002):

(78)  a.  Tuntuu   siltä    että    Maija        voittaa
          feel-3sg  it-abl  that   Maija-nom  win-3sg
      b.  (?) Se tuntuu   siltä    että Maija     voittaa
          feel-3sg it-abl   that    Maija-nom  win-3sg
          'It feels as if Maija will win'
      c.  Sitä   leikki   laspia        kadulla
          exp   play    children   in-street
          'There are children playing in the street'

There is a further property of Finnish that should be noted here, and correlates with the properties of the C system in this language (see also Koeneman, Chapter 3). As Vainikka and Levy point out, Finnish does not seem to tolerate verb-initial structures with third-person subjects. When the verb and the subject invert, another constituent, which must obligatorily be a nominal, appears in first position (79b, c). On the other hand, XP-fronting is not permitted with first and second person (79a).

(79)  a.  *?Palkankorotusta   pyysin            heti
           raise-par               ask-past-1sg   immediately
           'I asked for a raise immediately'
      b.  Palkankorotusta   pyysi             Lisa
           raise-par              ask-past-3sg   Liisa-nom
           'Liisa asked for a raise immediately'
      c.  *Ilmeisesti on tämän kirjan kirjoittanut Graham Greene
           evidently has this book written Graham Greene
           'G. G. has evidently written this book'        (Koeneman, Chapter 3)

---

[20] Note here that it is necessary that the verbal agreement is pronominal, i.e. it links to pronouns/ makes distinctions for all persons, so as to block languages such as German from exhibiting partial pro-drop properties, since their verbal paradigm makes partial person distinctions.

TABLE 5.7. Differences between Hebrew and Finnish

| Language | Spec,EPP | Spec,FP2 | Expletive[21] | DR | VSO |
|----------|----------|----------|-----------|----|----|
| Hebrew | −/+ | ? | (+) | −/+ | − |
| Finnish | −/+ | + | (+) | −/+ | + |

Koeneman (Chapter 3, and references therein) proposes that the ungrammaticality of (79c) has to do with the fact that adverbs are not very felicitous as topics. Holmberg and Nikanne (2002) also emphasize the discourse-configurational nature of the language. In terms of the proposal adopted here, we can account for the above contrast as follows. Since V-raising is not sufficient to check the EPP in (79b), an XP must be situated in the specifier (see also Koeneman). Given that the higher specifier in Finnish is of a double nature, i.e. it can host topicalized elements as well, and adverbs do not make felicitous topics, only an NP can be fronted. In the case of first and second person, however, verbal agreement is sufficient to check the EPP, and hence the presence of an XP is not permitted.

Table 5.7 summarizes the differences between Hebrew and Finnish. Note here that the reason why Finnish permits VSO orders (e.g. 79b) is related to the fact that it licenses spec,FP2. As Holmberg and Nikanne point out (2002), this position is not strictly associated with the subject, but objects can also appear there.

To conclude, in this section I argued that different parameter values are assigned to different persons, the result being that the languages show different syntax for certain members of their verbal paradigm. The result in both cases is that the language as a whole shows the properties identified in section 5.1.2. to a varying degree.

## 5.5 Conclusions

I have discussed certain differences among languages that are generally grouped together as being pro-drop. It was shown that these languages have a number of non-uniform aspects. While in certain cases, for example in Hebrew and Finnish, the verbal morphology is responsible for the partial pro-drop property of the language, i.e. person specification, in the case of Italian the differences cannot be reduced to differences in morphology, though this may function as a cue (e.g. second person subjunctive). I attempted to

---

[21] It should be kept in mind that the Hebrew expletive is not exactly like the English *there*.

identify the structural properties that are the source for these differences. I followed the view that being pro-drop means that V-movement checks the EPP, that SVO orders involve CLLD-ed subjects, and that inverted structures lack expletives and show no DR effects. The varying degree to which the languages show the properties of pro-drop correlates with the varying degree to which (a) their morphology checks EPP, i.e. is pronominal (Hebrew, Finnish), and (b) an XP can be present in the specifier checking EPP, correlating with DR effects in inverted orders (Italian, Hebrew, Finnish).

In Hebrew and Finnish, in those parts of the paradigms where verbal agreement cannot be interpreted as pronominal, no pro-drop is allowed. As a result, these languages show a mixed behaviour with respect to the other properties associated with pro-drop languages. In Italian, partial evidence exists that spec,EPP is occupied in certain cases by a maximal projection. Hence again the language behaves unlike Greek and Spanish with respect to the properties in section 5.1.2.

An additional feature which correlates with the availability of VSO orders, i.e. transitive inverted orders, is the presence of doubling, as well as that of an extra functional specifier in the split IP. If neither is present, the language will not permit VSO orders. An extra specifier is present in, for example, Finnish, but not in Italian. In this respect Finnish is similar to Irish in permitting XP movement to a further lower specifier than the spec, EPP position specifier in the IP domain, resulting in case-checking. Doubling is not available in Italian, which hence lacks the VSO order altogether.

# 6

# Asymmetrical Pro-Drop in Northern Italian Dialects

CECILIA POLETTO

## 6.1 Introduction

In this chapter I intend to address two basic questions concerning the role of overt morphology in the syntactic process of pro-drop.

The two questions are intrinsically related in a more general perspective aiming to determine how much the presence of overt morphology influences syntactic processes. The empirical domain ranges over subject agreement, subject clitics, and pro-drop in some Northern Italian dialects, which will be compared with well-known analyses of the diachronic development of French. The picture that will emerge from this investigation will support the view that overt morphology can only favour a given syntactic process, but has no direct role in triggering the development of a given syntactic strategy. This result agrees with the observation made by Alexiadou (Chapter 5 above) and Speas (Chapter 2 above), who also arrive at the conclusion that morphology is a necessary but not a sufficient condition for the emergence of null subjects in a given language.

The first question, which has been much debated in the literature, is: does agreement morphology have immediate import for the selection of the pro-drop parameter? I will consider an analysis in the original spirit of Rizzi's (1986a) work and compare it with a possible solution in minimalist terms, showing that they are equivalent from the empirical point of view.

This work assumes the view of Alexiadou and Anagnostopoulou (1998) and Alexiadou (Chapter 5) of pro-drop as EPP checking via head movement of an inflected verb carrying pronominal (or better person) features. It concentrates on the details of how a given head can be marked as +pronominal. In this sense it could also be compatible with a theory like the one proposed by Speas (Chapter 2), but it aims at rendering more precise the definition of 'strong' or

'+pronominal' agreement, which, as we will see, is not a morphological concept at all, but a syntactic one.

The second question is: why and how can asymmetric pro-drop systems (i.e. systems with pro-drop only for some persons) exist?

Various cases of partial pro-drop systems have been reported—notably cases like Hebrew described by Shlonsky (1990; 1997) and Finnish (see Koeneman, Chapter 3 above): there are cases where pro-drop is possible only for first and second person but not for third person, and, vice versa, cases in which only third-person null subjects are allowed (see Kayne (2000), who proposes that pro can only be a third-person pronoun). A distinction between first and second person on the one hand and third person on the other is indeed plausible and has a long tradition in the literature on the topic; the first who proposed it is, to my knowledge, Benveniste (1966),[1] who considered third person as 'non-person', a definition which we might translate in formal terms as lacking a feature, or being marked as [−deictic].[2]

The systems we describe and analyse here are more complex, because the split between pro-drop and non-pro-drop persons runs across the first and second person singular and plural, and hence shows a finer distinction within the domain of deictic persons. Moreover, the licensing conditions seem to vary from one person to another: some persons display null subjects when C° is strong, others when I° is. I will call this phenomenon 'asymmetric' pro-drop. Furthermore, the asymmetry among persons has nothing to do with the connection between verbal morphology and the pronominal system which has been noted for partial pro-drop systems. As we will see, asymmetric pro-drop clearly calls for an explanation based on the feature composition of the persons of the verb, not in terms of morphological ambiguity between agreement markers and pronouns. In order to account for the distribution of null subjects in Northern Italian dialects we must resort to a more refined distinction within the domain of [+deictic] persons, namely first and second person singular and plural. We will adopt an analysis of person features which has become quasi-standard by now (see e.g. Manzini and Savoia, forthcoming; Bianchi 2004) in the precise formulation proposed by Poletto (2000): 'person' is not a primitive notion but derives from a combination of the plus

---

[1] An anonymous reviewer points out that the same distinction is also found in Conklin's analysis of Hanunoo pronouns: H. Conklin, 'Lexicographic treatment of folk taxonomies', in S. Tyler (ed.), *Cognitive Anthropology: Readings*, New York; Holt, Rinehart & Winston, 1969, pp. 41–59.

[2] Here the term [−deictic] is used in the sense of Poletto (2000): first and second persons are [+deictic] because they refer to persons present in the relevant context, while third person is [−deictic] because it signals somebody who is not present in the relevant context (although he/she/they might be physically present in the same place where the conversation is taking place).

and the minus for [speaker] and [hearer]; moreover, as again originally suggested by Benveniste (1966), and by other scholars in more recent times, first person plural is not the plural of first person singular, and second plural can be the plural of second singular but can also result from the combination of second singular with something else. We will further refine this picture on the basis of the observation that first and second person plural share a number of properties that single them out as a subclass inside the domain of the deictic persons. I will also explore the relation between inflection and elements located in the CP domain, which contribute to the occurrence of null subjects and try to provide an account for the interaction between 'strong inflection' and 'strong C°'.

The chapter is organized as follows: in sections 6.2 and 6.3 I provide a diachronic excursus on the evolution of asymmetrical pro-drop in Middle French and Middle Northern Italian dialects (NIDs), starting from the characteristics of medieval Romance.

In section 6.4 I examine the behaviour of some modern NIDs, taking into account what has changed with respect to the Renaissance system. Section 6.5 contains a theoretical proposal in the traditional framework which captures both the development and the synchronic distribution of null subjects in NIDs. In section 6.6 I compare a traditional and a minimalist solution, showing that they are both empirically adequate although they make use of different theoretical tools. The two structural configurations relevant for the asymmetrical pro-drop system are government (1a) and spec-head agreement (1b).

(1)  a. $[_{C^\circ}$ $V_i$ $[_{AgrSP}$ $[_{SpecAgrS}$ pro$[_{AgrS^\circ}$ $t_i]]]$
      |_____|  licensing configuration
     b. $[_{C^\circ}$ $V_i$ $[_{AgrSP}$ $[_{SpecAgrS}$ pro$[_{AgrS^\circ}$ $t_i]]]$
        |_____|  licensing configuration

The analysis of NIDs[3] through a period that goes from the medieval (on the basis of Benincà (1984; 1988) and Roberts (1993)) to the modern one permits us to reach the following conclusions:

(a) Capitalizing on the work quoted above we will see how the medieval system (where licensing of a null subject was performed by an inflected verb in a government relation, hence from I° in C° governing SpecAgrS) developed into asymmetric systems where:

---

[3] Throughout this chapter I will refer to the Romance domain, including French and the NIDs, as North-Western Romance (NWR), as these languages share crucial properties and diachronic tendencies that distinguish them from Spanish, Catalan, and Southern Italian, to which we will refer to as Southern Romance (SR).

- some verbal forms were strong enough to license a null subject by spec-head agreement (as in (1b)), hence pro-drop was found in all syntactic contexts;
- others still required a strong feature in C°, so pro-drop was possible only when this additional condition was satisfied.

(b) The asymmetry is still visible nowadays:

- those persons that used the configuration in (1b) remained pro-drop;
- those persons that used the configuration in (1a) developed subject clitics.

(c) In some languages the inflected verb never plays any role in the licensing of a null subject, which is performed by a clitic. However, the clitic system still reflects the asymmetry of the Renaissance one: some persons use a clitic in the configuration (1a), others in the configuration (1b).

This will lead us to make some general claims on the split among persons revealed by this diachronic evolution.

## 6.2  V to C, Haiman's generalization, and middle North Western Romance (NWR)

Let us first consider the rise of asymmetrical pro-drop systems (which only admit null subjects for a subset of persons) from a diachronic perspective, and start our investigation by presenting Haiman's (1974) diachronic generalization on the development of subject clitics. Haiman notes that the split within Romance that distinguishes French and NIDs from other Romance languages stems from a property that was already present in the medieval period. He proposes the following generalization:

(2)   The Romance languages that were V2 in the medieval period developed subject clitics when they lost the V2 property.

According to Haiman, then, French and the NIDs—which have developed subject clitics—were the only Romance languages that clearly displayed V2 in the medieval stage. However, much subsequent work, starting from Benincà (1988), who proposes that all Romance varieties including Spanish and Portuguese were V2, to Fontana (1993) for Old Spanish, and Fischer (2002) for Old Catalan, has shown that all Romance languages had some V2 properties in the medieval period. V2 is a complex phenomenon which includes at least two superficial characteristics: subject inversion of the 'Germanic' type, in which the subject occurs between the auxiliary and the past participle, and the so-called 'linear restriction', according to which the inflected verb can only be preceded by a single constituent. It is well known that V2 languages can vary with respect to the domain in which they admit V2: some Germanic languages admit V2 only in main contexts, others have generalized V2 also to many embedded domains (including some wh contexts).[4] Romance languages obeyed more or less strictly the linear restriction (within the same language there can be variation according to the period considered) but they all share the property of subject inversion. Considering V2 at a more abstract level, i.e. as a structure resulting in essence from movement of the V higher than the subject position (SpecAgrS or SpecT according to the analysis chosen), the generalization is that in all medieval Romance languages the inflected verb had this property, and it is precisely to the loss of this property that scholars refer when they say that Romance lost V2 after the medieval period. The long debate on whether V2 targets a low CP or a high IP projection in Old Romance languages is irrelevant to the purpose of the present work.[5] For the moment, it is sufficient to note that Haiman's generalization cannot be maintained in its original form, even though it expresses the intuition that the development of subject clitics must have been connected to a property that was possessed only by NWR and that was somehow related to the V2 system.

We will therefore propose a reformulation of Haiman's generalization that has more to do with the way null subjects were licensed in Old Romance than with the V2 phenomenon *per se*. Even if all Old Romance languages were V2, there is another characteristic that distinguished NWR from the other Romance languages. Since the work by Benincà (1983), Dupuis (1988), Hirschbühler (1990), Vance (1989; 1995), Adams (1987b), and Roberts (1993), it is well known that a distinction concerning the licensing of null subjects cuts across Old Romance languages: while Old Spanish and Old Southern Italian varieties display pro-drop in all contexts[6] (provided the verb is finite), Old NWR can only have a null subject when the inflected verb has moved to C°—hence in main clauses and in a subset of embedded clauses, i.e. those involving

---

[4] For a detailed description of the split inside Germanic see Vikner (1995). Old Romance displayed V2 also in embedded domains, including relative clauses similarly to Yiddish and Icelandic, but not in embedded interrogatives.

[5] One might try to trace the distinction between NWR and the rest of the Romance domain noted by Haiman on the basis of the position targeted by V2. Nevertheless, this would be only a necessary and not a sufficient condition for understanding what is behind Haiman's generalization. We believe that the crucial property for understanding the partition inside Romance created by the development of subject clitics has to do with the licensing of pro-drop, which might in turn be different according to the target of V2, a further development that we will not pursue here.

[6] We are leaving aside inflected infinitives here, which are a tangential phenomenon to our topic.

a CP head higher than Focus/*wh*P.[7] If the inflected verb does not move
to C°, a subject pronoun has to appear. The following examples illustrate
the point for French (3) and NIDs (4)[8] (the null subject is signalled by an
underscore _ ):

(3) a. Si errerent   _       tant   en tele    maniere
       so wandered (they)  much  in such-a  way
       qu'   il      vindrent en la    praerie   de  Wincestre   (Artu 16, 66)
       that  **they**  came     in  the   meadow   of   Winchester
       'They wandered much until they came to the meadow of Winchester'

    b. mes     toutevoies  s'en     reconforterent _      au plus biau qu'  il
       but     nevertheless refl of-it consoled          (they) as best       that **they**
       porent (Artu 2, 8)
       could
       'Nevertheless they consoled themselves as best they could'

(4) a. E così   ne          provò _     de più cari ch'elli avea[9] (Old Florentine, 13C, Schiaffini)
       And   so of-them  tested (he)  some-of-the most dear that he had
       'And so he tested the most expensive ones he had'

    b. e      seria_ stado        plu      biado s'elo avesse   possedù    lo reçimento
       and   would_have-been more    happy if he had   possessed   the power
       de   la    soa    mente    (Old Venetian, 1370)
       of   the   his    mind
       'And he would have been more tranquil if he had been sane'

(5) Or    te       mostrerai _    Dominidè,  que  tu   lo    veras (Serm. Sub. I 116)
    now  to-you  will-show (I)  God, (so)   that  you  him  will-see
    'Now I will show you God, so that you will see him'

(3a) represents a clear case, as it strikingly distinguishes Old Florentine (from
now on referred to as Old Italian) from modern Standard Italian: in modern
Italian the subject of an embedded clause can have a null subject and is

---

[7] Roberts (1993 and references) considers two distinct periods in Old French: the older one, in
which pro is licensed through government by an additional AgrS2 head, and the second one (which
includes the second half of the 13th century), in which pro is licensed through government by the
inflected verb in C°, and hence depends on V2. We will take into account only the second period,
because it is parallel to the NIDs and because the data coming from the earlier one could be subject to
debate as to their interpretation.

[8] All examples reported here are taken from Benincà (1984: 10; 1988: 12 ff.). For a statistical
treatment of the French data we refer to Roberts (1993 and references).

[9] Although the particle *e* 'and' is found at the beginning of the clause, the sentences reported here
are not coordinations. The particle *e* in Old Italian is used as a Null Topic licenser: when *e* is present at
the beginning of a clause, this has the same Topic as the preceding sentence (see Benincà and Poletto
(2002) for a detailed description of the phenomenon, which is quite pervasive); therefore a considerable number of examples begin with an *e*.

interpreted as coreferent with the subject of the main clause. This is not the case in Old Italian, where the pronoun is lexically realized in the embedded clause. On the other side, pro-drop is allowed when the inflected verb moves to C° as in main contexts.

Old Spanish and Old Southern Italian, on the contrary, are just like their modern counterpart in this respect, as null subjects are found in all contexts, not only when the inflected verb has moved to C°:

(6) Spanish

     et    desque _ llegaron     assu padre a Cananea (Fontana 1993)
     and   when (they) arrived   at the father in Cananea
     'and when they arrived at his father's house in Cananea'

(7) Southern Italian

     a. et    li    Romani   fece incontenente    quelo ke _ li dixe
                                   (*Le Miracole de Roma*, 25)
       and   the   Romans   made immediately   what that (they) them told
       'and the Romans immediately did what they had been told'
     b. et incontenente _   fo aperto lo celo    (*Le Miracole de Roma*, 65)
       and immediately (it) was open the sky
       'and immediately the sky cleared'

Benincà (1984; 1988) notes this distinction between the two pro-drop systems within Romance; we refer here to her work for a more detailed picture of the data.

Let us for the moment leave aside the theoretical problem underlying the two different pro-drop systems, and reconsider Haiman's generalization from this perspective. We can reformulate it in the following way:

(8) Only those languages that had pro-drop depending on I to C have developed subject clitics when V2 was lost.

In this way Haiman's generalization makes sense within the present framework, because it is not directly dependent on the V2 phenomenon which existed in all Old Romance languages, but is mediated by the pro-drop system, which was parasitic on V2 only in NWR. Therefore, the development of subject clitics does not depend directly on V2, but is a straightforward consequence of the loss of the pro-drop licensing context.

More precisely, we can conceive the insertion of subject pronouns as the only alternative device to satisfy the EPP feature in TP once the pro-drop licensing context was lost with the loss of the V2 property, namely verb raising to a position higher than TP/AgrSP. These pronouns, then, have further developed into weak elements (in modern French) or even to inflectional heads (in the majority of the NIDs).[10] If this line of reasoning is correct, we predict that NWR should have become totally non-pro-drop immediately after the loss of V2 (i.e. in the Renaissance period), giving rise to a symmetric system with subject pronouns for all persons, like modern French. Alternatively, they might have developed into the complementary symmetric system, becoming totally pro-drop languages, like modern Italian; this could result from a new licensing context for pro through spec-head with the inflected verb. Neither prediction is borne out. As we will see, both cases are unattested in the period immediately following the loss of V2. Instead, NWRs have developed asymmetrical pro-drop systems. Some of them still maintain this type of system, which gives us the advantage of testing our predictions on a living language. The analysis of these systems is presented in sections 6.3 and 6.4.

## 6.3  The development of French and Northern Italian

### 6.3.1  *The Renaissance period*

In the Renaissance period both Middle French and Middle NIDs developed asymmetrical pro-drop; null subjects were allowed in all contexts (main and embedded clauses) for some persons, while other persons had a more restricted pro-drop system. As anticipated in the introduction, the split between the persons that are pro-drop in embedded declaratives and those that are not cuts across the deictic persons. This section on French essentially reports what Roberts (1993) and other authors quoted there (e.g. Adams 1987b; Hirschbühler and Junker 1988; Vance 1989) have stated on Middle French, and does not contain any original research. Here, the analysis of Middle French is instrumental to our analysis of the development of subject clitics and pro-drop restrictions in NIDs.

Let us first consider the schema illustrating the situation in Middle French as it is presented by Roberts (1993). He notes that V2 is not lost altogether, but that some V2 contexts still remain stable even after the medieval period: he assumes that V2 was completely lost by the beginning of the sixteenth century. The loss of V2 is, however, not abrupt: there is a period in which V2 is still optionally possible, though no longer obligatory.

From the fourteenth century on the French texts present:

- an increased number of V>2 orders;
- an increase in subject-initial clauses;

---

[10]  Probably Franco-Provençal varieties have a system more similar to French than to other NIDs, as standard tests on coordination suggest.

- a decrease in inverted subjects (which were clear positive evidence for the acquisition of V to C): Vance (1989: 157) notes that the class of adverbs that allow for non-inverted subject increases dramatically.

Roberts draws the conclusion that the V2 system is weakening and that, although V2 structures are still possible, V2 is no longer obligatory. Given that pro-drop depended in Old French on I to C, we expect some changes in the pro-drop system as well. There are indeed such changes: in Middle French the class of contexts that allowed null subjects is apparently enlarged, but the possibility of licensing a null subject becomes sensitive to the person of the verb.

Vance (1989) shows that in Middle French there are three contexts for null subject licensing: matrix V1, embedded V1 clauses, and embedded V2 contexts.

As for matrix V1 clauses of the type in (9), Roberts (1993: 147ff.) assumes that they are AgrSPs, and not CPs; hence when CP is not realized, the head of AgrS (which is the highest head in the structure) can license pro in the structural relation of spec-head agreement:

(9)  a.  Et  me       dist   l'on  depuis
         and to-me   says   one   since...
         'And one tells me since...'

  b. Se   appensa de faire     ung amy    qui  a  son besoing la   secourrait
     refl. thought of making   a    friend who to her need     her   would-help
     'And she thought of getting a friend who would help her if needed'

These cases are analysed by Roberts as AgrPs because they do not obey the Tobler–Mussafia law,[11] and because subject-initial clauses were (according to his general analysis of Middle French) AgrSPs.

Other contexts in which pro-drop is licensed are V1 embedded clauses. However, in non-wh contexts the only persons that can be pro-drop are first and second plural (see Hirschbühler (1992: 77ff.) for second person and Vance (1989: 219ff.) for first person):[12]

---

[11] The Tobler–Mussafia law says that a clitic pronoun cannot be found in first position in the clause: it either has an XP or requires the verb to raise in front of it.

[12] Vance (1989: 167, 239), from whom the examples are quoted, also reports one case of first person singular, which could be relevant for the comparison with the NIDs, where also first person singular works like first and second person plural. Given that only one case is reported, however, I will leave this aside here. The texts examined by Vance and quoted are here *Le Petit Jehan de Saintré* and *La Queste del Saint Graal.*

(10)  Mais  que         soions  en la chambre,  nous rirons
      but   when (we)    are     in the room,     we will-laugh
      'But when we are in the room, we will laugh'

(11)  Madame, je feroie  tuout ce   que me        vouldriés commander
      madame, I  will-do all   that which me (you) wish    to-command
      'Madame, I will do everything you tell me'

According to Roberts (1993: 180ff.), the distribution of pro in Middle French is thus the following:

(12)  a. Any pro is possible when AgrS is the highest head (i.e. no CP is
         projected).
      b. Any pro is possible in wh embedded clauses.
      c. In non-wh, non-V2 embedded contexts only first and second
         person plural pro is possible.

Roberts's analysis is thus that, while pro was licensed under government in Old French, it is licensed either by government (in V2 contexts and wh embedded clauses) or by spec-head agreement in Middle French V1 matrix clauses, in declarative non-V2 embedded clauses.

In the sixteenth century, French lost pro-drop entirely. Roberts proposes that this loss is connected to the loss of pro-drop licensing through government. His hypothesis is the following: in Middle French two distinct structural configurations could license pro: government and spec-head agreement (see (1a, b)). When the government licensing configuration was lost, the Agr head (being −pronominal) was not strong enough to become the unique pro licenser. Hence, pro-drop was lost entirely, due to the disappearance of the government licensing condition. We will see that some Northern Italian dialects have never lost licensing through government and still have a system similar to the Renaissance one.

### 6.3.2 Renaissance Northern Italian

A partially parallel system is found in Renaissance Venetian and Paduan (sixteenth century; cf. also Poletto (1995) for Renaissance Milanese and Bergamasco): some persons have regular pro-drop licensed via spec-head agreement, others have pro-drop licensing only when C° has strong features.

Given that the texts considered here belong to the sixteenth century, we do not expect to find any instances of residual V2, and hence there is no licensing of pro through the 'old' V2 system.

In fact, Renaissance Venetian and Paduan are similar to their modern counterpart in that they are no longer V2, except for some residual contexts (main interrogatives, optative and counterfactual clauses) which are the same that allow V2 in the modern varieties (see e.g. Munaro 1999). They present an asymmetric system, however, like the one described in section 6.3.1 for French, in particular the cases in (12b, c): some persons (first and second person plural and first person singular) are regularly pro-drop both in main and in embedded clauses; others are sensitive to a strong feature in $C°$.

As Vanelli (1987) notes, in this period null subjects are more numerous in embedded than in main clauses. So the situation is reversed with respect to the medieval period, where pro-drop was licensed only by V to C, which generally occurred in main contexts: Vanelli does not draw any distinction between persons, but the persons sensitive to strong $C°$ are second singular, and third person singular and plural. In particular, null subjects for these persons are found only in embedded clauses when an element like *si* 'if', a wh operator, or a subjunctive complementizer occupies $C°$.[13]

The other persons (first singular and plural and second plural) are regularly pro-drop in all domains, including main and embedded interrogative and declarative clauses. The following examples illustrate regular pro-drop of first person singular and plural and second person plural in main clauses, where, due to the loss of V2, $C°$ is not strong.[14]

(13)  a. Ve suplico ...               (Calmo 72)[15]
         (I) you pray,
         'I pray you'
      b. Havemo buo notitia che ...   (Calmo 129) ...
         (we) have had news that ...
         'We heard that ...'
      c. Dirè    a         Ser Zuan che ...  (Ruz. 107)
         (you+pl.) will-say to Sir Z. that ...
         'You will tell Sir Z. that ...'

---

[13] Venetian and Paduan differ from French in that main contexts never allow pro-drop of second singular and third person singular and plural. However, the period considered here is the 14th century and not the 14th–15th. This might be an indication that pro-drop in V1 main clauses in Middle French is still connected to the V2 system, and not to spec-head agreement as Roberts suggests.

[14] Throughout this chapter I provide no statistical indications. The reason is that statistical data concerning the occurrence of pronouns are not relevant in this case, given my claim that their occurrence depends on the syntactic configuration. Once the right syntactic configuration is selected, the system is completely regular.

[15] The texts examined for this period are the first 100 pages of a collection of letters written by the scholar Andrea Calmo (*Le Lettere*) and his comedy *La Spagnola* for Venetian. For Paduan, the first 100 pages of Ruzante's collection of plays was used. For philological reasons, only the sentences spoken by the character played by Ruzante were considered.

The same is true in embedded wh contexts:

(14)  a. Quando      aspetemo    suto          (Calmo 111)
         when (we)    expect      dry weather
         'When we need dry weather...'
      b. Co      avesse  ben         dissenao      (Calmo 73)
         when    (I)     had well   dined
         'When I had finished eating...'
      c. Si volè                     scambiar    tuto        (Calmo 94)
         if (you+plr)   want   to exchange   everything
         'If you want to change everything...'

Second person singular and third person singular and plural only have pro-drop when C° is strong. The following cases are residual wh contexts in which C° contains a [+wh] (16) or a subjunctive feature (15) (which is much rarer and we just mention it here for completeness):

(15)  Dirè a Ser Zuan che _ la guarda ben (Ruz. 107)
      (you) will say to Sir Zuan that (he) it+fem. looks+subjunctive well
      'You will tell/ask to Sir Z. to look after her well'

(16)  a. si_      no resta      altro
         if (it)  not remains   anything else
         'if nothing else is left'
      b. com fa l'orsa      quando_   se      guz      gi ongi (Ruz. 105)
         as does the bear   when (she)  herself  sharpens  her claws
         'as the bear does when it sharpens its claws'
      c. che uta la zente co _            li      vede, se ghe inchina (Calmo 75)
         that all the people when (she) them  sees,   refl. bows
         'that everybody bows when they see them'
      d. si             farae        megio ...   (Ruz. 102)
         whether (they)  would-do   better
         'whether they would better have'

Examples of subject pronouns (in bold) when licensing via a strong C° is lacking are the following:

(17)  a. El m'ha lagò le cavale ...        (Ruz. 78)
         he to-me has left the horses ...
         'He left me the horses'
      b. El e      par      che   l    sarave      cossa giusta  (Calmo 111)
         it to-me  seems   that   it   would-be   thing right
         'This seems to me to be the right thing'

   c.  Un passo i no farè        (Ruz. 74)
       a   step   I not will-do
       'I will not move'
   d.  Te no vissi mà        (Ruz. 91)
       you not saw never
       'You never saw'

The same is true for postverbal subjects, which require a subject pronoun in the preverbal position:[16]

(18)  El viene    quel so   fraelo      (Ruz. 94)
      he comes   that his  brother
      'That brother of his is coming'
(19)  L'è    sta     suspeso    le prediche   al   Sior Geronimo   (Calmo 15)
      it is  been   suspended  the sermons  for  Sir Geronimo
      'The sermons to Sir G. have been suspended'

Summing up, we have the following distribution of null subjects in Renaissance Venetian and Paduan:

| (20) | *Main clauses* | *Embedded −wh* | *Embedded +wh* |
|---|---|---|---|
| 1sg. | + | + | + |
| 1pl. | + | + | + |
| 2pl. | + | + | + |
| 2sg. | − | − | + |
| 3sg. | − | − | + |
| 3pl. | − | − | + |
| pro postverbal subject | − | − | + |

In order for this description of the facts to be correct, we need to show that the subject pronouns occurring when pro was not possible were not clitic heads at this stage of evolution, but real XPs. Following Vanelli (1987), who applies the standard tests of relative ordering with negation (21a–f) and lack of subject clitic doubling (21g, h), we can show that third-person subject pronouns at this stage were not clitic heads, but at most weak pronouns in the sense of Cardinaletti and Starke (1999):

---

[16] Real expletive subjects can either be pro-drop or have a subject pronoun; expletive pro co-occurring with postverbal subjects requires the preverbal pronoun. This shows that there must be a difference between the two contexts—a line of research which is potentially very interesting, but which I will not develop here.

(21)  a.  E no podeva tior          (Calmo 66)
          not could take
      b.  ... che te   no   vissi mà    (Ruz. 91)
          ... that you not see never
          'that you never saw'
      c.  La no vaga   a mio conto    (Calmo 79)
          she not goes on my behalf
          'She cannot go on my behalf'
      d.  El no puol eser altrimenti  ca benedeto   (Calmo 94)
          he not can be   other        than blessed
          'It can only be blessed'
      e.  E no     se          inganemo   (Calmo 66)
          we not   ourselves   mistake
          'We are not wrong'
      f.  ... c'un passo i      non farè      (Ruz. 74)
          ... that a step they   not will-make
          'I will not move'
      g.  Ognon    vorà        acomodarse de si   bela      stampa (Calmo 66)
          everybody will-want take            of such beautiful picture
          'Everybody will want such a nice picture'
      h.  Un'arma longa fa   star    indrio   el   so   nemico (Calmo 96)
          a weapon long makes stay   behind   the  his  enemy
          'A long weapon keeps the enemy away'

A survey of a great number of varieties belonging to this domain would surely strengthen our observations; but in many cases this is not possible because of the lack of texts from this period for many dialects. Nevertheless, we can conclude that the asymmetrical pro-drop system splits the persons into two classes: those that require an additional strong feature overtly realized within the CP domain and those that do not. Moreover, it seems that the split does not run according to the most plausible and well-attested person division, i.e. first and second versus third, as is the case with partial pro-drop quoted in the introduction, but includes only part of the deictic persons, first and second plural probably being the core case, with the possible addition of first person singular.

Furthermore, it is a fact that not all NIDs have developed such an asymmetric pro-drop system when they have lost V2; at this stage of development some dialects already display what will become invariable clitics in the modern dialects, in part or throughout the whole paradigm. We examine here another Veneto dialect, Polesano, which represents an interesting case for understanding the split inside the paradigm we are investigating,[17] because the split among persons is found even though a subject pronoun is always present. (Bolognese seems to have the same system during the same period; we use here examples from Polesano because it has maintained the system throughout its evolution.)

In this dialect there are no cases of pro-drop during the Renaissance, in the sense that a pronoun (in bold) is always present, also for first person singular and plural and second person plural:

(22)   a. **A** digh dunca  (Polesano)
          I    say then
       b. **T**   m  insegn
          you me teach
       c. **Al** vegnia
          he came
       d. **La**   s      lamintava
          she  self  complained
       e. **A**  v          pusì mo pinsar vu
          you yourself   can now think YOU
       f. che   **i**    j           diseven ...
          that  they  to-him   said
       g. **l'**intraviegn
          it happened

Note that a subject pronoun is present even for non-referential subjects as in (22g).

(23) shows that also in Polesano, as already illustrated for Venetian and Paduan, subject pronouns are not clitic heads at this stage, but real XPs; (a) the subject pronoun is not present when a DP subject is realized; (b) the subject pronoun occurs before the preverbal negative marker (contrary to their modern counterparts); (c) a subject pronoun can be omitted in coordinated structures (contrary to their modern counterparts).

(23)   a. Una zentildona de    Guascogna andò pelegrinando ... (Polesano)
          a    lady        from Guascogna went pilgrimage
          'A lady from Guascogna went on a pilgrimage'

---

[17] The data are all taken from the *Novella del Re di Cipro*, a translation of one of Boccaccio's short novels collected in the Renaissance by the scholar Lionardo Salviati and published in 1875, together with many more contemporary versions by the philologist Giovanni Papanti.

    b.  La   non   truvava   luogh
         she   not    found    place ...
         'She could not find a place'
    c.  la   i        andò  dinanz   e     si _      i        diss
         she  to-him  went  in-front  and  so (she)  to-him  said
         'She came in front of him and said'

On the other hand, it seems that in Polesano the clitic *a*, which appears with first person singular and plural and second person plural, already has the properties it displays in the modern dialects: it always clusters with the complementizer (cf. (24)), while this is not the case with other pronouns.

(24)  a.  cha     possa imparar
         that+I  can    learn
      b.  cha     intend
         that+I  understand

Leaving aside the problem of the categorial status of subject pronouns in this period, it is a fact that pro-drop is never found in this language; but note that the subject pronoun of first person singular and plural and second person plural is an invariable element, *a*, which is found in the same contexts where in Venetian and Paduan we find pro-drop. The particle *a* is clearly not a pronoun expressing person and number features, as is the case for second person singular and for third person singular and plural. Evidently, the element *a* is not a well-behaved subject pronoun but must be realized for purely syntactic reasons, given that it does not seem to have any morphological distinction. Hence, the split between the two sets of persons remains, although it surfaces in a different form. Moreover, the clitic *a* in modern NIDs has been analysed as a CP element occurring inside the CP domain (cf. Benincà 1983; Poletto 2000), not as a true subject clitic within IP. Because of the lack of data in the corpus it is not possible to show incontrovertibly that at this point in the history this element was already within CP. Nevertheless, the data in (24) seem to suggest that it already had the status of a CP element. We will leave this question open, noting that if this were true we would have another case in which a strong C allows null subjects.

## 6.4 The modern stage

As is well known, French has lost both pro-drop types, the regular and the CP-dependent one; it has become a non-pro-drop language. Nevertheless, French has two series of subject pronouns, weak and strong. Moreover, the subject pronouns currently analysed as weak pronouns are the ones that can occur in the preverbal subject position (see Cardinaletti and Starke 1999), while the strong forms are found in dislocated or focalized positions.

Note, however, that no systematic morphological change occurred from Middle to modern French in the verb agreement paradigm; more precisely, first and second person plural are still morphologically distinct from the other persons, and nevertheless they have an obligatory subject pronoun in the same way as the other persons. We will show that the same thing occurred in Venetian and Paduan, which have changed their syntactic system without any change in verbal morphology. On the other hand, Polesano too has changed its system for second person singular without changing its morphology. Therefore, our first question concerning the effect of agreement morphology on the availability of null subjects is already answered: morphology is not the immediate trigger for null subjects. We will come back to this in section 6.5. For the moment we simply state that the loss of null subjects is not always connected to a morphological loss in the paradigm.

### 6.4.1 *Modern Polesano*

As already noticed by Benincà (1983) for Paduan and by Poletto (1996) for Polesano, NIDs have developed different types of subject clitic. Leaving aside finer distinctions, which exist but are not relevant here, we can follow Poletto (1996) in splitting the class of subject clitics into two main groups: clitics that are within IP and clitics directly merged in the CP domain. I will also follow the analysis that both clitic groups are heads in the NIDs. The tests distinguishing between the two groups have by now become standard and have already been mentioned in section 6.3; we will summarize them here.

(a) The first test is the position of the clitic with respect to the preverbal negative marker: while IP clitics occur after the preverbal negative marker, CP clitics occur before it:

(25)   a. A    no vegno   (Polesano (Loreo dialect))
          SCL  not come
          'I do not come'
       b. No la    vien
          not SCL  comes

This split is straightforwardly explained by the hypothesis that some clitics are in CP and others in IP, although the test provided by negation is still 'too gross' to provide clear evidence for the exact position of the two types: there might be subject clitics in IP which occur higher than NegP but lower than CP (and in fact there are such cases, although not in the dialects we consider here: cf. Poletto (2000)). So, this test simply shows that this type of clitic is higher than 'agreement' subject clitics, but it does not show yet where the clitic is located.

(b) A second test is the possibility of repeating the clitic in coordinated structures including an object:

(26)  A      canto co ti    e     balo co lu          (Loreo)
      SCL    sing with you  and   dance with him
      'I sing with you and dance with him'

(27)  a. *La    magna patate   e beve vin
          SCL   eats   potatoes and drinks wine
      b. *Ti    magni  patate    e bevi vin
          SCL   eat    potatoes  and drink wine

The clitic *a* can be omitted in the second conjunct of a coordination, while IP clitics are necessarily repeated. Once again, the coordination test shows that there are at least two types of subject clitics, but does not constitute strong evidence in favour of the idea that some clitics are merged within the CP domain.

(c) The test that clearly reveals that this is the correct hypothesis is the clustering with the complementizer (already mentioned in section 6.3 for Renaissance Polesano):

(28)  a. Ara ch'a        vegno (Loreo)
         look that-SCL  come
         'Look, I am coming'
      b. *Ara che a vegno

(29)  a. No so           s'a        vegno
         not know        if+SCL     come
         'I do not know whether I will come'
      b. *No so se a vegno

(30)  a. Ara    che el    vien      (Loreo)
         look   that SCL  comes
         'Look, he is coming'
      b. Ara ch'el vien

The contrast between (28b)/(29b) and (30a) shows that clustering with the complementizer is obligatory only for the *a* clitics, and can only be explained by saying that it is the complementizer itself that is merged lower than the clitic and then adjoined to it.[18] The three tests mentioned above consistently point to the direction that *a* is located higher than the IP clitics.

---

[18] The possibility of (30b) is a different type of phenomenon, a purely phonological process due to *allegro* speech.

(d) Further evidence in favour of the hypothesis of splitting subject clitics into two classes, one of which is merged in the CP domain, is provided by the fact that CP clitics are incompatible with other typical CP elements, like wh-items and focalized constituents (as originally noted by Benincà (1983) for Paduan):

(31)   a. *Cossa a voto?
         What  a want-you?
         'What do you want?'
       b. *Mario a go visto, no Piero
         Mario a have seen, not Piero
         'I have seen Mario, not Piero'

(e) Furthermore, a CP head like the temporal complementizer *co* is incompatible with *a*, while its XP counterpart is not. This shows that *a* is located inside the CP domain, but also that it is a head, not an XP, as it interferes with other C° heads.

(32)   a. *Co a vegno
         when a come
         'When I come'
       b. Quando   ch' a vegno
         when        that a come
         'When I come'

We will not pursue this further here, referring to Poletto (2000) for further discussion on this topic; the status and the position of subject clitics here is instrumental to the analysis of null subjects.

If subject clitics are heads in Polesano, in a traditional account this means that this is also a pro-drop language. Nevertheless, it cannot be pro-drop in the same sense that Standard Italian is, because the subject clitic is obligatorily present when no DP subject is realized. The paradigm of simple present in modern Polesano is illustrated in (33):

(33)   a. a magno
         I eat
       b. a te magni
         you eat
       c. el/la magna
         he eats
       d. a magnemo
         we eat
       e. a magnè
         you eat

    f.  i/le magna
       they eat

(34)  a.  a piove
        it rains

      b.  a pare
        it seems

      c.  A ga telefonà Nane
        it has phoned Nane
        'Nane has phoned'

Apparently nothing has changed with respect to the Renaissance period: one could still assume that null subjects are never allowed in this dialect, because there is always an element preceding the inflected verb. Moreover, the asymmetric system is still operative, as some persons have the invariable clitic *a*, others a subject pronoun carrying morphological distinctions.

However, we have shown that both IP and CP clitics are heads, while at least IP clitics were not in the Renaissance system, so something must have changed.

Moreover, a crucial difference between the Renaissance system and the modern system which becomes evident comparing the two paradigms in (33) and (22) is that second person singular only had a subject pronoun in the Renaissance, while today it requires both the CP and the IP clitic, as the sequence in (33b) shows.

In the next section I will propose that the subject clitics in these dialects are connected to licensing and/or identification of pro, as they 'support' the inflected verb in either licensing, licensing and identifying, or identifying a null subject; this view can also be translated into minimalist terms.

For the moment, let us simply conclude with the following observations: the system we have here is neither the Standard Italian one, where the inflected verb is always strong enough to license null subjects, nor the non-pro-drop one of French, where there is always a weak (or maybe clitic) pronoun and the inflected verb is never strong.

Moreover, this system still looks asymmetric, because for some persons the clitic resembles real subject pronouns as it morphologically encodes person and number features, while for other persons it looks like an expletive element of some sort.

### 6.4.2 *Modern Paduan and Venetian*

After the Renaissance period, the contexts of licensing through a feature overtly expressed on C° have been lost. However, modern Paduan and Venetian have also maintained an asymmetric system, in the sense that a null subject is licensed in two different ways across the verbal paradigm. Once again, second person singular and third person singular and plural require a subject clitic:[19]

(35)  a.  ti magni
          you eat
      b.  el magna
          he eats
      c.  i magna
          they eat

In Paduan and Venetian, as in the majority of the NIDs, the status of the subject pronoun has changed: it is no longer a real subject XP but a head. What has not changed is the weak (or −pronominal) status of the inflected verb, which was unable to license a null subject of second person singular and third person singular and plural in the medieval and Renaissance period and which still is: the subject clitic is present because inflection is not strong enough in the case of second person singular and third persons.

As for the other three persons, once again, nothing has changed with respect to the Renaissance period: first person singular and plural and second person plural have maintained their ability to license a null subject in all contexts, and they still retain it:[20]

(36)  a.  magno
          I-eat
      b.  magnemo
          we-eat
      c.  magnè
          you+pl.-eat

We can conclude that, although all the NIDs have lost the possibility of pro-drop licensing when C° is strong, Venetian and Paduan have maintained the original split between the persons which originated in the passage from the medieval system of pro-drop licensing by I in C° to the Renaissance system.

---

[19] The examples are taken from Venetian, but Paduan has the same system as far as pro-drop licensing is concerned.

[20] Paduan also has a clitic element *a*, which has a different distribution with respect to the one described above for Polesano. As Benincà (1983) proposes, it is a Topic marker located inside a Topic position.

## 6.5  A general picture

### 6.5.1  *A survey of the data*

In this section I begin by summing up the data gathered from the investigation of the NWR evolutionary path. I will then try to draw some conclusions concerning the two main questions raised in the introduction by analysing the evolution of Paduan, Venetian, and Polesano and comparing it to French.

The starting point of the analysis is Haiman's intuition (1974) that the birth of subject clitics depends on a property already shared by French and NIDs at their medieval stage, which sets them apart from other Old Romance languages. While Haiman identified this property with V2, on the basis of work by Benincà (1983), Vanelli et al. (1985), and other authors mentioned above, it has been shown that the correct connection with the development of subject clitics does not involve V2 *per se* but a different type of null subject licensing, which in turn depended on V2. So, languages like Spanish, Catalan, and Southern Italian varieties, which had null subject licensing by the inflected verb similar to their modern counterparts, have maintained null subjects with no variation.

NWR was different because null subject licensing was possible only in V2 contexts. During the Renaissance period NWR lost the V2 property, and as a consequence the null subject licensing context had to change. NWR did not immediately become totally non-pro-drop, as might have been expected, but developed what we called asymmetrical pro-drop systems in two forms, depending on the variety. In the first type (French, Venetian, Paduan) second-person singular and third-person singular and plural null subjects were licensed when C° contained a strong feature; otherwise a subject pronoun of the non-clitic type was used (see Vanelli (1987) for further arguments in favour of the phrasal status of subject pronouns at this stage). First-person (singular and) plural and second-person plural null subjects were licensed by means of the inflected verb, as is regularly the case in modern Standard Italian.

In the second type (Polesano, Bolognese) there were apparently no null subjects: a subject pronoun was always phonetically realized. Nevertheless, we saw that there are reasons to suspect that the invariable clitic *a* occurring with first person singular and plural and second person plural was already a CP element which licensed a null subject rendering C° strong. Second person singular and the third persons used subject pronouns, which were non-clitic subject pronouns (as shown by tests concerning doubling and ordering with a preverbal negative marker). As will be discussed in section 6.5.2, this system is particularly relevant for the analysis of null subject licensing because it clearly shows that, although C° is involved in the process, it cannot be the element that identifies the features of the null subject, being invariable.

The modern stages of these languages present three distinct developments: (a) Standard French has totally lost null subjects (although spoken French looks more similar to the NIDs). Both licensing by strong $C°$ and licensing by strong $I°$ are absent in the modern language. Nevertheless, first and second person plural have maintained their morphological distinctions. According to Roberts (1993) this is due to the fact that, in order to license pro only by spec-head agreement, verbal inflection has to be pronominal, and this was not the case in French, which lost pro-drop entirely.

(b) Venetian and Paduan have maintained an asymmetric system: some persons have null subjects licensed directly by the inflected verb in $I°$, others need a subject clitic head. Licensing by a strong $C°$ has disappeared in these varieties, replaced by a constant use of the subject pronoun. Subject clitics have become heads, which occupy head positions higher than $T°/AgrS°$ but still within the IP domain. Licensing by strong $I°$ for first person singular and plural and second person plural has remained constant.

(c) Polesano has partially maintained null subject licensing by $C°$. It has developed a system in which a subject clitic is always necessary for the licensing of null subjects. Some subject clitics are located in IP, the invariable clitic in CP. The two distinct positions of the clitic element still reflect the split between persons typical of the Renaissance asymmetric systems. Licensing by strong $I°$ was never an option in this variety, although the morphological distinctions on verbal inflection are similar to those of Venetian, Paduan, and French.

Through the examination of asymmetrical pro-drop systems and of their development we conclude that the syntactic system can change even though overt morphology does not. Languages like French, Venetian, and Paduan directly show that strong morphology on the verb can, but need not, license null subjects. French has developed into a non-null subject language, while Venetian has maintained an asymmetric system. In neither case has verbal morphology been altered. In Polesano, strong inflection never played a role, although the necessary morphological distinctions were (and still are) present. The answer to the first question we raised in the introduction is that the relation between morphology and syntax is only one-way: strong morphology on a head can 'feed' syntactic properties as null subject licensing, but this is not necessarily the case. Strong morphology is thus not a sufficient condition for null subject licensing across Romance languages.[21] The same conclusion is reached by Speas and Alexiadou (Chapters 2 and 5 above).

---

[21] This conclusion is compatible with the proposal of Roberts (1993) that, in order to be able to license pro, verbal inflection has to be +pronominal (i.e. have an inflectional ending for all persons and have at most one syncretism in the paradigm). Polesano inflection is +pronominal, but still it does not license pro.

Let us now try to make sense of the evolutionary path described above and see what it can tell us about the pro-drop property and the relation between C° and I°, which are the two heads that seem to be involved in the process of null subject licensing.

### 6.5.2 *The interaction between I° and C°*

The authors who have worked on the phenomenon of pro-drop licensing in medieval French and NIDs (Benincà 1983; Adams 1987b; Roberts 1993) propose that in medieval NWR pro is licensed by government and not by spec-head agreement, a solution which has also been proposed for cases of expletive pro-drop licensing in V2 languages like German (see Vikner 1995). Given that NWR was V2 in the medieval period this seems a plausible hypothesis. Note, however, that expletive pro in German is found both in main and in embedded clauses and does not depend on I to C, but just on the C° head being realized. Medieval NWR is different from German because it does not only require that C° is filled by some phonetically realized category; the head in C° also has to be the inflected verb. Benincà (1983) originally noted that in medieval NWR it is only when the inflected verb raises to C° via V2 that pro can be licensed, otherwise a subject pronoun is required. Hence, the structural condition for pro-drop licensing according to this view is:

(37)   Pro is licensed iff:
    (a) the inflected verb has (+ finite) strong features;
    (b) the inflected verb governs pro.

Given that the inflected verb could govern pro only when it raised higher than T°, the system of pro-drop in NWR depended on V2. As noted above, the loss of the V2 property affected also the pro-drop system, giving rise to the asymmetric system and to different types of subject clitic.

Let us first examine the Polesano system, which is the most conservative one. Renaissance Polesano has simplified the condition in (37) to a government condition:

(38)   Pro is licensed iff it is governed by a strong head.

In Polesano the inflected verb was never strong enough to license pro, which was either licensed by an element in C° (*a*) or not licensed at all, in which case a pronoun was required. Expletive subjects, first person singular and plural and second person plural, were licensed by C°, which was strong when it contained *a*. Referential pro was also submitted to an identification requirement, which was performed by the inflected verb, given that C° does not have any overt agreement features in this language.

As for third person singular and plural and second person singular, the inflected verb was probably not even strong enough for identifying a null subject. Therefore, a subject pronoun was required. As we have seen, subject pronouns were not clitic heads in this period, but real pronouns located in subject position.

The Polesano system is the one that looks like German, because the licensing condition is just the same.[22] Still, there is a fundamental difference with respect to Germanic pro-drop licensed by $C°$: in Germanic languages we never find referential pro. Hence, the identification requirement is not met, even in those cases in which verbal morphology has enough distinctions. In our terms: in the Germanic languages the inflected verb can never identify pro; in Polesano it can. In other words, verbal inflection apparently always plays a role in Romance null subjects, which is not the case in the Germanic domain.[23]

Summing up: pro was licensed by strong $C°$, referential subjects were identified by inflection. When inflection was unable to identify a null subject, a pronoun was inserted. The asymmetric system of Polesano arose as a consequence of two facts: (a) the head which formally licensed the null subject had no identification features; (b) not all persons could identify the null subject. Subject pronouns (from which subject clitics originated) were required in this case.

The other system we have found in NWR in the Renaissance period is the one of French, Paduan, and Venetian. In this system, first and second person plural (and first person singular in Venetian and Paduan) were always pro-drop in all contexts, second person singular and third persons only when $C°$ contained some feature. It is plausible to interpret the first type as being licensed by strong inflection and the second as being licensed by strong C. In other words, these languages have split the two conditions in (37), changing an 'and' to an 'or' function: pro is licensed either when the inflected verb is strong or when $C°$ is strong:

---

[22] In German the complementizer is strong enough to license pro; in Polesano *a* is present also in embedded domains. The clustering between *a* and the complementizer noted above could be a way of rendering the complementizer itself strong.

[23] Note that in Germanic varieties there are cases of agreeing complementizers which express subject features. In the Romance languages these cases are extremely rare, the only cases possibly being Friulian examples which change the vowel of the complementizer according to the person of the subject. French *qui* is something different, as it does not change according to the person features of the subject, but simply signals that the XP extracted from the sentence is the subject. The possibility of agreeing complementizers might be connected to the fact that there is no identification of a null subject from $I°$ in the Germain domain.

(39) a. C° is a pro-drop licenser iff it is strong.
  b. The inflected verb in T°/AgrS° is a pro-drop licenser iff it is strong.

The definition of strength is given in (40):

(40) a. C is strong when it contains a feature different from the unmarked one.[24]
  b. Agr is strong when it contains a morphologically realized + person and +number feature.

(39) provides the theoretical means of explaining why an apparently costly system like the asymmetric one should exist. The verbal forms which could be reanalysed as strong by virtue of their feature composition (see below) became null subject licensers, giving rise to 'regular' pro-drop similar to modern Standard Italian. Those inflectional forms that could not be analysed as strong were non-pro-drop unless another head was strong, namely C°. A null subject could be licensed either by spec-head agreement or by government. The identification requirement was always performed by the inflected verb, as C° had no agreement features. As already noted for Polesano, this means that we do not have to equate the possibility of identifying a null subject with the possibility of licensing a null subject. The cases of null subject licensing by C° and identification by I° in Renaissance NWR constitute the clearest case that overt person and number agreement features do not play any role in the selection of a head as null subject licenser.

Let us now turn to the modern systems: French, Venetian, and Paduan have lost the possibility in (40a): licensing by C° is no longer attested. Typical contexts of licensing by strong C° as embedded interrogatives now require a subject clitic:

(41) a. No so    cossa che *(te)  ga fato    (Paduan)
     not know  what that (you)  have done
     'I do not know what you did'
  b. No so    cossa che *(el)  ga fato
     not know  what that he    has done
     'I do not know what he did'

As for the other possibility given in (40b), Venetian and Paduan maintained it, while French lost it. So, in Paduan and Venetian first and second person plural are pro-drop, in French they are not. First person singular is

---

[24] Following many recent proposals (e.g. Roberts and Roussou 2002), I assume that declarative is the unmarked value. Hence, the [+wh] feature in C° renders it a null subject licenser.

also pro-drop in Paduan and Venetian, but it already was in the Renaissance period (contrary to French—see above).

One additional change that has occurred in all NIDs is that the subject pronouns, which were not clitic heads in the Renaissance, have become clitics in the modern varieties. This is true not only of Venetian, Paduan, and Polesano, the dialects considered here, but also of the vast majority of the NIDs (excluding Franco-Provençal varieties and V2 Romantch and Rhaetoromance of the Dolomites).

A possible explanation for this change has to do with a 'regularization' of the asymmetric system: in the Renaissance period French, Venetian, and Paduan could have null subjects across the whole paradigm, even though the licensing conditions of a null subject were different according to the person. The loss of null subject licensing through government by strong $C°$ should have given rise to a real asymmetric system, where only some persons (i.e. those that admitted licensing by a strong $I°$) could have a null subject. Probably the fact that subject pronouns became clitic heads has to do with this asymmetry: becoming heads, subject clitics created a new type of null subject licensing (and identifying) performed by a head which is not $T°/$AgrS$°$, but a higher one. In other words, the null subject licensing (and identifying) process by the clitic head is similar to the one performed by $C°$, because the head is higher than $T°/$AgrS$°$, but, by contrast with licensing by $C°$, the subject clitic can also identify referential null subjects, and this is probably done in a spec-head agreement configuration.

As for modern Polesano, this dialect has changed its system in a very limited way. Expletive and referential pro of first person singular and plural and second person plural is licensed by *a* in $C°$. Referential pro is still identified by verbal inflection. Third person singular and plural are now regular cases of pro-drop, as discussed above: the licenser and identifier is a clitic head located higher than the inflected verb, but still in the IP domain (as the tests discussed in section 6.4 show). Second person singular is a special case. In the Renaissance period it was similar to third persons; now it requires both a clitic IP head and the $C°$ clitic *a*. We can say that in this case the $C°$ clitic licenses the null subject and the IP clitic identifies it. Verbal inflection probably plays no role here (see below for a discussion on the special requirements of second person singular).

One interesting consequence of the analysis of Polesano is that we have to divorce null subject licensing from nominative case assignment. Roberts (1993) explicitly proposes that the change in the null subject parameter, on a par with the loss of V2, depends on a change in the nominative assignment possibilities: in the medieval period case could be assigned by the inflected verb in C° through government, while in the Renaissance period nominative could only be assigned through spec-head agreement. Null subjects were also licensed through government in the medieval period; subsequently this possibility was lost, and replaced by licensing through spec-head agreement (where possible). Modern Polesano has lost V2, and this tells us that nominative case assignment through government is no longer possible. However, pro is still licensed in a government configuration by the *a* clitic in the CP domain: hence, null subject licensing is not directly connected to case assignment, and a head can still remain a pro-drop licenser even when it has lost its case-assigning ability.

We can sum up the three evolutionary stages examined for second person singular and third person singular and plural across all NWR as follows:

- Medieval stage: the inflected verb in C° licenses a null subject through government and identifies referential null subjects.
- Renaissance stage: a strong C° head licenses a null subject through government. Identification of referential null subjects is performed by verbal inflection.
- Modern stage: a clitic head licenses (and identifies) the null subject.

This analysis also captures Haiman's intuition that subject clitics and the loss of Verb Second were somehow connected, although the connection is only indirect. Subject clitic heads originate from a reanalysis of full pronouns, which in turn were obligatory because the V2 context of pro-drop licensing had been lost. The reanalysis of pronominal XPs as heads permitted a generally uniform system in the NIDs, where a null subject is always licensed, although the licensing conditions change, and still reflect the original split between strong and weak forms internal to the verbal paradigm.

The definition of strength in (40) still leaves a problem: why is it the case that just first and second person plural can be considered strong while other persons cannot? The case of second person singular, whose inflected verb is morphologically distinct in the NIDs, shows that being strong does not simply depend on morphological distinctions. A number of morphological phenomena isolate first and second person plural in the Romance languages. For instance, they use a different root from all other persons with irregular verbs like *andare*; very often first- and second-person singular pronouns are compound forms of the bare pronoun plus the form *altri* 'other' in the NIDs, yielding forms like *noialtri, voialtri*: 'we + other', 'you + other', and this induces us to consider them as a natural subclass inside the domain of deictic persons. Moreover, Chinellato (2001) has shown that agrammatical patients have more problems with producing these two persons than with all the others, including third person plural. This has probably to do with the fact that they have the most complex feature composition: all other persons result from the combination of the plus and minus of at most two features. Among the deictic persons first and second singular are respectively [+speaker], [−hearer] and [−speaker], [+hearer]. In the non-deictic persons, i.e. the third, there is only a distinction of number among singular and plural. First and second person plural require the most complex feature composition, including hearer and speaker, but also something more, as first person plural can express [+speaker], [+hearer] but can also include a third person, and second person plural can also result from the combination of a deictic and a non-deictic person. One might think of translating this 'heaviness' in their feature composition in terms of verb movement and assume that these two verbal forms raise higher than the others, and that this is the reason why they license null subjects in a higher functional head, on a par with subject clitics. However, if we adopt the relative position of adverbs as a test, as has traditionally been done since Pollock (1989), we find no difference between first and second person plural and the other persons. This does not mean that this hypothesis has to be discarded, because there might be no adverbs intervening in this area. However, given that we lack empirical evidence in favour of this hypothesis, we propose it as a possibility, leaving it for future research in which our tests concerning verb movement will be more refined.

One further research path that could shed light on the feature composition of the various persons is the one indicated by Renaissance Venetian and Paduan, where first person singular goes with first and second person plural: the extension to first person singular must not be considered pure chance. There are several cases of morphological spreading of forms which go from the first person singular to the first person plural (for instance, reflexive and object clitics in Lombard and Veneto dialects use a first-person singular form also for the first person plural, and some French dialects use the form *je* 'I' for the first person plural clitic pronoun). Hence, it seems that also the class of persons including first person singular and first and second person plural is a natural one, and it is very likely that it is first person plural that constitutes the 'bridge' between first person singular and second person plural.

Second person singular deserves special treatment within the NIDs: as Renzi and Vanelli (1983) originally noted, if a dialect has only a subject clitic, this is second person singular, and is not connected to the presence of distinct morphology on the verb. Moreover, we saw that in modern Polesano, the inflected verb is not sufficient to identify a null subject licensed by *a*. A morphologically distinct subject clitic (*te*) is obligatory. It seems that second person singular requires additional morphological material in order to be identified. Even standard Italian subjunctives require a second-person pronoun when the forms are ambiguous among first, second, and third person singular, but do not require it for third or first person (see Cardinaletti and Starke 1999). The fundamental reason why second singular should display such a requirement or 'morphological redundancy' is still obscure, but must somehow be connected to the feature composition of this person, being more marked than first person.

We can therefore single out a number of natural subclasses according to their feature composition within the verbal paradigm:

- The first split is the one that becomes evident in partial pro-drop: first and second person versus third persons.
- Another natural subclass includes first person singular and plural which combine + and − deictic features.
- The third natural class includes first person singular and plural marked as +speaker.
- The last class might be first and second person singular, with second singular being more marked in the opposition between speaker and hearer.

Many morphological spreading phenomena found in Romance probably follow these natural classes.

## 6.6 Minimalist views on null subject licensing

In this section I will briefly consider two possible alternative solutions in minimalist terms, neither of which makes use of the notion of government. Both solutions share the assumption originally proposed by Alexiadou and Anagnostopoulou (1998) that pro-drop is due to a mechanism of feature checking: the head of TP is endowed with an EPP feature which needs to be checked by an appropriate element; in pro-drop languages the inflected verb can check the EPP feature moving to the head of T°. Null subject licensing therefore amounts to feature checking, and we do not need to postulate the existence of a null pronoun in the Spec of TP that has the same characteristics as overt pronouns.[25] Even the definition of 'null subject' would thus be misleading, as there are no null subjects in SpecTP at all, but simply a different way of checking a syntactic feature.

The first solution that comes to mind to account for the diachronic path described above exploits verb movement. One could update the original

---

[25] This proposal has also been made by various other authors (e.g. Manzini and Savoia 1997).

observation made by Benincà (1983) and assume that the EPP feature of a given F°, in our case TP, is checked in Romance by the inflectional features which overtly raise up to F°, pied-piping the verb that hosts them. The difference between NWR and the other Romance languages would lie in the F° that is endowed with the EPP feature: in NWR it would be a projection higher than T° but lower than C°. In the other Romance languages like Spanish or Portuguese it would be T°.[26] Therefore, in NWR the EPP feature could be checked by the inflected verb moving through F° only when the verb is moving to the V2 position; otherwise, the inflected verb would remain in T°, a subject pronoun would be inserted in SpecF, and EPP checking would be performed in this way. In the other Romance languages, T° is always reached by the inflected verb, and hence the EPP feature would always be checked by the verb and never by a pronoun.[27]

However, there is at least one good reason not to choose this reformulation in terms of movement of the relation between C° and the lower FP. Our system has to derive medieval pro-drop but also its further evolution. In the Renaissance period it seems that it is not V to C that licenses pro-drop, but C° itself: we saw that the original observation made by Vanelli (1987), that embedded contexts in this period allow more null subjects than main contexts, depends on the fact that a null subject was licensed by a strong C°, endowed with wh- (or modal in the case of subjunctive) features. Hence the fact that C° can license a null subject when it contains a wh-element constitutes a direct counterargument to the minimalist analysis based on movement: it is not possible to account for the Renaissance pro-drop system by assuming that it is due to an EPP feature checked by means of verb movement on its path to C°.[28] The Polesano system, which has systematically null subject licensing by a CP clitic, would also be problematic: once again one could assume that the clitic *a* is merged in F° where it checks the EPP feature

---

[26] This solution is reminiscent of the proposal of Roberts (1993) of an additional AgrS projection in early Old French.

[27] Note that this hypothesis needs an additional assumption: that the EPP feature does not trigger overt movement but can only be checked parasitically when the inflected verb moves for independent reasons (i.e. because of other features checking) to the relevant head.

[28] A way to solve the problem and account also for the Renaissance system in terms of movement would be to assume that all the contexts of null subject licensing have V to C movement. Hence, in wh-embedded contexts, the typical context of null subject licensing in this period, the verb should raise higher than in embedded declaratives. Given that there is no empirical evidence in favour of this hypothesis—indeed there seems to be evidence to the contrary—we are left without an account for the Renaissance asymmetric systems in which a strong C° is directly involved in null subject licensing. Here C° licenses a null subject even when it does not contain the inflected verb but an XP, which has no reason to move through F°, being a wh-element and directly targeting its operator position; in the case of yes/no questions the problem is even clearer, as the interrogative complementizer (on a par with the null operator in its Spec) is directly merged in CP and does not move from the inside of the clause.

and then raises up to C°, but there is no empirical evidence for that either. It seems that the status of C° as null subject licenser is crucial in NWR.[29] We come back to the problem that a movement analysis straightforwardly explains V2 and medieval null subject, but not the further evolution of the phenomenon.

Another possible solution which does not exploit movement is the following: licensing by C° is a sort of an 'optical illusion' due to the fact that C° overtly shows what the features of the whole phase and of the inflected verb are. In other words, the morphological evidence that the inflected verb is strong enough to license a null subject can be provided by the inflectional endings or 'at a distance' by C°, whose strong features are transferred to the inflected verb by virtue of a feature-sharing mechanism which ensures that all the extended projections of the verb share the same feature composition. One could exploit the Agree operation, which is part of the movement complex operation as proposed by Chomsky (2001a), and assume that it has to apply to all functional heads within a phase. Agree requires matching: two elements match when they have identical (or better non-distinct) features. Hence, 'match' is not strictly speaking identity, but non-distinctness: the two matching categories have to have the same feature (independently of its interpretable or uninterpretable value).[30] Agree is subject to locality conditions: an intervening potential element *c* prevents matching of two more distant *a* and *b*.

Given that between I and C there is no potential intervener, the operation of Agree can apply, with I° having an uninterpretable feature matched by the interpretable feature in C°; by means of this relation, too, the EPP feature in I (or T°) could be checked, yielding null subjects.[31] In other words, Agree in the new framework is a substitute for the notion of government, which has been used in section 6.5 following traditional accounts. The analysis proposed in section 6.5 can thus be transferred to a minimalist framework by means of the substitution of government by Agree.

This is a welcome result, because (at least in this case) we have an analysis with the same empirical coverage with a less complex theoretical burden: the

[29] Note that it would not be possible to assume that it is CP itself that is endowed with an EPP feature in these contexts, because this analysis has already been proposed by Haegeman (2000) and Roberts (2004) and accounts for V2 contexts, not for null subjects.

[30] According to Chomsky (2001a), Agree applies in narrow syntax to uninterpretable features that enter into agreement relations with interpretable features. Agree is activated by an uninterpretable feature, which must be deleted under an agreement relation; the agreement relation removes the uninterpretable feature from the narrow syntax, allowing derivations to converge at LF.

[31] Note that this is a restatement in new terms of the old idea that null subjects are licensed by C°: it is C° that has the interpretable feature and transfers it to I° by virtue of the Agree operation.

notion of government has been eliminated, and Agree is anyhow necessary because it is involved in the complex operation of movement.

This analysis makes use of a mechanism that must be in any case incorporated into every theory: feature sharing between I° and C°.

## 6.7 Conclusion

Having been a major topic in the 1980s, pro-drop has been recently neglected in the syntactic studies (a notable exception is Ackema and Neeleman (2000), in addition to the articles quoted above). This is partly due to the fact that within the minimalist approach Agreement projections do not exist. The reason for such a move is that they do not encode any real semantic feature, but simply a syntactic relation, which can also be expressed in terms of spec-head agreement within a given functional projection, i.e. without the need of an independent head. However, we have seen that in NWR null subjects do not depend only on the inflected verb, but are clearly connected to the type and number of subject clitics and to the internal feature composition of a given person of the paradigm. We have seen that the NIDs we examined here seem to be asymmetrical pro-drop systems. Moreover, the asymmetry does not cut between first and second person on one side and third person on the other, as one might plausibly think on the basis of Kayne's recent proposal that pro can only be third person and that first and second person are different. The distinction running through the verbal paradigm in the NIDs forces us to draw a more detailed analysis of the feature composition of each person: first and second person plural have been proposed as strong because their feature composition is more complex than that of all other persons, as it combines features of the deictic persons (first and second) with features of the non-deictic persons (third singular and plural). Furthermore, we have seen that first person singular seems to be connected to first person plural, and modern Polesano *a* also shows that there is a split between first and second persons and third persons of the type already noted in other languages. Second person singular has a special status and needs redundant morphology: the reason why this is so still remains a mystery.

Moreover, I have first presented an analysis of the development of NWR null subjects in terms of a traditional proposal that exploits the notions of government and spec-head agreement. Two possible ways of eliminating government have been presented in section 6.6, the one based on the operation Agree being more promising.

# Part III
## Interpreting Empty Arguments

# 7

# Agreement Phenomena in Sign Language of the Netherlands

INGE ZWITSERLOOD AND INGEBORG VAN GIJN

## 7.1 Introduction

For some years, linguists have tried to account for the occurrence and interpretation of null arguments by relating them to (rich) agreement (among others Taraldsen 1980; Chomsky 1981; Rizzi 1982). However, numerous problems were encountered. Some languages (such as German) appear not to allow null arguments, even though they have rich agreement systems. Other languages (such as Chinese) do allow null arguments, but have no agreement at all. For the latter type of languages, alternative analyses have been suggested, in which not agreement, but a null topic, recovers the content of the null argument (Huang 1984; Raposo 1986). Signed languages complicate matters even more due to the fact that they allow null arguments with all verbs but, although they have a rich agreement system, only a subset of verbs can have agreement marking. Lillo-Martin (1986; 1991) suggests a combined recovery strategy for the content of null arguments in American Sign Language (ASL): agreement and null topics. Since then, new facts have come forward, which we will address here and which we will relate to the matter of the recovery of null arguments.

We discuss the agreement system and verb types of signed languages with special reference to Sign Language of the Netherlands (NGT). In contrast to previous analyses we argue that the φ features person and number do not play a role in the verb agreement system and the pronominal system of signed languages. We claim that the only two relevant types of φ features in signed

We would like to thank two anonymous reviewers and the audience at the UiL OTS Workshop, 'The Role of Agreement in Argument Structure', Utrecht, 31 August–1 September 2001, for valuable comments. We are grateful to Handicom, the designers of the sign drawing programme 'Sign PS', for their kind permission to use a demonstration version of this programme.

languages are gender and location. Verb semantics determines which of the two types of agreement fills an agreement slot. We further show that besides agreement verbs that show agreement for their complete θ grid and verbs that show no agreement at all, verbs occur that have agreement for some of their arguments only. In NGT (as in ASL) null arguments can occur with all verb types, in the right pragmatic contexts. This means that agreement in NGT does not represent argument structure (Jelinek 1984; Chapter 9 below; Baker 1996), and that agreement cannot be the only device to recover the content of null arguments. We extend Lillo-Martin's proposal, which is based on Huang (1984), and incorporate ideas by Raposo (1986) and Huang (1995) to explain the linking and the recoverability of (multiple) null arguments within a discourse.

Since the start of the linguistic investigation of signed languages in the 1950s and early 1960s (Tervoort 1953; Stokoe 1960), both similarities and differences between signed and spoken languages have been found. Like words in spoken languages, signs are built up of smaller units comparable to phonemes in spoken languages. By uttering signs in a linear string a sentence can be formed. Prosody, expressed by systematic non-manual behaviour, determines the sentence type. For example, raised eyebrows and a lowered chin signal that a sentence is a yes/no question, whereas a wrinkled nose and a raised chin signal a wh-question (Baker-Shenk and Cokely 1980; Coerts 1992). A difference between spoken and signed languages is the use of signing space in the latter for the expression of pronouns, verb agreement, and spatial relations. Signing space is the space around the signer and various discourse referents. We will explain this use of signing space in section 7.2.1.

The structure of the chapter is as follows. In the next section we will explain how agreement works in signed languages, using data from NGT. Furthermore, we will discuss what φ features are relevant in NGT and what different types of verbs occur. We will focus on null arguments in NGT in section 7.3. In this same section we will review the proposals that have been made in the literature to explain the occurrence of null arguments. These proposals can be divided into two: sentence-internal accounts versus discourse-based accounts. In section 7.4 we give an integrated account of null arguments in signed languages and introduce an identification hierarchy for null arguments. Our findings are summarized in section 7.5.

## 7.2  The agreement system of NGT

Many languages have a system of verb agreement: a systematic marking on the verb that refers to a referent of that verb. The most common case is an affix that carries (a subset of) the φ features (features of person, number, and gender) of the referent. Such affixes form paradigms. As we will show in section 7.2.2, signed languages use special means of referent marking on the verb: verb agreement is expressed by locations in signing space (see also Padden 1988; Bos 1993; Janis 1995; Mathur 2000; Meir 2002). Besides this, there is also a small set of verbs that take gender agreement markers. This will be explained in section 7.2.3. The set of NGT verbs that show agreement is limited (section 7.2.4). In section 7.2.5 we discuss the type of agreement marking that occurs on particular verbs. In section 7.2.6 we discuss the possibility of yet another way to mark agreement in signed languages, viz. by non-manual markers. We adjust the universal set of φ features in such a way that the agreement features of all (spoken and signed) languages are captured in section 7.2.7.

### 7.2.1 *Referential locations*

Verb agreement involves particular locations in signing space. Some locations, viz. those of the discourse participants (such as the signer, the addressee, and other referents) that are actually present at the time of the utterance, are fixed: they are determined by the locations they occupy (in practice, often a location just in front of their body is used). When a referent is not physically present, this person or object is assigned an abstract location in signing space. There are several ways to assign a location to a referent. One of these is making the sign for the referent and subsequently pointing to a particular location in signing space, as in (1).[1] This is called 'localization'.[2]

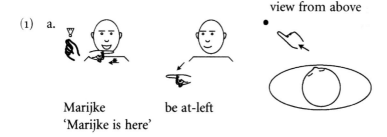

view from above

(1)   a.

Marijke       be at-left
'Marijke is here'

---

[1] In our examples we do not use the gloss notation that is often used in the signed language literature. We choose to give as close a representation of the structure of the signs as possible. This is done by drawing the signs. The front-view drawings are mirror images of a signer; the views from above include the signer and dots representing referents. When we cite examples by other authors, we will use their notation. It is conventional to use capitals for signed language glosses, subscripts for agreement morphology, and superscripts for aspect morphology. Usually, prosodic sentence-marking is indicated in a separate line above the gloss (sequence). In some of our examples we will use this prosodic marking above the pictures of the sign sequence.

[2] The pointing signs that are used in localization of a referent have the same form as pronouns. We distinguish between these signs by glossing the former as 'be at-x' and the latter as 'prn-x'.

b.

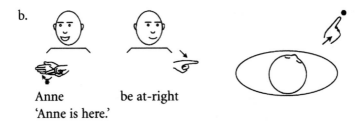

Anne          be at-right
'Anne is here.'

After localization, the referent and the location are connected, until a new discourse topic is introduced. The locations for physically present and non-present referents are used in the verb agreement system as well as in the pronominal system. Basically, every point in signing space can be used as a possible location, not only those on the horizontal plane.[3]

### 7.2.2 Location agreement

As in most signed languages investigated hitherto, a subset of verbs in NGT can show agreement with one or more of its referents (Bos 1990; 1993). This is done in the following ways. First, a verb can be made near the location of a referent in signing space. In (2a) the intransitive NGT verb for 'to wait' is shown in its citation form: it is made in *neutral* signing space (neutral signing space is the space in front of the signer, to which no referents are connected), and in an inflected form (2b), where it is expressed near the location of a referent.

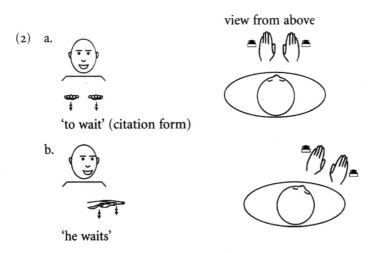

view from above

(2)    a.

'to wait' (citation form)

b.

'he waits'

---

[3] In everyday conversation it is quite rare to use more than three or four different locations per discourse, which is probably due to memory and perceptual limitations. Still, these three or four locations can be anywhere in signing space.

Secondly, some transitive verbs in NGT can show agreement with two arguments by means of two locations. The movement and/or the orientation of the verbs are adjusted in order to include the two locations of both referents. (3b, c) are examples of the inflected NGT verb for 'to visit' in which the movement of the sign is directed from the location of the subject (x) towards the location of the object (y).

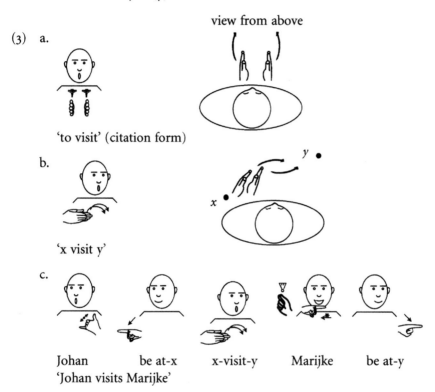

view from above

(3)  a.

'to visit' (citation form)

b.

'x visit y'

c.

| Johan | be at-x | x-visit-y | Marijke | be at-y |

'Johan visits Marijke'

As we will explain in section 7.2.7, we claim that inflected verbs have one or more abstract location features which are coindexed with those of the referents taking a role in the event described. We call this 'location agreement.'

### 7.2.3  *Gender agreement*

In a subset of NGT verbs, viz. those verbs that express motion, location, and existence of a referent, the hand configuration is determined by characteristics of the referent such as its shape or animacy. Often the hand configuration globally reflects the shape of the referent. This is illustrated in (4).

(4)  a.

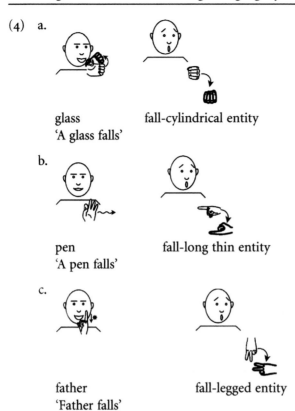

glass            fall-cylindrical entity
'A glass falls'

b.

pen             fall-long thin entity
'A pen falls'

c.

father          fall-legged entity
'Father falls'

If a signer wants to express that a particular entity falls down (e.g. a glass) the signer will use a hand configuration that matches the cylindrical shape of a glass (4a). If the referent that is falling is a long, thin entity (e.g. a pen) he will use an extended index finger (4b), and if the entity is a human being or an animal, usually a hand configuration with two extended fingers is chosen (4c).

In (4), alongside the hand configuration, there are DPs referring to the falling referent. These DPs are in a fixed position before the predicate.[4] Because of this, the hand configuration cannot be analysed as an incorporated argument of the verb.[5] Clearly, the hand configuration indicates a referent involved in the event expressed by the verb. The set of meaningful hand configurations that can be used to represent referents on these predicates

---

[4] In some cases, the referent noun is mentioned in the previous discourse and does not occur within the same sentence as the predicate. We analyse this as an empty noun occurring in the same sentence, which will be explained in more detail in section 7.4.

[5] As we will see in section 7.3.1, DPs in NGT cannot be analysed as adjuncts as is done by Jelinek (1984) and Baker (1996).

form a small, closed class. Furthermore, they appear obligatorily on verbs of motion, location, and existence. For this reason we consider these hand configurations to be agreement markers, following Supalla (1982), Glück and Pfau (1998; 1999), and Zwitserlood (2003a). This analysis is not uncontroversial, however. In the previous signed language literature, these hand configurations are usually described as 'classifiers' but no further account of these elements is provided. For spoken languages it is claimed that classifiers are not agreement markers, because the set of classifiers in a language is often very large, and classifiers are not obligatory (Croft 1994; Corbett 1991). However, in view of the above-mentioned characteristics of meaningful hand configurations, we reject this claim, at least for signed languages.

We call hand configuration agreement 'gender agreement', because the semantics of the genders and the assignment of noun referents to these genders is reminiscent of those in the gender agreement system found in Bantu languages. Within the set of gender agreement markers, we distinguish between *subject* and *object* agreement. Subject gender agreement markers occur only on intransitive verbs. The hand configurations involved in subject gender agreement can be described by the features [animate], [legged], [straight], [small], [flat], and [volume] in NGT.[6] These hand configurations and their features are shown in Table 7.1.[7]

Object gender agreement markers occur only on transitive verbs. They represent referents that are being manipulated by another entity. We have found no need to distinguish the features [legged], [animate], or [volume] in these markers. However, it proves necessary to posit a feature [control], in order to capture the measure of control exerted in the manipulation of a referent. The object gender agreement markers are illustrated in Table 7.2.

Some examples of verbs showing object gender agreement are shown in (5).

(5)  a.

Johan      book      he-move down-flat entity
'Johan puts a book down'

---

[6] The feature [+legged] indicates that the referent has legs, the feature [+straight] that the referent is not bent; the feature [+volume] indicates that the volume of the referent is represented as opposed to its outline. The features [animate], [small], and [flat] are self-evident. If a feature value is not relevant for a particular agreement marker, this cell is left empty.

[7] In this table, we do not include allophonic and free variation that can sometimes be observed in the choice of a particular hand configuration.

TABLE 7.1.    Hand configurations involved in subject gender agreement in NGT

| Hand configuration | Features | | | | | |
|---|---|---|---|---|---|---|
| | Animate | Legged | Straight | Small | Flat | Volume |
| | | | + | − | − | + |
| | | | + | − | + | + |
| | | | − | − | − | − |
| | | | − | + | − | − |
| | | | − | + | + | − |
| | | | − | − | + | − |
| | | | + | − | + | − |
| | | | + | − | + | + |
| | | | | | | + |
| | + | | | | | |
| | | + | | | | |

b.

Johan        glass            he-move down-cylindrical entity
'Johan puts a glass down'

TABLE 7.2. Hand configurations involved in object gender agreement in NGT

| Hand configuration | Features | | | |
|---|---|---|---|---|
| | Straight | Small | Flat | Control |
| | + | − | − | − |
| | − | − | − | − |
| | + | − | − | − |
| | − | − | + | − |
| | − | − | + | + |
| | − | + | + | + |
| | + | + | − |
| | + | − | + | − |
| | + | − | − | + |
| | + | + | − | − |
| | + | + | | + |

c.

|   |   |   |
|---|---|---|
| Johan | pen | he.move down-thin entity |
| 'Johan puts | | |
| a pen down' | | |

It may be necessary to expand the gender agreement features in order to capture the agreement hand configurations in other signed languages as well. For instance, it is proposed that in Taiwanese Sign Language and Japanese

Sign Language (Smith 1989; Fischer and Osugi 2000) there are specific hand configurations for male and female human beings, and American Sign Language (Supalla 1982; 1986) has a specific hand configuration for vehicles.

### 7.2.4 *Mismatches between argument structure and agreement markers*

We saw in sections 7.2.2 and 7.2.3 that NGT verbs can show subject agreement and object agreement (location *and* gender agreement). In the case of ditransitives the predicate can even show agreement for the subject and for both objects, as in the sign for 'to give' (6), which has location agreement for the subject and indirect object, and gender agreement for the direct object.

(6)

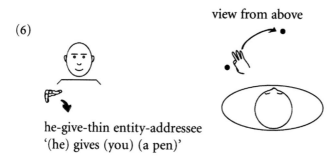

he-give-thin entity-addressee
'(he) gives (you) (a pen)'

However, not every verb shows agreement for all of its arguments. Some verbs do not show agreement at all.[8] It is, however, not the case that it is always the subject or always the object that is left unspecified by agreement. Let us look at some examples. In the set of intransitive verbs the verb can show location or gender agreement for its argument, as has already been shown for the NGT verb for 'to wait' in (2) that shows location agreement, and the verb for 'to fall' in (4), that shows gender agreement. But there is also a group of intransitives that shows no agreement, as in the predicate that expresses 'to be poor' (7). This predicate has the same form for all types of referents.

(7)

'I/you/he/she/we/they am/is/are poor'

---

[8] Note that in the signed language literature much attention is given to agreement verbs. Because of this, one may get the impression that the set of agreement verbs is the most attested type of verb in signed languages. In NGT, however, this set of verbs is rather small compared to the group of non-agreement predicates. Interestingly, though, it seems as if, over time, some non-agreement verbs tend to become inflecting for one or more arguments. A discussion on the possible consequences of this fact is outside the scope of this chapter.

Alongside transitive verbs that show agreement for both arguments, as in the sign for 'to visit' in (3), there are also transitive verbs that do not show agreement for every argument.[9] For example, the verb for 'to find' (8a) has no subject agreement, and the verb for 'to meddle' (8b) has no object agreement. Moreover, the verb for 'to love' in (8c) shows no agreement at all.

(8)   a.                      b.                      c.

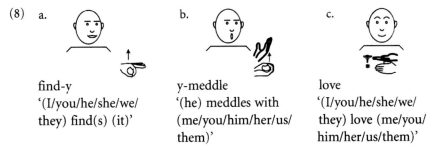

find-y                   y-meddle                love
'(I/you/he/she/we/       '(he) meddles with      '(I/you/he/she/we/
they) find(s) (it)'      (me/you/him/her/us/     they) love (me/you/
                         them)'                  him/her/us/them)'

The same holds for ditransitive verbs: some of these verbs only agree with a subset of their arguments. The verb for 'to send' in (9a) has agreement for its subject and indirect object only. Both are expressed by location agreement. Conceptually, the verb expresses the motion of an entity, so a gender agreement marker for the direct object should be possible. However, this argument is not expressed on the verb. The verb for 'to sell' (9b) only agrees with one of its arguments, and the verb for 'to rent' (9c) does not show any agreement marking.

(9)   a.                      b.                      c.

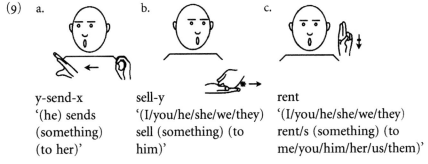

y-send-x                 sell-y                  rent
'(he) sends              '(I/you/he/she/we/they) '(I/you/he/she/we/they)
(something)              sell (something) (to     rent/s (something) (to
(to her)'                him)'                   me/you/him/her/us/them)'

For spoken languages it is often assumed that a lacking agreement morpheme is actually a zero morpheme. Such an analysis is not possible for NGT, because there are no deficit paradigms. First, for verbs such as that for 'to send' in (9a), the direct object could be referred to by gender agreement (as is the case in the

---

[9] Bos (1994) observes that signers can make use of an auxiliary to indicate the (human) referents of a transitive predicate. Logically, this auxiliary would be used when a verb agrees with only a subset or none of its arguments. However, the use of this auxiliary is not restricted to these verbs; it is also used with fully inflected verbs.

sign for 'to give'). However, it does not show agreement for the direct object. The assumption of a deficit agreement paradigm would force us in this case to posit, not one zero morpheme, but zero morphemes for the whole paradigm of possible referents. Second, anticipating the discussion on location agreement in section 7.2.7, it is not possible to indicate a paradigm at all for this type of agreement.

Explanations of argument–agreement mismatches in the signed language literature are given by phonological and morphological accounts. For instance, Zwitserlood (2003a) uses a phonological explanation, in which she assumes that non-agreement verbs or partially agreeing verbs are (partially) phonologically specified for location and/or hand configuration, in contrast to fully agreeing verbs. This phonological analysis may even have a morphological basis (see Zwitserlood 2003b), in that the location and hand configuration slots contain morphemes with specified phonological features. Therefore, these slots cannot be used for agreement morphology. An alternative analysis is provided by Meir (2002), who relates the (location) agreement possibilities to the presence of a directional morpheme (DIR) in the predicate. We will not further pursue this issue here.

### 7.2.5  Which agreement marking on which verb?

We have described two kinds of agreement in NGT, location and gender agreement. We saw that verbs can show location agreement only, as in the verbs for 'to wait' in (2) and 'to visit' in (3), or gender agreement only, as in the verb for 'to fall' (4). However, combinations of location and gender agreement are possible too, as we have seen in the verb for 'to give' in example (6). Another example of this is the verb for 'to move' in (10), where the hand configuration refers to a person (Johan) and the locations to the places involved (home and school).

(10)

view from above

school.move.animate entity.house
'(Johan) goes (home from school)'

The type of agreement marking that a verb will take for its referents can be predicted from its semantic roles. First, a note on argument structure must be made here. Usually, the semantic roles Source, Goal, and Location are not considered arguments, but adjuncts (although some verbs subcategorize for a spatial argument). However, since in signed languages it is possible to make use of space, spatial expressions play a much more prominent role than in spoken languages. Verbs that express the motion, existence, or location of a referent in space show agreement marking (location agreement) with spatial arguments. Therefore, we claim that in signed languages Source, Goal, and Location are verbal arguments. For example, the locations in (10), viz. that of the school and that of the house, are agreement markers for the Source and Goal arguments respectively.

The patterns observed in signed languages are the following: Agents, Patients, Recipients, Sources, Goals, and Locations are expressed by location agreement. Theme arguments (arguments that are in a state or location, or that are undergoing a motion: Gruber (1976); Jackendoff (1987)) are expressed by gender agreement.

(11)    Agent, Patient, Recipient, Source, Goal    → locus agreement

      Theme    → gender agreement

Although the semantic roles determine the type of agreement, we will use the grammatical notions 'subject' and 'object' when we refer to the agreement slots in the remainder of this chapter.

### 7.2.6 *Non-manual agreement*

Neidle et al. (2000) claim that there is an additional way to mark agreement in ASL, which they call non-manual agreement. This is because this kind of agreement is expressed by non-manual markers, viz. head tilt for subject agreement and eye gaze for object agreement. An example is shown in (12) below, in which the head is tilted towards the right: to the location of the subject referent. The signer's eye gaze is directed towards the left: the location of the object referent.

view from above

(12)    a.                    b.

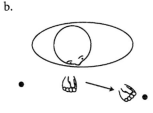

$_x$give$_y$ (something)          (Neidle et al. 2000: 65, fig. 5.1)

Neidle et al. claim that these non-manual markers have a fixed scope. Following Chomsky (1995), they assume two functional projections for agreement above VP. They further claim that the non-manual agreement markers are associated with the agreement features in the heads of these agreement projections. With this they can explain that the non-manual agreement markers start before the signing of the predicate. The subject agreement marker starts before the object agreement marker, because AgrS dominates AgrO. These markers obligatorily spread over their c-command domain. This is illustrated in (13).

(13)

$$[[ + \text{agr}_i][[ + \text{agr}_j]\text{VP}]_{\text{Agr}_O\text{P}}]_{\text{Agr}_S\text{P}} \qquad \text{(Neidle et al. 2000: 66, ex. 3)}$$

For NGT this analysis is not applicable. First, we observe that eye gaze and head tilt do not always occur in the environment of a non-agreement predicate with null arguments where they would be required. Second, if they occur in this context these non-manual markers appear not to have a fixed domain. In other words, there appears to be no systematic correlation between the expression of the non-manual marking and its presupposed scope. This is illustrated in (14).

(14)

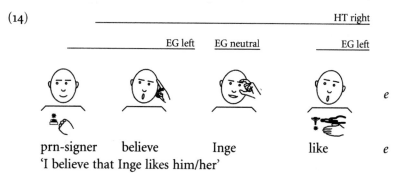

prn-signer   believe   Inge   like   e
'I believe that Inge likes him/her'

In (14) the head tilt (HT) to the right that refers to the embedded subject 'Inge' already begins on the matrix verb for 'to believe', of which 'Inge' is not the subject. The eye gaze (EG), which is towards the location of the null object to the left, occurs two times. The first occurrence starts during the matrix verb and extends over the boundary between the matrix and complement clause. The domain of the null object is not constituted by both clauses together. The second occurrence starts *during* the complement verb to which the null argument belongs, not *before* the predicate, as predicted by Neidle et al. In another instance (15), the non-manual markers are reversed: the eyes gaze to the location of the subject (left) and the head tilt is towards the right, which is the location of the null object.

(15)

she-tell-signer    prn-she        want        e    learn        know
'She$_i$ tells me that she$_i$ wants to learn to know him$_j$'

Even if we assume that the head tilt marks object agreement instead of subject agreement in this case, it is puzzling that it already appears above the matrix verb ('want'), instead of before the verb sequence 'to learn–to know' of which the null object is an argument. Thus, if the non-manual markings eye gaze and head tilt occur at all in NGT, they do not systematically mark subject and object agreement. Therefore we do not consider these markers as agreement markers.[10]

### 7.2.7  Relevant φ features

We now turn to a discussion of the relevant φ features in signed languages. Most researchers of signed languages assume that these languages have person and number features (e.g. Padden (1988) and Rathmann and Mathur (2003) for ASL, Bos (1990; 1993) for NGT, Glück and Pfau (1999) for German Sign Language, Sutton-Spence and Woll (1999) for British Sign Language). However, the presence of a grammatical category person has been questioned. With Lillo-Martin and Klima (1990) and Keller (1998) we argue that there is no formal distinction between 'persons'. We therefore claim that this category does not exist in signed languages. Furthermore, we claim that signed languages (at least, NGT) have no grammatical category number. We will first discuss the category 'person', then the category 'number'.

The person distinction in the pronominal system of signed languages has been linked to the use of locations in signing space. A sign that is directed

---

[10] For ASL, the non-manual agreement analysis appears to be somewhat problematic, too. In the first place, as Neidle et al. (2000) themselves indicate, they are not obligatory. That is, they are only obligatory in case null arguments occur with non-agreeing verbs. In the second place, Thompson and Emmorey (2003) show that eye gaze in ASL also occurs in contexts where it has no agreement interpretation, which makes it a hard task for the addressee to figure out whether it should be interpreted as agreement or not.

towards the location of the signer is taken to be the 'first person' pronoun, a sign that points to a location opposite the signer is the 'second person' pronoun, and the various other locations in signing space indicate 'third person' pronouns, as in Figures 7.1 and 7.2.

Some have claimed that the *direction* of the movement is distinctive for every person. The movement of the 'first person' pronoun is always directed towards the signer; the 'second person' pronoun points away from the signer; and any 'third person' pronoun moves towards positions at the left or at the right of the signer. However, not the movement, but rather the *location* of the referent is involved in the pronominal system. Moreover, the locations of the referents are not fixed as in Figure 7.1. Rather, the positions of the addressee and non-discourse participants vary with the discourse situation. For instance, the addressee can be next to the signer, and a non-discourse participant can be opposite the signer. Thus, it is nearly impossible to make a formal distinction between 'second person' and 'third person' pronouns.

Meier (1990) claims that ASL only has a distinction between 'first person' and 'non-first person'. However, other observations make clear that there is no

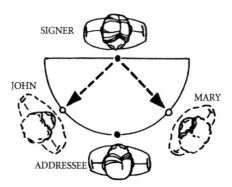

**Figure 7.1**    Reference in signing space (Lillo-Martin and Klima 1990: 193, fig. 10.2)

PRONOUN 'me'    PRONOUN 'you'    PRONOUN 'John'    PRONOUN 'Mary'

**Figure 7.2**    Person distinction in the pronominal system of ASL (Lillo-Martin and Klima 1990: 192–3, figs. 10.1, 10.2)

unique 'first person' pronominal, either. In the first place, Lillo-Martin and Klima (1990), as well as our own data, show that it is possible to assign the signer and the addressee arbitrary locations in signing space (even though this is a rather marked situation).[11] These locations can be used in further discourse in the pronominal system as well as in the verb agreement system. At the same time the physically real locations of signer and addressee can be used in the usual way for pronominal reference. It is impossible to capture this in common personal pronominal systems without adding extra information. In the second place, locations do not change along with changes in conversational perspective (Ahlgren 1990). This is illustrated by the following example. In English, if person A and person B are talking to each other and person A is speaking at the moment, the pronoun *I* will refer to person A and the pronoun *you* will refer to person B. If the conversational perspective changes, i.e. person B starts to speak, the pronoun *I* will no longer refer to person A but to person B, and the pronoun *you* refers to person A and not to person B. If person A and person B are talking with each other in NGT they will use their locations for grammatical reference. Thus, if person A is signing he will point to person B if he wants to convey the meaning of English *you.* Person B will use the same location to convey the meaning of English *I* when he takes on the conversational role of speaker. Therefore, we claim that the locations used in the pronominal system and in verb inflection are absolute. This means that a location that is linked to a referent is constant during a discourse. Thus, this type of agreement is location-deictic, not person-deictic.

For the reasons mentioned above, we argue that signed language pronouns and location agreement markers do not distinguish a grammatical category 'person'. Instead, these systems make use of a grammatical category 'location'. As stated in section 7.2.1, basically every location in signing space can be used for reference marking. If one assumes that locations are morphemes, this would mean that signed languages have an infinite set of location morphemes. It is unlikely that the lexicon would contain a set of morphemes with an infinite number of forms. The locations do not show a paradigm like the category 'person' in spoken languages, because of this infiniteness. We therefore assume that there is one abstract feature [locus], extending a proposal by Lillo-Martin and Klima (1990) for locations within the pronominal system to include the verb agreement system. Lillo-Martin and Klima argue that ASL has only one pronoun, which consists of a pointing gesture towards a location in signing space. A referent is connected to a location (an

---

[11] See Van Hoek (1996) for the same phenomenon with 'third person' pronouns in signed languages.

R-locus) in the sense of Chomsky (1981). When the referent is physically present, the R-locus is automatically coindexed with the referent. When a referent is not physically present or the signer chooses to connect it with a different location, it is assigned an arbitrary R-locus in signing space, which can be used in further discourse. Lillo-Martin and Klima assume that the association of the referents and R-loci takes place in Discourse Representation Structures (DRSs) in the sense of Kamp (1981), Heim (1982), and Roberts (1985) (in spoken languages R-indexing happens covertly, whereas in signed languages the index is visible). This analysis elegantly accounts for the referential phenomena in signed languages, not only in the pronominal system but also in the verb agreement system.

With respect to gender agreement, this type of agreement does not show person distinctions either. All discourse participants with the same gender features are expressed by the same hand configuration.

Concerning the category 'number', we claim that there is no systematic distinction between singular and plural. With respect to nouns, NGT does not take an obligatory plural marker when they refer to plural referents. In contrast to what has been claimed before (Koenen et al. 1993), plural referents are not necessarily marked by repetition of the sign. Although there are several ways for a signer to indicate plural referents, e.g. by numeral incorporation[12] or by localization of the referents in signing space, these are not systematic number markers on the noun.[13]

Regarding verbs, many languages obligatorily mark plural referents (sometimes in a portmanteau affix in which person and number features are combined). This does not hold for NGT.[14] There are several ways to mark plurality of referents, depending on the viewpoint of the signer, but these are not obligatory. These ways are illustrated in (16).

Views from above

(16)   a.        b.        c.

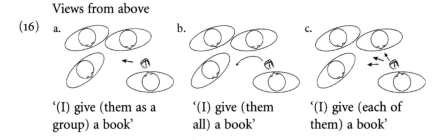

'(I) give (them as a        '(I) give (them        '(I) give (each of
group) a book'             all) a book'           them) a book'

---

[12] Numeral incorporation is the replacement of the hand configuration by a hand configuration that indicates a number. This is restricted to a subset of the nominals, viz. those that have a hand configuration that consists of an extended index finger, and to a limited set of numbers (one to ten).

[13] See Nijhof and Zwitserlood (1999).

[14] The same is argued by Keller (2000) for German Sign Language.

If the signer considers multiple referents as a group, he will use an agreement form that is in no way distinct from the 'singular' form. He will direct the verb movement towards a central location in the group of referents, as in (16a). When a signer wants to indicate which referents are intended, he incorporates the locations in signing space that have been assigned to these referents. This can be done in a sweeping movement including all of these locations, as in (16b). If the signer wants to indicate that each of the individual referents is involved, the verb is repeated and the repeated motions are directed towards the locations of all of the intended referents (16c).

Both signed and spoken languages express verb agreement, but in different ways. Agreement markers in spoken languages contain person, number, and gender features, whereas those in signed languages contain gender and locus features. For these reasons, we conclude that the universal set of φ features, consisting of features for person, number, case, and gender, that has been assumed so far needs to be extended with a locus feature. Thus, φ features have to be distributed over spoken and signed languages, as in Table 7.3.

TABLE 7.3. φ features for spoken and signed languages

| Spoken languages | Signed languages |
| --- | --- |
| Person | – |
| Number | – |
| Case | – |
| Gender | Gender |
| – | Locus |

As far as we are aware, locus features are not attested in the verb agreement systems of spoken languages. The fact that locus is one of the most prominent φ features in signed languages may be due to the visual-gestural articulatory-perceptual channel (as opposed to the oral-auditory channel of spoken languages), or, in other words, due to the use of signing space in signed languages to express spatial relations, pronominals, and agreement.

### 7.2.8 *Summary*

In contrast to what is known about agreement in the world's languages, agreement morphology in NGT is not a regular mapping of the arguments of the verb: some verbs agree with all of their arguments, other verbs agree with only a subset of their arguments, and a third group of verbs does not show any agreement at all. We have shown that no zero agreement morphemes can be assumed in NGT. Furthermore, we have argued that the grammatical categories person and number do not play a role, and we have modified the universal set of φ features by adding the locus feature.

## 7.3 Licensing of null arguments

In this section we will discuss the licensing possibilities of null arguments in languages as a background for the discussion of the licensing of null arguments in NGT. We will discuss several proposals from the literature to account for null arguments. These can be divided into two types: sentence-internal accounts and discourse-based ones. But first we will give some information about contexts in which null arguments appear in NGT.

### 7.3.1 Null arguments in NGT

In NGT, arguments can, but need not, be expressed overtly. Not only is it possible to leave the subject of the sentence unexpressed, but the object(s) can be left unexpressed, too. Null arguments occur in the presence of agreement, as in (17).

(17)    a. *e*                           *e*

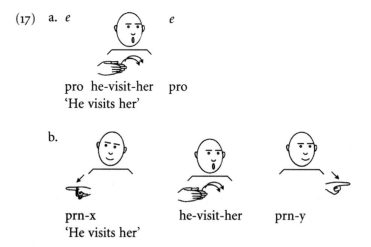

pro  he-visit-her    pro
'He visits her'

b.

prn-x                he-visit-her       prn-y
'He visits her'

Furthermore, null arguments also occur in the absence of agreement. The only restriction seems to be that the referents are clear from the context (linguistic or deictic) as in (18).

(18)   (Context:   Does Alinda like that skirt?)
       Answer:   $e_i$

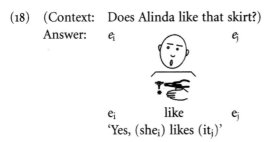

       $e_i$          like          $e_j$
       'Yes, (she$_i$) likes (it$_j$)'

Interestingly, this phenomenon is optional in signed languages. In other words, there is not necessarily a difference in emphasis or focus, as in Spanish, whether an argument is expressed overtly or not. Compare (17) with (19).

(19)   a. *e*        visita a   María                        (Spanish)
          'He/she   visits     María'
       b. Él        visita a   María
          '*He*    visits     María'

Structures such as (17) might, at first glance, be considered to be pronominal argument phenomena (Jelinek 1984; Chapter 9 below). That is, agreement morphemes are considered to be the arguments of the predicate, whereas overt DPs are considered adjuncts. However, this analysis is not possible for NGT. First, verb inflection cannot be regarded as representing the verb's arguments, because of the occurrence of null arguments in the absence of agreement. Thus, in such cases there is no element that represents the arguments. Second, DPs in NGT cannot be analysed as adjuncts. Evidence for this comes from the fact that the word order is fixed. Although variation is possible in the order of the verb and the object, the subject must be expressed sentence-initially, i.e. the NGT basic word order is SOV or SVO.[15] Hence there is a structural relation between the subject and the object. Moreover, in contrast to pronominal argument languages, DPs in NGT cannot be discontinuous. In other words, NGT is a configurational language or, in terms of Jelinek, a lexical argument language.

### 7.3.2 *Sentence-internal accounts*

Several proposals have been made in the literature to explain the occurrence of null arguments. Some proposals account for null arguments within the sentence, whereas other proposals seek a sentence-external explanation. We will start with a discussion of the former. The possibility of null arguments

---

[15] Coerts (1994a; 1994b) claims that the basic word order in NGT is SOV. Our data suggest that it can be either SOV or SVO.

in a language is often explained by the occurrence of a rich agreement paradigm in that language (Taraldsen 1980; Chomsky 1981; Rizzi 1982). It is argued that in such languages null arguments are permitted because the agreement is rich enough to identify or license the null arguments: the pro-drop parameter. Italian and Spanish are the most cited examples of this type of language.

We saw that agreement in signed languages is extremely rich, but only with those verbs that show agreement. This is especially the case in locus agreement, because the morphemes have unique reference as a result of overt indexing (see section 7.2.7). Ambiguities of the following sort that could arise in Spanish do not exist in signed languages with locus agreement. In a Spanish discourse in which Juan and Enrique have been introduced, the sentence in (20) would cause ambiguity, since it would not be clear which of them (or perhaps even another person) has visited María. The third person agreement on *visitar* can refer to any third person referent, including Juan and Enrique.

(20)   *e* visita    María                                        (Spanish)
       'he/she visits    María'

In a similar discourse in NGT, María, Juan, and Enrique each have their own R-locus in signing space: Juan is localized at location x, María at location y, and Enrique at location z. The NGT verb for 'to visit' starts at the locus of the referent that visits María and ends at the locus of María, and thereby unambiguously indicates who exactly is the one who visits María (see (21)).[16]

(21)   a.                              b.

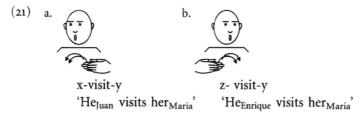

       x-visit-y                     z- visit-y
       'He$_{Juan}$ visits her$_{María}$'    'He$_{Enrique}$ visits her$_{María}$'

Agreement in signed languages would thus be rich enough to identify or license null arguments. In NGT, however, null arguments can also occur in environments where there is no agreement, as in (18). From this we must conclude that agreement cannot identify or license all null arguments. Exactly

---

[16] This does not imply that there are no ambiguities in signed language pronominal marking. Ambiguities are of a slightly different kind.

this point has been part of proposals made by Lillo-Martin (1986; 1991) for ASL, to which we will turn in section 7.4.1.[17]

A sentence-internal proposal for the licensing of null arguments in the absence of agreement (e.g. in Chinese) comes from Jaeggli and Safir (1989a). Their Morphological Uniformity Condition (MUC) states that null arguments, in this case null subjects, are permitted in languages that have a morphologically uniform paradigm, i.e. a paradigm that consists of either only uninflected verbs or only inflected verbs. Obviously, the MUC cannot account for the NGT phenomena either, since NGT has agreement *and* non-agreement verbs. As a matter of fact, analyses that make use of verbal paradigms (e.g. Rohrbacher 1994; Speas 1994; Koeneman 2000) cannot account for the data from signed languages at all, since, as we have seen in 7.2.7 above, it is impossible to state a paradigm of verb locus agreement.

Summarizing, not all null arguments in signed languages can be licensed sentence-internally by agreement. We will discuss additional, discourse-based licensing strategies in the next section.

### 7.3.3 *Null arguments and discourse*

Huang (1984) was the first to link the occurrence of null arguments to discourse. His analysis is based mainly on data from Chinese, a language that does not have verb agreement. He proposes a special account for null arguments in discourse-oriented languages such as Chinese, in contrast to sentence-oriented languages such as English. According to him a null argument is either pro or a variable. Pro is coindexed with the closest nominal element (Generalized Control Rule).[18] The nominal element can be a DP or an agreement marker. Variables, on the other hand, are traces left by movement of a zero topic to a sentence-initial topic position. Huang assumes that at LF' there is a rule which coindexes such an empty topic with an appropriate preceding topic made available by the previous discourse or pragmatic context. Examples of both analyses are presented in (22) and (23).

---

[17] Recall that in section 7.2.6 we discussed the proposal by Neidle et al. (2000) about non-manual agreement. This proposal was made to account for the occurrence of null arguments in the absence of manual agreement: null arguments are, in their analysis, *always* licensed by agreement, either manual or non-manual. However, as discussed in section 7.2.6, we refute their analysis.

[18] Closest is defined by Huang (1984) as follows: A is closer to B than C is iff A c-commands B but C does not c-command B. Furthermore, for two nodes A and C, both of which c-command B, A is closer to B than C is if A but not C occurs within the same clause as B, or if A is separated from B by fewer clause boundaries than C is.

(22)  The null argument is pro:

a. Zhangsan$_i$    xiwang    [$e_i$    keyi    kanjian    Lisi]
    Zhangsan    hope        can    see        Lisi
    'Zhangsan hopes that (he$_i$) can see Lisi'

b. * Zhangsan$_i$    xiwang    [Lisi    keyi    kanjian    $e_i$]
    Zhangsan    hope    Lisi    can    see
    'Zhangsan hopes that Lisi can see (him$_i$)' (Huang 1984 : 538, ex. 22)

(23)  The null argument is a variable:

[$_{Top}e_i$],    [Zhangsan    shuo    [Lisi    bu    renshi $e_i$]]
        Zhangsan    say        Lisi    not    know
'Zhangsan says that Lisi didn't know him' (Huang 1984: 542, ex. 34).

In (22a) we see that the subject of the embedded sentence can be pro (in Chinese the embedded subject is the only argument that can be pro), because its content can be recovered by the matrix subject which is the closest nominal element. An object in an embedded sentence cannot be recovered by the same process, because there is a closer possible antecedent, viz. the subject of the embedded clause. Coindexation with this antecedent results in a violation of principle B of the Binding Theory, which renders the clause ungrammatical (22b). (23), in which the object is not bound by the matrix subject but by an empty topic, is grammatical.

Huang links his null topic analysis to a more general parameter that distinguishes between discourse-oriented and sentence-oriented languages. Discourse-oriented languages have the following characteristics (Tsao 1977 cited in Huang 1984): (a) they have discourse anaphora, viz. the anaphor can be bound in the discourse; (b) they allow Topic NP Deletion, viz. deletion of the content of a topic can take place under identity with a topic in the previous discourse (thus creating a topic chain); and (c) they have topic-prominent structures. However, linking the null topic account to the discourse-oriented versus sentence-oriented parameter is not unproblematic. As outlined by Authier (1988), null objects in KiNande (a Bantu language spoken in Zaire) that occur in the absence of verbal object agreement should be analysed as variables. Yet KiNande conforms to only one of the three characteristics of discourse-oriented languages: it has discourse anaphora but it has no rule of deleting NP topics that results in a topic chain, and it has no topic-prominence structures. The last-mentioned characteristic poses yet another problem. Authier suggests that the topic-prominence characteristic fails to distinguish between sentence-oriented and discourse-oriented languages in general, because sentence-oriented languages like English can have topic-prominence structures, too. Thus, it appears that the assumption of a parameter that links the discourse-oriented versus sentence-oriented status of languages to the possibility of having null topics is not correct. Therefore, we adopt an alternative view on this possibility, namely the rule of Predication parameter that is proposed by Raposo (1986) on independent grounds.

Raposo (1986) formalizes Huang's proposal based on data from European Portuguese. In European Portuguese null direct objects occur, but the language has no verbal object agreement. The content of these null objects is recoverable from the linguistic or pragmatic context. Raposo claims that null objects are variables that result from moving an empty category to spec,CP, where it becomes an operator and locally A'-binds the null object. Evidence for a movement analysis comes from null object constructions that obey Subjacency (e.g. the Sentential Subject Constraint), that induce ungrammaticalities under violations of the Doubly Filled COMP filter, and that allow parasitic gaps (*pg*), as illustrated in (24).

(24)    (Context: People are talking about a new IBM personal computer.)
   a. *Que a IBM venda $e_i$ a particulares surpreende-me
      'That IBM sells $e_i$ to private individuals surprises me'
   b. *[Para qual dos filhos]$_j$ é que a Maria comprou $e_i$ $t_j$ ?
      'For which of her children did Mary buy $e_i$ ?'
   c. Vi $e_i$ na TV sem reconhecer $pg_i$
      'I saw $e_i$ on TV without recognizing $pg_i$' (Raposo 1986: 382–4, exx. 18, 22, 23a)

Raposo claims in addition that a null topic is base-generated outside CP and that it is assigned an arbitrary index that differs from the index assigned to the operator and its trace, as represented in (25) (adapted from Raposo 1986: 380, ex. 15).

(25)    [$_{TOP}e_i$] [$_{CP}$OP$_j$ [a Joana viu $t_j$  na  TV  ontem]]
                          Joana saw  on  TV  yesterday
        'Joana saw *e* on TV yesterday'

According to Raposo (1986: 385), 'The discourse or context-bound interpretation of these sentences is thus provided by this rule, identifying the index of the zero topic with the index of the null operator and the trace it A'-binds, deriving a representation in the LF' component of the grammar.' Raposo suggests the parameter in (26) to distinguish between languages like European Portuguese and Chinese on the one hand and languages like English and French on the other.

(26)   The rule of Predication of the LF' module of the grammar may
       (may not) refer to a pragmatic topic (Raposo 1986: 385, ex. 24).

The parameter in (26) refers to special properties of the rule of Predication. In particular, in European Portuguese and Chinese the rule is open to pragmatics, viz. LF' is directly linked to pragmatics, whereas this is not the case in English and French. Thus, the rule of Predication appears to be independently motivated and does not encounter the problems Huang's parameter was confronted with. Therefore, for signed languages we will adopt Raposo's analysis, in particular the parameter he proposes for the licensing and identification of null arguments.

## 7.4 An integrated account for null arguments in signed languages

### 7.4.1 *Two identification procedures for null arguments*

Like NGT, ASL has a set of verbs that take agreement markers, but also verbs that do not have agreement markers. Both types of verb can, however, occur with null arguments. Null arguments can be both subjects and objects. Lillo-Martin (1986; 1991) discusses the licensing and identification of the null arguments in ASL, basing her analyses on Huang (1984). She claims that in ASL two identification procedures of null arguments are at work. In the first place, there is identification by agreement. Since ASL has subject and object agreement, both subject and object null arguments can be identified by the rich agreement system. Where agreement is present, the null argument is pro. Pro obeys the Generalized Control Rule: the empty pronominal is coindexed with the verb agreement. If no agreement is present but there is another nominal element present, then pro can be coindexed with that element, as is the case with null embedded subjects.

In the second place, Lillo-Martin argues that null arguments that occur in an environment where no agreement or other nominal element is present are variables left by movement of an empty or an overt topic which is coindexed with an appropriate preceding topic (Huang 1984).[19] She shows that these arguments must indeed be wh-traces, since they obey principle C of Binding Theory, Subjacency and the Empty Category Principle (ECP). Since ASL is a discourse-oriented language, this second identification device is permitted.

---

[19] In signed languages, topics are marked by several non-manual and manual characteristics, such as raised eyebrows, a lowered chin, a hold or lengthening of the sign (see Coerts 1992 and references cited there; Aarons 1994 for ASL). Note that we have not found a distinction between moved and base-generated topics, in contrast to Aarons.

The occurrence of two different null arguments in ASL and Lillo-Martin's analyses are illustrated by the following part of a signed narrative (adapted from Lillo-Martin 1991: 81, ex. 53),[20] in which the daughter is the topic of the narrative.

(27)   ONE   DAY,   $_a$DAUGHTER   NOTHING   #D-O,   $_a e$   DECIDE   $_a e$

WALK   $_{b-c}$WOODS.   $_a e$   $_b$WALK$_c$,   $_d$PRONOUN   $_a e$   SEE$_d$   $_d$FLOWER,

$_a e$   PICK-UP$_d$   $_d$ *pro,*   $_a e$   SEE$_e$   $_e$WATERFALL,   $_a e$   $_c$WALK$_e$, $_a e$

FASCINATED$_e$   $_e$*pro,*   $_a e$   LOST$^{[resultative]}$.

'One day, the daughter had nothing to do, so (she) decided to take a walk in the woods. (She) walked around, and saw some flowers there, and picked (them) up; (she) saw a waterfall, and walked (near it); and (she) was so fascinated (by it) that (she) became lost.'

Thus, in (27) two object pros occur that are identified by verb agreement (as can be seen from the corresponding subscripts): the null objects in the clauses '$_a e$ PICK-UP$_d$ $_d$*pro*' and '$_a e$ FASCINATED$_e$ $_e$*pro*'. All other null arguments refer to the daughter who is the topic of the narrative. These latter empty categories mark the sites of a topic that is deleted under identity with a topic in a preceding sentence, resulting in a topic chain. The empty categories are called zero topics or variables.

Lillo-Martin's approach appears to account in a structured way for the ASL facts. We will adopt her account in our analysis of the NGT facts, but suggest some improvements in order to account for the following issues. First, Lillo-Martin argues for ASL to be discourse-oriented. However, in section 7.3.3 we saw that there are several problems with linking the discourse-oriented parameter with the proposed characteristics of this parameter and with the identification and licensing of null arguments. Therefore, identification should instead be formalized within the proposal by Raposo (1986).

Second, as we claimed in section 7.2.3, some verbs take a gender agreement marker.[21] Thus, agreement may identify more null arguments than was previously thought. For example, in the ASL predicate for 'to walk', occurring three times in (27), the hand configuration (probably) reflects the characteristic 'legged' of the argument 'daughter', and, as a consequence, is

---

[20] We have inserted e for all empty variables and pro for all empty pronominals, as proposed by Lillo-Martin (1991).

[21] Lillo-Martin mentions the type of verb that has these markers (usually called 'spatial verbs' in the literature), but regards only the loci in these verbs as possible agreement markers, not the hand configurations.

a gender agreement marker.[22] This means that the three null arguments occurring with the predicate for 'to walk' are probably pros licensed by gender agreement morphology, instead of empty variables (as proposed by Lillo-Martin).[23]

### 7.4.2 Null arguments in NGT

Like Lillo-Martin, we claim that null arguments in the presence of agreement are pros that are identified by the $\varphi$ features of the agreement marker. As discussed above, we consider both locus and gender morphemes as agreement markers that can identify or license null arguments. For NGT null arguments that occur in the absence of agreement, we adopt Raposo's (1986) analysis outlined above. This means that, in the case of a transitive verb that shows agreement for its subject only and where both arguments are null, the null subject is pro (the content of which is recovered by the verb agreement), while the null object is a variable left by movement of an empty category to spec,CP, where it becomes an operator. The operator and the trace that it A'-binds are linked to the pragmatic topic by a rule of Predication at LF'. Below we will illustrate some possibilities of null arguments in NGT.

(28)    (Context: Inge has R-locus x, and Roland has R-locus y)

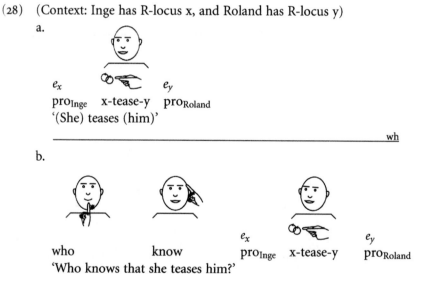

    a.

$e_x$               $e_y$
$\text{pro}_{\text{Inge}}$  x-tease-y  $\text{pro}_{\text{Roland}}$
'(She) teases (him)'

    b.

who        know    $e_x$           $e_y$
                        $\text{pro}_{\text{Inge}}$  x-tease-y  $\text{pro}_{\text{Roland}}$
'Who knows that she teases him?'

---

[22] Unfortunately, from the gloss notation it cannot be ascertained whether this hand configuration is actually used.

[23] Lacking subjacency data on this issue from ASL, we cannot prove that the null arguments occurring with these types of verb are true pros.

The verb in (28a) shows agreement for its subject and object. The null arguments in the sentence are pros, licensed by the verb agreement. This can be concluded from (28b), where sentence (28a) is embedded under a wh-island without violating subjacency. In contrast to this, the null argument in (29a) is an empty variable, viz. a wh-trace left by movement of an empty category to spec,CP.

(29)     (Context: Inge has R-locus x, at the signer's right.)

a.

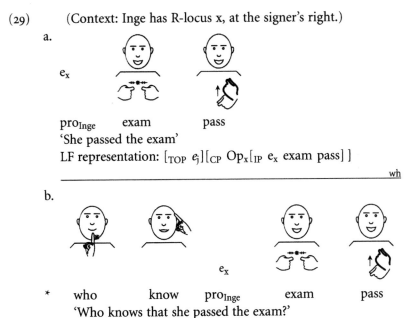

pro$_{Inge}$     exam          pass
'She passed the exam'
LF representation: $[_{TOP}\ e_j][_{CP}\ Op_x[_{IP}\ e_x\ exam\ pass]\ ]$

wh

b.

*     who          know     pro$_{Inge}$     exam          pass
'Who knows that she passed the exam?'

In (29a) the verb carries no agreement marking that licenses the empty subject. According to the analysis in section 7.3.3, the empty subject is licensed by an empty operator. The rule of Predication links the operator and its trace to an empty topic. This is corroborated by (30b), where sentence (30a) embedded under a wh-island violates subjacency.

Our analysis of hand configurations as gender agreement is confirmed by the fact that the null arguments referred to by gender agreement are pros, licensed by this type of agreement, as is shown in (30).

(30)   a.

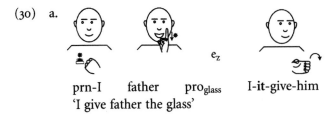

prn-I     father     pro$_{glass}$     I-it-give-him
'I give father the glass'

b.

Marijke      know      who      pro   father   I-it-give-him
'Marijke knows who gives father the glass'

Since the sentence in (30b) does not show a subjacency violation, the embedded empty direct object must be pro. It is licensed by gender agreement.

### 7.4.3 A note on topicality

In the case of more than one null argument in the absence of agreement, we have to assume that a clause has more than one empty operator and more than one null topic. Although sentences with multiple topics are not common in Germanic languages, other languages allow at least two topics, such as Chinese (Huang 1984). Sentences with two topics are also attested in ASL (Lillo-Martin 1986; 1991; Aarons 1994; Neidle et al. 2000). This is possible in NGT too, as can be seen in the examples in (31) and (32).

(31) ——————————————— topic  ——————————————— topic

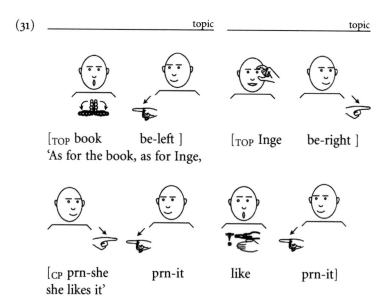

[TOP book      be-left ]    [TOP Inge      be-right ]
'As for the book, as for Inge,

[CP prn-she      prn-it      like      prn-it]
she likes it'

(32)

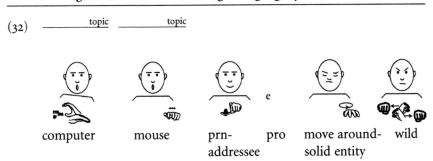

computer    mouse    prn-        pro    move around-    wild
                     addressee          solid entity

'As for the computer, as for the mouse, you move (it) around so wildly!' (*NSDSK* 1999)

This infers that two empty topics can be assumed as well. Along the lines of Rizzi (1997) we can assume furthermore that there are two functional projections above IP instead of one CP (for expository reasons we call them both CP). Both empty operators occupy a spec,CP position. The LF representation of a sentence with two null topics looks like (33).

(33)

$[_{TOP}e_i][_{TOP}e_j][_{CP}Op_k[Op_m[t_k$ ⟨face image⟩ $t_m]]]$

$e_k$        like        $e_m$

'(Inge) likes (the book)'

It is as yet unclear whether sentences with three null arguments and no agreement occur in NGT. In the current analysis we would have to assume three (empty) topics in these sentences. Since we have not come accross such sentences in our data, we will refrain from discussing this possibility here.[24]

### 7.4.4 *Determining the recoverability mechanisms*

As discussed in 7.2.4, most verbs in NGT do not show agreement marking. Other verbs take agreement markers, but some of these agree only with a subset of their arguments. The spoken languages treated in the literature on the occurrence of null arguments show more consistent agreement patterns. This means that in identification and licensing mechanisms for null arguments these languages are more straightforward as well. Null subjects are licensed either by subject agreement or by the matrix subject or a null

---

[24] Neidle et al. (2000) reject the possibility of having three topics for ASL.

operator. Null objects are identified either by object agreement, or by a null operator. For instance, Campos (1986) argued for Spanish that null indefinite objects are variables, because Spanish has no object agreement. We know that subjects in Spanish are licensed and identified by subject agreement. Thus, two mechanisms can be at work in Spanish to recover the content of two null arguments of the same verb in (34b).

(34)    a. ¿Compraste e café?
         pro buy-2P    coffee
         'Did (you) buy coffee?'
      b. Sí, e   compré *e*
         yes, pro buy-1P.PAST t
         'Yes, (I) bought (some)' (adapted from Campos 1986: 354, ex. 2)

In signed languages the licensing and identification mechanisms are not as straightforward, since they depend on the agreement properties of the verb. This was shown in (28) and (29), where the null subject was licensed by agreement and a (null) topic, respectively. This may indicate that the null arguments in signed languages have to be identified by the closest possible element that can function as the referent.

We propose an identification procedure of null arguments (pros and variables) using the heuristic identification procedure as suggested by Huang (1995). Huang gives a discourse-pragmatic solution for the identification of null arguments. A null subject or null object is identified by a sentential topic if such a topic is available. Generally, a c-commanding antecedent is preferred over a non-c-commanding antecedent. But if there is no topic in the sentence that qualifies as a possible identifier, the previous clause will be examined for a possible identifier, until the topmost clause. If there is still no possible identifier, the null argument will be interpreted as 'arbitrary'.[25] Huang's analysis stresses the fact that the interpretation of the null argument should be in conformity with our knowledge of the world. Such an account works well with respect to the recoverability of multiple variables.

The proposed identification hierarchy is situated at LF and LF'. We assume that LF' forms the last stage towards pragmatics within LF. At LF, a null argument seeking to identify with a referent starts out at the left-hand side of the hierarchy. The null argument first looks for agreement for its identification. If agreement is not available, it will go on looking for a local subject or a local object. In these three cases, the null argument is a pro. If these identifiers

---

[25] As distinct from pro$_{arb}$.

are not available, the null argument will look for an appropriate sentential topic. In this case, the null argument is a variable, bound by the sentential
topic. If a sentential topic is not available either, the null argument is
identified by a discourse topic in the following way. The variable is bound
by an empty operator. For every variable-empty operator chain there is a null
topic that is linked with a discourse topic. The rule of Predication works in
combination with the right-hand part of the identification hierarchy. It makes
sure that the indices of a zero topic linked to a discourse topic are identified
with the right variable-null operator chain. If there is no discourse topic
available either, the null topic of a variable-empty operator chain is identified
with the speaker, or it gets an arbitrary interpretation otherwise. In all cases,
world knowledge plays an important role.

(35)   Identification hierarchy of a null argument
       agreement < local subject < local object < sentential topic <
       discourse topic < speaker < arbitrary interpretation
       / world knowledge

   We have discussed two types of null argument in NGT: pros and variables.
The type of null argument depends on the agreement possibilities of the verb.
Null arguments are recovered according to the universal identification hier-
archy in (35), using the closest possible identifier.

## 7.5 Concluding remarks

In this chapter we have proposed that signed languages may have two types of
agreement: locus agreement and gender agreement. The distribution of these
two agreement types among agreement verbs can be predicted by the verb
semantics. The Theme argument of motion verbs is expressed by gender
agreement only. All other arguments (Agent, Patient, Recipient, Source,
Goal, and Location) are always expressed by locus agreement. Locus agreement is realized by directing the movement and/or orientation of a verb
towards the loci of the referents in signing space, or by expressing the verb
at the locus of a referent in signing space. Gender agreement is realized in
signed languages by hand configuration morphemes on the predicate. On the
basis of the class of hand configurations that is used in NGT gender agreement, we have proposed a first characterization of this type of agreement by
means of the features [animate], [legged], [straight], [small], [flat], [volume],
and [control]. We did not adopt the analysis of Neidle et al. (2000) that the
non-manual marking that in some cases accompanies verbs is agreement for
NGT.

We also claimed that the φ features for person and number do not play a role in verb agreement in signed languages. Instead we proposed that the relevant φ features in signed languages are locus and gender. The universal set of φ features should be extended in order to include the locus feature as well.

With regard to verbs in signed languages, we demonstrated that the current classification of verbs in signed languages in agreement verbs on the one hand and non-agreement verbs on the other is not sufficiently fine-grained. Besides agreement verbs and non-agreement verbs, a third set of verbs should be recognized with predicates that show agreement for some arguments of their θ structure only.

We showed that all arguments of every verb from every class can be null in the right context. From this we concluded, with Lillo-Martin (1986; 1991) for ASL, that agreement is not the only mechanism that is active in signed languages to recover the content of null arguments. We adopted Lillo-Martin's analysis for two kinds of null argument in signed languages, viz. pros and variables, and extended her analysis to verbs with an 'incomplete' agreement pattern. As opposed to Lillo-Martin, we do not link the null topic analysis to the parameter that distinguishes between discourse-oriented and sentence-oriented languages, as was done first in Huang (1984), because of problems concerning the characteristics that differentiate between these types of language. Instead, we adopted Raposo's (1986) proposal and associate the null topics in NGT to the rule of Predication parameter. The rule of Predication has to be assumed on independent grounds to account for the interpretation of constructions such as purposive clauses and relative clauses (Chomsky 1980; 1982). Raposo parametrizes this rule so that it either can or cannot refer to a pragmatic topic.

Although our conclusions from section 7.2 are not in accordance with the common analysis of agreement phenomena in signed languages, we would like to generalize our conclusions to most signed languages that have been investigated until now, on the basis of what is reported in the literature about these languages with respect to the use of signing space for verb agreement and the different verb types that occur.[26] Unfortunately, this same literature

---

[26] See Bergman and Wallin (1985) and Wallin (1996) for Swedish Sign Language; Bos (1990) for NGT; Bouchard and Dubuisson (1995) for Quebec Sign Language; Collins-Ahlgren (1990) for Thai Sign Language; Corazza (1990) and Pizzuto et al. (1990) for Italian Sign Language; Engberg-Pedersen and Pedersen (1985) and Engberg-Pedersen (1993) for Danish Sign Language; Fourestier (1999) for Catalan Sign Language; Hoemann et al. (1985) for Brazilian Sign Language; Glück and Pfau (1999) and Keller (1998) for German Sign Language; Meir (1998) for Israeli Sign Language; Oviedo (1999) for Colombian Sign Language; Schmaling (2000) for Hausa Sign Language; Sutton-Spence and Woll (1999) for British Sign Language; Vasishta et al. (1985) for Indian Sign Language; and Vermeerbergen (1996) for Flemish Sign Language.

does not discuss the occurrence of null arguments, except for the literature on ASL. Therefore, we are slightly reserved in generalizing our conclusions from section 7.4 to all signed languages. We would instead like to present them here as analyses for NGT (and ASL) only, which still need to be verified for other signed languages.

# 8

# 'Arbitrary' Pro and the Theory of Pro-Drop

PATRICIA CABREDO HOFHERR

Since Rizzi's influential work (1986a) on pro-drop, it has been generally assumed that null subject pronouns pattern together depending on their θ-role. The idea is that null pronouns bearing a full θ-role need more content identification than null pronouns bearing a quasi-θ-role or no θ-role at all (section 8.1).

In what follows I will discuss evidence showing that the possibility of pro-drop is not directly dependent on the θ-role borne by the pronoun (section 8.2). In particular I present data from different languages[1] that allow null third-person pronouns with so-called arbitrary reference even though anaphoric third-person argumental pro is not available.

In order to account for the split between arbitrary and anaphoric null pronouns I propose a modification of Rizzi's theory of pro-drop. I argue that anaphoric and non-anaphoric pro should be distinguished, and I propose that the two types of pro-drop are content-identified by two different types of agreement (section 8.3).

Finally, in section 8.4, I examine some predictions of the present analysis.

I want to thank Ildikó Tóth for many discussions on arbitrary pronominals. I am indebted to Jean-Marie Marandin and two anonymous reviewers for many comments on an earlier version of this work, which have led to significant improvements. I particularly want to thank Brenda Laca for her detailed comments. I am very grateful to Nisrine Al-Zahre, Nora Boneh, Gilles Boyé, Adil El Ghali, Ora Matushansky, and Kristiina Saarinen for help with their native languages. All errors and misinterpretations are my responsibility.

[1] In the examples, the languages are indicated as follows: Bav= Bavarian, Fi= Finnish, Fr= French, Ge= German, Gr= Greek, Ice= Icelandic, It= Italian, MH= Modern Hebrew, Sp= Spanish, Ru= Russian. The following abbreviations are used in the glosses: m(asculine), f(eminine), fut(ure), acc(usative), inf(initive), gen(itive), par(titive), ela(tive), neg(ation), pres(ent); sg=singular, pl=plural.

## 8.1 Rizzi's theory of pro-drop

Since Rizzi (1986a) it has been generally accepted that null pronouns are subject to two separate licensing requirements, formal licensing and content identification.

(1)  a.  Formal licensing: pro is governed by $X_y$
         (where X is a governing head of type y).
     b.  Content identification: Let X be the licensing head of an occurrence of pro: then pro has the grammatical specification of the features on X coindexed with it. (Rizzi 1986a: 519–20)

Rizzi further points out that languages do not necessarily allow pro-drop for all types of subject pronouns (partial pro-drop). In particular, there are languages that have null subject pronouns with weather predicates, but not with referential subjects. Rizzi proposes that the possibility of having a null pronoun is dependent on the θ-role and distinguishes three types of pro-drop:

(2)  Three types of pro-drop (Rizzi 1986a)
     a.  referential pro: null pronouns bearing a full θ-role;
     b.  quasi-argumental pro: null pronouns bearing a quasi-θ-role;
     c.  expletive pro: null pronouns bearing no θ-role.

According to Rizzi's theory of pro-drop, the difference between these three types of null pronoun lies in their feature content. For referential pro to be licensed, the features [person] and [number] have to be identified. For the content identification[2] of quasi-argumental pro it is sufficient to identify the [number] feature, while for expletive pro no features have to be identified.

(3)  Content identification (Rizzi 1986a)
     a.  referential: identify the feature [person] and [number];
     b.  quasi-arguments: identify the feature [number];
     c.  expletives: no features need to be identified.

Rizzi notes that any language capable of identifying the feature content of referential null subjects should also allow null pronouns with fewer features

---

[2]  See Tóth (2000) for a detailed discussion of the difference between *content assignment* to pro and *content identification* of pro. In Toth's terms the present analysis assumes content assigment to a formally licensed null pronoun. Since this distinction does not bear on the following discussion, I will retain Rizzi's term 'content identification' in what follows.

and therefore admit quasi-argumental and expletive pro-drop. Rizzi's theory of content identification therefore predicts an implicational hierarchy among the three types of pro-drop.

(4)  Rizzi's pro-drop hierarchy
     referential pro  →   quasi-argumental pro  →   expletive pro
     full θ-role          quasi-θ-role              no θ-role

Rizzi's proposal has been the starting point for many studies of pro-drop systems in typologically diverse languages. These studies have led to some modifications of his original proposal. In particular, it has been pointed out that in Finnish and Modern Hebrew the referential pronouns are split into two classes with respect to pro-drop: first and second person pronouns can be null, while the third person pronouns bearing a full θ-role have to be lexicalized (see e.g. Holmberg and Nikanne (1999; 2000) for Finnish and Borer (1980) for Modern Hebrew).

In order to account for these pro-drop patterns, refinements of Rizzi's licensing conditions for referential pro have been proposed (see e.g. Holmberg and Nikanne (1994) for Finnish, Shlonsky (1997) for Modern Hebrew, and Vainikka and Levy (1999) for a comparison of both languages).

Less attention has been paid to a split among the referential third person pronouns with respect to pro-drop. In what follows, I will examine the behaviour of antecedentless third person null pronouns (so-called 'arbitrary pro'),[3] and I will present data from four languages showing that these pronouns are clearly different from anaphoric third person pronouns with respect to pro-drop.

## 8.2  'Arbitrary' pro-drop in full theta positions

The data presented in this section show that arbitrary third person pronouns may differ from anaphoric third person pronouns with respect to pro-drop. I will discuss four languages with partial pro-drop systems: Modern Hebrew, Finnish, Russian, and Icelandic.

All four languages have quasi-argumental pro-drop: as the following examples show, the subject of weather predicates is null.

---

[3] Following the terminology familiar from the literature, I use the term 'arbitrary pronoun' to refer to pronouns without an antecedent. It must be stressed, however, that the term 'arbitrary pro' for non-anaphoric null pronouns is misleading, since (i) non-anaphoric readings do not form a homogeneous class and (ii) non-anaphoric null pronouns clearly differ from uncontrolled PRO (arbitrary PRO): see the discussion in section 8.3.2 below.

(5)  a. Kar                          (MH; Shlonsky 1997: ex. 7–30a)
        cold
        'It is cold'
     b. Sataa⁴                       (Fi)
        rains
        'It is raining'
     c. Segodnja xolodno/teplo   (Ru)
        today      cold/warm
        'Today it is cold/warm'
     d. Rigndi   igaer?            (Ice; quasi-argumental pro)
        rained   yesterday
        'Did it rain yesterday?'

With respect to referential pro-drop the four languages differ. Icelandic and Russian do not have referential null subjects (see Holmberg and Platzack (1995) for Icelandic and Franks (1995 and references) for Russian).⁵ Finnish, in contrast, has partial referential pro-drop: it allows first and second person null subject pronouns, while anaphoric third person pronouns have to be lexical (see Holmberg and Nikanne 1994).

(6)  a.   (Minä)  puhun     suomea (Fi)
          (I)     speak.1sg Finnish
     b. * (Hän)   puhuu     suomea
          (s)he   speaks.3sg Finnish
     c. * (He)    puhuvat   suomea
          they    speak.3pl Finnish

The most complex pattern is observed in Modern Hebrew, where the possibility of pro-drop varies with the tense of the verb. The present tense, historically derived from a participial form marked for number and gender only, does not license first, second, or third person pro-drop (see Borer 1980; Shlonsky 1997). The past and future forms, in contrast, are inflected for person, number, and gender and allow null first and second person subjects,

---

⁴ In Holmberg and Nikanne (1994), the use of a subject *se* is indicated as optional with weather verbs. My Finnish informant does not accept the subject *se* with weather verbs. She marginally accepts *se* if the weather verb is embedded under an emphatic expression. The alternation zero/*se* might therefore be comparable to a phenomenon that is observed in French and German where the subject of weather predicates can alternate with a deictic expression under emphasis: *il/ça pleut* (Fr), *es/das regnet* (Ge), 'it/that rains'.
⁵ Null subjects are possible in spoken Russian; these null surface subjects behave like null topics and not like null pronouns (cf. Matushansky 1998).

while third person subjects have to be lexical (unless they are controlled by an antecedent in a superordinate clause; see Borer (1989)). In all four languages arbitrary (i.e. antecedentless) third person pronouns differ from anaphoric third person pronouns with respect to pro-drop.

As pointed out by Shlonsky (1997), in Modern Hebrew arbitrary third person plural pronominals are null in all tenses. Unlike the first and second person and third person anaphoric pronouns, arbitrary third person plural pronouns are null in the present tense (see (7a)).

(7) a. be-šavu'ot    'oxlim       givna    (MH; Borer 1998)
     in-Pentecost eat.benoni.mpl cheese
     'One eats cheese in Pentecost'
  b. moxrim      Sam kartisim
     sell.benoni.mpl there tickets
     'They(arb) sell tickets there'    (Shlonsky 1997: ex. 7–30b)

In the past and future, the third person plural arbitrary pronouns are null in contrast with the third person plural anaphoric pronouns, which have to be lexical:

(8) maxru       šam    kartisim   (MH)
    sell.past.3mpl there   tickets
    'They(arb) sold tickets there.'   (Shlonsky 1997: ex. 7–29b)

The same split between arbitrary and anaphoric third person pronouns can be found in Finnish. The arbitrary pronoun in Finnish takes third person singular morphology but does not pattern with the referential third person singular pronouns. Unlike the third person singular referential anaphoric pronouns, which have to be lexical, arbitrary pronouns are null (see Hakulinen and Karttunen (1973) for more examples):

(9) Metsästä    löytää    helposti mustikoita
    forest-ELA find.3sg easily    blueberries-PAR
    'One finds blueberries easily in the forest'
    (Fi; Vainikka and Levy 1999: ex. 43)

In Russian, arbitrary third person plural subjects also have to be null, differing from the other referential pronouns. In examples like the following, the lexical third person plural subject pronoun *oni* is impossible with an arbitrary inter-pretation:

(10) vo Francii (*oni) edjat ulitok    (Ru)
     in France (they) eat.3pl snails
     'In France, they(arb) eat snails'

As discussed in Sigurðsson (1989; 1990), Icelandic also allows arbitrary null subjects under certain circumstances:

(11)  Eg vissi  ekki  að    aetti   að   fara  svona  oft    til  Graenland
      I   knew   not   that  should  to   go    so     often  to   Greenland
      'I did not know that one should go so often to Greenland'
      (Ice; Sigurðsson 1990: ex. 28a)

The distribution of arbitrary third person pro as compared to referential and quasi-argumental pro in the languages discussed here can be summarized by Table 8.1.

The arbitrary pronouns in the examples discussed above occupy the subject position of predicates such as *sell tickets, eat snails, find blueberries*, which are clearly assigned a θ-role. This implies that the contrast between arbitrary and anaphoric referential pronouns with respect to pro-drop cannot be captured in terms of a difference in the type of θ-role along the lines of (3) above. In the following sections I will therefore propose an alternative analysis in order to account for the split between anaphoric and non-anaphoric third-person pronouns with respect to pro-drop.

## 8.3  An alternative analysis

The data discussed in the previous section show that third person null pronouns bearing a full θ-role do not form a homogeneous class. In order to account for this observation I will develop an alternative to Rizzi's typology of pro-drop repeated here.

(12)  Three types of pro-drop (Rizzi 1986a)
      a.  referential pro: null pronouns bearing a full θ-role;
      b.  quasi-argumental pro: null pronouns bearing a quasi-θ-role;
      c.  expletive pro: null pronouns bearing no θ-role.

TABLE 8.1. Distribution of arbitrary third person pro vs. referential and quasi-argumental pro

|  | 1/2 pro | 3 anaphoric pro | 3 arb pro | weather pro |
|---|---|---|---|---|
| Finnish | Yes | No | Yes | Yes |
| MH past/future | Yes | No | Yes | Yes |
| MH present | No | No | Yes | Yes |
| Russian | No | No | Yes | Yes |
| Icelandic | No | No | Yes | Yes |

I propose to replace Rizzi's distinction based on the θ-role by a distinction between (a) deictic, (b) anaphoric, and (c) non-anaphoric null pronouns. The pronouns of first and second person singular and plural are deictic containing reference to the speaker and the hearer; the distinction between anaphoric and non-anaphoric pronouns therefore applies only to third person pronouns.

(13)   Three types of pro-drop (modified)
  a. deictic pro: null pronouns marked [+speaker]/ [+hearer];
  b. anaphoric pro: null third person pronouns that take up
     a discourse referent previously introduced in the discourse;
  c. non-anaphoric pro: null third person pronouns that do not take
     up a discourse referent previously introduced in the discourse.

The grammatical distinction between anaphoric and non-anaphoric pronouns is independently motivated. Languages such as Bavarian and Frisian have grammaticalized this distinction on the definite determiner. The non-anaphoric form (glossed det.NA) is used with proper names, unique entities, and kind-referring NPs, while the anaphoric form (glossed det.A) is used with entities introduced in the discourse (see Ebert (1970) for Frisian; Krifka et al. (1995) for Bavarian):

(14)   a. Da/     *dea   Kare    is    kema                       (Bav)
          det.NA  det.A  Karl    has   arrived                    (proper name)
       b. Da/     *dea   Kini    is    gschtoabm
          det.NA  det.A  king    has   died                       (unique entity)
       c. Da/     *dea   Schnaps  is   deia
          det.NA  det.A  Schnaps  is   expensive                  (kind-referring NP)
       d. I   hab   a Bia   un    an   Schnaps    bschdait.
          I   have  a beer  and   a    schnapps   ordered
          Dea/    *da    Schnaps  war   deia                      (anaphoric NP)
          det.NA  det.A  schnapps  was   expensive

The class of non-anaphoric third person pronouns includes quasi-arguments and arbitrary third person plural: in both cases the pronoun does not pick out an already established discourse referent. This grouping of quasi-arguments and arbitrary third person plural is consistent with the evidence from the languages examined in the previous section. The data show that, with respect to pro-drop, the arbitrary third person pronouns are more similar to quasi-argumental pronouns than to anaphoric argumental third person pronouns. This observation has been explicitly made by Shlonsky

(1997) for Modern Hebrew, and this author considers arbitrary pro and quasi-argumental pro as members of a single class that he terms 'quasi-referential pronouns'. The present analysis gives an explicit formulation of the intuition underlying Shlonsky's proposal: the similarity between the two types of pronoun is reduced to the fact that both lack an antecedent.

Following Rizzi's theory of pro-drop, I assume that any instance of a null pronoun needs formal licensing. As in Rizzi's analysis, I therefore propose to derive the difference between the different types of pro-drop from differences at the level of content identification. More precisely, I propose that anaphoric and non-anaphoric third person pronouns differ with respect to the features that have to be identified by agreement:

(15) Content identification (modified)
   (i) Deictic pro arises with agreement that identifies φ features including a feature [+speaker] or [+hearer] (first/second person pronouns).
   (ii) Anaphoric third person null pronouns arise with an agreement morpheme identifying the full set of φ features person, number, and gender.
   (iii) Non-anaphoric third person null pronouns arise with agreement that only identifies a subset of φ features.

The following sections develop the mechanisms of content identification that apply to non-anaphoric third person pro.

Section 8.3.1 develops the clause in (15iii) identifying the subsets of features that give rise to non-anaphoric pro-drop. I will argue that two different subsets of φ features identified by agreement account for the difference between (i) non-anaphoric non-human third person pro (quasi-arguments) and (ii) non-anaphoric [+human] third person pro (arbitrary third person plural pro).

In section 8.3.2 I will examine the case of non-anaphoric [+human] third person plural pro in more detail. I will argue that (at least) five types of non-anaphoric [+human] third person plural pro have to be distinguished (section 8.3.2.1).

In order to account for the different types of non-anaphoric third person plural pro I propose that for the content identification of arbitrary null pronouns the subset of φ features identified by the agreement combines with further licensing mechanisms that yield the different arbitrary readings identified in section 8.3.2.1. These further licensing mechanisms are discussed in section 8.3.2.2.

### 8.3.1 Two types of deficient φ feature

In the previous section I have proposed that non-anaphoric third-person pronouns form a class with respect to pro-drop by virtue of having a partial set of φ features. The class of non-anaphoric lexical pronouns includes (i) expletives (appearing e.g. with inverted subjects), (ii) quasi-arguments (e.g. subjects of weather predicates), and (iii) arbitrary third person subjects. The existence of null quasi-arguments and null arbitrary third person pronouns is motivated by the fact that these null pronouns are syntactically active—for example, with respect to control and binding. The existence of null expletives is more problematic, since its principal motivation is theoretical: expletive pro provides an element that satisfies the requirement that every finite clause have a syntactic subject in a specific structural position (EPP). Rizzi gives German as an example of a language that has only expletive pro. I have argued for an analysis of German without empty subject pronouns elsewhere (see Cabredo Hofherr 1999), and I will therefore assume that expletive pro does not exist.

The distinction between quasi-arguments and arbitrary subjects corresponds to a morphological difference in languages that have non-anaphoric readings with third person singular and plural pro:[6] weather predicates appear with the third person singular, while arbitrary third person plural subjects appear with the third person plural.

(16)  a. 3sg non-anaphoric pro: quasi-arguments (e.g. subjects of weather verbs); and
      b. 3pl non-anaphoric pro: arbitrary 3pl subjects.

In what follows I will argue that, while third person singular and third person plural agreement may both identify subsets of φ features, the subsets identified differ with respect to the [number] feature.

The third person agreement form is uncontroversially the prototypical agreement form. It appears as a default with weather predicates (17a), extraposition (17b), and also with nominal agreement morphology, as e.g. non-agreeing participles (17c):

(17)  a. Llueve.    (Sp)
         (it) rains.3sg
         'It is raining'

---

[6] In the following discussion I will leave aside Finnish and Icelandic, since in these languages only the 3sg pro seems to be available (see Hakulinen and Karttunen (1973) for Finnish, Sigurðsson (1989) for Icelandic).

    b. Parece        que Juan no  quiere venir.
       (it) seems.3sg that Juan not wants come.inf
       'It seems that Juan does not want to come'
    c. Tus    hermanas  han       venido.
       your   sisters.3fpl  have.3pl  come.msg
       'Your sisters have come'

The third person singular agreement appearing in these examples does not contribute any obvious semantic content.

    The third person plural verbal agreement that allows the non-anaphoric readings of third person plural pro is of a different type, since it contributes to the interpretation. First, the arbitrary subject is unspecific but [+human], and, secondly, in certain languages the arbitrary subject is third person excluding speaker and hearer (for further discussion see section 8.3.2.1 below).

    A pattern resembling that of arbitrary third person plural subjects can be found with the nominal agreement in the examples in (18): (i) without an antecedent the interpretation is human (see Corblin (1995) for French) and (ii) the morphological features are third person plural.

(18)   a. los grandes, los chicos     (Sp)
        los fuertes (los = mpl)
    b. die Grossen, die Kleinen    (Ge)
        die Starken (die = pl)
    c. les grands, les petits       (Fr)
        les forts (les = pl)
        'the big (ones), the small (ones)
        the strong (ones)'

I propose that both third person agreement forms appearing with non-anaphoric pro have in common that their specification for [number] is deficient.

    The difference between the third person singular and the third person plural lies in the fact that third person singular deficient agreement is uncountable, corresponding to a mass noun, while third person plural deficient agreement is countable, corresponding to a count noun. This proposal is supported by the following generalization.

    Cross-linguistically, in the interpretation of non-anaphoric forms that are not marked for gender, the distinction between singular and plural corresponds systematically to a distinction between mass/inanimate and count/human interpretation respectively:

(19)   a. Beaucoup a     été  dit    (Fr)
        'Much    has.3sg been said'  (sg, inanimate)

   b.  Beaucoup   ont      été   tués /   vus
      'Many       have.3pl  been  killed /  seen'   (pl, human)

(20)  a.  Poco se   sabe      de  él   (Sp)
      little refl  know.3sg  of  him
      'Little is known of him'  (sg, inanimate)

   b.  Pocos       vinieron  a verlo
      little.mpl   camp.3pl   to see him
      'Few came.3pl to see him'  (pl, human)

(21)  a.  Much has been done   (sg, inanimate)

   b.  Many have been killed  (pl, human)

I propose that the difference between count and mass status of the pronoun associated with the deficient agreement is due to their specification for the [number] feature.

While the third person plural deficient agreement has an underspecified [number] feature, the third person singular deficient agreement has no [number] feature at all. For the third person plural deficient agreement the slot for the [number] feature is present, but the value is not specified by the agreement morpheme and has to be retrieved from the context. For the third person singular deficient agreement the [number] feature is simply absent and therefore never assigned a value.

With respect to the [person] feature, the deficient third person plural agreement may vary cross-linguistically. The non-anaphoric third person plural readings in Spanish exclude speaker and hearer, while this is not the case for Russian or Modern Hebrew (see section 8.3.2). I propose to analyse this difference as a difference in feature content of the third person plural agreement with an underspecified [number] feature: while the deficient third person plural agreement in Spanish is marked for [third person], the third person plural agreement in Russian and Modern Hebrew is not marked for [person]. I will remain neutral as to the question whether the [person] feature is underspecified (i.e. filled in by the context) or completely absent.

Notice that the difference between the non-anaphoric third person plural readings coincides with a difference in the verbal morphology. Russian and Modern Hebrew both have tenses that do not mark [person] but only [gender] and [number]—namely, the Russian past and the Modern Hebrew present. In Spanish, in contrast, all tenses mark person distinctions.

The deficient third person singular agreement, in contrast, yields a mass interpretation: this interpretation automatically excludes speaker and hearer since mass interpretation is inanimate. I therefore propose that the third person singular deficient agreement that appears with weather predicates is not marked for [person].

Given the preceding discussion, the third person plural deficient agreement is more complex than the third person singular agreement in that it is under-specified for [number], while in the third person singular deficient agreement the [number] feature is absent.

Furthermore, the third person plural deficient agreement may have a value for [person], namely [third person], while the third person singular deficient agreement does not have a [person] feature. If the third person singular deficient agreement has neither [number] nor [person] features, the only feature contributed by the agreement is the characteristic feature of nominals, presumably [+N].

Summarizing, I propose that non-anaphoric pro may arise with two types of deficient agreement. These two types of agreement differ crucially with respect to their specification for the feature [number]. This difference is reflected in a difference with respect to the mass versus count status of the non-anaphoric pronouns identified by the deficient agreement.

The feature [+human] is not a specific property of non-anaphoric third person plural pronouns, but falls under a wider generalization that non-anaphoric third person plural forms are interpreted by default as referring to humans, while the non-anaphoric third person singular forms are interpreted as inanimate. According to the analysis proposed here, this is related to the fact that mass interpretation is related to inanimacy while countable interpretation is related to the feature [+human].[7]

(22)   a. 3sg deficient agreement contains the feature: +N
           no number feature ⇒ mass ⇒ inanimate interpretation by default
       b. 3pl deficient agreement contains the features:
           (i) +N, underspecified number (e.g. Russian) or
           (ii) +N, 3rd person, underspecified number (e.g. Spanish)
           number feature present ⇒ count ⇒ human interpretation by default

### 8.3.2 The analysis of non-anaphoric third-person plural pro

In the preceding section I have proposed that the feature [number] allows us to distinguish two types of deficient agreement yielding two types of non-anaphoric pro: third person singular quasi-argumental pro and third person plural non-anaphoric ('arbitrary') pro.

---

[7] This correlation is visible in certain languages where plural is obligatory only for [+human] entities, e.g. Kriyol as discussed by Kihm (2006).

The non-anaphoric readings of third person plural pronouns do not form a uniform class, however. As I will argue in section 8.3.2.1, five types of non-anaphoric third person plural pronouns have to be distinguished. In order to account for the different readings of non-anaphoric third person plural, I propose that the content identification due to the agreement morpheme combines with further interpretive mechanisms, discussed in section 8.3.2.2.

**8.3.2.1** *A classification of non-anaphoric third-person plural readings*   In the present section I summarize the classification of third person plural non-anaphoric readings proposed in Cabredo Hofherr (2003). I will briefly present the criteria that this classification is based on and present cross-linguistic data that support the distinctions drawn in the classification.

I then briefly summarize some properties of the non-anaphoric third person plural subjects that will play a role in the analysis proposed in section 8.3.2.2.

I will assume the classification of non-anaphoric third person plural subjects into five types:

(23)   (I)   Specific existential reading (temporally anchored):
             Tocan a la puerta
             '(They) knock.3pl at the door' (=someone is knocking … )
       (II)  Vague existential reading (not temporally anchored):
             Han encontrado una motocicleta en el patio
             '(They) have.3pl found a motorbike in the courtyard'
       (III) Inferred existential reading (inferred from a result):
             Aquí han comido mariscos
             'Here, (they) have.3pl eaten seafood' (=someone)
       (IV)  Corporate reading (predicates with a designated subject:
             see Kaerde (1943)):
             Volvieron a aumentar el IVA
             '(They) raised the VAT again'
       (V)   Universal/locative reading (licensed by a locative):
             En España hablan español
             'In Spain, (they) speak.3pl Spanish'[8]

This classification takes several factors into account.

The first division is between the readings (23.I–III) and the readings in (23.IV, V): while the former can be roughly paraphrased by existential quantification

---

[8] This class covers the core cases of the quasi-universal readings in the sense of Cinque (1988). Notice, however, that, depending on the locative and the predicate it combines with, the group defined by the locative expression need not be quasi-universal:
(i) En este colegio enseñan       ruso.
    in  this school (they) teach.3pl Russian

(by using a subject corresponding to 'someone'), the latter cannot. Relying on this difference I will distinguish the existential readings (23.I–III) from the non-existential readings (23.IV, V).

The three existential readings can be further differentiated depending on the anchoring of the event in time. While the specific existential reading in (23.I) is anchored to a particular point in time, vague existential and inferred existential readings in (24.II) and (24.III) only imply that an event of the type described has taken place (see Casielles Suárez (1996) for a similar distinction). I will assume that in the specific existential reading (24.I) the event is anchored to a deictic point in time, while the vague and the inferred existential readings (24.II, III) are obtained by existential quantification over event instantiations. The inferred existential reading matches the vague existential reading in that it does not imply an anchoring of the event to a precise point in time. Nevertheless, the inferred existential reading in (23.III) has to be distinguished from the vague existential reading in (23.II) since it is subject to further restrictions. The inferred existential reading is only possible if the event can be inferred from a perceivable result (compare the discussion in Tóth (2000)).

Data from French further support the distinction between the existential readings. First, the French third person plural pronoun *ils* cannot have a specific existential interpretation while the vague existential reading is possible.

(24)   a.   Ils nous attaquent                                  (Fr)
\*'Someone is attacking us'
OK 'They.anaphoric are attacking us'   (specific exist.\*)
b.   Ils ont trouvé une moto dans la cour
'They have found a motorbike in the   (vague exist.OK)
courtyard'

Secondly, the evidence from French suggests that the vague existential and the inferred existential reading have to be distinguished: while the vague existential reading is possible for French *ils*, the inferred existential reading is not.[9]

(25)   Ici ils ont mangé des fruits de mer   (Fr)
\*'Here they have eaten seafood'   (inferred exist.\*)

Syrian Arabic further confirms the independent status of the inferred existential reading: in Syrian Arabic the specific existential[10] and the vague

---

[9] The closest equivalent to an inferred existential reading involves the use of the impersonal pronoun *on*:
(i) Ici   on   a   mangé des fruits de mer.   (Fr)
here ONE has eaten   seafood.
[10] My informant preferred the impersonal passive to a specific existential 3pl pro.

existential readings are possible, while the examples corresponding to an inferred existential reading were rejected by my informant.

In Spanish, the inferred existential reading (23.III), unlike the vague existential reading, systematically appears with a locative and the perfect *haber*, 'have' + past participle. The constellation in Spanish suggests that the inferred reading is linked to the properties of the perfect, and in particular its evidential readings, which are beyond the scope of this chapter. I will therefore leave the inferred existential reading aside in the analysis of arbitrary third person plural readings given in section 8.3.2.2.

Apart from the three existential readings, the classification in (23) distinguishes two non-existential readings: the corporate reading and the universal/locative reading (23.IV, V).

The corporate reading (23.IV) arises with predicates such as *deliver the mail, operate on patients, raise taxes* which are associated with a designated group carrying out the activity (e.g. postmen, doctors, and governments). Pesetsky (1995) coined the term 'corporate' to refer to '[a] pronoun [that] picks out some socially designated group of people, prototypically governments, bosses, criminals, or shopkeepers'. Pesetsky further suggests that the existential arbitrary readings are in fact corporate readings. As pointed out by Tóth (2000), this cannot be maintained, since Hungarian and Spanish allow existential readings with predicates that do not have a designated subject (e.g. *sing, knock on the door*).

The fact that in French the corporate reading is possible, while the specific existential reading is not, provides a second argument in favour of a distinction between the two readings. As already mentioned, the French third person plural pronoun *ils* cannot have a specific existential interpretation (see (24a)); the corporate reading, in contrast, is possible (see Kleiber 1994):[11]

(26)  Ils ont encore augmenté les impôts　(Fr; Kleiber 1994)
　　　 'They raised taxes again'　　　　　　 (corporate reading)

Finally, the universal/locative reading differs from the corporate reading in two ways: (i) it does not impose a restriction on the type of predicate, and (ii) it depends on the presence of a locative expression.

Table 8.2 summarizes the properties of the non-anaphoric readings discussed in this section. Before turning to the analysis of the five readings that I have distinguished, I will briefly summarize the main properties of non-anaphoric third person plural readings that will play a role in the discussion.

---

[11] Kleiber calls the corporate reading 'collective' (Fr. *collectif*).

TABLE 8.2. Non-anaphoric third person plural readings

| Properties | Specific-ex. (I) | Vague-ex. (II) | Inferred ex. (III) | Corporate (IV) | Univ./loc. (V) |
|---|---|---|---|---|---|
| Paraphrase by ex. | | | | | |
| quantification | yes | yes | yes | no | no |
| Anchoring to a particular | | | | | |
| point in time nec. | yes | no | no | no | no |
| Inference from a | | | | | |
| result nec. | no | no | yes | no | no |
| Perfect tense nec. (in Sp) | no | no | yes | no | no |
| Predicate with | | | | | |
| designated subject | no | no | no | yes | no |
| Locative nec. | no | no | no | no | yes |
| *Possible for* | | | | | |
| Fr *ils* | no | yes | no | yes | yes |
| Sp 3pl pro | yes | yes | yes | yes | yes |
| Syrian Ar 3pl pro | yes | yes | no | yes | yes |

The most striking property of non-anaphoric third person plural subjects is that they necessarily refer to humans: even if the selectional properties of the predicate force a non-human subject, the only available interpretation is pragmatically anomalous with a [+human] subject.

(27)  Aquí ladran en la mañana                    (Sp)
      'Here, (they[+human]) bark in the morning'

A second property often pointed out for non-anaphoric third person plural pronouns is the fact that they exclude speaker and hearer (see Suñer (1983) for Spanish third person plural pro, Kitagawa and Lehrer (1990) for English *they*, and Kleiber (1994) for French *ils*).

This property crucially distinguishes the third person plural arbitrary interpretation in Spanish, French, and English from arbitrary PRO and the impersonal uses of the second person (English *you*, French *tu*, Spanish pro.2sg/*tú*) that do not exclude the speaker (cf. Hernanz 1990; Kitagawa and Lehrer 1990).

However, the exclusion of speaker and hearer is not generally valid for third person non-anaphoric readings. The non-anaphoric plural null pronoun in Russian and in Modern Hebrew need not exclude the speaker and the hearer, as indicated by the translation by *one* in the following examples.

(28) a. vo   Francii  [ ]        edjat    ulitok   (Ru)
        in   France   (they)    eat.3pl  snails
        [ ]  ix   kladut  v  sol'na  celij  den' i   gotovjat   s
        (one) them put.3pl in salt on whole day and prepare.3pl with
        chesnokom
        garlic (univ/loc)
        'In France, (they) eat snails. One puts them in salt for a whole
        day and prepares them with garlic'
    b. be-šavu'ot [ ]   'oxlim          givna     (MH; Borer 1998)
        in-Pentecost    eat.benoni.mpl  cheese
        'One eats cheese in Pentecost'

The third property concerns the [number] feature. For the non-anaphoric
third person plural pronouns the interpretation is not necessarily [plural]: the
existential readings do not imply a plurality (see e.g. Suñer (1983) for Spanish,
Cinque (1988) for Italian):

(29) a. "'¡Que me matan!" Así clamaba una liebre infeliz que se miraba
        en las garras de un águila altanera. (Samaniego, *Fábulas* I,5,
        quoted in Bello (1847))
        ' "That they kill me!" So lamented an unhappy hare that found
        itself in the claws of a haughty eagle.'
    b. Lo hanno cercato: era un signore anziano        (It; Cinque 1988)
        'They have been looking for him: it was an
        elderly man'

The discussion in this section has dealt with the classification of non-
anaphoric readings of third person plural pronouns, be they lexical or null.
As the Spanish examples in (24) show, the five readings distinguished here are
all attested for null third person plural pronouns. In the following section
I will discuss the further licensing mechanisms that yield the different non-
anaphoric readings.

8.3.2.2 *Further content identification*  According to the analysis presented in
section 8.3.1, non-anaphoric [+human] readings arise with a deficient form of
third person plural agreement. I have argued in the preceding section that an
analysis of non-anaphoric third person plural pro has to account for five types
of reading. I therefore propose that the interpretation of non-anaphoric third
person plural null pronouns depends on two further factors apart from the φ
feature content.

The first factor is the semantic ambiguity of pronouns. Pronouns can
function either as a definite plural, denoting a unique maximal group, or as
an indefinite, introducing a variable into the semantic representation.

The translation as a definite plural is motivated by the parallel behaviour of definite plurals and plural pronouns. Both can be used anaphorically, implying contextual uniqueness and maximality of the referent group. For definite plurals anaphoricity and uniqueness can be dissociated as discussed above (see (14)), and I therefore assume that the same dissociation is possible for plural pronouns, resulting in pronouns that refer to a unique maximal group without being anaphoric.

The translation as a variable is independently motivated by bound variable readings of pronouns.

The second factor lies in further mechanisms of content identification. A non-anaphoric third person plural pronoun that is translated as a unique maximal group receives a corporate or a universal/locative reading, depending on the mechanism of content identification of the group. For non-anaphoric third person plural pronouns that are translated as a variable, the specific and the vague existential readings arise through existential closure.

(30)  Third person plural pro translated as:
      a. a variable → existential readings;
      b. a definite plural → non-existential reading.

In the following sections I will discuss separately the means of content identification for the translation of the plural null pronoun as a maximal group and as a variable.

### 8.3.2.2.1 Third person plural referring to a unique maximal group.

In what follows I examine the content identification for the translation of the third person plural pronoun as a unique maximal group. This translation gives rise to the two non-anaphoric readings that are not existential: the corporate and the universal/locative reading.

The analysis proposed here assimilates the subjects of the universal/locative and the corporate reading to definite NPs. Such an analysis is further supported by the comparison of null third person plural subjects with a universal reading with lexical NPs in generic sentences. The example (31a) with a non-anaphoric third person plural pro subject has a reading comparable to (31b) with a plural definite NP in that both state a habit or a recurrent pattern. The example (31c) with an indefinite singular subject differs from both (31a) and (31b) in that it implies a modal component of obligation. This contrast is not dependent on the contrast between singular and plural, as the example in (31d) shows: the definite singular, unlike the indefinite singular, does not necessarily imply a modal reading of obligation.

(31)   a. En España, se acuestan temprano   (Sp)
'In Spain   (they) go to bed early'
b. En España, los niños   se   acuestan   temprano
in   Spain   the   children   refl   lie-down   early
'In Spain children go to bed early'
c. En España, un niño se acuesta temprano
'In Spain a child (modal: should) go to bed early'
d. En España, el bebé de la familia se acuesta temprano
'In Spain the baby of the family goes to bed early'

As we have seen in section 8.3.2.1, the non-anaphoric readings of null third-person plural pronouns exclude speaker and addressee in Spanish, while in Russian and Modern Hebrew this restriction does not hold. In languages where the non-anaphoric third person plural agreement is not marked for person, the non-anaphoric third person plural pro can receive an interpretation corresponding to 'people in general', 'one'.

As pointed out by Kleiber for French non-anaphoric *ils*, in languages where the non-anaphoric third person plural pronouns exclude the speaker and the hearer such pronouns cannot have the reading of 'people in general', since such a reading would include the speaker and the addressee. Under the assumption that a simple third person plural pronoun cannot refer by default to a semantically complex group like *everyone but you and me*, it is then necessary to restrict the reference of the unique maximal group to exclude the hearer and the speaker. The corporate and universal readings arise through different restricting mechanisms.

The first possibility is that the predicate is associated with a designated subject, namely a group typically carrying out the activity: this gives the corporate reading. A second restricting mechanism is provided by the identification of the group by a locative expression that functions like an I-level predicate (see Condoravdi 1989; Casielles Suárez 1996): this results in the universal/locative reading.

As pointed out by Tóth (2001), not any predicate identifying a group is possible; the sentence in (32a), for example, does not have a reading comparable to (32b):

(32)   a. De viejos   necesitan       más ayuda (Sp; Toth 2001)
of old.3mpl (they.anaphoric) need more help
'In old age, they need more help' (non-anaphoric reading*)

Compare:

   b. Los viejos necesitan más ayuda
      'The old need more help'

I propose that this is due to the fact that the adverbial expression *de viejos* in (34a) is interpreted as a restricting when-clause, *when (they are) old*. Such a restriction does not give individuals, however, but temporal stages with a certain property that could apply to any individual, in particular the speaker and the addressee. Consequently, a restriction of this type does not provide a group that excludes speaker and addressee, and therefore such an expression cannot content-license non-anaphoric third person plural pro.

Extending Kleiber's (1994) analysis for French, the present analysis treats the collective and the universal arbitrary reading as definites that denote a unique maximal group. The group is unique in the context and identifiable through the locative or the designated subject associated with the predicate. The unspecific interpretation is due to the fact that the individual members of the group are not identified.

The present analysis of the subject of the corporate reading as a definite plural accounts for the fact that these examples cannot be translated felicitously using the indefinite *'someone'* as a subject. The existential flavour of the corporate reading is due to the fact that it is not necessary that the entire collective entity take part in the event for a sentence like those in (33) to be judged true (see Kleiber 1994).

(33)   a. Jean a touché les feuilles de l'arbre
          'Jean touched the leaves of the tree'
       b. Les Américains ont débarqué sur la lune en 1969   (Fr; Kleiber 1994)
          'The Americans landed on the moon in 1969'

The analysis proposed here cannot explain, however, why locatives are the privileged means of defining a group that is not lexically associated with the predicate. In principle the following temporal expressions should be able to define groups of people that exclude speaker and hearer: nevertheless these examples are less acceptable than examples with a locative adjunct, even if they are clearly better than the example (32a):

(34)   a. En la edad media sólo tomaban cerveza              (Sp)
          porque el agua estaba contaminada
          'In the Middle Ages (they) only drank
          beer because the water was contaminated'         (non-anaphoric: ?*)

  b. Durante el servicio militar aprenden a utilizar un arma
    'During the military service (they) learn to use a gun'
                (non-anaphoric: ?*)

Compare:

  c. En la mili aprenden a utilizar un arma
    'In the military (they) learn to use a gun' (non-anaphoric ok)

The contrast between locatives and other adjuncts may be due to the fact that locatives share properties with nominal subjects. In locative inversion structures, for example, locatives have been argued to occupy the subject position (see e.g. Bresnan 1994). This affinity between locatives and nominal subjects may provide a lead to an explanation for the restriction to locative adjuncts for universal readings of non-anaphoric third person plural subjects. I leave this question open here.

**8.3.2.2.2 Third person plural translated as a variable.** In the present section I propose two mechanisms of content identification for the translation of the third-person plural pronoun as a variable. As I have said above, I will set the inferred existential reading aside, since the analysis of this reading is probably dependent on the analysis of the perfect, which is beyond the scope of the present paper.

 We have seen above that the specific existential reading and vague existential reading can be dissociated in a language like French. Consequently, the two readings must rely on separate licensing mechanisms that may be available independently. I suggest that both the specific and the vague existential reading arise through existential closure taking scope over the subject. The difference between the two readings is analysed as a scope difference. The specific existential reading arises through existential closure of the VP (Heim 1982). This existential closure only gives an existential reading if the subject is within VP. The vague existential reading, on the other hand, relies on existential quantification over the event as a whole, taking scope over Tense.

 If this analysis is correct, the difference between French *ils* and Spanish third person plural pro with respect to the specific existential reading can be traced back to a syntactic difference. In French, subject pronouns occupy a VP-external subject position (spec,IP, with subsequent phonological cliticization onto the verb), and therefore subject pronouns are not in the scope of the default existential closure that applies to the VP. In Spanish, null pronouns occupy the VP-internal position and can stay in the scope of existential closure at the VP-level. If existential closure takes scope over VP, the value for Tense can still be specified, yielding a temporally anchored interpretation.

Given that the present analysis admits that non-anaphoric third person plural pronouns can be translated as a variable, it may seem puzzling that unselective binding by 'if/when'-clauses or Q-adverbs cannot license a generic reading in a language like Spanish. In this respect third person plural pro contrasts with lexical indefinite NPs. Notice, however, that since speaker and hearer have to be excluded, the unselective binding with 'if/when'-clauses or Q-adverbs cannot give an interpretation corresponding to people in general (see the discussion above). Since 'if/when'-clauses and Q-adverbs do not define a group excluding the speaker and hearer, however, they cannot license a universal non-anaphoric reading.

If this argumentation is correct, this predicts that in Russian and Modern Hebrew, where the third person plural does not necessarily exclude the speaker and the addressee, null subjects should be licensed by 'if/when'-clauses and Q-adverbs. I have not been able to check this prediction.

## 8.4 Anaphoric arbitrary subjects and further questions

So far I have only considered non-anaphoric readings in isolation. Two types of phenomenon show that unspecific readings in isolation have to be kept separate from cases where several instances of unspecific readings co-occur. The first phenomenon concerns two instances of null pronouns co-occurring within a sentence, illustrated in Modern Hebrew and in Finnish.

As shown by Borer (1989), Modern Hebrew admits null subject pronouns with third-person inflection that are co-referent with a c-commanding DP in the main clause:

(35)  Tal 'amar          le-'itamar   še-[ ]  ya cli'ax (MH; Shlonsky 1997)
      $Tal_i$ said.past.3msg  to-$Itamar_j$  that-($pro_{i/j/*k}$) 3msg-succeed.fut
      'Tal said to Itamar that he (Tal or Itamar) is going
      to succeed'

This option is only available (as pointed out by Shlonsky) if the verb in the matrix clause is past or future (i.e. marked for person). This example shows that further licensing mechanisms for null third person pronouns are available with a local antecedent. Given the analysis of non-anaphoric readings here, it is therefore possible that a null third person pronoun with an unspecific interpretation is licensed by an unspecific antecedent in the matrix clause. In such a configuration the second arbitrary subject would be dependent on a local arbitrary antecedent.

A second example of locally co-occurring null third person pronouns can be found in Finnish. Hakulinen and Karttunen (1973), in their discussion of generic third person singular null pronouns in Finnish, identify several licensing conditions that are necessary to license a generic null third person singular. They show that the presence of a pronoun with an non-anaphoric reading in the superordinate clause may license another null pronoun with the same interpretation in a 'that'-clause, even if the licensing conditions for the second null pronoun are not fulfilled:

(36) Tässä työssä [ ] vaaditaan, että [ ] osaa ruotsia
'This work requires of you that
you know Swedish'
(Fi; Hakulinen and Karttunen 1973: ex. 31b)

A second phenomenon that may independently allow null third person subjects with an unspecific reading is anaphoric dependency on an unspecific antecedent. This case is illustrated by the following fragments taken from Spanish:

(37) a. En esta mina pro trabajan mucho. pro Despiertan a las 5 y media, pro salen a las 6 de la mañana y pro regresan a las 8 de la noche, y si pro llegan más tarde, el capataz se enfada con ellos. Y a fines del mes les pagan una miseria
'In this mine (they) work a lot. (They) wake up at 5 o'clock, (they) leave at 6 in the morning and come back at 8 at night, and if (they) arrive later, the supervisor gets annoyed with them. And at the end of the month (they) pay them a pittance'        (univ/loc OK)
b. Salen a las 6 de la mañana y regresan a las 8 de la noche
'(They) leave at 6 in the morning and come back at 8 at night'        (univ/loc *)
c. En esta mina trabajan mucho
'In this mine (they) work a lot'        (univ/loc OK)

(38) a. En Francia pro comen caracoles. pro Los ponen en sal durante 12 horas y después pro los preparan con mantequilla y ajo
'In France (they) eat snails. (They = people in France) put them in salt for 12 hours and then (they) prepare them with butter and garlic'(univ/loc OK)
b. pro Los ponen en sal durante 12 horas
'(They) put them in salt for 12 hours'        (univ/loc *)

The locative that licenses a universal reading is only present in the first sentence of fragments (37a)/(38a); nevertheless the unspecific reading is taken up by the boldface pronouns in the later sentences even though the necessary locative is not present locally. In isolation such examples do not receive an arbitrary reading, as (37b) and (38b) show. Notice that even object pronouns (*les*) and strong pronouns that occur as complements of prepositions (*ellos*) can take up the unspecific reference of the non-anaphoric subject in the first sentence.

As the comparison of (37a) and (37b) shows, pronouns that cannot have a non-anaphoric reading in isolation can receive an unspecific interpretation in a fragment where they co-occur with a subject that satisfies the licensing conditions for a non-anaphoric reading (cf. (37c)). The same behaviour can be observed with the corporate reading, as illustrated in (39).

(39)  a. Ayer arreglaron mi computadora. **pro** Llegaron a las 10 de la
      mañana y se fueron a las 6 de la tarde
      'Yesterday (they) repaired my computer. (They) came at 10 in the
      morning and left at 6 in the evening'                     (corp OK)
    b. pro Llegaron a las 10 de la mañana y se
      fueron a las 6 de la tarde
      '(They) came at 10 in the morning and
      left at 6 in the evening'                                  (corp *)

I propose that the boldface pronouns in (37a), (38a) and (39a) are not to be analysed as instances of non-anaphoric third person plural pronouns. The interpretation of these pronouns is unspecific, since they are anaphoric to an unspecific antecedent. The same unspecific interpretation may arise with lexical pronouns in English, as in the following example:

(40)  Alguien/un sicópata asesinó a Holmes. pro Lo esperó aquí,
      le disparó y después llevó el cadáver hasta el río, donde lo
      encontró la policía
      'Someone/a madman killed Holmes. (He) waited for him here,
      shot him and then dragged the body to the river, where the
      police found it'

The third person singular pro in the second sentence and the corresponding pronoun *he* in the gloss refer to an unspecific individual, since in both cases the pronouns are co-referent with the unspecific subject, *someone / a madman*, of the first sentence in the fragment.

In view of the data that I have just discussed, I have based the discussion in the previous sections on isolated examples of non-anaphoric readings in order to exclude interference by the type of reading that has a non-anaphoric flavour but is not itself non-anaphoric.

Now, if the distinction anaphoric/non-anaphoric pro proposed here is justified, this predicts that in languages that do not have anaphoric third-person pro there should be no arbitrary third person plural pro by co-reference with a vague antecedent as in the Spanish examples (37), (38), and (39).

According to my Russian informant this prediction is correct for Russian, as the following examples show.

(41)  vchera   (*oni) mne pochinili kompjuter                (Ru)
      yesterday (they) me.dat repaired.3pl computer
      *(*oni) prishli v 10 chasov ...                         (corp)
      (they) came.3pl at 10 o'clock

(42)  a.  Na etom zavode (*oni) mnogo rabotajut              (Ru)
          in this factory (they) much work.3pl
          *(*oni) prixodjat v 6 chasov utra ...
          (they) come.3pl at 6 o'clock morning.gen
      b.  vo Francii (*oni$_i$) edjat ulitok
          in France (they) eat.3pl snails
          *(*oni$_i$) ix kladut v sol' na celij den' i gotovjat s chesnokom
          (they) them put.3pl in salt on whole day and prepare.3pl with garlic
                                                             (univ/loc)

According to my Russian informant, the subject of the first sentence in (42b) cannot be taken up either by a lexical or by a null third person plural pronoun. If the subject of the second sentence in (42b) is a null third person plural pronoun, this pronoun does not take up the subject of the first sentence (i.e. roughly 'people in France, the French'), but can only be understood as an instruction to prepare snails (corresponding to a sentence with the subject *one* in English).

In Modern Hebrew, the prediction is only partially borne out. As predicted by the present analysis, a third person plural null subject with corporate interpretation cannot be taken up by a null third person plural pronoun: in (43) the anaphoric subject of the second sentence has to be a lexical third person plural pronoun *hem*.

(43)  'etmol      [ ]      tiknu     li      'et  ha-maxšev     (MH)
      yesterday  (they)  repaired  to-me  acc  the-computer
      ??(hem)    ba'u     be-'eser  ve-halxu  be-šeš  ba-'erev
      they       came    at-ten    and-left  at-six  at-night  (corp)
      'Yesterday they repaired my computer'

In the first example with a locative licensing the universal/locative reading in
(44), the null subject in the second sentence is not interpreted as anaphoric on
the third person plural pro in the first sentence. As in Russian, the only reading
for a null third person plural subject is that of a general instruction, a recipe.

(44)  be-carfat  [ ]        'oxlim    šablulim  (MH)
      In-France  (they)    eat.3mpl  snails
      [ ]        samim     'otam     be-melax  le-mešex  yom
      (they)     put.3pl   them      in-salt   for-one   day
      ve-'az     [ ]        mevašlim  'otam     be-šum
      and-then   (they)    cook.3mpl them      in-garlic  (univ/loc)

For the second example of a reading licensed by a locative expression, Modern
Hebrew differs from Russian, however: in the example (45), the non-
anaphoric third person plural null subject of the first sentence can be taken
up by third person plural null pronouns in the subsequent discourse.

(45)  ba-maxane  ha-ze,     [ ]       'ovdim     harbe  (MH)
      in-camp    the-this, (they)    work.3mpl  much
      [ ]  kamim be-šeš ba-boker,  [ ]  matxilim
      (they) get-up  at-6  in the morning, (they) start
      la'avod be-Seva
      working at-7 o'clock
      ve-[ ]      lo        mafsikim  'ad ševa  ba-'erev
      and (they) only      finish    at 7      in the evening
      ve-be-sof   ha-xodeš            [ ]       mekablim
      and-at the-end  of the month  (they)    earn
      saxar 'aluv
      (a) miserable wage                         (univ/loc)

The present analysis does not provide an explanation for this contrast in
Modern Hebrew. Further investigation of the role of the locative could shed
light on the difference between the two locative readings, but I have to leave
this question open here.

Notice that even in languages that have anaphoric third person null
subjects, not all non-anaphoric subjects can be taken up by a null pronoun,
as illustrated by the specific existential subject in (46):

(46)  Tocan        a la  puerta. *pro  Quieren entrar      (Sp)
      (they) knock at the door.  (they) want     come-in.inf (specific exist.)

In Russian and Modern Hebrew the specific existential reading cannot be taken up by a following third person plural pronoun either, be it null or lexical.

(47)  a.  (*oni)  stuchat.  *pro/*oni  xotjat  voiti            (Ru)
          (they)  knock.   (they)     want  come-in.inf
      b.      dofkim ba-delet.    *pro/*hem rocim le-hikanes (MH)
          (they) knock  at-the door. (they)     want come-in  (specific exist.)

The preceding examples show that the different readings of non-anaphoric third person subjects differ with respect to discourse transparency: while the corporate readings can be taken up in the discourse in Spanish and in Modern Hebrew, the third person plural specific existential reading cannot be taken up in either of the languages considered here.

In the present section I have presented data showing (i) that null third person pronouns in a finite subordinate clause can be licensed by an antecedent in the matrix clause independently of the possibility of anaphoric pro-drop, and (ii) that third person plural pronouns can receive an unspecific reading by co-reference with a non-anaphoric antecedent.

I have further argued that not all readings of non-anaphoric third person plural pronouns are discourse-transparent when introducing a referent into the discourse: the data from Spanish, Russian and Modern Hebrew suggest in particular that the specific existential reading does not introduce a discourse referent.

## 8.5 Conclusion

In examining non-anaphoric readings of third person plural pronominals, I have given arguments showing that non-anaphoric third person plurals do not pattern with anaphoric third person plural pronouns with respect to pro-drop. In fact, the distribution of non-anaphoric third person plural is closer to that of quasi-argumental subjects than to that of anaphoric argumental third person pro. In order to account for this observation, I have proposed replacing Rizzi's typology of pro-drop based on the type of θ-role by a typology based on the distinction between anaphoric and non-anaphoric pro.

According to the analysis proposed here non-anaphoric pro arises with deficient agreement that only identifies a subset of φ features. Developing this hypothesis, I have argued that there are two types of deficient agreement. The deficient third person singular agreement does not contain number or person features and functions like a mass noun being interpreted as inanimate by default. The deficient third person plural agreement, by contrast, may be marked for third person or not, depending on the language, but is always underspecified for number and behaves on a par with count nouns, its default interpretation being [+human].

In order to account for the different types of non-anaphoric third person plural pro I have further proposed that third person plural pronouns can be translated either as referring to unique maximal groups, comparable to definite plurals, or as variables, comparable to indefinites.

As a consequence of the latter, certain non-anaphoric third person plural readings resemble indefinites (specific and vague existential reading), while others resemble definite plurals (corporate and universal/locative reading).

Finally, I have discussed some predictions of the present analysis concerning the occurrence of third person null pronouns that are anaphoric on a non-anaphoric antecedent.

# Part IV
# Non-configurationality

# 9

# The Pronominal Argument Parameter

ELOISE JELINEK

## 9.1 Introduction: defining the parameter

The goal of this chapter is to distinguish a class of Pronominal Argument (PA) languages from the larger class of pro-drop languages. There is considerable typological variation across languages with respect to the distribution of subject and object agreement and clitics (Alexiadou, Chapter 5 above; Alexiadou and Anagnostopoulou 1998: 493–5). One variety is found in Egyptian Arabic, where the verb agrees in person and number with the subject, permitting pro-drop of subject NPs.

(1)   a. il-walad daras      b. daras
           DET-boy 3ms:studied     3ms:studied
           'The boy studied'         'He studied.'

Subject NPs never occur without agreement but may be omitted in context, when definite and familiar. There is no object agreement; object clitics alternate with full DPs in object positions.

I dedicate this chapter to the memory of Ken Hale, his contributions to linguistic theory, and his work to preserve minority languages. Earlier versions of some of the material here are presented in Hale et al. (2003). I thank the members of the organizational committee for the Workshop on Agreement in Argument Structure held at the University of Utrecht in 2001—Peter Ackema, Patrick Brandt, Maaike Schoorlemmer, and Fred Weerman—for inviting me to the workshop, and for their kind hospitality. This chapter could not have been written without the help of Mary Willie. I am grateful to Mark Baker, David Basilico, Andrew Carnie, Richard Demers, Helen de Hoop, Barbara Partee, Montserrat Sanz, Elly van Gelderen, Robert Young, and particularly Andrew Barss and Heidi Harley, for their help and counsel. I thank the anonymous reviewers for this volume for their very helpful comments.

(2)  a.  šuft-aha                          d.  šuft bint
         1sg:saw-3fsg                          1sg:saw girl
         'I saw her'                           'I saw a girl'
     b.  šuft il-bint                       e.  *šuft-aha bint
         1sg:saw DET girl                      1sg:saw-3fsg girl
         'I saw the girl'                      *'I saw her girl'
     c.  šuft-aha, il-bint
         1sg:saw-3fs DET girl
         'I saw her, the girl (that is)'

Examples (2b, d) show that object DPs may occur without coreferent clitics. In this language type, there is a subject–object asymmetry: there is no co-occurrence of object clitics and object DPs, unless the latter are definite, and occur in a kind of 'afterthought' adjunct position (2c). The right-adjoined, non-argument DP in this construction type is called an 'anti-topic' by Lambrecht (1994: 203).

(3)  He's a nice guy, your brother

There are languages such as Spanish, where there is subject agreement, and object clitics may co-occur with some—but not all—object DPs; an animacy hierarchy plays a role. Other kinds of agreement include that seen in sign languages; Van Gijn and Zwitserlood (Chapter 7 above) show that, in the Sign Language of the Netherlands, it is not the $\varphi$ features of person and number that play a role in the verbal agreement system, but rather the features of gender and location.

What I want to consider here is yet another parametric type of agreement system. These are languages where there is *no* subject–object asymmetry with respect to agreement, and both subject and object are always represented by some overt pronominal element (either affix or clitic). Coreferent DPs may be present for either argument, but need not be if reference is unambiguous in the context. An example from Navajo:

(4)  a.  Yiyiiłtsà
         3sObj:3sSubj:saw
         'He saw him'
     b.  (Diné) ('ashkii) yiyiiłtsà
         man  boy  3sObj:3sSubj:saw
         '(The man,) (the boy,) he saw him'

The subject–object pronominal inflection is absolutely necessary for grammaticality, while the adjoined nominals are present only when the speaker judges that they are needed to establish reference. Either or both DPs may be omitted; the Navajo sentence typically has at most one DP. Thompson (1996: 95) found in a count of sentences in printed material that only one out of a sample of 294 Navajo transitive sentences had more than one DP. Since the pronouns are obligatory for the sentence, while the DPs are not, it is arguable that the former are the arguments, while the latter are topic-like adjuncts. Languages of this type, with *no* DPs in A-positions, are what I have called 'Pronominal Argument' languages (Jelinek 1984: 43–4; 1995: 487–8); and Baker (1996: 21–2; 1995b: 83–9) has designated 'polysynthetic'. Pronominal Argument languages are found in various language families, including Athabaskan, Salish, and Pama-Nyungan. This chapter will focus on data from Navajo (Southern Athabaskan) and Lummi (Straits Salish) to provide evidence in favour of this typological contrast. I present three lines of evidence on the Pronominal Argument parameter—data that demonstrate how this class of languages differs from the class of pro-drop languages.

Navajo and Lummi differ in many important respects. Lummi is a verb-initial language, Navajo is verb-final. Both have inflectional clitic strings where various functional categories are marked. In Lummi these strings are in the 'Wackernagel' second position; in Navajo they are prefixed to the verb at spell-out. The subject and object pronouns are included in these inflectional strings. A major feature of inflectional elements in Pronominal Argument languages is that they are *all* backgrounded and discourse-anaphoric; in order to emphasize a semantic feature in the domain of tense/aspect or modality, it is necessary to use a 'periphrastic' expression, a lexical item that can be focused. In Lexical Argument (LA) languages, on the other hand, both pronouns and DPs serve as arguments, and any constituent can be given focus via intonation—'light' verbs or auxiliaries, modals, even some affixes, can have contrastive stress (*RE-copy*, *UN-tie*). If there are any DPs at all in A-positions, then the language does not fall into the Pronominal Argument category.

Neither Lummi nor Navajo shows noun incorporation; since there are no NPs in object position, it is impossible for DPs to move from this position to the verb. Both these languages have a small closed list of noun roots (typically referring to body parts etc.) that may take part in complex verb formation. In Lummi grammar they are termed 'lexical suffixes', and often do not correspond morphologically to a semantically equivalent free root. In Navajo they are even more limited (see Hale et al., 2003). In contrast, some pro-drop languages—those that have both object clitics and object DPs in alternation—do show Noun Incorporation.

I propose that this parametric contrast has to do with the nature of the mapping between argument structure and information structure—the organization of old versus new information in the clause in these languages. Old information is topical; new information has focus.[1] In Pronominal Argument languages, morphosyntactic status directly reflects information status: pronouns are topical, unstressed discourse anaphors referring back to a referent earlier in the clause or in the discourse. New information is presented in the form of lexical items—predicates or DPs that carry inherent focus and stress. Consider the following construction:

(5)   Niiłtsá              (Navajo)
      1sgObj-1sSUBJ-saw
      'I saw you'

In this sentence, the affixed pronouns are both familiar and topical; both are backgrounded and unstressed as old information. In a comparable construction in English, either pronoun may be stressed.

(6)   a. *I* saw you
      b. I saw *you*

How do languages like Lummi and Navajo solve the problem of placing focus on a pronominal argument? The only way to produce the equivalent of (6a, b) in Navajo is to add a freestanding contrastive focus pronoun in an A-bar position preceding the verb sentence, as shown in (7). These pronouns always carry a contrastive reading.

(7)   a. Shí niiłtsá
         '*I*, I saw you'
      b. Ni niiłtsá
         '*You*, I saw you'

Note that the inflected verb, with its arguments, does not change when a contrastive independent pronoun is present. It is impossible to produce a verb without its full complement of arguments, inflectional affixes, in Navajo. Focus can be added to an argument only via a Contrastive Focus element. This is the core difference between Pronominal Argument languages and Lexical Argument languages; in a PA language the verb complex always

---

[1] The terms 'topic' and 'focus' have been used with reference to the information structure of the sentence, as in work by Diesing (1992: 49–53), Hajičová et al. (1998: 102–21), and numerous others. In this tradition, that part of the sentence that is familiar and presuppositional is classed as topical, established in the discourse, while what is new information in the context of the sentence belongs to the focus. Basilico (1998) extends the thetic/categorical contrast to the topicalization of goal arguments within the object array in dative movement.

represents a complete predicate/argument complex, with backgrounded, unstressed pronominal arguments—old information—while the verb stem itself is new information. In contrast, in an LA language such as English, verbs appear without affixed arguments and a pronoun may freely receive contrastive intonation. Intonation is not used to mark argument focus in PA languages. Affixed pronouns are always backgrounded, and lexical roots have normal (default) focus.

Compare the situation in Spanish. Spanish has subject agreement with pro-drop, and object clitics. Independent subject pronouns can be added to the subject-inflected verb to add emphasis, along with stress on the independent pronoun.

(8)  a.  Te   ví
         you:OBJ I-saw
     b.  *Yo* te   ví
         *I* you:OBJ I-saw
         '*I* saw you'        (contrastive focus on the subject)

In order to place contrastive focus on the object pronoun, however, it is necessary to add an oblique, *non-argumental* contrastive object phrase:

(9)  c.  Te        ví    *a tí*
         you:OBJ I-saw  (OBL) *you*
         'I saw *you*'

Where there is an inanimate DP object, it is impossible to use a coreferent object clitic:

(10)  Leí el mensaje   (*Lo leí el mensaje)
      'I read the message'

PA languages differ in using the 'add-on' adjunct strategy to mark contrastive focus with *all* subjects and objects, since the pronominal inflection is always present.

Information structure is a feature of universal grammar; all languages have some means of marking this level of the interpretation of the sentence. Chomsky (2001b) gives Topic and Focus syntactic status as functional projections. In PA languages, DP adjuncts appear at Topic/Focus operator positions, while the pronouns appear at functional projections associated with the subject and object cases.

In LA languages, information structure contrasts are largely expressed in intonation contrasts, and traditionally have been set aside as 'post-syntactic'. In PA languages the mapping between argument structure and Topic/Focus articulation is expressed in the morphosyntax, not by intonation. In this chapter, I present three lines of evidence on the PA parameter—data that demonstrate how this class of languages differs from the class of pro-drop languages. These are:

1. *The absence of pro-drop.* PA languages completely lack the agreement relation, involving subjacency, that licenses pro-drop. Affixed pronouns serve as arguments, and contrastive pronouns and DPs are syntactic adjuncts to the predicate/argument complex. These adjuncts need not occur next to the pronouns.

2. *Contrasts in case marking.* PA languages have distinct sets of case options available to pronouns, on the one hand, versus 'full' DPs, on the other (Jelinek 1998: 339–41; 2000b: 53). The pronouns have the kinds of grammatical case that appears on direct arguments. In contrast, DPs cannot carry grammatical case; they may appear with a lexical case, as oblique objects of prepositions or case particles. DPs in PA languages may also be case-less predicate nouns or topical adjuncts.

3. *The absence of determiner quantification.* PA languages completely lack determiner quantification, which functions to fix quantifier scope to an A-position. Since PA languages have no DP in (direct) A-positions, they rely upon adverbial quantification exclusively. Furthermore, the default reading of nominals in these languages is definite; only in a few marked contexts are indefinite readings possible. Since the restriction on a determiner quantifier is stated in a simple indefinite noun, these quantifiers are excluded in PA languages.

Let us begin with a consideration of the question of pro-drop.

## 9.2 The absence of agreement and pro-drop in Pronominal Argument languages

We will see that, while there are some syntactic agreement relations in these languages, we do not find the kind of relation between terms generally recognized as agreement, where there are matching φ features between constituents in a subjacency relation. In these languages, there are no independent pronouns that perform this function. In Lummi, there are no freestanding pronouns that match the pronominal arguments in the φ feature of person. In Navajo there is only the set of contrastive focus pronouns that are limited to A-bar positions. Let us first review argument structure in Lummi.

### 9.2.1 *Subject clitics and object suffixes in Lummi*

Lummi is a predicate-initial language with a second-position clitic string where tense/aspect, mood, and modality are marked, and the subject clitics appear (Jelinek 2000a: 216–18). The Subject clitics are last in the second-position clitic string, and are always unstressed. The main-clause subject markers are seen in the examples in (11):

(11)    a.   Ye'=ł'ə'=sən
          go=PAST=1sgNOM
          'I left'
     b.   Ye'=ł'ə'=l
          go=PAST=1plNOM
          'We left'
     c.   Ye'=ł'ə'=sxʷ
          go=PAST=2sgNOM
          'You (sg.) left'
     d.   Ye'=ł'ə'=sxʷ helə
          go=PAST=2plNOM
          'You (pl.) left'
     e.   Yye'=łə'=0
          go=PAST=3ABS
          'He/they (definite, referential) left'
     f.   Ye'=łə'=0    cə wet
          go=PAST=3ABS DET person
          'He/they left, the person(s).'
          (Somebody/some people left.)

Example (11e) cannot be used to mean 'Somebody left'. In order to convey 'somebody', it is necessary to use a construction like (11f). The Ø is a third-person absolutive pronoun, the only phonologically null pronoun in any Lummi paradigm. I conclude that this Ø is not a result of pro-drop, since the φ features of this null argument are fixed: it is always third-person absolutive, and does not vary ('agree') in φ features in context. Aside from the phonologically null third-person absolutive, all arguments in all Lummi clause types are overt—there are no control phenomena and no PRO or pro.

(12)   S-λ̓i'-əs=lə'=0                 kʷ     ye'=əs
       NOMLZR-wish-3POSS=PAST=3ABS   DET   go-3SUBORD SUBJ
       'It was his wish that he go' (He wanted to go)

Third person is overt (*-əs*) in the adjoined subordinate clause in (12). There is no copula in any paradigm in the language. Lummi predicates are overtly marked as to valence by one of a small closed set of transitivizers (a 'light' verb) at a functional projection where transitive and intransitive constructions are derived. The transitivizer licenses object suffixes. These object suffixes are incorporated into the verb and, according to phonological rules, may sometimes carry the main word stress. There are no freestanding subject or object pronouns that agree in person with these pronominal arguments. Examples:

(13) a. Nəp-t-oŋəs=sx$^w$
        advise-TRANS-1sgACC=2sgNOM
        'You advise me'
    b. Nəp-t-oŋəɬ=sx$^w$
        advise-TRANS-1plACC=2sgNOM
        'You advise us'

In these examples, the main stress of the sentence is on the complex predicate word, including the object pronoun, while the subject is unstressed. This is consistent with the information status of these pronouns: the object is included in the predicate, which is the new information that constitutes the focus; the subject is topical and backgrounded. The predicate (Root + Transitivizer + Object, if any) in a Lummi sentence raises to a Focus position at the head of the clause, in COMP. It is followed by the INFL clitic string, which may include an overt mood marker.

(14)

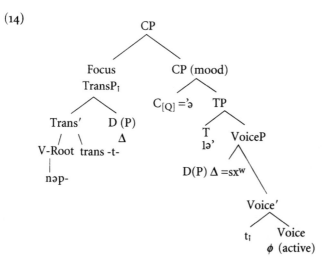

Nəp-t-0='ə=lə'=sx$^w$?
advise-TRANS-3ABS=Q=PAST=2sNOM
'Did you advise him?'

The absolutive, by definition, refers either to an intransitive subject (11e) or to a transitive object (14). There is a case 'split' in Lummi, of the most commonly seen variety: first and second person (the speech act participants) are NOM/ACC, while third person is ERG/ABS (Jelinek 1993). The third-person ERG argument is phonologically overt (-s):

(15)  Nəp-t-s=lə'=0
      advise-TRANS-3ERG=PAST=3ABS
      'He advised him' (definite third-person pronominal arguments)

There is a person hierarchy in Lummi. The case split and person hierarchy make it possible for both ACC and ERG to be morphologically internal arguments, suffixed to the verb—note that the ERG argument, like the object suffixes, precedes the tense clitic—and Lummi permits only one internal argument in a transitive sentence. (As we will see, there are no ditransitive constructions.) Therefore, it is impossible to have a construction of the type seen in (16a), where both an ACC and an ERG argument are present, in either order:

(16)  a.  *Nəp-t-s-oŋəɬ  (or:  *nəp-t-oŋəɬ-s)
          [*he advises us]
      b.  Nəp-t-ŋ=ooŋəɬ
          advise-TRANS-PASSIVE=1plNOM
          'We are advised'

Constructions like (16a) are excluded. It is necessary to use the Passive (16b) as an approximate equivalent.

DPs, optional additions to the clause in adjunct positions, may be added only to clauses that contain an ABS or ERG pronoun.

(17)  Ye'=lə' =0          cə    si'em
      go=PAST=3ABS    DET   elder
      'He left, the elder'

In transitive sentences, two DPs may be added; however, there is ambiguity, indicating that neither DP is in an A-position. They are adjuncts, anti-topics.

(18)  Nəp-t-s= lə'=0                       cə si'em    cə nə-men
      advise-TR-3ERG= PAST=3ABS    DET elder    DET my-father
      'He advised him, the elder, my father'
      'My father advised the elder' or 'The elder advised my father'

Some Straits languages (e.g. Lushootseed) permit only one DP adjunct to transitive sentences. All Straits Salish languages show ambiguity when two DP adjuncts are present. In the feature of free word order for any DP adjuncts, the Straits Salish languages may be termed 'non-configurational'. Without matching freestanding pronouns, there can be no agreement or pro-drop in Lummi. The affixes and clitics are simply incorporated arguments. One could invoke a full set of null subject and object pronouns just in order to 'pro-drop' them—pronouns that would never be visible in any environment—but we would have no evidence on their putative order in the clause, in addition to the other problems raised by such a move.

### 9.2.2 *The contrastive focus demonstratives*

If Pronominal Arguments in Lummi are necessarily backgrounded, how is focus placed on an argument? Lummi solves this problem in an interesting way, which provides evidence in support of the PA parameter. Like all the Salish languages, Lummi is rich in lexical roots that mark various deictic features such as position in time and space. There is a set of demonstrative lexical roots that mark the semantic features of person, which do not carry the grammatical φ feature of person. Significantly, they are *third-person* in syntax, and have inherent focus, like other deictic roots. We may call them pronouns, if we keep in mind that they do not have the grammatical feature of person, only the lexical feature.

(19)    Person  1      2         3
        SG      ʼəs    nəkʷə     niɫ
        PL      ni,əɫ  nəkʷiliyə  nəniɫiyə

These words are comparable to deictic expressions like *the former* and *the latter*, which also have inherent focus (Diesing and Jelinek 1995: 170). Like all other roots, they appear either (1) in clause-initial position, to form a clausal predicate followed by the clitic string, or (2) under the scope of a determiner, to form DPs. They cannot occur in either subject (clitic) or object (affixal) positions. They occur only in focus constructions and in oblique adjuncts. Example (20) shows an oblique DP built on a contrastive focus (CF) demonstrative:

(20)    Leŋ-t-ŋ= sxʷ          ʼə    cə      ʼəs
        see-TR-PASS=2sNOM     OBL   DET:M   BE:ME
        'You were seen by ME (masculine)'

The determiner *cə* marks masculine gender. (Gender is not marked in the pronominal affixes and clitics.) Straits Salish employs DPs built on CF demonstratives in constructions requiring first-, second-, or third-person oblique arguments, as in (20), since the Oblique marker takes scope *only* over Determiner Phrases, producing oblique adjuncts.

Example (21) shows a CF demonstrative, nəkʷə 'be you', functioning as a main-clause predicate. This CF demonstrative is followed by an evidential clitic, yəxʷ. There is a null third-person absolutive subject. This clause is followed by a DP with the determiner marked feminine, and the noun *ten* 'mother' preceded by the first-person singular possessive pronoun.

(21)   Nəkʷə = yəxʷ=0        sə   nə-ten
       BE:YOU=EVID=3ABS DET:F   1sPOSS-mother
       'It must be YOU,         (who are) my mother'

These roots undergo various derivational and inflectional processes.

We have seen that, in non-finite or Subjunctive adjoined subordinate clauses, there is overt third-person subject inflection.

(22)   Čte-t-ŋ =sən          kʷə   nəkʷ-əs
       ask-TRANS-PASS=1sNOM   DET   BE:YOU-3SBD SUBJ
       'I was asked if it was YOU'

(23)   Xʷən-ŋ       cə Bill    kʷə   nəkʷ-əs
       do/act-MIDDLE   DET Bill   DET   BE:YOU-3SBD SUBJ
       Bill acted for YOU (in your place; acting as you)

Like other lexical roots, they may be transitivized:

(24)   Nəkʷə-txʷ=0
       BE:YOU-CAUS:TRANS-3ABS
       'Make/let it be YOU.' (YOU do it) (Saanich; Montler 1991: 55)

The crucial role of these CF demonstratives is to provide a grammatical mechanism for focusing referents, since the pronominal arguments cannot receive contrastive stress. Compare:

(25)   a. Leŋ-t-oŋəs=ɫə'=sən
          see-TR-2ACC=PAST=1sNOM
          'I saw you' (no CF)
       b. Nəkʷə =ɫə'=0    cə   leŋ-t-ən
          BE:YOU=PAST=3ABS DET see-TR-1sSBD
          'YOU were the one I saw' (CF)
       c. Leŋ-t-0=lə'=sən    cə   nəkʷə
          see-TR-3ABS=PAST=1sNOM DET BE:YOU
          'I saw the one that was YOU' (CF)

Example (25c) could be used when recognizing someone in a crowd.

The contrastive focus demonstratives have the semantic features of person and number found in the pronominal arguments, together with a feature that we gloss with the copula: 'be you', 'be me', etc. This feature is simply a result of functioning as a predicate. In sum, these CF demonstratives undergo various inflectional and derivational processes, appearing as the root of the predicate in both main and subordinate clauses, but never appear in A-positions. Note that they cannot occur with the PAs that mark the grammatical $\varphi$ features of person, as in (26).

(26)  a.  *Nk$^w$ = sx$^w$             b.  *'ə s=sən
          BE YOU=2sgNOM                  BE I=1sgNOM
          [*you are you]                 [*I am I]
      c.  *Leŋ-t-oŋəs=lə'=sən    cə   nək$^w$ə
          see-TR-2sgACC= PAST=1sNOM DET BE:YOU
          '*I saw you, the YOU'

Compare (26c), which is excluded, with (25c), where a *third*-person object PA is coreferent with the second-person CF demonstrative. Since a PA may never co-occur with a coreferent CF demonstrative, any possibility of agreement and pro-drop with these forms is excluded. We have already rejected the possibility that the third-person Ø absolutive pronoun is PRO, since its features do not vary in context or as the result of 'control'. I conclude that Lummi lacks argument agreement and pro-drop.

### 9.2.3  *Contrastive pronouns in Navajo*

The situation in Navajo, the second PA language that we will compare briefly with Lummi, is somewhat different. As we saw above in (7), Navajo has a set of freestanding 'emphatic' pronouns, in addition to incorporated PAs, but these two pronoun sets do not alternate in A-positions. The independent pronouns have the $\varphi$ features of person and number, but they occur only with the PAs in a special CF construction. Their function is the same as the CF demonstratives in Lummi. Their syntax is different; the Navajo Contrastive pronouns are confined to a particular left-peripheral (clause-initial) operator position where CF is marked. They never occur in A-positions. DPs in Navajo occupy topic and focus operator positions that have scope over the PAs marked on the inflected verb, while the independent pronouns occupy the CF position. Navajo is a discourse configurational language (Hale et al. 2003).

Kiss (1995: 6) groups discourse configurational languages into subtypes, depending on whether there are left-peripheral operator positions for (1) topic, (2) focus, or (3) both. Kiss notes that there are also languages (e.g.

Finnish (Vilkuna 1995: 248)) where there is a clause-initial position for contrast. Etxepare (1998: 65–8) argues that Basque has this kind of CF position. Navajo also has this feature, and this sentence-initial CF position is the *only* place where the freestanding pronouns may occur.

(27)  a.  Yááłti'                b.  Shí yààłti'
          1sSubj-spoke          I    1sSubj-spoke
          'I spoke'             'I, [*I'm* the one who] spoke'

The independent contrastive pronouns do not have Case, and may bind any PA that matches in φ features. In (27b) the subject argument in an intransitive has contrastive focus. In a transitive sentence, either argument, regardless of grammatical relation, may have contrast.

(28)  a.  Shí    niisisdlą́ą́d
          *I*    2sObj-1sSubj-believed
          'I, I believed you. (*I'm* the one who believed you)'
      b.  Ni    niisisdlą́ą́d
          *YOU*  2sObj-1sSubj-believed
          '*YOU*, I believed you (*You're* the one I believed)'

9.2.3.1 *Navajo contrastive pronouns are not arguments*  Evidence for this statement includes the fact that it is impossible to include more than one independent pronoun in a simple sentence. In (29) below, both arguments cannot be given contrastive focus—the two independent pronouns cannot both appear in the sentence-initial position.

(29)  *Shí   ni   niisisdlą́ą́d
       *I*   *YOU*  2sObj-1sSubj-believed
       '*I believed *YOU*'

We have seen that an independent pronoun must appear first in the clause, in the contrast position, no matter what the grammatical relation of the coreferent pronominal argument. In ditransitives, any argument may be given CF by an independent pronoun. Note that the verb complex following the contrastive pronoun is identical in (30a, b, c), a ditransitive construction where the incorporated PP is leftmost in the complex verb.

(30)  a.  Shí    nich'i'yíł'aad
          I    2sg-to-3Obj-1sSubj-sent
          'I, *I* am the one who sent him to you'
      b.  Ni    nich'i'yíł'aad
          *YOU*  2sg-to-3Obj-1sSubj-sent
          '*You*, *you* are the one I sent him to'

c. Bí   nich'i'yiɬ'aad
   HE 2sg-to-3Obj-1sSubj-sent
   'He, he's the one I sent to you'

Along with an independent pronoun in the contrastive focus position, a Navajo sentence may contain DP in the topic and focus operator positions.

(31) a. Shí ashkii naaltsoos shich'i' áyiilaa
     I   boy   book   1sg-to   3OBJ-3Subj-sent
     'I, I'm the one, the boy sent the book to me' [*me*]
   b. *Ashkii shí naaltsoos shich'i' áyiilaa
      boy   I   book   1sg-to   3OBJ-3Subj-sent
   c. *Ashkii naaltsoos shí shich'i' áyiilaa
      boy   book   I   1sg-to   3OBJ-3Subj-sent

Examples (31b, c) are excluded. The contrastive pronoun must appear in sentence-initial position, although it is coreferent with the goal argument marked on the dative postposition—*ch'ii'* 'to'. (Here the PP is not incorporated.) In (31a) it is the presence of the contrastive pronoun in the sentence-initial pronoun that places focus on the first-person goal; there is no phonological or other focus marking on the PA that is the object of the postposition—the gloss is just marking the interpretation here. I conclude that this is not an agreement relation of the kind that licenses pro-drop, since there is no subjacency relation between the contrastive pronoun and the postpositional object.

The examples in (29–31) provide evidence that the freestanding contrastive pronouns in Navajo, as in Salish, do not occupy A-positions.

*9.2.3.2 DP in the contrastive focus position*    There is also a CF particle *ga'* that may be used with a DET P in the sentence-initial CF position.

(32) At'ééd   ga'   ashkii   naaltsoos   bich'i'   áyiilaa
     girl     CF    boy      book        3-to      3OBJ-3Subj-sent
     'The girl, the boy sent her [*her*] the book'

## 9.3 Case-marking options and 'dative movement'

The second line of evidence on the PA parameter has to do with case assignment. These languages show an interesting distribution of case marking that follows directly from argument type. Since arguments are limited to the morphologically integrated affixes and clitics, and DPs are not (direct) arguments, we must predict different kinds of case option for PAs and DPs. In languages where both pronouns and 'full' DPs can occupy A-positions, there should be no such difference in case marking. This turns out to be the case. In both Lummi and Navajo (as in all PA languages), case distribution is as follows:

(33)   a.   PAs, carry grammatical case, the cases carried by direct arguments.
      b.   Determiner Phrases may carry oblique lexical case, the cases carried by adjuncts, certain prepositional objects and the like.

This contrast constitutes strong evidence for the existence of a typological parameter. In PA languages, animate goals are the crucial case. Lummi and Navajo show a split in the distribution of dative case according to animacy. In effect, we might say that animate goals in these languages undergo 'obligatory dative movement' to the status of direct objects, while inanimate and other non-pronominal goals and destinations do not show 'goal advancement', but appear as obliques. Let us first consider the semantic and syntactic properties of dative movement in universal grammar.

### 9.3.1 *Dative movement*

I use the traditional term 'dative movement' (DM) to refer informally to contrasting sentence pairs of the following kind:

(34)   a.   John gave a book to Mary
      b.   John gave Mary a book

In (34a), the goal is syntactically oblique; in (34b) the goal argument, *Mary*, precedes the theme, and there is no oblique marker (the preposition *to* in (34a)). However, it is not always possible to employ DM. Bresnan (1982) and Oehrle (1978) noted the role of animacy in constraints on DM in English:

(35)   a.   The lawyer sent a letter to Ellen
      b.   The lawyer sent Ellen a letter

(36)   a.   The lawyer sent a letter to Chicago
      b.   ## The lawyer sent Chicago a letter

While (35b) is fine, (36b) is excluded unless *Chicago* refers to a person or perhaps an institution, a set of people, not a place. Thus, in English only animates can undergo dative movement. Animate goals are typically affected in ways that inanimates are not. Consider the following contexts:

(37)   Q: What happened to Ellen?
      A: The lawyer sent Ellen a letter

(38)  Q: What happened to Chicago?
      A: ## The lawyer sent Chicago a letter

In addition, there are other constraints on the Dative in English that appear to be lexical in nature, and less obviously related to animacy. Compare:

(39)  a. They donated a book to the library
      b. *They donated the library a book
      (The goal, *library*, is not affected as an animate would be.)

(40)  a. He whispered a warning to his friend.
      b. *He whispered his friend a warning.
      (The theme, *warning*, is affected by the act of whispering.)

This lexical constraint appears most commonly with verbs of Latinate origin. These verbs have a lexical semantic property in common: they are more specific with regard to the manner of the exchange taking place. The manner of this exchange can imply a particular effect on the theme argument immediately following the verb. Again, goal arguments that do not advance are not significantly affected, as compared to the goal arguments that undergo DM.

Basilico (1998: 542–6) provides an insightful analysis of DM in terms of the relative topicality of the two object arguments. The effect of DM is to make familiar, presuppositional goal arguments 'topical' within the object array. Basilico's analysis puts the 'advanced' goal at a transitive functional projection (corresponding to the vP, or VP 'shell'). Familiar goals are backgrounded with respect to themes, which are in the sentence-final focus position.

In the next sections, we will consider some examples of DM in PA languages. The important point here is that, in these languages, DM is never a free discourse option; that is, the speaker cannot choose between alternative utterances, as in (46), to alter the information structure of the clause.

(41)  a. John gave a book to me
      b. John gave me a book

In (41b), DM has placed the familiar animate goal in a backgrounded position. Now compare:

(42)  John gave *me* a book

In (42), a shift in the intonation peak has given the goal contrastive focus, 'overriding' the effect of DM. Recall that, in PA languages, contrastive intonation is never used to mark focus. In accord with the dative split, the grammar makes use of obligatory goal 'advancement' for pronouns. There are no sentences corresponding to (41a); only the (41b) type appears. This means that PAs have one kind of case, while DPs have another, when they function as goals or destinations. In contrast, while animacy plays a role in the distribution of DM in English, the pronoun/DPs split is not the determining factor; either a pronoun or a DP may be backgrounded.

### 9.3.2 Datives in Lummi

Lummi has no ditransitive constructions, no verbs that select for two obligatory objects. Animate goals are obligatorily 'advanced' to the status of direct object. The item exchanged may optionally be identified by adding an oblique nominal. In (47), the root 'oŋəs 'give' appears with the auxiliary verb -t, one of the small closed set of Transitivizers:

(43)  'oŋəs-t-s=lə'=0                     ('ə  cə sčeenəxʷ)
      give-TRANS-3ERG=PAST=3ABS    OBL DET salmon
      'He gifted them ([with] a/the salmon/fish)'

In the corresponding passive (48), the semantic goal is further 'promoted' to subject:

(44)  'oŋəs-t-ŋ=lə'=0                     ('ə  cə sčeenəxʷ)
      give-TRANS-PASS=PAST=3ABS    OBL DET salmon
      'They were gifted ([with] a/the salmon)'

A second oblique nominal may be added to identify the 'implicit' agent of a passive. Again, neither oblique nominal is in an A-position, and their order is free. Ambiguities are resolved in context: in the next example, the hearer judges it unlikely that the second interpretation is intended.

(45)  'oŋəs-t-ŋ=lə'=0                ('ə cə sčeenəxʷ)    ('ə cə si'em)
      give-TR-PASS=PAST=3ABS    OBL DET salmon    (OBL DET chief)
      a. 'They were gifted with the salmon by the chief'
      b. ## 'They were gifted with the chief by the salmon'

Nominal adjuncts in Lummi function as anti-topics, occurring after the initial predicate and clitic string. Without a nominal, the sentence is interpreted as having a definite third-person pronominal argument—the absolutive.

(46)  'oŋəs-t-0=lə'=sxʷ                   (cə xʷləmi)
      give-TR-3ABS=PAST=2sgNOM      DET Lummi
      'You gifted them, (the Lummi)' [You gave them something.]

In the corresponding passive, the semantic goal argument is subject:

(47)  'oŋəs-t-ŋ=lə'=0                     (cə xʷləmi)
      give-TR-PASS=PAST=3ABS              DET Lummi
      a.  'They were gifted, the Lummi' [They were given something]
      b.  *They were given, the Lummi [* they were given away]

There are no oblique pronouns or pronominal objects of prepositions in
Lummi (Jelinek 1998: 341). The single oblique marker occurs only with
nominals (including the contrastive demonstratives). Inanimate destinations
are oblique nominals, optional adjuncts.

(48)  Ye'=lə'=0          ('ə cə swi'iłč)
      go=PAST=3ABS       OBL DET lake
      'He went (to the lake)'

Crucially, inanimate destinations cannot be 'advanced'. In sum, PAs are backgrounded, oblique nominals are given focus, and the morphological status of
these terms reflects their status in information structure.

### 9.3.3 Datives in Navajo

Oblique arguments in Navajo are marked with postpositions. Young and
Morgan (1987: 26–36) identify some seventy-seven postpositions in Navajo.
Young and Morgan (1976: 19–26) recognized two classes: the postpositional
enclitics and the (ordinary) postpositions. Postpositional enclitics attach
directly to nouns, deriving oblique adjuncts:

(49)  a.  'olta'-dę'ę'        b.  hooghan-di
          school-from             home-at
          'from school'          'at home'

The ordinary postpositions differ in requiring a pronominal object as an
argument, and form a complex with the inflected verb; they may be phonologically incorporated into the verb word. They mark backgrounded goals.

(50)  a.  Yá jiłbéézh              b.  Béeso naa ní'ą̨'
          3-for 3Obj:3Subj:boils       dollar 2sg-to 1sg:gave
          'He is boiling it for him'   'I gave you a dollar'
      c.  Nich'i'yíł'aad
          2sg-to-3Obj-1sgSubj-sent
          'I sent him to you'

Example (50a) shows the benefactive; (50b) the dative. Example (50c) shows
an incorporated postposition, *ch'i'* 'to, toward', and its object. Willie (1991:
93–5) calls those postpositions (50) which have pronominal objects and may

attach to the verb 'grammatical' postpositions. She classifies the postpositional enclitics (49) that attach to the object as the 'lexical postpositions'.[2] The grammatical postpositions and their object pronouns appear at a vP projection left of (above) the direct object. Here is another example of an incorporated postpositional phrase:

(51)  Łi'į'      yeinílóóz
      horse    3-to:3Obj:3Subj:led
      'The horse, he led it to him'

Example (52) shows a schematic outline of a tree for the sentence in (51) (see Harley et al. (forthcoming) for a technical exposition).

(52)

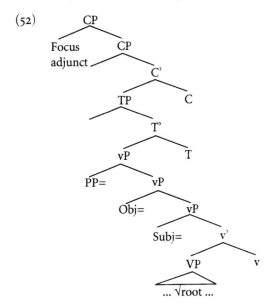

² Willie (1991) lists the following frequently used grammatical postpositions that occur only with pronominal objects:
(i)  a. -aa  ' to'  (Dative)
     b. -ts'ą' ą'  'from' (take away from)   (Malefactive)
     c. -á  'for'  (Benefactive)
     d. -ł  'with, together'  (Comitative)
The class of lexical postpositions, which occur only with nominals, includes the following directional or locative elements:
(ii)  a. -di  'at'                        d. –dę' ę' 'from'
      b. -gi  'at' (less productive)   e. -góó 'to'
      c. -dóó 'from'                   f. -ji 'to','as far as'
A few locative postpositions may occur with both animate and inanimate goals (Willie 1991: 39–44).

For a related analysis of the Navajo verb, see Hale (2003: 12). The Navajo verb has more than a dozen prefix positions, including numerous aspectual, modal, and adverbial projections, which we will not attempt to describe here. The grammatical PPs are initial in the verbal complex, whether phonologically integrated into the verb word or freestanding. This postposition–verb complex is the domain of the inverse voice alternation (Willie and Jelinek 2000: 265–78), a major feature of Navajo syntax.

Whether preceding the verb or phonologically incorporated into it, grammatical postpositional phrases are at the topmost argument projection. Other examples of postpositions: the grammatical postpositional phrase *yaa* in (53) marks motion towards a discrete entity.

(53)  'awéé'   jooł   yaa   yíłmáás
     baby   ball   3-to   3ACC-3NOM-rolling
     'She is rolling the ball to the baby'

The lexical postposition *góó* in (54) marks motion towards an inanimate area.

(54)  Kinłání-góó   déyá
     Flagstaff-to   1sNOM-go:Future
     'I will go to Flagstaff'

This postposition is not used with an animate individual:

(55)  *'awéé'-góó   jooł   yíłmáás
     baby-to   ball   3ACC-3NOM-rolling
     'She is rolling the ball to the baby'

Unless an areal reading is implied:

(56)  Shimá sání-góó   déyá
     grandmother-to   1sNOM-go:Future
     'I will go to my grandmother's place'

In (57), the verb–postpositional complex contains subject, theme, and goal pronouns. It also contains three DPs; this would occur in a very unusual discourse context, where all the referents need to be identified.

(57)  Asdzání at'ééd   naaltsoos   yaa   yiní'ą'
     woman girl   book   3-to   3ACC-3NOM gave
     'The woman, the girl, the book, she gave it to her'

When more than one DP adjunct is present, as in (57), they must be ordered according to the Navajo animacy hierarchy, not in terms of putative grammatical relations. This hierarchy ranks referents as follows:

(58)   supernatural>adult human>child>infant>large animal>small
       animal>insect>inanimate

If less than the full complement of DPs are present, as is typically the case, the
hearer must rely on context and real-world knowledge to decide who gave
what to whom. Notice that the PP *yaa* is not adjacent to the DP that the
pronoun is coreferent with, *at'ééd*—the PP must precede or adjoin the verb. If
only one DP is present, it directly precedes the verb sentence.

(59)   Naaltsoos   ya      yiní'ạ̀'
       book         3-to    3ACC-3NOM gave
       'The book, she gave it to her'

(Navajo pronouns do not mark gender or animacy; the features are used in
the glosses here to aid in reference.) Since books do not give or receive, we
know that 'book' is the transferred item. Now consider:

(60)   Mary,   ya      yiní'ạ̀'
               3-to    3ACC-3NOM gave
       'Mary, she gave it to her'
       'She gave it to Mary' or
       'Mary gave it to her'

This sentence is ambiguous; the hearer has no way of knowing if the singular
DP represents the agent or the goal, since, without the other animate DP, he
does not have enough information about the referents to make use of the
animacy hierarchy. He is forced to rely on context.

To place focus on an object in Navajo, accusative or dative, there must be a
lexical item (NP or contrastive pronoun) in the Focus position before the
complex verb. For example, 'wh-words' carry inherent focus, and the answer
to a 'wh-question' includes a focused lexical item that supplies the requested
information.

(61)   a.   Ha'át'íí-sh   naa yiní'ạ̀'
            what-?        2s-to 3ACC-3NOM gave
            'What did she give you?'

       b.   Naaltsoos shaa yiní'ạ̀'
            book         1s-to 3ACC-3NOM gave
            'She gave me a book'      (focus on the theme)

(62)   a.   Hái-sh yaa yiní'ạ̀'
            who-? 3-to 3ACC-3NOM gave
            'Who did she give it to?'

   b. At'ééd   yaa yiní'ą'
      girl     3-to 3ACC-3NOM gave
      'She gave it to the girl'   (focus on the goal)

Wh-words in Navajo occur in the same Focus positions that other nominal operators may occupy. The wh-words in (61a) and (62a) show an interrogative or modal suffix -*sh* that carries contrastive focus. Questions in Navajo do not have a distinct intonation; the question particles -*sh* (second position, or after the first constituent) and *da'* (clause initial) serve this purpose. Note that in (61b) the adjoined nominal is coindexed with the ACC pronoun; in (62b) the nominal is coindexed with the DAT pronoun. The speaker places focus on either argument by adding a lexical item that is coindexed with it— only lexical items have focus. The examples in (61) and (62) are evidence that the focus position preceding the verb–postpositional complex is not an A-position. The speaker cannot alter the focus status of either a pronoun or a nominal, since there is a strict correlation between their information structure status and their morphosyntactic properties.

### 9.3.4 Summary on Case options

In Pronominal Argument languages, where information structure is marked overtly in the morphosyntax, there is no 'optional' dative movement; instead, we find syntactic constraints on the distribution of the dative. In Lummi, goal pronouns are direct objects; only DP may be marked oblique. In Navajo, the structural cases, the accusative plus the (postpositional) dative and benefactive cases, appear with PAs at vP projections, and there is a class of lexical postpositions that derive oblique DP.

(63)   a. In Pronominal Argument languages, the Case options for pronouns and DPs differ, since only pronouns occur in A-positions.
       b. In Lexical Argument languages, pronouns and DPs show the same range of case markings, since both may appear in A-positions.

In PA languages, nominals appear at topic/focus projections, while the PAs appear at functional projections associated with the subject/object cases. We have seen that these languages show a rigid mapping between information structure and argument structure in the morphosyntax: affixed pronouns are backgrounded or topical, and only lexical items have focus as new information in context.

So far, we have identified two features that PA languages have in common, as opposed to LA languages: (1) the absence of agreement and pro-drop, and (2) the absence of any productive dative movement, along with distinct sets of case options for Pas and Dps. Finally, I want to turn to the third and most important line of evidence in support of the PA Parameter to be surveyed here: the absence of determiner quantification in PA languages.

## 9.4 Quantifiers in Lummi and Navajo

Lummi and Navajo show many similarities in the expression of quantificational notions that follow from the fact that they are PA languages. We will identify briefly the salient features wherein languages differ from LA languages in this domain of the grammar.

### 9.4.1 *Determiner versus adverbial quantification*

Investigations of parametric contrasts in the expression of quantification in natural language (Bach et al. 1995) have shown that, while all languages have adverbial quantification (Lewis 1975), only some languages have determiner quantification. Some examples of this contrast in English:

(64)   a. Determiner quantification: *most children, every child, three children, few children.*
       b. Adverbial quantification: *always work, never work, work often, just work.*

Languages with PAs have been claimed to lack determiner quantification; Straits Salish (Jelinek 1995: 487–8), Mohawk (Baker 1995: 21–2), Asurini do Trocará (Damaso Vieira 1995: 701–3), and Navajo (Faltz 1995: 283–4; Hale et al. 2003) are examples. Determiners in Lummi and Navajo are restricted to demonstratives that do not mark definiteness, number, count versus mass, or any quantificational notions. Quantification in PA languages is limited to adverbials, predicates, and certain morphological processes marking aspect (Jelinek and Demers 1997: 303).

### 9.4.2 *'Strong' versus 'weak' quantifiers*

In addition to this contrast in the syntactic expression of quantificational notions, there is a semantic contrast between two classes of quantifiers that is language-universal. This is the 'strong' versus 'weak' distinction (Milsark 1977).

(65)   a. Strong quantifiers range over the members of some presupposed set.
       b. Weak quantifiers (including cardinality expressions) assign number or numerical size (few, many) to the members of a set.

Examples from English determiners:

(66)   a. Strong: *most children, every child.*
       b. Weak: *three children, many children.*

This semantic contrast has many syntactic reflexes. For example, strong quantifiers cannot occur in existential contexts, while weak quantifiers can.

(67)   a. *There are most children/every child in the garden
       b. There are many/three children in the garden

In PA languages, the strong quantifiers are adverbial. In Lummi, the strong quantifiers have a special syntax, not shared by other adverbs.

(68)   Mkʷ =łə'=0        'əw' t'iləm   cə 'ŋən' ŋənə
       ALL=PAST=3ABS   LINK sing    DET children
       'They all sang, the children'

The strong quantifiers are linked to a following predicate by a conjunctive (LINK) particle, *əw*. The quantifier is followed by the second position clitic string.[3] An example of a different adverbial quantifier, showing variable scope, is given in (69).

(69)   λe'=sən              'əw'     t'əm'-t-0
       AGAIN/ALSO=1sNOM   LINK    hit-TRAN-3ABS
       'I hit him again/ I also hit him' ('in addition')

Since the strong adverbial quantifiers in Lummi have operator scope over the rest of the sentence, they are subject to interpretations with variable scope of the quantifier. Compare:

---

[3] An interesting analogue with the syntax of strong quantifiers in Lummi is provided by English constructions such as *I'm good and tired*, and *It's nice and clean*. Here there are quality words, functioning as quantifiers, linked by a conjunction to the following predicate. Because of the external position of the adverbial quantifier with respect to the sentence in Lummi, the surface syntax parallels the 'tripartite structure' defined for the semantic structure of quantified contexts. The tripartite structure contains a quantifier in an operator position, a restriction on the quantifier, and the nuclear scope. In the mapping between this tripartite structure and the syntax, it is universally the case that, in complex sentences, the main clause corresponds to the nuclear scope, and the restrictor to the subordinate clause (Hajičová et al., 1998: 60–72). These authors argue that this tripartite semantic structure reflects the focus component of the grammar. In Straits syntax, the main clause precedes any subordinate clauses, and thus the clause with nuclear scope precedes the restrictive clause in the surface syntax. The syntax of sentences with strong adverbial quantifiers in Straits Salish provides evidence that there are languages where the tripartite semantic structure of these sentences is 'grammaticalized' or overt in the surface syntax.

(70) Mək<sup>w</sup>= 'əw' p'əq cə speq'əŋ

ALL (x)  LINK  white (x)  DET flowers (x)

a. 'All the flowers are white'

b. 'The flowers are completely white [not parti-coloured]'

This Lummi sentence has the two readings of the English sentence *The flowers are all white*, which is also ambiguous between (70a) and (70b). However, Lummi lacks the distinction between the two sentences (70a, b) without employing complex multi-clause constructions—since the quantifier can occur in only one position.

In Navajo also, strong quantifiers are adverbial, and show variable scope, as in the following example:

(71) 'ałtso yíshį'į'

3OBJ-1sgSUBJ-dyed black

'I finished dyeing it/them black' or 'I dyed all of it/them black'

Weak quantifiers never appear as adverbial quantifiers. In both Lummi and Navajo, there are existential verbs or particles that are used to introduce new and indefinite referents into the discourse. Both languages also have predicates marking cardinality. (Lummi has no copula; Navajo does.)

(72) Čəsə'=ł

two=1pSUBJ

'We are two (in number)'  (Lummi)

(73) Táá' niilt'é

three 1pSUBJ-be

'We are three (in number)'  (Navajo)

Faltz (1995: 283–4) argues that Navajo quantifiers are 'floating'—i.e. not in construction with nouns—and constitute adjuncts in their own right. Weak quantifiers in these languages are either clausal predicates or adjectival in function.

Navajo nouns, apart from a few referring to human beings, are not marked for number. If a quantifier appears between two nominals in a Navajo sentence, it may be interpreted with either, evidence that it is adverbial in function:

(74) Má'íí ałtso dibé baayijah

coyote all sheep 3Obj-3PlSubj-ran away

a. 'The sheep were chased by all the coyotes'

b. 'All the sheep were chased by the coyotes'

A 'weak' quantifier such as *t'oo ahoy"i* 'many' has the same distribution.
In both Lummi and Navajo, the default reading of DPs is definite. It is only
in a few existential or other marked contexts that they can receive an indefinite reading. Since the restriction on a determiner quantifier is stated with a
simple indefinite noun, this excludes determiner quantification in these
languages. Examples are from Lummi (75) and Navajo (76):

(75)  a.  Leŋ-t-0=sən                     cə     sčeenəxʷ
          see-TRANS-3ABS=1sgNOM   DET    fish
          'I see the fish'
      b.  Ni'-0              cə     sčeenəxʷ
          there-3sgNOM   DET    fish
          'There are fish' (existential), or 'The fish are there'

(76)  a.  Dibé      yish'į̇
          sheep    see:3Obj:1sgSubj
          'I see the sheep'
      b.  Dibé      hólo'
          sheep    exist
          'There are sheep'
          (This is also a common way to convey: 'We have sheep')

Navajo also has a particle *léi'* that can be used to derive an indefinite:

(77)  a.  Ashkii    yááłti'
          boy      3Subj:spoke
          'The boy (familiar, presuppositional) spoke'
      b.  Ashkii ła'    yááłti'
          boy one      3Subj:spoke
          'One of the (presupposed set of) boys spoke'
      c.  Ashkii léi'    yááłti'
          boy some     3Subj:spoke
          'A/some/a certain boy (ambiguous) spoke'

### 9.4.3 *Summary on quantifier type in Pronominal Argument languages*

There is no determiner quantification in either of the PA languages we are
reviewing here. DPs are not in (direct) A-positions, and the function of
determiner quantification is to fix the scope of a quantifier to a particular
A-position. Weak quantifiers in these languages are verbs or adjectives; strong
quantifiers are adverbial. And the default reading of nouns in PA languages is
definite, while the restriction on a determiner quantifier across languages is
stated in a simple indefinite.

## 9.5 Concluding remarks

We have identified three major syntactic differences between the class of Pronominal Argument languages, on the one hand, and the class of Lexical Argument languages, on the other.

(78)  a. PA languages do not show the agreement relation that licenses pro-drop; some LA languages do. In an LA language, only definite arguments are pro-dropped, and the corresponding agreement elements are backgrounded. Similarly, in PA languages, a PA is backgrounded. PA languages have special contrastive focus elements that make it possible to place contrastive emphasis on a PA.
   b. In PA languages, there is no 'optional' dative movement. Pronouns and DP differ in case options, since only the former are in (non-oblique) A-positions. In LA languages, these two classes of referring expressions do not differ in case options, since they occupy the same A-positions, and dative movement is freely employed to mark focus.
   c. PA languages lack determiner quantification, while LA languages do not, since (1) determiner quantification functions to restrict the scope of a quantifier to a particular A-position, and DPs do not occupy A-positions, and (2) there are no simple indefinite nouns to serve as restrictors on determiner quantifiers.

While these features are absent in PA languages, they are present in pro-drop languages: agreement, 'optional' dative movement with the same case options for DPs and pronouns, and determiner quantification. The distribution of these traits clearly differentiates the two language types. There are many other syntactic features shared by PA languages that are outside the scope of this chapter. Some of the major parametric differences are:

(79)  a. There is no DP- or wh-movement from A-positions, since these constituents are excluded from A-positions.
   b. There is no noun incorporation from an object position.
   c. There are no embedded clauses, only adjoined subordinate clauses; in contrast, in LA languages, embedded clauses are nominalized constructions in A-positions.
   d. There is no inter-clause raising of subjects and objects.
   e. Reflexives do not function as emphatics, since they are incorporated pronominal arguments that exclude focus.

    f. There is no V or VP ellipsis, no infinitival verb forms, no control phenomena, etc. A verb always appears with its pronominal arguments.

In sum: the three syntactic features considered here, and the fact that their distribution is the same in genetically unrelated PA languages, provides conclusive evidence in support of the Pronominal Argument hypothesis. Lummi and Navajo represent a parametric option in which the grammar maps information structure directly onto the syntax by requiring pronouns—discourse anaphors that are old information—to be incorporated and unstressed, while lexical items—as items new in the context—have focus. Navajo does not make use of intonation contours in expressing information structure contrasts, but relies on morphosyntactic structure to express the Topic/Focus articulation of the clause. Recent spectrographic work by McDonough (2003: 203–6) shows that questions and other focus constructions do not have distinct intonation contours in the language.

In LA languages, the constraints on dative movement are lexical, having to do with animacy. Freestanding pronouns and DPs are equal under DM. Both pronouns and DPs can have any case or voice role, or any level of focus. We have seen that, in Lummi and Navajo, there is no 'optional' DM; rather, animate pronominal goals carry 'grammatical' case, while inanimate DP goals carry an oblique lexical case. Finally, the fact that both languages lack determiner quantification is definitive evidence in support of the claim that DPs are excluded from argument positions. These major parametric contrasts follow from differences in the mapping between information structure and morphosyntactic structure in PA versus LA languages. In PA languages, the information structure status of a constituent can be read directly from its morphosyntactic status.

# 10

# On Zero Agreement and Polysynthesis

MARK C. BAKER

## 10.1 Introduction

Research on non-configurationality and polysynthesis in the tradition of Jelinek (1984; 1993; 1995) and Baker (1996) assigns great significance to the presence of pronominal agreement morphemes on verbs and other θ role assigners. My Polysynthesis parameter, for example, says that every argument of a predicate must be expressed by morphology on the word that contains that predicate:

(1) The Polysynthesis parameter (informal version, Baker 1996: 14)
Every argument of a head element must be related to a morpheme in the word containing that head (a pronominal agreement morpheme or an incorporated root).
Yes: Mohawk, Nahuatl, Southern Tiwa, Mayali, Chukchee, (Mapudungun) . . .
No: English, Spanish, Chichewa, Japanese, Quechua, Turkish, (Kinande) . . .

This chapter was made possible thanks to a trip to Argentina in October 2000, to visit the Universidad de Comahue in General Roca, Argentina. This gave me a chance to supplement my knowledge of Mapudungun from secondary sources (Augusta 1903; Smeets 1989; Salas 1992) by consulting Argentine experts on this language (Pascual Masullo, Lucía Golluscio, and Roberto Aranovich), and by interviewing their Mapuche consultants, as well as members of the Mapuche community whom we met in Junín de los Andes, Argentina. Special thanks go to Pascual Masullo for making this trip possible. I also thank those who attended my class on polysynthesis at Universidad de Comahue, the audience at the workshop on agreement and argument structure held at Utrecht University in August–September 2001, and four anonymous reviewers for their comments. More recently, since completing the first version of this article in 2002, I have had the pleasure of corresponding about these matters in some detail with Elisa Loncon Antileo of the Universidad Autónoma Metropolitana in Mexico City, a linguist and native speaker of Mapudungun. This has led to several improvements in the empirical basis for this work, and a few new ideas, and I am very grateful to her for this input. The Kinande data in this article were collected from Ngessimo Mutaka during his visit to Rutgers University in the spring of 2001. All remaining faults in this work are my own responsibility.

Pronominal agreement morphology is the single most important way of satisfying this requirement, the other way being incorporation. (1) implies that, in a polysynthetic language like Mohawk, all verbs necessarily agree with subjects, objects, and indirect objects, except perhaps for the special case when the direct object is incorporated into the verb. This accounts elegantly for paradigms like the following, found also in languages like Nahuatl and Chukchee:[1]

(2)  a.  *Ra- nuhwe'-s    ne    owira'a  (Mohawk; Baker 1996: 21)
         MsS-like-HAB    NE    baby
         'He likes babies'
     b.  Shako-nuhwe'-s        (ne    owira'a)
         MsS/FO-like-HAB       NE    baby
         'He likes them (babies)'
     c.  Ra-wir-a-nuhwe'-s
         MsS-baby-Ø-like-HAB
         'He likes babies'

A transitive verb in Mohawk must contain an object agreement morpheme (2b) or an incorporated noun root (2c); an example like (2a) that contains neither is ruled out by (1).

Pronominal agreement is also syntactically significant in a second way: when it is present it is taken to induce dislocation of any overt NP associated with the agreement, as in (3) (from Baker (2003a); see also Baker (1996: 83–9)).

(3)  [In a certain class of languages], a verb X agrees with an overt NP Y if and only if Y is in a dislocated, adjunct position.

---

[1] Abbreviations used include the following: Ø, epenthetic vowel; AFF, affirmative; APPL, applicative; ASSOC, associative particle; ASP, aspect; AUG, augment vowel; CAUS, causative; CIS, cislocative; CL(+number), noun class (Bantu); CP, complementizer phrase; DIR, directional; DIST, distributive; DS, dative subject; FACT, factual mood; FCT, factitive; FOC, focus particle; FUT, future tense; FV, final vowel (Bantu); HAB, habitual; IMPER, imperative; IND, indicative mood; INST, instrumental case/postposition; INV, inverse; IP, Infl phrase, i.e. the core clause; ITR, iterative; IVN, instrumental nominalizer; LK, linker particle; LOC, locative; NE, particle introducing NPs in Mohawk; NEG, negative; NOML, nominalizer; NP, noun phrase; NPST, nonpast tense; NRLD, nonrealized tense; OM, object marker; PAST, past tense; PLUR, plural; POSS, possessive particle; PRES, present tense; PRT, particle; PUNC, punctual aspect; REP, reportative; SM, subject marker (Bantu); ST, stative aspect; T, tense (unspecified); TR, transitivizer; VP, verb phrase. Agreement markers, when not simply given as OM or SM, are complex forms that indicate person (1, 2, or 3) or gender (M, F, N), followed by number (s, d, or p), followed by series (S for subject or O for object). For more information about what these categories refer to, see the original sources.

Agreed-with NPs are found not in canonical argument positions, but rather in positions adjoined to the clause, and their syntactic properties are like those of clitic left-dislocated NPs in Romance languages (see Cinque 1990). Among other things this means that the NPs can appear in any order, on either side of the clause, and can be omitted without rendering the clause incomplete. In short, full agreement creates a particular kind of non-configurational syntax.

The causal relationship between agreement and dislocation is a bit abstract for languages like Mohawk, which have the 'Yes' value of the Polysynthesis parameter. Since every argument is agreed with and every argument is dislocated, it is hard to be sure that the one property causes the other. Bantu languages such as Chichewa and Kinande illustrate the connection more clearly. These languages have the 'No' value of the Polysynthesis parameter. Subject and object agreements are thus possibilities in these languages, but not requirements. One can therefore see more clearly that dislocation of the object is correlated with presence of object agreement on the verb, as shown in (4) from Chichewa (Mchombo, pers. comm.) and (5) from Kinande.

(4)　a. Mdyerekezi　[$_{VP}$ a-ku-námíz-a　　abúsa　(tsópáno)]
　　　 devil　　　　 SM-PRES-deceive-FV　priests　now
　　　 'The devil is deceiving the priests (now)'
　　 b. Mdyerekezi　[$_{VP}$ a-ku-námíz-a　　(tsópáno)]　abúsa
　　　 devil　　　　 SM-PRES-deceive -FV　now　　　 priests
　　　 'The devil is deceiving the priests (now)'

(5)　a. N-a-gul-a　　　　 eritunda
　　　 1sS-PAST-buy-FV　fruit
　　　 'I bought a fruit'
　　 b. Eritunda,　n-a-ri-gul-a
　　　 fruit　　　 1sS-PAST-OM-buy-FV
　　　 'The fruit, I bought it'

Bresnan and Mchombo (1987) provide evidence from word order and from a rule of phrasal phonology known as High Tone Retraction that the object *abúsa* 'priests' is contained in the verb phrase in (4a) but not in (4b). The distinction is more obvious in Kinande, which allows only left dislocation. The presence of agreement thus has an unsubtle effect on word order in this language: unagreed-with objects immediately follow the verb (5a), whereas agreed-with objects (if present at all) come at the front of the sentence as a whole (5b). Such facts give (3) a solid grounding. This implies that agreement has important syntactic effects, at least in a significant class of languages.

Together (1) and (3) have approximately the same effect as Jelinek's well-known Pronominal Argument hypothesis (1984), apart from a few technical differences concerning whether the affix in question is itself a pronoun (Jelinek's view) or only the licenser of a null pronoun in a normal argument position (my view). Because of these differences, Jelinek refers to the relevant morphemes on the verb as 'pronominal' affixes, whereas I call them 'agreement' affixes. I maintain my usage in this chapter, but the reader should realize that the difference is a relatively minor one. See Baker (2003a) for a proposed parameter that distinguishes languages like Bantu, in which agreement always goes hand-in-hand with dislocation, from Indo-European languages, in which it does not.

This general programme for analysing non-configurational polysynthetic languages depends in a crucial way on the ability to recognize null agreement affixes. It is clear that not every argument in a polysynthetic language is associated with a manifest agreement morpheme on the verb. Mohawk verbs, for example, seem not to agree with third-person neuter inanimate objects. The agreement prefix in the transitive sentence in (6a) is no different from the one on the intransitive sentence in (6b). Thus the presence of a neuter object has no effect on the verbal morphology. (6c) makes the same point in a different way, showing that incorporating the neuter object does not change the agreement borne by the verb. (6c) is different from (2c) in this respect, where incorporation of the object changes the agreement prefix because the object-agreement factor becomes unnecessary.

(6)  a. Sak   *ra*-nuhwe'-s        ne   atya'tawi
        Sak   MsS-like- HAB    NE   dress
        'Sak likes the dress'
     b. Sak   *ra*-rast-ha'
        Sak   MsS-draw-HAB
        'Sak is drawing'
     c. Sak   *ra*-[a]tya'tawi-tsher-a-nuhwe'-s
        Sak   MsS-dress-NOML-Ø-like-HAB
        'Sak likes the dress'

A more serious case, perhaps, concerns the theme objects of double object constructions. These can only be third-person neuter NPs in Mohawk, and they too have no influence on the verb morphology. This is shown by the fact that the version with the theme incorporated has the same prefix as the version without the theme incorporated:

(7)  a. Sak   wa-hiy-u-'                          ne   ashare'
        Sak   FACT-1sS/MsO-give-PUNC   NE   knife
        'I gave Sak the knife'

   b. Sak   wa-hiy-a'shar-u-'
       Sak   FACT-1sS/MsO-knife-give-PUNC
       'I gave Sak the knife'
   c. *Sak  t-a-hiy-u-'                  ne   owira'a
       Sak   CIS-FACT-1sS/MsO-give-PUNC  NE  baby
       'I gave Sak the baby'

The agreement prefix in (7a) is also identical to the one found on a simple monotransitive verb with a first-person singular subject and a masculine singular object (*wa-hi-yena-'* FACT-1sS/MsO-catch-PUNC 'I caught him'). Examples like (7a) are found quite routinely in most polysynthetic languages. Some linguists (notably Austin and Bresnan (1996: 242–3)) have used them to argue against the Polysynthesis parameter or the Pronominal Argument hypothesis. But proponents of such theories are generally unmoved. We say that (6a) has an object agreement and (6b) does not; this is just difficult to observe because the form of the agreement happens to be Ø in this case. Similarly, we say that (7a) has a third agreement in it, but triple-agreement forms are possible only when the third morpheme is a Ø. In one sense, this seems perfectly reasonable, since nearly all linguists, descriptive and theoretical, acknowledge the presence of zero agreement morphology in some cases. But, if it is used too freely, this gambit can look suspicious. If one can appeal to zero morphology whenever one likes, ideas like the Polysynthesis parameter and the Pronominal Argument hypothesis could become untestable. Therefore, proving that there is a distinction between the presence of null agreement and the absence of agreement—and learning how to tell which is which—are urgent tasks for evaluating this family of ideas.

    In the remainder of this chapter I propose to investigate this general issue by way of a case study of Mapudungun, a polysynthetic language of the Chilean and Argentinean Andes (Augusta 1903; Smeets 1989; Salas 1992). This language is interesting in that it has an overt third-person object agreement marker *fi*, and this marker seems to be optional, as shown in (8).

(8)  a. Nü-n     mapu  (Smeets 1989: 19)
        take-1sS  land
        'I took land'
     b. Nü-fi-n      mapu
        take-OM-1sS  land
        'I took the land'

In this respect, Mapudungun seems similar to the Bantu languages shown in (4) and (5) and unlike Mohawk and other true polysynthetic languages. But I will argue that appearances are deceptive here. Agreed-with objects show very different syntactic behaviour from unagreed-with objects in the Bantu languages, whereas in Mapudungun there is no detectable syntactic difference. On the contrary, objects in clauses in which the verb bears *fi* have the same behaviour as objects in clauses in which the verb does not. Moreover, both classes of objects have a syntax comparable to that of agreed-with objects in Bantu languages, not the syntax of unagreed-with objects in Bantu. From this I conclude that it is reasonable to posit an agreement marker in (8b), the shape of which is Ø. Mapudungun thus provides an example of Ø agreement and Kinande an example of absence of agreement. This distinction, which the Polysynthesis parameter and the Pronominal Argument hypothesis depend on, is therefore seen to be valid.[2]

This comparison between Mapudungun and Kinande raises an interesting learnability problem. How can children acquiring a language learn the very subtle distinction between absence of agreement and presence of null agreement, given only simple grammatical sentences? Normally Ø morphology is posited in cases of obvious paradigmatic 'holes'—cases in which every cell of a paradigm but one has an overt morpheme. But there is no such hole in the Mapudungun paradigm, since the child learns that third-person objects go with *fi* agreement. There must, then, be a less direct way of acquiring this knowledge. I argue that the Polysynthesis parameter can play a crucial role in this. The child is exposed to other kinds of evidence that Mapudungun is a polysynthetic language but Kinande is not—evidence comes from noun incorporation, causative patterns, and the nominalization of embedded clauses. This evidence could, in principle, be enough to tell the child that the Polysynthesis parameter is set 'Yes' in Mapudungun, but 'No' in Kinande. They can then infer that there must be a Ø object marker in (8a), but there is no pressure to infer this for (4a) or (5a). Children's natural conservatism thus leads them to assume no null affix in Bantu. If this proposed solution to the logical problem of language acquisition is supported by empirical studies of the actual course of language acquisition, it will show that 'macroparameters' like (1)—parameters that are not local to particular constructions but shape whole languages in a global way—are psychologically real and play an important role in how children come to have the language that they do.

But first I must show that the distinction is real.

---

[2] The overall theme of this article is very similar to that of Mithun (1986). She too argues that some languages that seem to lack agreement markers really do lack them, whereas others actually have phonologically null agreement markers. The languages she considers and the tests she uses to establish this result are quite different, however.

## 10.2 Null agreement versus absence of agreement

### 10.2.1 *Agreement and pro-drop*

Agreement has long been associated with pro-drop phenomena. Languages that have rich agreement paradigms typically do not require a full NP argument in the agreed-with position, because (depending on one's theory) the agreement morpheme either counts as a pronoun in its own right or else licenses the presence of a null pronoun. When a language that is otherwise a pro-drop language happens to lack an agreeing form for a particular combination of person, number, and tense, an overt noun phrase is sometimes required in just such environments; Hebrew (Borer 1986) and Irish (McCloskey and Hale 1984) are two prominent examples of this. Thus, agreement is generally required in order to have a null pronominal interpretation in languages that have agreement at all (Jaeggli and Safir 1989a).

(9)   If a language has agreeing forms, then agreement is needed to license a null pronoun.

This statement is silent about whether a language with no agreement at all will have pro-drop: some do (e.g. Chinese) and some do not (e.g. Edo). And there are problematic borderline cases. Nevertheless, something like (9) seems to be true in many languages.

Kinande fits very well with this general picture. The verb in the main clause in (10a) bears object agreement, and this clause is understood as having a pronoun that refers back to 'potatoes', the object of the conditional clause. In contrast, the verb in the main clause in (10b) has no object agreement, and this clause cannot be interpreted as containing an object pronoun. The second verb in (10b) can be understood only as an intransitive verb that means 'to do the cooking'.

(10)   a.   Ng-u-li-gul-a          ebitsungu, Kambale a-luandi-*bi*-kuk-a
             if-2sS-NPST-buy-FV  potatoes    Kambale SM-FUT-OM-cook-FV
             'If you buy potatoes, Kambale will cook them'
       b.   #Ng-u-li-gul-a        ebitsungu, Kambale a-luandi-kuk-a
             if-2sS-NPST-buy-FV  potatoes    Kambale SM-FUT-cook-FV
             Only as: 'If you buy potatoes, Kambale will do the cooking'

Mapudungun is different in this regard. A transitive verb that bears the object marker *fi* but has no overt NP object is interpreted as having a pronominal object, as expected. But so too is a transitive verb that does not bear *fi*. This is illustrated elegantly by the following minimal pair taken from a single page of a narrative text (Smeets 1989: 600). The story as a whole consists of reminiscences of the teller's father. The two sentences contain the same verb, but it is inflected with *fi* in the second case and not in the first. In spite of this difference, both are understood as having third-person singular pronouns that refer to the narrator's father, the subject of the text as a whole:

(11)  a.  Fey-mu     fiy     ta     yepa-le-r-pu-y-iñ                   iñchiñ
          that-INST   PRT    PRT    take.after-ST-ITR-LOC-IND-1pS     we
          'In this respect we take after him [our father]'
      b.  yepa-ntu-nie-r-pu-*fi*-y-iñ          kümé   dungu-mu       yiñ   kon-küle-al
          take.after-...-LOC-OM-IND-1sP        good   matter-INST    we    enter-ST-NOML
          'We take after him [our father] in that we get involved in good things'

There are approximately four or five examples of this kind in the 125 pages of texts in Smeets (1989), and at least that many in Salas (1992). There are two instances in the second sentence in (12a), both referring back to the NP 'cattle' found at the end of the first sentence (Smeets 1989: 513). (12b) is a similar example from Augusta (1903: 288).

(12)  a.  ... pichi-ke   ngül-üm-nie-rki-y                plata   ngilla-ya-m       kulliñ
          little-DIST    join-CAUS-ASP-REP-IND/3sS      money   buy-FUT-NOML      cattle
          '... little by little he saved money to buy cattle'
          Ngilla-ye-m        elfal-ke-fu-y                  ñi    pu     wenüy-mew
          buy-DIST-NOML      entrust-HAB-ASP-IND/3sS        POSS  PLUR   friend-INST
          'Whenever he bought [some], he used to entrust [them] to his friends'
      b.  Küpal-i-mi         kofke?     Küpal-n
          bring-IND-2sS      bread      bring-IND/1sS
          'Did you bring bread? (Yes,) I brought it/some'

These facts, taken together with the principle in (9), strongly suggest that Mapudungun has a Ø object agreement but Kinande does not.[3]

### 10.2.2 *Agreement and word order*

It is well known that languages with extensive agreement systems often tolerate a significant degree of freedom of word order, unlike lightly inflected

---

[3] An anonymous reviewer points out that there are other possible theoretical interpretations of the data in (11) and (12). It could be that the null object is not a pro, but rather the trace of a null topic operator (see Huang (1984) on Chinese and Japanese and Raposo (1986) on Portuguese). I have not tried to construct the subtle examples needed to distinguish these possibilities, but I think it is unlikely that this alternative analysis will prove correct. Note, for example, that the discourse properties of (11) and (12a) are different. In (11), the understood object does refer to the topic of the text as a whole, so a null topic analysis is not implausible. But in (12) the understood object does not refer to the topic of (this stretch of) the text; rather, the subject 'he' does. So a null topic analysis is less plausible for this example. Indeed, Mapudungun has a special 'inversion' construction which is used precisely when the object is topical and the subject is third person (Smeets 1989), and that morpheme is not used in (12b). See Baker (2003b) and sources cited there for an analysis of object 'topicalization' in Mapudungun.

English, which is a rigid SVO language. Mohawk, for example, has agreement with both subject and object, and permits the major constituents of the clause to come in any order (Baker 1996). Chichewa is a particularly interesting case in this regard, because object agreement is optional. Bresnan and Mchombo (1987) show that, when object agreement is absent, the object must be right-adjacent to the verb, as in English. The agreed-with subject, in contrast, can be on either edge of the clause. When object agreement is present, then any order of subject, object, and verb is acceptable, as in Mohawk. These patterns are summarized in (13) (all the sentences have the same meaning as (13a)).

(13)  a. Njuchi  zi-na-(wa)-lum-a  alenje
          bees    SM-past-OM-bit-FV  hunters
          'The bees stung the hunters'
      b. Zi-na-(wa)-lum-a      alenje    njuchi
          SM-past-OM-bit-FV    hunters    bees
      c. Alenje    zi-na-*(wa)-lum-a    njuchi
          hunters   SM-past-OM-bit-FV   bees
      d. Alenje    njuchi    zi-na-*(wa)-lum-a
          hunters   bees      SM-past-OM-bit-FV
      e. Njuchi    alenje     zi-na-*(wa)-lum-a
          bees      hunters    SM-past-OM-bit-FV
      f. Zi-na-*(wa)-lum-a    njuchi    alenje
          SM-past-OM-bit-FV   bees      hunters

Chichewa thus demonstrates a perfect correlation between agreement and freedom of order. Subjects are always agreed with and can always come on either side of the verb; objects can be agreed with and can appear on either side of the verb only when they are. This gives us the following crude working generalization:

(14)  In head-marking languages, an argument X is freely ordered with respect to the verb only if the verb agrees with X.

Consider now word order in Mapudungun. Subjects are always agreed with in Mapudungun,[4] and both subject–verb and verb–subject orders are possible—indeed common—on all accounts (see e.g. Smeets (1989: 454–9) and Rivano

---

[4] Verbs always agree with their subjects in person features, but it is quite common for third-person plural subjects to appear with third-person singular agreement on the verb, instead of with plural agreement (see Loncon Antileo, forthcoming, for some discussion). It is not clear whether number agreement is simply optional, or if something more systematic is at work; either way, I take this to be a minor caveat. Inanimate third-person plural NPs also trigger singular agreement in Mohawk and many other native American languages, so this is not unique to Mapudungun.

Fischer (1991)). (15) shows that the understood object can also come either before or after the verb when the object marker *fi* is present, as expected.

(15)  a. Ngilla-fi-n      kiñe  waka    (Elisa Loncon Antileo, pers. comm.)
         buy-OM-1sS    one   cow
         'I bought a (certain) cow'
      b. Kiñe  waka   ngilla-fi-n
         one   cow    buy-OM-1sS
         'I bought a (certain) cow'

Statistically speaking, the verb–object order is much more common than the object–verb order, maybe by a factor of 8:1. This has led to the claim that verb–object order is basic in Mapudungun (e.g. Smeets 1989; Loncon Antileo, forthcoming). However, object–verb order is certainly also grammatical, particularly when the object is 'newsworthy' new information. An example from a text is:

(16)  Fewlá  wariya-ülmen  küdaw-el-me-fi-y-iñ    (Smeets 1989: 490)
      Now    town-rich      work-APPL-LOC-OM-IND-1pS
      'Now we went to work for rich townsfolk'

The idea that the pragmatics of 'newsworthiness' influences word order in polysynthetic languages with no basic word order intrinsically defined by the syntax is familiar from Mithun (1987); Mapudungun does not seem significantly different from the polysynthetic languages she discusses in this regard. Nor do agreed-with objects need to be adjacent to the verb. Rather, they can be separated from the verb by (for example) an adverb; compare (17) with (4b) in Chichewa.

(17)  Pe-fi-y        pun   che,  ñuwi-i-ke-fi-y  (Smeets 1989: 483–4)
      see-OM-IND/3S  night  people  get.lost-CAUS-HAB-OM-IND/3S
      '[When] they [spirits] see people in the night, they make them get lost'

All this is consistent with the descriptive generalization in (14).

Unlike in Chichewa, however, Mapudungun word order is at least as free when the overt object marker *fi* is absent.[5] Apart from the absence of *fi*, the examples in (18) are identical to those in (15).

---

[5] In fact, object–verb order is quite a bit more common when the verb does not have the object marker *fi* than when it does in the texts I have studied from Smeets (1989) and Salas (1992). My guess is that this is an interaction between the fact that the object comes before the verb only if it is 'newsworthy', which often means it is indefinite, and the fact that *fi* tends to be used with objects that are definite or at least specific. The pragmatic factors that tend to encourage object–verb order thus overlap substantially with those that tend to discourage the use of *fi*. But these are tendencies of usage, not firm grammatical rules.

(18)  a. Ngilla-n   kiñe   waka   (Elisa Loncon Antileo, pers. comm.)
          buy-1sS    one    cow
          'I bought a cow'
      b. Kiñe   waka   ngilla-n
          one    cow    buy-1sS
          'I bought a cow'

A textual example of the less frequent object–verb order is shown in (19).

(19)  Feytachi   fücha-ke    witran-alwe    nie-y          re    pu     ülmen
        that        big-DIST    visitor-soul   have-IND/3S   only  PLUR   rich
        che...
        people
        'Only rich people have these big soul-visitors [a kind of guardian spirit]'

These patterns fall immediately into place if Mapudungun has a null object agreement as well as the overt agreement *fi*, whereas Chichewa does not.

The generalization in (14) will not do as a theoretical principle, of course. The theories of non-configurationality in Jelinek (1984), Baker (1996), and related work connect word-order facts like these to the pro-drop facts discussed in the previous section. We know that clauses in languages such as Chichewa and Mapudungun are complete without any overt NPs, and that the arguments of the verb in such a clause are inherently pronominal thanks to the presence of agreement morphology on the verb. We can suppose that the same is true in clauses that contain overt NPs. These overt NPs thus have the status of dislocated phrases, which are adjoined to the clause as extra 'topics' and the like. Even configurational languages like English allow such dislocated expressions to occur on either edge of the clause, as long as pronouns are present in the relevant position(s) inside the clause:

(20)  a. That cow, I bought it in town last week
      b. I bought it in town last week, that cow

The idea, then, is that the syntax of 'simple' clauses in Mohawk, Chichewa, and Mapudungun is comparable with that of dislocated clauses like those in (20) in English, except for the minor difference that the pronominal arguments are null/realized as agreement on the verb.[6] This is the underlying source of free word order in head-marking languages, I claim.

---

[6] Technically, clitic left dislocation as found in the Romance languages is a more exact parallel to the structure of clauses with agreement in Mohawk or Mapudungun than ordinary left dislocation in English is. See Cinque (1990: ch. 2) for a comparison of clitic dislocation with 'ordinary' dislocation, and Baker (1996: ch. 3) for a detailed comparison between clitic dislocation in Romance languages and clause structure in polysynthetic languages. Among other things, this has the consequence that freely ordered NPs are found in a full range of embedded clauses in Mapudungun (Smeets 1989: 465), not just in matrix clauses and other root-like environments. I downplay the distinction between the different types of dislocation in the text purely for expository reasons.

This perspective also gives us a way of addressing the fact that word order is freer in some head-marking languages than in others. Kinande, for example, is like Chichewa in that the object NP must be right-adjacent to the verb when there is no object marker. But, as already mentioned in section 10.1, Kinande is more restrictive than Chichewa in that, when the object marker is present, an associated NP can come only at the beginning of the clause, not at the end:

(21)   a. N-a-(*ri)-gul-a        eritunda
          1sS-T-OM-buy-FV   fruit
          'I bought a fruit'
       b. Eritunda,   n-a-*(ri)-gul-a
          fruit        1sS-T-OM-buy-FV
          'The fruit, I bought it'

This difference can be described by saying that Kinande allows only left dislocation, whereas Mapudungun and Chichewa (like Mohawk and English) allow both left and right dislocation. The same parametric difference can be observed with subjects: agreed-with subjects appear on either side of the clause in Mapudungun (Smeets 1989: 454–5) and Chichewa (13), but they can come only before the verb in Kinande:

(22)   a. Omukali   mo-a-sat-ire
          woman      AFF-3sS/T-dance-ASP
          'The woman danced'
       b. *Mo-a-sat-ire              omukali
          AFF-3sS/T-dance-ASP   woman
          'The woman danced'

I thus take the deeper property that underlies (14) to be (23) (repeated from (3)).[7]

(23)   In [a certain class of] languages, an argument X is dislocated if and only if the verb agrees with X.

Dislocation in turn produces free word order to varying degrees in different languages, depending on whether they allow both left and right adjunction of topic NPs. (Word order is also not quite as free in Mapudungun as it is in

---

[7] Agreement does not imply dislocation in all languages; for example, agreed-with subjects do not act as though they are dislocated in Indo-European languages like Greek and Spanish, at least when they are postverbal. (Alexiadou and Anagnostopoulou (1998) argue that preverbal subjects in these languages are also dislocated, although this is controversial.) See Baker (2003a) for a proposed parameter that has (23) as a consequence in languages like the Bantu ones but not in languages like Spanish and Greek.

Mohawk or Chichewa, and the difference can be attributed to a parameter concerning adjunction; I discuss this briefly in section 10.2.7 below.)

In Baker (1991; 1996), I pushed this line of reasoning a bit further, arguing that the reason why agreement forces dislocation in these languages is because it absorbs the case features of the head that it attaches to (Tense for subject agreement; the verb (or v) for object agreement). As a result, overt NPs cannot appear in the corresponding argument positions; only null NPs like pro or trace can. Overt NPs can appear only in clause-peripheral positions, to which the case filter does not apply. But this layer of the analysis is not particularly crucial to my topic here. To detect null agreement as opposed to absence of agreement, all that is needed is for there to be some kind of principled relationship between agreement—which one cannot always observe—and dislocation—which one can observe by looking at word order.

### 10.2.3 *Agreement and content questions*

The statement in (23) has other testable syntactic implications. It is known, for example, that wh-phrases can appear *in situ* in many languages, but they cannot be dislocated. This contrast is clearly seen in Kinande: wh- *in situ* is possible if and only if there is no object marker on the verb:

(24)  a. Kambale   a-gul-a       ebihi?
          Kambale   SM/T-buy-FV   what
          'What did Kambale buy?'
       b. *Ebihi   Kambale   a-bi-gul-a?
          what      Kambale   SM/T-OM-buy-FV
          'What did Kambale buy?'

The reason behind this contrast is presumably that wh-expressions are less than fully referential. As such, they cannot form a binding chain with a pronominal argument. This in turn means that they are not licensed in dislocated positions (Cinque 1990; Baker 1995; 1996).

Turning to Mapudungun, (25a) shows that, when the object marker *fi* is present, wh- *in situ* is impossible, as expected.

(25)  a. *Pe-fi-y-mi         chem?
          see-OM-IND-2sS   what
          'What did you see?'
       b. Chem   pe-fi-y-mi?
          what    see-OM-IND-2sS
          'What did you see?

(25b), in contrast, is grammatical. I claim that here the wh-expression is not left-dislocated (as it is in (24b)), but rather has undergone true wh-movement to spec,CP—a special specifier position that is universally at the left periphery of the clause. Only an NP with +wh-features can undergo such movement; ordinary, non-interrogative NPs cannot. When true wh-movement takes place, the empty category in the argument position is a wh-trace (i.e. a variable), not an inherently pronominal pro. Hence, the wh-expression does not need to be inherently referential to form a binding chain in this example.[8]

Consider now questions that do not have the object marker *fi*. Unlike Kinande, wh- *in situ* is bad in Mapudungun even when *fi* is omitted, as shown in (26a) (compare with (24a)).

(26)   a. *Pe-y-mi     chem?
          see-IND-2sS   what
          'What did you see?'
       b. Chem    pe-y-mi?
          what    see-IND-2sS
          'What did you see?'

The ungrammaticality of (26a) is explained if it contains a Ø object agreement marker. This object marker forces dislocation of the object by (23), and a dislocated NP cannot be a wh-expression. The badness of (26a) is then on a par with (25a) and (24b).[9] (26b) shows that the sentence becomes grammatical if wh-movement to spec,CP takes place, as expected.

---

[8] The need to explain the contrast between (25a) and (25b) is one of my motivations for saying that morphemes like *fi* are agreements, rather than incorporated pronouns, as Jelinek's version would have it. If *fi* were always intrinsically pronominal, then it should be incompatible with the non-referential wh-expression in both (25a) and (25b). But if *fi* is really an agreement element, the difference can be explained. In (23a), *fi* agrees with pro, and pro is inherently incompatible with the wh-expression. In contrast, *fi* in (23b) agrees with a nonpronominal wh-trace and there is no violation.

An anonymous reviewer points out that NPs that do not have intrinsic wh-features can undergo A-bar movement in some languages. They can undergo topicalization in English and Portuguese but not in Italian, and they can undergo focalization in English and Italian but not in Portuguese. Subtle theoretical considerations led me to say that neither focalization nor topicalization exists as such in languages like Mohawk, but only clitic dislocation (which can be associated with a variety of pragmatic values) (Baker 1996: chs. 2, 3). If focalization and topicalization were possible in Mohawk, then one could not derive the complete absence of non-referential quantifiers and NP anaphors in the language; these non-referential NPs could be possible if and only if they underwent topicalization or focalization—which is not what is observed. Mapudungun is identical to Mohawk in these respects. It would, however, be worthwhile to do a more fine-grained analysis of the left periphery in polysynthetic languages than I have ever attempted; see Legate (2002) for such a study of non-configurational (but not polysynthetic) Warlpiri.

[9] There is a difference between Mapudungun and Kinande at work here as well: agreed-with objects can undergo wh-movement in Mapudungun, but not in Kinande, as shown in (i):

By itself, this is not the strongest argument imaginable. It is perfectly possible that wh- *in situ* is ruled out in Mapudungun for reasons that have nothing to do with agreement and dislocation, as in English. But the facts in (26) are at least consistent with my hypothesis about zero agreement, inasmuch as they are identical to the facts in (25) with overt agreement. The exact parallelism suggests that the verb in (26) also bears an object marker in the syntax.

If this line of reasoning is correct, it has an even stronger consequence than the others we have seen so far. My first two arguments suggest that Mapudungun has a Ø object agreement. This one points to the further conclusion that the Ø object agreement is required on transitive verbs that have no other object agreement. If the Ø object agreement were merely an option, then (all things being equal) the string in (26a) should be possible without that marker, as (24a) is in Kinande. Apparently, then, some kind of agreement is required in Mapudungun. This suggests that Mapudungun really is a polysynthetic language in the sense of (1), even though this is partially concealed on the surface. I return to this in section 10.3.

### 10.2.4 *Agreement and non-referential noun phrases*

Wh-expressions are not the only noun phrases of dubious referentiality that are incompatible with dislocation. Various quantified noun phrases and nonspecific indefinites also have this property (Rizzi 1986b; Cinque 1990). As a result, non-referential quantified NPs are systematically absent in languages like Mohawk, in which all NPs are agreed with and dislocated (Baker 1995; 1996).

This contrast too shows up language-internally in Kinande. Common nouns in Kinande usually consist of three morphemes: a noun root, a gender/number prefix, and a pre-prefixal vowel. For example, the usual word meaning 'thing' is *e-ki-ndu* (AUG-CL7(SG)-thing). This pre-prefix is known as the 'augment vowel' in the Bantu literature. A two-morpheme version of common nouns also exists, consisting of only the gender/number prefix and the noun root. This short form of the noun has a limited distribution and a

---

(i) Ebihi  byo   Kambale  a-(*bi)-gul-a?
    what  FOC   Kambale  SM/T-OM-buy-FV
    'What did Kambale buy?'

I believe this to be of little significance. Since the Polysynthesis parameter in (1) holds in Mapudungun, there is no choice but to agree with a wh-expression. Kinande's 'No' setting of the Polysynthesis parameter means that agreement is not required, so it is possible to have wh-movement of objects without object agreement. Furthermore, when it is possible not to agree with a wh-expression, it seems to be preferred not to do so. This last observation is supported by the so-called anti-agreement effect found with subject questions in a variety of languages (see e.g. Ouhalla 1993).

special semantics: it is possible only in the domain of negation or some other scope-bearing element, and it is interpreted as an existentially quantified expression with narrow scope (Progovac 1993). These properties are illustrated in (27).

(27) a. Omukali   mo-a-gul-ire          *(e)-ki-ndu
        woman     AFF-SM/T-buy-ASP      AUG-CL7-thing
        'The woman bought something'
     b. Omukali   mo-a-teta-gul-a                  ki-ndu
        woman     AFF-SM-NEG/PAST-buy-FV          CL7-thing
        'The woman didn't buy anything' ¬($\exists$ x (thing(x))
           [woman bought x])

The crucial fact for current purposes is that there is no agreement with the augmentless non-referential object in (27b). When a suitable object marker is included and the object is dislocated, the augmentless version of the noun is impossible:

(28) *Ki-ndu,      omukali   mo-a-teta-ki-gul-a
     CL7-thing     woman     AFF-SM-NEG/PAST-OM-buy-FV
     'Anything, the woman didn't buy it'

The sentence becomes possible if *ki-ndu* is replaced by *e-ki-ndu*; in that case the NP is referential, and the whole sentence means 'The thing, the woman did not buy it.' This is just as we expect; the contrast between (27b) and (28) is like the English contrast between *I bought nothing* and *Nothing, I bought it.*

Mapudungun is systematically different. It has an NP-internal element *rumé* (Smeets 1989: 96), which is often translated as 'any' and appears in the scope of negation to express a narrow scope existential reading, as shown in (29).

(29) Pe-la-n        metawe   rumé
     see-NEG-1sS    vessel   any
     'I did not see any vessel'

One might naturally think of this as the Mapudungun equivalent of (27b) in Kinande. But, unlike the Kinande example, the existential expression is not limited to a particular syntactic position; it can come before the verb as well as after it:

(30) Metawe   rumé   pe-la-n
     vessel   any    see-NEG-1sS
     'I didn't see any vessel'

Assuming that the correct theory of free word order in head-marking languages is in terms of dislocation, then at least one of (29) and (30) shows that NPs with *rumé* can be dislocated in Mapudungun. Put another way, seemingly non-referential expressions have the same freedom of word order as any other (non-wh) NP in Mapudungun.

Even more tellingly, both orders are also possible when the object marker *fi* is included:[10]

(31)  a.  Metawe    rumé    pe-la-fi-n
          vessel    any     see-NEG-OM-1sS
          'I didn't see any vessel'
      b.  Pe-la-fi-n            metawe    rumé
          see-NEG-OM-1sS       vessel    any
          'I did not see any vessel'

This shows that it is a mistake to analyse NPs like *metawe rumé* as inherently non-referential expressions, on a par with augmentless NPs like *kindu* in Kinande. Rather, these must be ordinary indefinite noun phrases, which have no inherent quantificational force. Some independent support for this is that *rumé* can occur in positive polarity environments too, in which case it means 'very' and the NP as a whole can be referential (e.g. *rumé küme wentru*, 'a very good man' (Smeets 1989: 95)). As indefinite NPs, nominals containing *rumé* can take part in ordinary pronominal anaphora, and thus can form binding chains in dislocation structures. At the same time, they themselves can be bound by other items in the environment that are inherently quantificational, making them nearly equivalent to quantificational expressions themselves by the level of logical form. This is exactly how Baker (1995) analyses putatively quantificational expressions in languages like Mohawk, following Heim's (1982) treatment of indefinite NPs in English.

Given this analysis, we do not have a genuine minimal comparison between Kinande and Mapudungun in this domain, because the stock of indefinite/non-referential NPs in the two languages is somewhat different. Even so, (29)–(31) show once again that sentences with *fi* in Mapudungun are not syntactically different from sentences without it. This is consistent with the claim that all transitive sentences in Mapudungun bear an object agreement, whether it is visible or not. In contrast, (27) and (28) give strong evidence that Kinande does not require a Ø object agreement.

---

[10]  Elisa Loncon Antileo (pers. comm.) reports that the *fi*-less examples like (30) sound better than (31a) out of the blue, but agrees with my other consultants that (31a) is grammatical. I assume that, to the extent that (31a) is dispreferred, this is because of the pragmatic tension between object–verb order and the use of *fi* mentioned in n. 5 above.

### 10.2.5 *Agreement and extraction from objects*

My last probe into agreement in Mapudungun concerns the possibility of wh-extraction from NP. Under ideal circumstances, it is possible to extract a question word out of a complex NP in English, so long as that NP is a direct object (32a). It is never possible to extract a question word out of a dislocated NP, however (32b). This is a subcase of the adjunct island effect, which bars movement out of adjoined phrases quite generally.

(32)   a. Who do you think Chris will paint a picture of – ?
       b. *Who do you think, a picture of –, Chris will paint it?

Suppose that we apply this test for dislocation to Mapudungun. The language has two kinds of complex NP that could be relevant: possessed NPs, which contain a particle that agrees with the possessor (Smeets 1989: 170–2), and a kind of noun–complement structure that has no overt agreement (Smeets 1989: 173–4).

(33)   a. Pe-(fi)-n        Maria   ñi       metawe
          see-OM-1sS    Maria   POSS   vessel
          'I saw Maria's metawe'
       b. Küpa-i-n        kiñe   truran   Antonio   ñi         pizza
          want-eat-1sS   one    piece    Antonio   3.POSS   pizza
          'I want to eat a piece of Antonio's pizza'

When the object marker *fi* is present, causing dislocation of the object by (23), we expect extraction out of the NP to be impossible, just as in (32b). (34) shows that this is correct.

(34)   a. ?*Iney   pe-fi-y-mi                      ñi        metawe?
          who      see-OM-IND-2sS         POSS   vessel
          'Who did you see the metawe of?'
       b. ?*Tuchi   pizza   küpa-i-fi-y-mi                  (kiñe)   truran?
          which     pizza   want-eat-OM-IND-2sS      one       piece
          'Which pizza do you want a piece of?' (complement extraction)

If Mapudungun did not have a Ø agreement, there would be nothing to force the dislocation of the object in similar sentences without *fi*. Then extraction from the object could be possible, the way it is in (32a). But this is not the case; objects in *fi*-less sentences are as much islands to extraction as objects in sentences with *fi*:[11]

---

[11] See Baker (1996) for discussion of why examples like (35a) are not plausibly ruled out by the same principles that bar *Whose did you see pot?* in English.

(35) a. ?*Iney pe-y-mi    ñi    metawe?
       who  see-IND-2sS POSS vessel
       'Of whom did you see the metawe?'        (possessor extraction)
     b. ?*Tuchi pizza küpa-i-y-mi      (kiñe) truran?
        which pizza want-eat-IND-2sS one    piece
        'Which pizza do you want a piece of?'   (complement extraction)

On the other hand, (35) is just what we expect on the hypothesis that Mapudungun has a Ø object marker in addition to *fi*, and like *fi* it forces all objects to be dislocated.[12]

### 10.2.6 *Conclusion*

The five arguments in this section so far all have the same logical structure. Whether an object marker is present or not has a profound influence on the syntactic behaviour of the object in Kinande, determining whether it can be omitted, where it appears in the clause, and whether it can be a wh-word or an augmentless noun phrase. This makes sense under two assumptions: (1) agreement is syntactically significant, licensing null pronominals and forcing dislocation of overt NPs, and (2) when one does not see an object agreement in Kinande, there is no object agreement. Mapudungun is quite different. There too, sentences may or may not have the object marker *fi*. But this morphological variation has no detectable syntactic effect: objects can be omitted, freely ordered, negatively quantified, require wh-movement if interrogative, and count as islands for extraction both with and without agreement. Moreover, the syntax of all objects in Mapudungun is comparable to the syntax of agreed-with, dislocated objects in Kinande, not to that of unagreed-with objects. Therefore, I conclude that Mapudungun has a Ø agreement marker. Like *fi* in Mapudungu and the various object markers in Kinande, it counts as/licenses a pronoun and absorbs the verb's case, making it impossible for an overt NP to appear in argument position. It is identical to other object markers in every way except for its special phonological form.

---

[12] One also cannot extract out of objects in Kinande (or other Bantu languages), even when no object marker is present. I claim that this is for a different reason. Kinande does not have NP complements, only possessors, and in Kinande there is no agreement with the possessor. Thus the trace of an extracted possessor is neither lexically governed nor governed by an agreement marker in Kinande, so the extraction violates the Empty Category principle (or its successor) quite apart from questions of whether the object as a whole is agreed with or dislocated.

(ii) *Kambale yo    n-a-seny-a     [olukwi (lwa)  –]
     Kambale FOC 1sS-T-chop-FV wood    ASSOC
     'It's Kambale that I chopped his wood'
     (Compare: *olukwi lwa Kambale* 'wood of Kambale')

### 10.2.7 *Addendum on word order in Mapudungun*

There seems to be one significant difference between Mapudungun and other 'full agreement' languages such as Mohawk and Chichewa. Whereas Mohawk and Chichewa allow any of the six logically possible orders of subject, object, and verb, Mapudungun seems not to allow orders in which the object appears further from the verb than the subject does. Both Rivano Fisher (1991) and Loncon Antileo (forthcoming) report that in sentences of the form NP1–NP2–verb, NP1 is always interpreted as the subject—even if this interpretation renders the sentence infelicitous. Similarly, in sentences with the order verb–NP1–NP2, NP2 is always interpreted as the subject. My experience with texts is compatible with this: examples with object–subject–verb or verb–subject–object order are either nonexistent or much rarer than the other word orders. This detail is not particularly threatening to my main line of argument, because it holds regardless of whether the verb bears the overt object agreement *fi* or not. But it would be good to have an idea on the table about why it holds, to allay any fears that this undermines the framework as a whole.

My suggestion about this is that Mapudungun is a little different from Chichewa, Mohawk, and some of the other languages studied in Baker (1996), in that it allows dislocated NPs to adjoin to VP as well as to IP. Baker (1996: 3.2.2) has already claimed that there was low-level cross-linguistic variation in exactly which categories a dislocated NP can adjoin to: some languages allow adjunction to CP and DP, for example, whereas others do not. Given this, it is not far-fetched to imagine that there is similar variation in whether VP can be adjoined to. Now, assuming that the subject pro resides in spec,IP in Mapudungun (see Baker 2003b), an NP that expresses the subject argument cannot avail itself of the opportunity to adjoin to VP. If it did, the NP would fall within the c-command domain of the subject pro, in violation of Condition C of the Binding Theory. So VP adjunction is *de facto* an option for NPs linked to an object position only. At the same time, we might think that, whenever VP adjunction is possible for an object, it is preferred to IP-adjunction—perhaps for economy reasons, because the length of the binding chain consisting of the dislocated NP and the object *pro* is as short as possible in this case.[13] Overall, then, in a language like Mapudungun, putative objects will

---

[13] There are other possible explanations as to why NPs linked to the object position cannot adjoin to IP. Baker (2003a) shows that NPs linked to the subject position can adjoin to IP in Kinande, but NPs linked to the object position cannot, but can only adjoin to CP. My explanation in that article was that phrases adjoined to IP had to be licensed by having the content of the IP predicated of them, and this predication is possible only for subjects, which are the highest elements in IP. This explanation for Kinande could be extended to the parallel fact in Mapudungun.

typically adjoin to VP and putative subjects to IP. This gives the effect that objects always come inside subjects, even though both are freely ordered and have the syntactic properties of adjuncts rather than arguments. A representation of a typical example (from Rivano Fisher 1991: 168) would look like this:

(36)  $[[_{\text{IP}} \ pro_i \ [[_{\text{VP}} \ \text{langum-(fi)-y} \ pro_{k\text{VP}}] \ \text{domo}_{k,*i\text{VP}}] \ _{\text{IP}}] \ \text{wentru}_{i,*k\text{IP}}]$
      kill-OM-IND/3sS  woman   man
   'The man killed the woman' NOT: 'The woman killed the man'

This fits well with the observed facts of Mapudungun.

 This approach also makes sense of another, more subtle way in which Mapudungun differs from Mohawk and other polysynthetic languages. Consider an example like the following in Mapudungun.

(37)  Nü-(fi)-y    $[_{\text{NP}}$ Antonio ñi  chaketa]
  take-OM-IND/3S Antonio  POSS jacket
  'He took Antonio's jacket'

Baker (1996: 2.1.1) shows that, in examples of this form in Mohawk, the name embedded in the complex NP associated with object θ role can be understood as being coreferential with the understood subject of the clause. I took this as evidence that what looks like a direct object in Mohawk is really a dislocated adjunct, adjoined to IP, and thus outside the c-command domain of the subject pro. But, in Mapudungun, the judgement is different: (37) cannot be interpreted as Antonio being the person who took the jacket as well as the person who owns it. The Mapudungun intuitions on this point are like the intuitions in configurational English, even though the language is clearly non-configurational in other respects. The difference follows automatically from the suggestion that Mapudungun allows adjunction to VP but Mohawk does not. The NP *Antonio ñi chaketa* in (37) is preferentially adjoined to VP, not IP, and in this position it falls within the c-command domain of the subject pro in spec,IP. Therefore, the subject pro cannot be interpreted as referring to Antonio, by Condition C. This confirms the VP-adjunction analysis of semi-free word order in Mapudungun.

 Finally, it is significant that the judgements about coreference in (37) are the same regardless of whether the overt object agreement *fi* is generated on the verb or not. This is additional confirmation that sentences with *fi* and sentences without it have the same syntactic structure in Mapudungun. If we accept that the structures with *fi* have agreement and dislocation, then so do the structures without it.

## 10.3  How could null agreement be learned?

We have seen that the subtle distinction between absence of agreement in Kinande and presence of null agreement in Mapudungun is well justified. In one sense this is not too surprising, since a wide range of linguists assume the existence of null agreement in at least some cases. But it is fair to ask how children could learn whether the language being spoken around them has a Ø agreement marker or not. We can assume that children are like good scientists in being conservative in how they posit null structure—that they assume nothing means nothing unless there is either clear evidence or an innate imperative to the contrary. If so, the task of Kinande-acquiring children is straightforward: they assume from the start that no audible object agreement implies no object agreement, and they never have cause to change their minds. Mapudungun-acquiring children have a harder task. They cannot know from the start that they are learning Mapudungun rather than Kinande, so they too must conservatively assume that there is no agreement in transitive clauses without *fi*. What kind of evidence could move them away from this assumption toward the truth?

The most common justification for a null morpheme is a paradigmatic gap. A linguist analyses the verbal morphology and realizes that there are overt agreement morphemes for every relevant category but one. The last category (often the one with least-marked features) necessarily corresponds to a verb form with no relevant morpheme. In these circumstances it is natural to complete the paradigm by assuming a Ø affix that enters into the same obligatory agreement relation that the overt affixes do. Spanish verbs present a typical case of this kind (Table 10.1). Whether this paradigm-based approach is a good or sufficient reason for positing a null morpheme need not concern us here. What makes the Mapudungun case particularly interesting is that its paradigm does *not* have a gap of this kind. There is, after all, an overt third-person object agreement—namely, *fi*. Every box in the Mapudungun

TABLE 10.1.  Subject Agr for *hablar* 'to speak'

|            | Sing.        | Pl.            |
|------------|--------------|----------------|
| 1st person | habl-[a]-o*  | habl-a-mos     |
| 2nd person | habl-a-s     | [habl-a-ís]**  |
| 3rd person | habl-a-(Ø)   | habl-a-n       |

*Theme vowel [a] deletes before another vowel.
**Used in European Spanish only.

paradigm is comfortably occupied by a visible agreement morpheme, just as in Kinande.[14] And yet children apparently learn that Mapudungun has a *second* third-person agreement form that alternates with the first—which is surely a marked and unusual state of affairs. And they learn this without being able to hear the second form, because it is Ø. How could they do this?

It is unlikely that Mapudungun children learn that the language has a Ø object agreement in the same way that we did in section 10.2, by considering evidence from pro-drop, word order, constituent questions, indefinite NPs, and extraction from objects. The impossibility of wh- *in situ* and of extraction from direct objects is the kind of obscure negative evidence that is unavailable to the child under standard assumptions. The facts concerning negative sentences containing *rumé* are as likely to deceive as to enlighten, because children must also learn that *rumé* marks a potentially referential noun phrase, not a fully non-referential one. Without this piece of information, they could hear sentences like (29) and mistakenly infer that Mapudungun permits the absence of an object agreement. The only relevant facts that could be directly observed in natural discourse are that *fi*-less verbs allow pro-drop of the object and that the object is freely ordered with respect to the verb. But even this would not be so easy to observe. Object–verb order is less common than verb–object order (Smeets 1989: 456–7); and how could a child be sure that a sporadic object-initial example was not the result of focus or topicalization movement? Similarly, pro-drop is less common without *fi* than with it, and how could a child be sure that the *fi*-less verb was not being used as an intransitive? As anecdotal evidence, I can add that for six months I simulated the experience of a child learning Mapudungun by having access only to grammatical, unsystematically presented examples (the texts and examples in Smeets (1989)), and I failed to acquire the Ø object agreement under those conditions. A couple of carefully constructed consultant sessions were enough to clarify the situation—but children never get this opportunity, and would not be able to make the most of it even if they did.

I suggest that the null agreement of Mapudungun can be learned indirectly, by way of the Polysynthesis parameter in (1). This parameter is a 'macro-parameter' which places substantive conditions on every clause of every sentence of a language. As such, it has a pervasive effect on the morphology and syntax. The various repercussions of having the 'Yes' setting of this

---

[14] In fact, the Mapudungun paradigm has a rather unusual topology, because the language has a person/animacy hierarchy constraint, such that the object cannot be first- or second-person in the context of a third-person subject. Thus, object markers have a very limited paradigm, and express only third person. I take this to be independent of the basic point at hand. See Grimes (1985), Arnold (1996), and Baker (2003b) for extensive discussion.

parameter are explored in great detail in Baker (1996). It so happens that Mapudungun has several other salient properties of a polysynthetic language, which do not directly concern object agreement. Kinande, in contrast, does not have these properties. I claim that these other signs of polysynthesis are sufficient for a child to conclude that Mapudungun (but not Kinande) is a polysynthetic language. The child can then deduce that every Mapudungun sentence must have complete agreement inflection, and fill in Ø agreement morphemes as required by this hypothesis. In essence, they could use the Polysynthesis parameter to learn about agreement in their language in a top-down fashion, rather than using agreement to learn the Polysynthesis parameter bottom-up.

Perhaps the most obvious effect of the Polysynthesis parameter apart from agreement is noun incorporation. Moving the nominal head of the direct object NP to adjoin it to the verb is the second way to have a morpheme that expresses the object inside the word that contains the verb. Mohawk sentences with transitive verbs thus have either object agreement or an incorporated noun, but they do not need to have both, as shown in (2). Baker (1996) further argues that the positive setting of the Polysynthesis parameter is the unique trigger for syntactic noun incorporation, without which it would not take place. (Since noun incorporation generally has the morphology of compounding, rather than affixation, no obvious morphological selection requirements are at work.) Now Mapudungun does, in fact, have noun incorporation, as shown in (38).

(38)  a.  ñi    chao    kintu-waka-le-y          (Salas 1992: 195)
         my   father   seek-cow-ST-IND/3sS
         'My father is looking for the cows'
         (paraphrase:  ñi    chao    kintu-le-y          ta chi  pu       waka)
                       my   father   seek-ST-IND/3sS   the     PLUR   cow
     b.  Are-tu-ketran-e-n-ew          (Smeets 1989: 421)
         borrow-TR-wheat-INV-IND/1sS-DS
         'He borrowed wheat from me'

Smeets (1989) gives the impression that this is a lexical phenomenon, of minor importance to the language as a whole. She devotes only two pages to the topic and refers to it as a form of compounding found only with familiar, institutionalized events and nonspecific objects, and noun incorporation is not common in her texts. But Salas describes noun incorporation in Mapudungun as 'very productive', and paraphrases (35a) in both Mapudungun and Spanish with a definite object. Salas also claims that the most traditional Mapudungun speakers actually prefer the incorporated version, and attribute the unincorporated version to Spanish influence. Salas's description is compatible with saying that noun incorporation in Mapudungun can be 'Type III' (discourse sensitive) noun incorporation within Mithun's typology (1984)—a type that Baker (1996) takes to be syntactic. I agree with Salas on this point. Not only is noun incorporation very productive, but the incorporated nouns take part in coreference relationships in discourse. (39) gives an example in which the incorporated noun in the first clause introduces a new discourse referent and the pronoun in the second clause refers back to it.

(39)  Ngilla-waka-n.    Fei wula   elu-fi-n        Pedro
      buy-cow-1sS      then       give-OM-1sS     Pedro
      'I bought a cow. Then I gave it to Pedro'

(40b) gives an example in which the incorporated noun in the last sentence has a definite interpretation, referring back to the unincorporated noun in the first sentence of (40a).

(40)  a. Müle-y          mate.     Mate-tu-nge
         exist-IND/3S    mate      mate-take-2sS/IMPER
         'There is mate (a vaguely tea-like infusion). Have some'
      b. Fem-la-ya-n.    Juan   furk-üm-mate-y
         do-NEG-FUT-1sS  Juan   be.cold-CAUS-mate-IND/3S
         'I won't do it. Juan let the mate get cold'

Noun incorporation in Mapudungun thus satisfies Baker's criteria (1996) for being syntactic (see Baker et al. (2005) for detailed discussion). And the existence of syntactic noun incorporation implies that Mapudungun is a polysynthetic language.

In contrast, there is no question of Kinande having noun incorporation of any sort. Examples like (41) are completely out.

(41)  *Kambale    mo-a-tunda-gul-ire
      Kambale     AFF-3sS/T-fruit-buy-ASP
      'Kambale bought (some) fruit'

So Kinande is not polysynthetic, as we knew.

A second characteristic of polysynthetic languages that is not directly related to agreement concerns morphological causatives. Polysynthetic languages typically do have morphological causatives—not surprisingly, given their overall morphological complexity. But the morphological causatives of polysynthetic languages are usually quite restricted. In particular, only intransitive verbs can be causativized in prototypical polysynthetic languages such as Mohawk, Mayali, and Chukchee. Without going into details, the intuition behind my (1996) account of this was that languages that are constrained by (1) can have difficulties with 'valence-increasing' processes like causative. Since causative formation increases the number of arguments that the verb-word takes without increasing the agreement resources that the verb can use to express arguments morphologically, problems potentially arise. The most straightforward response to this difficulty is to avoid it, by having a type of causative construction that applies only to intransitive verbs.[15] A morphological causative process that applies to intransitive verbs creates at most a monotransitive verb, which it is within the powers of any polysynthetic agreement system to handle.

Mapudungun causatives behave just like those of canonical polysynthetic languages in these respects, to judge by the rather detailed study of Golluscio (2001). In addition to a less productive, potentially lexical causative *m*, Mapudungun has a productive causative affix *(e)l*. This can attach to intransitive verb roots, as in (42a). Mapudungun also has a causative morpheme *fal*, which can attach to transitive verbs, but gives them a passive-like meaning, in which the agent of the lower verb is not expressed. What Mapudungun does not have is productive uses of *(e)l* or *fal* with a transitive verb root in which both the subject and object arguments of the lower verb are expressed, along with the causer argument that comes in along with the causative affix. (42c), for example, cannot have a causative reading (but only an applicative one).

(42)  a. Kidaw-el-fi-i-n          Pedro
         work-CAUS-OM-IND-1sS   Pedro
         'I made Pedro work'
      b. ñi    patron    ngütrüm-fal-e-n-ew
         My    boss      call-CAUS2-INV-1sS-DS
         'My boss had me called'
      c. #Nentu-l-me-a-fi-n              ta    ñi    poñi
         take.out-CAUS-DIR-FUT-OM-1sS   PRT   his   potato
         'I made him dig out (his) potatoes'
         (OK as benefactive applicative: 'I dug potatoes for him')

---

[15] Other, rarer options are available. For example, Southern Tiwa allows causatives of transitive verbs, but only if the object of the transitive verb has been incorporated. Nahuatl allows causatives of transitive verbs but only if the lower verb has undergone passive. Both these strategies can be seen as ways of productively detransitivizing the lower verb so that it can be retransitivized by causative (Baker 1996: ch. 8).

Rather, the causative of a transitive verb in Mapudungun is usually rendered with a periphrastic construction that has two distinct verbs. Mapudungun is in this respect like canonical polysynthetic languages such as Mohawk.[16]

Kinande, however, is not like this. As in other Bantu languages, transitive verbs in Kinande can form morphological causatives in a very productive fashion:

(43)  Mo-n-a-seny-es-irie           Kambale  y'    olukwi
      AFF-1sS-T-chop-CAUS-ASP        Kambale  LK    wood
      'I made Kambale chop the wood'

Once again, Mapudungun can be recognized as a polysynthetic language apart from agreement paradigms, whereas Kinande cannot.

The last consequence of the Polysynthesis parameter that I discuss here concerns embedded clauses. Baker (1996: ch. 10) shows that the Polysynthesis parameter creates pressure for a polysynthetic language not to have embedded clausal complements (CPs). CPs do not bear person/number/gender features, so they cannot be agreed with; nor do they have a lexical head that can be incorporated. They thus have no way to satisfy the condition in (1). Polysynthetic languages respond to this pressure in a variety of ways. Some nominalize embedded clauses so that they can be agreed with on a par with ordinary NP objects (e.g. Nahuatl). Others incorporate a special noun that acts as a classifier for the clause (Mohawk). Still others apparently eschew clausal complementation entirely (Nunggubuyu). Mapudungun clearly behaves like a polysynthetic language in this respect. All embedded clauses must be nominalized by one of several affixes, the unmarked one being *n* (Smeets 1989: 238–9; Salas 1992: 161–2). One clear reflex of this nominalization is that the subject of the embedded clause is marked as a possessive expression. Another reflex, more to the point, is that the embedded clause can trigger agreement on the verb—either *fi* or Ø. Complement clauses in Mapudungun can never have a fully verbal head that is inflected for tense/mood and subject agreement. These properties are illustrated in (44).

---

[16] An anonymous reviewer points out that the badness of (42c) is also a kind of negative evidence, which may not be available to the child learning the language. Perhaps that is right—in which case the other polysynthetic properties mentioned must be enough to set the parameter in (1). But I would not be surprised if a kind of indirect negative evidence were available in morphological learning that is not available in syntactic learning. Children clearly remember words, and maintain lists of them in a way that they do not do for full sentences. They can learn morphemes and their subcategorization properties only by comparing words that they have heard and abstracting out the pieces that are in common. Now the internalized list of complete words that a Mapuche child uses to learn causative *(e)l* will contain only intransitive verb roots. I tentatively assume that a child can notice this and can draw the conservative conclusion that *(e)l* can attach only to intransitive verb roots.

(44)  a. Ayü-(fi)-n        Maria      ñi        amu-n
         like-OM-1sS       Maria      POSS      go-NOML
         'I like (it) that Maria left'   (lit. 'I like it, Maria's leaving')
      b. *Ayü-(fi)-n    Maria    amu-y
         like-OM-1sS    Maria    go-IND/3s
         'I like (it) that Maria left'

Again, Kinande is different in this regard. Kinande allows tensed CP complements with verbal complementizers and no hint of nominalization:

(45)  Mo-ba-nyi-bw-ire      ba-ti    Kambale  mo-a-gul-ire       eritunda
      AFF-3pS/T-1sO-tell-ASP  3p-that  Kambale  AFF-3sS/T-buy-ASP  fruit
      'They told me that Kambale bought fruit'

Such clauses cannot trigger object agreement on the Kinande verb—but then
agreement is not required, because Kinande is not a polysynthetic language.

   Overall, then, children learning Mapudungun are presented with various
kinds of evidence that Mapudungun is a polysynthetic language. Some of this
evidence concerns agreement and related phenomena: the fact that subject
agreement is required on finite verbs, the fact that object agreement occurs,
the fact that word order is free and that null anaphora is common. Other
evidence does not have anything to do with agreement directly: that noun
incorporation is possible, that morphological causatives are formed only from
intransitive verbs, that embedded clauses are nominalized. Taken together,
this range of facts justifies the global assessment that Mapudungun is a
polysynthetic language in the sense of (1). If it is a polysynthetic language,
then every transitive verb that does not have an incorporated object must bear
an object agreement. But there is no audible object agreement in some
sentences. Such sentences must therefore contain an object agreement
attached to the verb, the pronunciation of which is Ø.[17]

   Contrast this with children learning a Bantu language like Kinande or
Chichewa. What they are exposed to in terms of agreement is not very
different: subject agreement is required on finite verbs in Bantu too, object

---

[17] Note that if a null element existed but were somewhere else in the clause—say a null pronoun in
the object position, or a null topic operator in spec,CP—then (1) would still not be satisfied. What is
required is a null morpheme on the verb, not just any kind of null expression of the object.

One might wonder why Mapudungun has the unusual choice of Ø vs. *fi* for third-person objects,
from the perspective of discourse structure and/or language change. One hint can be gleaned from the
literature. The overt object agreement marker *fi* is said to be an incorporated version of the very
common pronoun/demonstrative particle *fey* (Smeets 1989: 193). As an affix, *fi* then might be a
comparatively new innovation in the language, which is gradually replacing the 'eroded' Ø form of
object agreement. The pressure to innovate a new, more apparent object marker might itself be
attributable to the Polysynthesis parameter.

agreement is possible, null anaphora is common, and free word order is found (especially in Chichewa). The only differences have to do with second-order correlations between these properties: the fact that free word order and object pro-drop are contingent on there being an overt object agreement. But these correlations could be due to accidental gaps in the data. The clearer difference in the linguistic experience of children learning Kinande or Chichewa is that they get no evidence outside the realm of agreement that the language is polysynthetic. There is no noun incorporation, morphological causatives are not restricted in transitivity, and embedded clauses are found without nominalization. African children can thus make an overall judgement that the language being spoken around them is not polysynthetic. As a result, there is no top-down expectation that agreement is required in every sentence. When these children hear sentences with no audible object agreement, they conservatively assume that those sentences do not contain object agreement. They acquire absence of agreement, rather than presence of null agreement. In this way, an otherwise difficult learning problem becomes solvable in principle, thanks to the Polysynthesis parameter.

It would, of course, require a separate study of the actual production and comprehension of children to determine whether this is in fact how they do learn the relevant properties. Such a study goes beyond what I can do at this point. But it is heartening to know that solving the problem of learning zero agreement is not impossible in principle.

## 10.4 Conclusion and implications

This case study has implications for ideas like the Polysynthesis parameter and the Pronominal Argument hypothesis at several levels.

First, the idea that there can be phonologically null agreement markers, which these ideas crucially depend on, has found support. A particularly interesting case of such a marker occurs in Mapudungun. Mapudungun allows overt agreement with third-person direct objects, in the form of *fi*, and this agreement has the expected effects of licensing pro-drop, allowing free word order, and forcing dislocation. But when overt object agreement is not present, the syntax of the clause is the same. This is strong reason to say that a null agreement marker is present in such cases. Mapudungun contrasts systematically with Bantu languages like Chichewa and Kinande. In these languages, whether an overt object marker appears or not does have a large impact on the syntax of the clause: the object acts as though it is dislocated if and only if the marker is present. This shows that having the option of leaving out an object agreement is quite a different matter from having a null object agreement, and both are attested in languages of the world. It is thus not possible to do without the theoretical device of Ø agreement. This result protects the infrastructure of theories like those of Jelinek and Baker, which depend on there being a very tight relationship between agreement and argument structure in some languages.

Second, I explored the question of how children, who have access only to positive evidence, unsystematically presented from a single language, could learn the subtle distinction between null agreement and absence of agreement. The answer, I suggested, is that this could be learned top-down, thanks to the Polysynthesis parameter. This parameter is a macro-parameter with wide-ranging impact on the syntax of a language. As a result, children can look at the overall character of the language they are learning to decide its setting. Once this is done, they can use their answer as a tool to evaluate gaps in an agreement paradigm, to see if they must be filled with Ø morphemes or not. If this is correct, then children are using syntactic parameters to learn morpho-logical paradigms, rather than the other way round, as has often been proposed in (for example) the literatures on pro-drop and verb movement. This has implications for the morphology–syntax interface. It suggests that syntax drives morphology, as in Distributed Morphology-style frameworks, rather than morphology driving syntax, as in more traditional, lexicalist theories. It also provides a new kind of support for the existence of macro-parameters like the Polysynthesis parameter. If there were no parameters that had a global effect on languages, then the kind of indirect learning that I have argued for would be impossible. There would be no legitimate reason for observing that 'this language, on the whole, looks polysynthetic, so therefore its verb paradigms must be such-and-such'. Questions of learning zero morphology would then be more difficult.

The kind of reasoning developed here has implications for the study of polysynthetic languages beyond the rather quirky case of Ø object agreement focused on here. Mapudungun is somewhat exceptional in having Ø agree-ment in more or less free variation with overt agreement for direct objects. But it is very common for languages to have a similar agreement gap in ditransitive sentences. The Polysynthesis parameter implies that there must, in some sense, be three agreements in such sentences (putting aside incorp-oration): agreement with the subject, with the direct object, and with the indirect object. But typically only two agreement morphemes show up overtly: one for the subject and one for the indirect object. The direct object is usually constrained to be third person and of unmarked gender, and it triggers no overt agreement (see (7) in Mohawk). Presumably this is the result of some kind of morphological constraint to the effect that in most languages a maximum of two distinct agreement 'factors' can be spelt out in the surface morphology. This looks like a more systematic and serious failure of agreement than the one we studied in Mapudungun. In particular, it is not sufficient to assume that Ø agreements can be learned by recognizing the holes in a paradigm, because there is no distinct ditransitive paradigm to begin with. One cannot recognize Ø agreement with third-person direct objects in the presence of indirect objects by parallelism with overt forms of agreement for first- and second-person direct objects in the presence of indirect objects, because there are typically no such forms. Sceptics of the Polysynthesis parameter/Pronominal Argument hypothesis conclude that there is no principled reason for saying that agreement is present in these cases. Nevertheless, the non-configurational effects of pro-drop, free word order, and dislocated syntax still apply to these apparently unagreed-with objects. (46) shows this for Mapudungun. (46a) shows that a simple ditransitive verb does not bear a third agreement morpheme (a second *fi*?) beyond what an ordinary transitive verb would have (see also Augusta 1903: 71). (46b) shows that the unagreed-with theme object can be pro-dropped (from Smeets 1989: 580). (46c) compared to (46a) shows that the theme object is freely ordered with respect to the verb. (46d) shows that wh- *in situ* is not allowed even for unagreed-with theme arguments.

(46) a. Iñché elu-fi-n        kiñe metawe Roberto
         I       give-OM-1sS one   vessel   Roberto
         'I gave Roberto a vessel'

     b. Ngilla-y      pichin mapu. Welu mapuche ngilla-ñma-la-fi-y
         buy-IND/3S little   land   but  Mapuche buy-APPL-NEG-OM-IND/3S
         'He bought a little land. But he did not buy it from a Mapuche'

     c. Kiñe metawe elu-fi-n        Roberto
         one  vessel  give-OM-1sS Roberto
         'I gave Roberto a vessel'

     d. *Elu-fi-y-mi           chem Roberto?
         give-OM-IND-2sS what Roberto
         'What did you give to Roberto?'

Similar facts hold in Mohawk and other polysynthetic languages. In short, there is generally no difference between the syntax of 'second objects' and that of other arguments, even though these second objects cannot be agreed with. Therefore, critics of the Pronominal Argument hypothesis conclude that this must be the wrong theory of non-configurational effects. And if they mean surface morphological agreement, their argument is correct.

But Mapudungun shows clearly that the Polysynthesis parameter should be interpreted as referring not to overt surface agreement, but rather to a notion of abstract, syntactic agreement. This agreement is related to surface agreement morphemes in systematic ways, but is not identical to it; rather, the syntactically significant agreements undergo the battery of impoverishment and readjustment rules of Distributed Morphology prior to being spelled as actual morphemes (Halle and Marantz 1993). The logic of objects in Mapudungun applies just as well to ditransitive constructions in a wide range of polysynthetic languages. Children get abundant evidence that Mapudungun and Mohawk are polysynthetic languages, without considering ditransitive clauses at all. They thus acquire the 'Yes' value for (1). When they see no overt agreement with the second object of a double object construction in a sentence like (46a), they are not particularly disturbed. Rather, they automatically posit a Ø agreement marker for the second object, and this induces non-configurational syntax in the usual way. In this domain, too, a global appreciation of the syntax can drive the learning of morphological details through the mediation of macro-parameters—not the other way around.

# References

Aarons, D. (1994). *Aspects of the Syntax of American Sign Language*. Ph.D. dissertation, Boston University.

Ackema, P. (2002). 'A Morphological Approach to the Absence of Expletive PRO', UCL Working Papers in Linguistics 14: 291–319.

—— and Neeleman, A. (2003). 'Context-Sensitive Spell-out', *Natural Language and Linguistic Theory* 21: 681–735.

Adams, M. (1987a). *Old French, Null Subjects and Verb Second Phenomena*. Ph.D. dissertation, University of California, Los Angeles.

—— (1987b). 'From Old French to the Theory of Pro Drop', *Natural Language and Linguistic Theory* 5: 1–32.

Ahlgren, I. (1990). 'Deictic Pronouns in Swedish and Swedish Sign Language', in S. D. Fischer and P. Siple (eds.), *Theoretical Issues in Sign Language Research*, vol. 1. Chicago: University of Chicago Press, 167–74.

—— Bergman, B., and Brennan, M. (eds.) (1994). *Perspectives on Sign Language Structure: Papers from the Fifth International Symposium on Sign Language Research, Salamanca (Spain), May 1992*, vol. 1. Leksand: Sveriges dövas riksförband.

Alexiadou, A. (1997). *Adverb Placement: A Case Study in Antisymmetric Syntax*. Amsterdam: Benjamins.

—— (1999). 'On the Properties of some Greek Word Order Patterns', in A. Alexiadou, G. Horrocks, and M. Stavrou (eds.), *Studies in Greek Syntax*. Dordrecht: Kluwer, 45–65.

—— (2000). 'Some Remarks on Word Order and Information Structure in Romance and Greek', in *Zentrum für allgemeine Sprachwissenschaft Papers in Linguistics (ZASPIL)* 20: 119–36.

—— (2003a). 'On Nominative Case Features and Split Agreement', in E. Brandner and H. Zinsmeister (eds.), *New Perspectives on Case Theory*. Stanford, Calif.: Center for the Study of Language and Information, 21–52.

—— (2003b). 'VSO and VOS: Microvariation in Pro-Drop Languages', MS, University of Stuttgart.

—— (forthcoming). 'On the Properties of VSO and VOS in (Some) Pro-Drop Languages', MS, University of Stuttgart.

—— and Anagnostopoulou, E. (1998). 'Parametrizing Agr: Word Order, V-Movement and EPP-Checking', *Natural Language and Linguistic Theory* 16: 491–539.

—— —— (2000). 'Clitic Doubling and Non-configurationality', *Proceedings of NELS* 30, 17–31.

—— —— (2001). 'The Subject-in-Situ Generalization and the Role of Case in Driving Computations', *Linguistic Inquiry* 32: 193–231.

Alexiadou, A. and Fanselow, G. (2000). 'On the Correlation between Morphology and Syntax: The Case of V-to-I', paper presented at the 15th Comparative Germanic Syntax Workshop, Groningen, Netherlands.

Anagnostopoulou, E. (1994). *Clitic Dependencies in Modern Greek*. Ph.D. dissertation, University of Salzburg.

—— (2003). *Double Object Constructions and Clitics*. The Hague: Mouton de Gruyter.

Anderson, S. (1992). *A-morphous Morphology*. Cambridge: Cambridge University Press.

Aoun, J., and Li, Y.-H. A. (1993). *The Syntax of Scope*. Cambridge, Mass.: MIT Press.

Ariel, M. (2000). 'The Development of Person Agreement Markers: From Pronoun to Higher Accessibility Markers', in M. Barlow and S. Kemmer (eds.), *Usage-Based Models of Language*. Stanford, Calif.: CSLI, 197–260.

Arnold, J. (1996). 'The Inverse System in Mapudungun and Other Languages', *Revista de lingüística teórica y aplicada* 34: 9–47.

Artstein, R. (1999). 'Person, Animacy and Null Subjects', in T. Cambier-Langeveld, A. Lipták, M. Redford, and E. J. van der Torre (eds.), *Proceedings of ConSole VII*. Leiden: Holland Institute of Linguistics, 1–15.

Auger, J. (1992). 'Français parlé et "fragmentabilité" des systèmes grammaticaux', paper presented at the XVᵉ Congrès International des Linguistes, Québec.

—— (1993). 'More Evidence for Verbal Agreement Marking in Colloquial French', in W. J. Ashby, M. Mithun, G. Perissinototo, and E. Raposo (eds.), *Linguistic Perspectives on the Romance Languages: Selected Papers from the 21st Linguistic Symposium on Romance Languages*. Amsterdam: Benjamins, 177–98.

—— (1996). 'Variation Data and Linguistic Theory: Subject Doubling in Québec Colloquial French', in A. Green and V. Motapanyane (eds.), *Proceedings of ESCOL 13*, 1–11.

Augusta, F. J. d. (1903). *Gramática Araucana*. Valdivia: Imprenta Central, J. Lampert.

Aulette, R. (1975). *201 Swedish Verbs*. Woodbury, N.Y.: Barron's.

Austin, P. and Bresnan, J. (1996). 'Non-Configurationality in Australian Aboriginal Languages', *Natural Language and Linguistic Theory* 14: 215–68.

Authier, J.-M. (1988). 'Null Object Constructions in KiNande', *Natural Language and Linguistic Theory* 6: 19–37.

—— (1992). 'A Parametric Account of V-Governed Arbitrary Null Arguments', *Natural Language and Linguistic Theory* 10: 345–74.

Bach, E., Jelinek, E., Kratzer, A., and Partee, B. (eds.) (1995). *Quantification in Natural Languages*. Dordrecht: Kluwer.

Baker, M. (1988). *Incorporation*. Chicago: University of Chicago Press.

—— (1991). 'On Some Subject/Object Non-asymmetries in Mohawk', *Natural Language and Linguistic Theory* 9: 537–76.

—— (1995). 'On the Absence of Certain Quantifiers in Mohawk', in Bach et al. (1995: 21–58).

—— (1996). *The Polysynthesis Parameter*. Oxford: Oxford University Press.

—— (2003a). 'Agreement, Dislocation, and Partial Configurationality', in Carnie et al. (2003: 107–34).

—— (2003b). 'On the Loci of Agreement: Inversion Constructions in Mapudungun', in M. Kadowaki and S. Kawahara (eds.), *Proceedings of NELS 33*. Amherst, Mass.: GLSA, 25–49.

—— Aranovich, R., and Golluscio, L. (2005). 'Two Types of Syntactic Noun Incorporation: Noun Incorporation in Mapudungun and its Typological Implications', *Language* 81(1): 138–76.

Baker-Shenk, C., and Cokely, D. (1980). *American Sign Language: A Teacher's Resource Text on Grammar and Culture*. Washington, DC: Clerc Books/Gallaudet University Press.

Barbiers, S. (forthcoming). 'Fronting in Imperative Clauses', in Van der Wurff (forthcoming).

Barbosa, P. (1995). *Null Subjects*. Ph.D. dissertation, MIT.

—— (1996). 'A New Look at the Null Subject Parameter', in J. Costa, R. Goedemans, and R. van de Vijver (eds.), *Proceedings of ConSole IV*. Leiden: Holland Institute of Linguistics, 375–95.

—— (2000). 'Clitics: A Window into the Null Subject Property', in J. Costa (ed.), *Portuguese Syntax*. Oxford: Oxford University Press, 31–93.

Basilico, D. (1998). 'Object Position and Predication Form', *Natural Language and Linguistic Theory* 16: 541–95.

Bátori, I. (1982). 'On verb deixis in Hungarian', in J. Weissenborn and W. Klein (eds.), *Here and There: Cross-Linguistic Studies on Deixis and Demonstration*. Amsterdam: Benjamins, 155–65.

Bauer, H., and Leander, P. (1922). *Historische Grammatik der hebräischen Sprache des Alten Testaments*. Halle: Niemeyer.

Beard, R. (1991). 'Lexeme-Morpheme Based Morphology: A General Theory of Inflection and Word Formation', Bucknell Occasional Papers in Linguistics 1. Lewisburg, Penn.: Linguistics Program, Bucknell University.

Bejar, S. (2003). *Phi-Syntax: A Theory of Agreement*. Ph.D. dissertation, University of Toronto.

Belletti, A. (1988). 'The Case of Unaccusatives', *Linguistic Inquiry* 19: 1–34.

—— (1990). *Generalized Verb Movement*. Turin: Rosenberg and Sellier.

—— (1999). 'VSO vs. VOS: On the Licensing of Possible Positions for Postverbal Subjects in Italian and Romance', paper presented at the Workshop on Inversion, May 1998, University of Amsterdam.

—— (2001). 'Aspects of the Low IP area', in L. Rizzi (ed.), *The Structure of CP and IP: The Cartography of Syntactic Structures*. Oxford: Oxford University Press, 16–51.

Bello, A. (1847). *Gramática de la lengua castellana*. Buenos Aires: Sopena. (8th edn. 1970.)

Benedicto, E. (1993). 'AGR, Phi-Features and V-Movement: Identifying Pro', in E. Benedicto and J. Runner (eds.), *Functional Projections*, University of Massachusetts Occasional Papers in Linguistics 17. Amherst, Mass.: GLSA, 1–18.

Benincà, P. (1983). 'Il clitico "a" nel dialetto padovano', in P. Benincà, M. Cortelazzo, A. Prosdocimi, L. Vanelli, and A. Zamboni (eds.), *Scritti linguistici in onore di Giovan Battista Pellegrini*. Pisa: Pacini, 25–32.

Benincà, P. (1984). 'Un'ipotesi sulla sintassi delle lingue romanze medievali', *Quaderni patavini di linguistica* 4: 3–19.

—— (1988). 'L'ordine degli elementi della frase e le costruzioni marcate: soggetto postverbale', in L. Renzi (ed.), *Grande grammatica italiana di consultazione*, vol. 1. Bologna: Il Mulino, 115–91.

—— (1995). 'Complement Clitics in Medieval Romance: The Tobler–Mussafia Law', in A. Battye and I. Roberts (eds.), *Clause Structure and Language Change*. Oxford: Oxford University Press, 296–325.

—— and Poletto, C. (2004). 'Topic, Focus and VT', in L. Rizzi (ed.), *The Structure of CP and IP: The Cartography of Syntactic Structures*, vol. 2. Oxford: Oxford University Press.

Bennis, H. (1986). *Gaps and Dummies*. Dordrecht: Foris.

—— (2000). 'On the Interpretation of Functional Categories', in H. Bennis, M. Everaert, and E. Reuland (eds.), *Interface Strategies*. Amsterdam: KNAW, 37–52.

—— (2004). 'Pronoms de la deuxième personne en néerlandais: contrastes en forme et en interprétation', *Franco-British Studies* 33–4: 10–22.

—— (forthcoming). 'Featuring the Subject in Dutch Imperatives', in Van der Wurff (forthcoming).

—— and Haegeman, L. (1984). 'On the Status of Agreement and Relative Clauses in West-Flemish', in W. de Geest and Y. Putseys (eds.), *Sentential Complementation*. Dordrecht: Foris, 33–53.

Benveniste, É. (1966). 'Structure des rélations de personne dans le verbe', in *Problèmes de linguistique générale*. Paris: Gallimard, 225–36.

Bergman, B., and Wallin, L. (1985). 'Sentence Structure in Swedish Sign Language', in W. C. Stokoe and V. Volterra (eds.), *Proceedings of the Third International Symposium on Sign Language Research. Rome, June 22–26 1983*. Rome/Silver Spring, Md.: CNR/Linstok Press, 217–25.

Berman, R. (1990). 'On Acquiring an (S)VO Language: Subjectless Sentences in Children's Hebrew', *Linguistics* 28: 1135–66.

Beukema, F., and Coopmans, P. (1989). 'A Government–Binding Perspective on the Imperative in English', *Journal of Linguistics* 25: 417–36.

Bianchi, V. (2004). 'On Finiteness as Logophoric Anchoring', in J. Guéron and L. Tasmovski (eds.), *Temps et point de vue/Time and Point of View*. Paris: Université de Paris X Nanterre, 213–46.

Blevins, J. (1995). 'Syncretism and Paradigmatic Opposition', *Linguistics and Philosophy* 18: 113–52.

Bobaljik, J. (2002). 'Syncretism without Paradigms: Remarks on Williams 1981, 1984', in G. Booij and J. van Marle (eds.), *Yearbook of Morphology 2001*. Dordrecht: Kluwer, 53–85.

—— (2003). 'Realizing Germanic Inflection: Why Morphology Does Not Drive Syntax', *Journal of Comparative Germanic Linguistics* 6: 129–67.

—— and Jonas, D. (1996). 'Subject Positions and the Role of TP', *Linguistic Inquiry* 27: 195–236.

Borer, H. (1980). 'Empty Subjects in Modern Hebrew and Constraints on Thematic Relations', in *Proceedings of NELS 10*. Ottawa: University of Ottawa, 25–37.

—— (1986). 'I-subjects', *Linguistic Inquiry* 17: 375–416.

—— (1989). 'Anaphoric AGR', in Jaeggli and Safir (1989a: 69–109).

—— (1995). 'The Ups and Downs of Hebrew Verb-Movement', *Natural Language and Linguistic Theory* 13: 527–606.

—— (1998). 'Deriving Passive without Theta Roles', in S. Lapointe, D. Brentari, and P. Farrell (eds.), *Morphology and its Relation to Phonology and Syntax*. Stanford, Calif.: CSLI, 60–99.

Bos, H. F. (1990). 'Person and Location Marking in Sign Language of the Netherlands: Some Implications of a Spatially Expressed Syntactic System', in S. Prillwitz and T. Vollhaber (eds.), *Current Trends in European Sign Language Research: Proceedings of the 3rd European Congress on Sign Language Research, Hamburg, July 26–29, 1989*. Hamburg: Signum, 231–46.

—— (1993). 'Agreement and Prodrop in Sign Language of the Netherlands', in F. Drijkoningen and K. Hengeveld (eds.), *Linguistics in the Netherlands*. Amsterdam: Benjamins, 37–48.

—— (1994). 'An Auxiliary Verb in Sign Language of the Netherlands', in I. Ahlgren, B. Bergman, and M. Brennan (eds.), *Perspectives on Sign Language Structure: Papers from the Fifth International Symposium on Sign Language Research*, vol. 1: 37–53.

—— and Schermer, G. M. (1995). *Sign Language Research 1994: Proceedings of the 4th European Congress on Sign Language Research, Munich, September 1–3, 1994*. Hamburg: Signum.

Bouchard, D. (1995). *The Semantics of Syntax*. Chicago: University of Chicago Press.

—— (1996). 'Sign Languages and Language Universals: The Status of Order and Position in Grammar', *Sign Language Studies* 91: 101–60.

—— and Dubuisson, C. (1995). 'Grammar, Order and Position of Wh-signs in Quebec Sign Language', *Sign Language Studies* 90: 1–23.

Brandi, L., and Cordin, P. (1989). 'Two Italian Dialects and the Null Subject Parameter', in Jaeggli and Safir (1989a: 111–42).

Bresnan, J. (1982). *The Mental Representation of Grammatical Relations*. Cambridge, Mass.: MIT Press.

—— (1994). 'Locative Inversion and the Architecture of Universal Grammar', *Language* 70: 72–131.

—— and Mchombo, S. (1987). 'Topic, Pronoun, and Agreement in Chichewa', *Language* 63(4): 741–82.

Britto, H. (2000). 'Syntactic Codification of Categorical and Thetic Judgments in Brazilian Portuguese', in M. Kato and E. Negrão (eds.), *Brazilian Portuguese and the Null Subject Parameter*. Madrid: Vervuert-Iberoamericana, 195–222.

Burzio, L. (1986). *Italian Syntax*. Dordrecht: Kluwer.

Cabredo Hofherr, P. (1999). 'Two German Impersonal Passives and Expletive Pro', *Catalan Working Papers in Linguistics* 7: 47–57.

Cabredo Hofherr, P. (2003). 'Arbitrary Readings of Third Person Plural Pronominals', in M. Weisgerber (ed.), *Proceedings of the Conference Sinn und Bedeutung 7*. Arbeitspapiere des Fachbereichs Sprachwissenschaften 114. Universität Konstanz, FB Linguistik (available under http://www.ub.uni-konstanz.de/serials/fb-sprach.htm).

Calabrese, A. (1992). 'Some Remarks on Focus and Logical Structures in Italian', in S. Kuno and H. Thrainsson (eds.), *Harvard Working Papers in Linguistics* 1: 91–127.

Cameron, R. (1992). *Pronominal and Null Subject Variation in Spanish*. Ph.D. dissertation, University of Pennsylvania.

Campos, H. (1986). 'Indefinite Object Drop', *Linguistic Inquiry* 17: 354–9.

Cann, R., and Tait, M. E. (1994). 'Raising Morphology: An Analysis of the English Auxiliary System', in C. S. Rhys, D. Adger, and A. von Klopp (eds.), *Functional Categories, Argument Structure and Parametric Variation*, Edinburgh Working Papers in Cognitive Science 9. University of Edinburgh, 1–23.

Cardinaletti, A. (1997). 'Subjects and Clause Structure', in L. Haegeman (ed.), *The New Comparative Syntax*. London: Longman, 33–63.

—— (2001). 'A Second Thought on *Emarginazione*: Destressing vs. Right Dislocation', in G. Cinque and G. P. Salvi (eds.), *Current Studies in Italian Syntax Offered to Lorenzo Renzi*. Amsterdam: North-Holland, 117–35.

—— (2002). 'Against Optional and Null Clitics: Right Dislocation vs. Marginalization', *Studia Linguistica* 56: 29–57.

—— (2004). 'Towards a Cartography of Subject Positions', in L. Rizzi (ed.), *The Structure of CP and IP: The Cartography of Syntactic Structures*, vol. 2. Oxford: Oxford University Press, 115–65.

—— and Starke, M. (1999). 'The Typology of Structural Deficiency: A Case Study of the Three Grammatical Classes', in H. van Riemsdijk (ed.), *Clitics in the Languages of Europe*. Berlin: Mouton de Gruyter, 145–233.

Carnie, A., Harley, H., and Willie, M. A. (eds.) (2003). *Formal Approaches to Function in Grammar: Papers in Honor of Eloise Jelinek*. Amsterdam: Benjamins.

Carstens, V. (1991). *The Morphology and Syntax of Determiner Phrases in Kiswahili*. Ph.D. dissertation, University of California, Los Angeles.

—— and Kinyalolo, K. (1989). 'Agr, Tense, Aspect and the Structure of IP', paper presented at GLOW Colloquium, Utrecht.

Casielles Suárez, E. (1996). '¿Es la interpretación arbitraria realmente arbitraria?', *Revista Española de Lingüística* 26: 359–77.

Chafe, W. (1976). 'Givenness, Contrastiveness, Definiteness, Subjects, Topics and Point Of View', in C. Li (ed.), *Subject and Topic*. New York: Academic Press, 25–56.

Chierchia, G. (1984). 'Anaphoric Properties of Infinitives and Gerunds', in M. Cobler, S. MacKaye, and M. Wescoat (eds.), *Proceedings of WCCFL 3*. Stanford, Calif.: CSLI, 28–39.

—— (1995). *Dynamics of Meaning: Anaphora, Presupposition and the Theory of Grammar*. Chicago: University of Chicago Press.

Chinellato, P. (2001). 'Agreement Disorders in Broca's Aphasia Sentence Production: A Bilingual Case Study', MS, University of Padua.

Chomsky, N. (1980). 'On Binding', *Linguistic Inquiry* 11: 1–46.

—— (1981). *Lectures on Government and Binding*. Dordrecht: Foris.

—— (1982). *Some Concepts and Consequences of the Theory of Government and Binding*. Cambridge, Mass.: MIT Press.

—— (1989). 'Some Notes on Economy of Representation and Derivation', in *MIT Working Papers in Linguistics 10*. Repr. in R. Freidin (ed.), *Principles and Parameters in Comparative Grammar*, Cambridge, Mass.: MIT Press, 1991.

—— (1992). 'A Minimalist Program for Linguistic Theory', MIT Occasional Papers in Linguistics 1, Cambridge, Mass.

—— (1994). 'Bare Phrase Structure', MS, MIT.

—— (1995). *The Minimalist Program*. Cambridge, Mass.: MIT Press.

—— (2001a). 'Derivation by Phase', in M. Kenstowicz (ed.), *Ken Hale: A Life in Language*. Cambridge, Mass.: MIT Press, 1–52.

—— (2001b). 'Beyond Explanatory Adequacy', MS, MIT.

Cinque, G. (1988). 'On *si* Constructions and the Theory of *arb*', *Linguistic Inquiry* 19: 521–82.

—— (1990). *Types of A-Bar Dependencies*. Cambridge, Mass.: MIT Press.

Coerts, J. A. (1992). *Nonmanual Grammatical Markers: an Analysis of Interrogatives, Negations and Topicalisations in Sign Language of the Netherlands*. Ph.D. dissertation, University of Amsterdam.

—— (1994a). 'Constituent Order in Sign Language of the Netherlands', in M. Brennan, and G. Turner (eds.), *Word-order Issues in Sign Language*. Durham: International Sign Linguistics Association, 47–70.

—— (1994b). 'Constituent Order in Sign Language of the Netherlands and the Functions of Orientations', in I. Ahlgren, B. Bergman, and M. Brennan (eds.), *Perspectives on Sign Language Structure: Papers from the Fifth International Symposium on Sign Language Research, Salamanca (Spain), May 1992*, vol. 1: 69–88.

Cole, P. (1987). 'Null Objects in Universal Grammar', *Linguistic Inquiry* 18: 597–612.

Collins, C. (1997). *Local Economy*. Cambridge, Mass.: MIT Press.

Collins-Ahlgren, M. (1990). 'Spatial-Locative Predicates in Thai Sign Language', in C. Lucas (ed.), *Sign Language Research: Theoretical Issues*. Washington, DC: Gallaudet University Press, 103–17.

Comrie, B. (1981). *Language Universals and Linguistic Typology*. Oxford: Blackwell.

Condoravdi, C. (1989). 'Indefinite and Generic Pronouns', *Proceedings of WCCFL* 8: 71–84.

Contreras, H. (1994). 'Economy and Projection', *ISRL 24*, University of Southern California and University of California, Los Angeles.

Corazza, S. (1990). 'The Morphology of Classifier Handshapes in Italian Sign Language (LIS)', in C. Lucas (ed.), *Sign Language Research: Theoretical Issues*. Washington, DC: Gallaudet University Press, 71–82.

Corbett, G. (1991). *Gender*. Cambridge: Cambridge University Press.

Corbett, G. (1994). 'Agreement', in R. Asher (ed.), *Encyclopedia of Language and Linguistics*. Oxford: Pergamon Press, 54–60.

Corblin, F. (1995). *Les formes de la reprise dans le discours*. Rennes: Presses Universitaires de Rennes.

Costa, J., and Galves, C. (2002). 'External Subjects in Two Varieties of Portuguese: Evidence for a Non-Unified Analysis', in C. Beyssade, R. Bok-Bennema, F. Drijkoningen, and P. Monachesi (eds.), *Romance Languages and Linguistic Theory 2000*. Amsterdam: Benjamins, 109–125.

Croft, W. (1994). 'Semantic Universals in Classifier Systems', *Word* 45: 145–71.

Culicover, P., and Jackendoff, R. (2003). 'Control Is Not Movement', *Linguistic Inquiry* 34: 493–512.

Damaso Vieira, M. (1995). 'The Expression of Quantificational Notions in Asurini do Trocará: Evidence Against the Universality of Determiner Quantification', in Bach et al. (1995: 701–20).

Davis, H. (1998). 'Person Splits, Phi-Features and Temporal Architecture', *GLOW Newsletter* 40: 83–4.

—— (2002). 'Identifying Agreement', *GLOW Newsletter* 44: 68–9.

DeGraff, M. (1993). 'Is Haitian Creole a Pro-Drop Language?', in F. Byrne and J. Holm (eds.), *Atlantic Meets Pacific*. Philadelphia: Benjamins, 71–90.

Den Dikken, M. (1992). 'Empty Operator Movement in Dutch Imperatives', in D. Gilbers and S. Looyenga (eds.), *Language and Cognition*, vol. 2. Yearbook 1992 of the research group for Linguistic Theory and Knowledge Representation of the University of Groningen, 51–64.

Deprez, V., and Pierce, A. (1993). 'Negation and Functional Projections in Early Grammar', *Linguistic Inquiry* 24: 25–67.

Diesing, M. (1990). 'Verb Movement and the Subject Position in Yiddish', *Natural Language and Linguistic Theory* 8: 41–79.

—— (1992). *Indefinites*. Cambridge, Mass.: MIT Press.

—— and Jelinek, E. (1995). 'Distributing Arguments', *Natural Language Semantics* 3(1): 123–76.

Doron, E. (1999). 'VSO and Left-Conjunct Agreement: Biblical Hebrew vs. Modern Hebrew', in A. Carnie and E. Guilfoyle (eds.), *The Syntax of Verb Initial Languages*. Oxford: Oxford University Press, 75–95.

—— and Heycock, C. (1999). 'Filling and Licensing Multiple Specifiers', in D. Adger, S. Pintzuk, B. Plunkett, and G. Tsoulas (eds.), *Specifiers: Minimalist Approaches*. Oxford: Oxford University Press, 69–92.

Drachman, G. (1997). 'Some Properties of Clitics with Special Reference to Modern Greek', in A. Alexiadou and T. A. Hall (eds.), *Studies on Universal Grammar and Typological Variation*. Amsterdam: Benjamins, 219–48.

Dupuis, F. (1988). 'Pro drop dans le subordonnées en ancien français', in P. Hirschbühler and A. Rochette (eds.), *Aspects de la syntaxe historique du français*, *Revue québécoise de linguistique théorique et appliquée* 7: 41–62.

Ebert, K. (1970). *Referenz, Sprechsituation und die bestimmten Artikel in einem nordfriesischen Dialekt*. Bredstedt: Nordfriisk Instituut.

Etxepare, R. (1998). 'A Case for Two Types of Focus in Basque', University of Massachusetts Occasional Papers in Linguistics 21: *Proceedings of the Workshop on Focus*. Amherst, Mass.: GLSA, 65–81.

Engberg-Pedersen, E. (1993). *Space in Danish Sign Language: The Semantics and Morphosyntax of the Use of Space in a Visual Language*. Hamburg: Signum.

—— and Pedersen, A. (1985). 'Proforms in Danish Sign Language', in W. C. Stokoe and V. Volterra (eds.), *Proceedings of the Third International Symposium on Sign Language Research, Rome, 22–26 June 1983*, 202–10.

Fabb, N. (1984). *Syntactic Affixation*. Ph.D. dissertation, MIT.

Faltz, L. (1995). 'Towards a Typology of Natural Logic', in Bach et al. (1995: 271–319).

Farkas, D. (1988). 'On Obligatory Control', *Linguistics and Philosophy* 11: 27–58.

Farrell, P. (1990), 'Null Objects in Brazilian Portuguese', *Natural Language and Linguistic Theory* 8: 325–46.

Ferdinand, A. (1996). *The Development of Functional Categories: The Acquisition of the Subject in French*. Ph.D. dissertation, Leiden University.

Fischer, S. (2002). *The Catalan Clitic System*. Berlin: Mouton de Gruyter.

Fischer, S. D., and Osugi, Y. (2000). 'Thumbs Up vs. Giving the Finger: Indexical Classifiers in NS and ASL', paper presented at the 7th International Conference on Theoretical Issues in Sign Language Research, 23–27 July, University of Amsterdam.

Fontana, J. (1993). *Phrase Structure and the Syntax of Clitics in the History of Spanish*. Ph.D. dissertation, University of Pennsylvania.

Foulet, L. (1919). *Petite syntaxe de l'ancien français*. Paris: Editions Champion.

Fourestier, S. (1999). 'Verben der Beweging und Position in der LSC: Eine Untersuchung von Komplexen Verben in der Katalanischen Gebärdensprache', *DasZeichen* 47: 84–100.

Franks, S. (1995). *Parameters of Slavic Morphosyntax*. Oxford: Oxford University Press.

Fukui, N. (1995). 'The Principles-and-Parameters Approach: A Comparative Syntax of English and Japanese', in T. Bynon and M. Shibatani (eds.), *Approaches to Language Typology*. Oxford: Oxford University Press, 327–72.

—— and Speas, M. (1986). 'Specifiers and Projection', *MIT Working Papers in Linguistics* 10: 128–72.

Giannakidou, A. (1997). *The Landscape of Polarity Items*. Ph.D. dissertation, University of Groningen.

Gilligan, G. M. (1987). *A Cross-Linguistic Approach to the Pro-Drop Parameter*. Ph.D. dissertation, University of Southern California.

Givón, T. (1975). 'Topic, Pronoun, and Grammatical Agreement', in C. Li (ed.), *Subject and Topic*. New York: Academic Press, 149–88.

Glück, S., and Pfau, R. (1998). 'On Classifying Classification as a Class of Inflection in German Sign Language', in T. Cambier-Langeveld, A. Lipták, and M. Redford (eds.), *Proceedings of ConSole VI*. Leiden: Holland Institute of Linguistics, 59–74.

—— —— (1999). 'A Distributed Morphology Account of Verbal Inflection in German Sign Language', in T. Cambier-Langeveld, A. Lipták, M. Redford, and E. J. van der Torre (eds.), *Proceedings of ConSole VII*. Leiden: Holland Institute of Linguistics, 65–80.

Golluscio, L. (2001). 'Syntax and Semantics of the Causative of Intransitive Constructions in Mapudungun', MS, University of Buenos Aires.

Goodall, G. (2001). 'The EPP in Spanish', in D. Davies and S. Dubinsky (eds.), *Objects and Other Subjects*. Dordrecht: Kluwer, 193–223.

Grimes, J. (1985). 'Topic Inflection in Mapudungun Verbs', *International Journal of American Linguistics* 51(2): 141–61.

Grimshaw, J. (1990). *Argument Structure*. Cambridge, Mass.: MIT Press.

—— (1997). 'Projection, Heads, and Optimality', *Linguistic Inquiry* 28: 373–422.

Grinstead, J.-A. (1998). *Subjects, Sentential Negation and Imperatives in Child Spanish and Catalan*. Ph.D. dissertation, University of California, Los Angeles.

Gruber, J. S. (1976). *Lexical Structures in Syntax and Semantics*. Amsterdam: North-Holland.

Guasti, M. T. (1996). 'On the Controversial Status of Romance Interrogatives', *Probus* 8: 161–80.

Guéron, J., and Hoekstra, T. (1988). 'T-chains and the Constituent Structure of Auxiliaries', in A. Cardinaletti, G. Cinque, and G. Giusti (eds.), *Constituent Structure*. Dordrecht: Foris, 35–99.

Haegeman, L. (2000) 'Negative Inversion, the Neg Criterion and the Structure of CP', in L. Horn and Y. Kato (eds.), *Negation and Polarity*. Oxford: Oxford University Press, 29–69.

—— (2003). 'Speculations on Adverbial Fronting and the Left Periphery', in J. Guéron and L. Tasmowski (eds.), *Temps et point de vue / Tense and Point of View*. Paris: Parix X/Publidix, 329–65.

—— and Ihsane, T. (2001). 'Adult Null Subjects in the Non-*Pro*-Drop Languages: Two Diary Dialects', *Language Acquisition* 9: 329–46.

Haiman, J. (1974). *Targets and Syntactic Change*. The Hague: Monton.

Hajičová, E., Partee, B., and Sgall, P. (1998). 'Focus, Topic, and Semantics', University of Massachusetts Occasional Papers in Linguistics 21: *Proceedings of the Workshop on Focus*. Amherst, Mass.: GLSA, 101–21.

Hakulinen, A. (1979). *Suomen Kielen rakenne ja kehitys* [The structure and development of the Finnish language]. Keuruu: Otava.

—— and Karttunen, L. (1973). 'Missing Persons: On Generic Sentences in Finnish', in *Papers from the Ninth Regional Meeting of the Chicago Linguistic Society*, Chicago: CLS, 157–71.

Hale, K. (2003). 'On the Significance of Eloise Jelinek's Pronominal Argument Hypothesis', in Carnie et al. (2003: 11–44).

—— Jelinek, E., and Willie, M. (2003). 'Topic and Focus Scope Positions in Navajo', in S. Karimi (ed.), *Word Order and Scrambling*. Malden, Mass.: Blackwell, 1–21.

—— and Keyser, S. J. (1991). 'On the Syntax of Argument Structure', MIT Lexicon Project Working Papers 34: MIT.

Halle, M., and Marantz, A. (1993). 'Distributed Morphology and the Pieces of Inflection', in K. Hale and S. J. Keyser (eds.), *The View from Building 20*. Cambridge, Mass.: MIT Press, 111–76.

Harley, H., and Ritter, E. (2002). 'Person and Number in Pronouns: A Feature-Geometric Analysis', *Language* 78: 482–526.

—— Willie, M., Barragan, L., and Tucker, V. (forthcoming). 'Light Verbs and the Mirror Principle', MS, University of Arizona.

Harris, J. (1991). 'The Exponence of Gender in Spanish', *Linguistic Inquiry* 22: 27–62.

Heim, I. (1982). *The Semantics of Definite and Indefinite Noun Phrases*. Ph.D. dissertation, University of Massachusetts, Amherst.

Hermon, G., and Yoon, J. (1990). 'The Licensing and Identification of Pro and the Typology of AGR', in *Proceedings of CLS 25*. Chicago: CLS, 174–92.

Hernanz, M. L. (1990). 'En torno a los sujetos arbitrarios de segunda persona del singular', in B. Garza and V. Demonte (eds.), *Estudios lingüísticos de España y de México*. Ciudad de México: Colegio de México / UNAM, 151–79.

Hird, G. (1977). *Swedish: An Elementary Grammar–Reader*. Cambridge: Cambridge University Press.

Hirschbühler, P. (1990). 'La légitimation de la construction V1 à sujet nul dans la prose et le vers en ancien français', *Revue québécoise de linguistique* 19: 32–55.

—— (1992). 'L'omission du sujet dans les subordonnées V1: Les Cent Nouvelles Nouvelles de Vigneulles et les Cent Nouvelles Nouvelles anonymes', *Travaux de linguistique* 24: 25–46.

—— (1995). 'Null Subjects in V1 Embedded Clauses in Philippe de Vigneulles Cent Nouvelles Nouvelles', in A. Battye and I. Roberts (eds.), *Clause Structure and Language Change*. Oxford: Oxford University Press, 257–91.

—— and Junker, M.-O. (1988). 'Remarques sur les sujets nuls en subordonnées en ancien et moyen français', in P. Hirschbühler and A. Rochette (eds.), *Aspects de la syntaxe historique du français*. Québec: Association Québécoise de Linguistique, 63–84.

Hoekstra, E. (1991). *Licensing Conditions on Phrase Structure*. Ph.D. dissertation, Rijksuniversiteit Groningen.

—— and Smits, C. (1997). *Vervoegde voegwoorden*. Cahiers van het P. J. Meertensinstituut 9. Amsterdam.

Hoemann, H. W., Hoemann, S., and Rehfeldt, G. K. (1985). 'Major Features of Brazilian Sign Language', in W. C. Stokoe and V. Volterra (eds.), *Proceedings of the Third International Symposium on Sign Language Research, Rome, 22–26 June 1983*. Rome/Silver Spring, Md.: CNR/Linstok Press, 274–80.

Holmberg, A., and Nikanne, U. (1993). *Case and Other Functional Categories in Finnish Syntax*. Berlin: Mouton de Gruyter.

—— —— (1994). 'Expletives and Subject Positions in Finnish', in M. Gonzalez (ed.), *Proceedings of NELS 24*. Amherst, Mass.: GLSA, 173–87.

—— —— (2002). 'Expletives, Subjects and Topics in Finnish', in P. Svenonius (ed.), *Subjects, Expletives and the EPP*. Oxford: Oxford University Press, 71–106.

—— and Platzack, C. (1991). 'On the Role of Inflection in Scandinavian Syntax', in W. Abraham, W. Kosmeijer, and E. Reuland (eds.), *Issues in Germanic Syntax*. Berlin: Mouton de Gruyter, 93–118.

Holmberg, A., and Platzack, C. (1995). *The Role of Inflection in Scandinavian Syntax.* Oxford: Oxford University Press.

Holton, D., Mackridge, P., and Philippaki-Warburton, I. (1997). *Greek: A Comprehensive Grammar of the Modern Language.* London: Routledge.

Hoonchamlong, Y. (1991). *Some Issues in Thai Anaphora: A Government and Binding Approach.* Ph.D. dissertation, University of Wisconsin, Madison.

Hopper, P., and Traugott, E. (1993). *Grammaticalization.* Cambridge: Cambridge University Press.

Huang, J. (1982). *Logical Relations in Chinese and the Theory of Grammar.* Ph.D. dissertation, MIT.

—— (1984). 'On the Distribution and Reference of Empty Pronouns', *Linguistic Inquiry* 15: 531–74.

—— (1989). '*Pro*-Drop in Chinese: A Generalized Control Theory', in Jaeggli and Safir (1989a: 185–214).

—— (1991). 'Remarks on the Status of the Null Object', in R. Freidin (ed.), *Principles and Parameters in Comparative Grammar.* Cambridge, Mass.: MIT Press, 56–76.

Huang, Y. (1995). 'On Null Subjects and Null Objects in Generative Grammar', *Linguistics* 33: 1081–1123.

Hulk, A. (1986). 'Subject Clitics and the Pro-Drop Parameter', in P. Coopmans, I. Bordelois, and B. Dotson Smith (eds.), *Going Romance: Formal Parameters of Generative Grammar II.* Dordrecht: ICP.

Hundertmark-Martins, M. T. (1998). *Portugiesische Grammatik.* Tübingen: Niemeyer.

Hung, H., Guilfoyle, E., and Travis, L. (1992). 'SPEC of IP and SPEC of VP: Two Subjects in Austronesian Languages', *Natural Language and Linguistic Theory* 10(3): 375–414.

Hyams, N. (1986). *Language Acquisition and the Theory of Parameters.* Dordrecht: Reidel.

—— (1989). 'The Null Subject Parameter in Language Acquisition', in Jaeggli and Safir (1989a: 215–38).

—— and Jaeggli, O. (1988). 'Null Subjects and Morphological Development in Child Language', MS, University of California, Los Angeles, and University of Southern California.

Jackendoff, R. S. (1987). 'The Status of Thematic Relations in Linguistic Theory', *Linguistic Inquiry* 18: 369–411.

Jaeggli, O., and Safir, K. (eds.) (1989a). *The Null Subject Parameter.* Dordrecht: Kluwer.

—— —— (1989b). 'The Null Subject Parameter and Parametric Theory', in Jaeggli and Safir (1989a: 1–44).

Janis, W. D. (1995). 'A Crosslinguistic Perspective on ASL Verb Agreement', in K. Emmorey and J. S. Reilly (eds.), *Language, Gesture, and Space.* Hillsdale, NJ: Erlbaum, 195–223.

Jelinek, E. (1984). 'Empty Categories, Case, and Configurationality', *Natural Language and Linguistic Theory* 2: 39–76.

—— (1993). 'Ergative Splits and Argument Type', in J. Bobaljik and C. Phillips (eds.), *MIT Working Papers in Linguistics* 18, 15–42.

—— (1995). 'Quantification in Straits Salish', in Bach et al. (1995: 487–540).

—— (1998). 'Prepositions in Northern Straits Salish and the Noun/Verb Question', in E. Czaykowska-Higgins and M. Dale Kinkade (eds.), *Salish Languages and Linguistics*. The Hague: Mouton, 325–46.

—— (2000a). 'Predicate Raising in Lummi, Straits Salish', in A. Carnie and E. Guilfoyle (eds.), *The Syntax of Verb Initial Languages*. Oxford: Oxford University Press, 213–33.

—— (2000b). 'Datives and Argument Hierarchies', in A. Carnie, E. Jelinek, and M. Willie (eds.), *Papers in Honor of Ken Hale*, MIT Working Papers in Endangered and Less Familiar Languages 1: 51–70.

—— and Demers, R. (1994). 'Predicates and Pronominal Arguments in Straits Salish', *Language* 70(4): 697–736.

—— —— (1997). 'Reduplication as a Quantifier in Salish', *International Journal of American Linguistics* 63: 302–15.

—— Midgette, S., Rice, K., and Saxon, L. (eds.) (1996). *Athabaskan Language Studies: Papers in Honor of Robert Young*. Albuquerque: University of New Mexico Press.

Jensen, J., and Stong-Jensen, M. (1984). 'Morphology is in the Lexicon!', *Linguistic Inquiry* 15: 474–98.

Kamp, H. (1981). 'A Theory of Truth and Semantic Representation', in J. Groenendijk, T. Janssen, and M. Stokhof (eds.), *Formal Methods in the Study of Language*. Amsterdam: Mathematisch Centrum, 277–322.

Kanerva, J. M. (1987). 'Morphological Integrity and Syntax: The Evidence from Finnish Possessive Suffixes', *Language* 63: 498–501.

Kärde, S. (1943). *Quelques manières d'exprimer l'idée d'un sujet indéterminé ou général en espagnol*. Uppsala: Appelbergs.

Kayne, R. (1994). *The Antisymmetry of Syntax*. Cambridge, Mass: MIT Press.

—— (2000). *Parameters and Universals*. Oxford: Oxford University Press.

Keller, J. (1998). *Aspekte der Raumnutzung in der Deutschen Gebärdensprache*. Hamburg: Signum.

—— (2000). 'AGR in der Deutschen Gebärdensprache', in H. Leuninger and K. Wempe (eds.), *Gebärdensprachlinguistik 2000. Theorie und Anwendung. Vorträge vom Symposium 'Gebärdensprachforschung im deutschsprachigem Raum', Frankfurt a.M., 11.–13. June 1999*. Hamburg: Signum, 33–66.

Kihm, A. (2006). 'Quelques notes à propos des groupes nominaux en Kriyol (créole portugais de Guinée Bissau)', in C. Dobrovie-Sorin (ed.), *Noms nus et généricité*. St Denis: Presses Universitaires de Vincennes.

Kinyalolo, K. K. W. (1991). *Syntactic Dependencies and the Spec-Head Agreement Hypothesis in Kilea*. Ph.D. dissertation, University of California, Los Angeles.

Kiss, K. E. (ed.) (1995). *Discourse Configurational Languages*. Oxford: Oxford University Press.

—— (1998). 'Identificational vs. Information Focus', *Language* 74(2): 245–73.

Kitagawa, C., and Lehrer, A. (1990). 'Impersonal Uses of Personal Pronouns', *Journal of Pragmatics* 14: 739–59.

Kleiber, G. (1994). *Anaphores et pronoms*. Louvain-la-Neuve: Duculot.

Koeneman, O. (2000). *The Flexible Nature of Verb Movement*. Ph.D. dissertation, Utrecht University.

Koenen, L., Bloem, T., and Janssen, R. (1993). *Gebarentaal. De Taal van Doven in Nederland*. Amsterdam: Nijgh & Van Ditmar.

Krifka, M., Pelletier, F., ter Meulen, A., Link, G., and Chierchia, G. (1995). 'Genericity: An Introduction', in G. Carlson, and F. J. Pelletier (eds.), *The Generic Book*. Chicago: University of Chicago Press, 1–124.

Kroeber, P. (1991). *Phrase Structure and Grammatical Relations in Tagalog*. Ph.D. dissertation, Stanford University.

Kuroda, Y. (1988). 'Whether We Agree or Not', *Lingvisticae Investigationes* 12(1): 1–47.

Lambrecht, K. (1994). *Information Structure and Sentence Form*. Cambridge: Cambridge University Press.

Landau, I. (2003). 'Movement Out of Control', *Linguistic Inquiry* 34: 471–98.

Lapointe, S. (1980). *A Theory of Grammatical Agreement*. Ph.D. dissertation, University of Massachusetts, Amherst.

Larson, R. (1988). 'On the Double Object Construction', *Linguistic Inquiry* 19: 335–92.

Lebeaux, D. (1988). *Language Acquisition and the Form of the Grammar*. Ph.D. dissertation, University of Massachusetts, Amherst.

Legate, J. (2002). *Warlpiri: Theoretical Implications*. Cambridge, Mass: MIT Press.

Levin, B., and Rappaport Hovav, M. (1995). *Unaccusativity*. Cambridge, Mass.: MIT Press.

Lewis, D. (1975). 'Adverbs of Quantification', in E. L. Keenan (ed.), *Formal Semantics of Natural Language*. Cambridge: Cambridge University Press, 3–15.

Lieber, R. (1992). *Deconstructing Morphology*. Chicago: University of Chicago Press.

Lillo-Martin, D. C. (1986). 'Two Kinds of Null Arguments in American Sign Language', *Natural Language and Linguistic Theory* 4: 415–44.

—— (1991). *Universal Grammar and American Sign Language: Setting the Null Argument Parameters*. Dordrecht: Kluwer.

—— and Klima, E. S. (1990). 'Pointing out Differences: ASL Pronouns in Syntactic Theory', in S. D. Fischer and P. Siple (eds.), *Theoretical Issues in Sign Language Research*, vol. 1. Chicago: University of Chicago Press, 191–210.

Loncon Antileo, E. (forthcoming). *Morfología y aspectos del mapudungun*. Mexico City: Universidad Autónoma Metropolitana.

Manzini, M. R. and Roussou, A. (2000). 'A Minimalist Theory of A-movement and Control', *Lingua* 110: 409–47.

—— and Savoia, L. (1997). 'Null Subjects without Pro', *UCL Working Papers in Linguistics* 9: 303–13.

—— —— (2002). 'Parameters of Subject Inflection in Northern Italian Dialects', in P. Svenonius (ed.), *Subjects, Expletives and the EPP*. Oxford: Oxford University Press, 157–200.

—— —— (forthcoming). *I dialetti italiani: morfosintassi*. Bologna: Il Mulino.

Mathur, G. (2000). *Verb Agreement as Alignment in Signed Languages*. Ph.D. dissertation, MIT.

Matushansky, O. (1998). *Le sujet nul à travers les langues*. Ph.D. dissertation, Université de Paris 8.

May, R. (1985). *Logical Form*. Cambridge, Mass.: MIT Press.

McCloskey, J. (1996). 'Subjects and Subject Positions in Irish', in R. Borsley and I. Roberts (eds.), *The Syntax of Celtic Languages: A Comparative Perspective*. Cambridge: Cambridge University Press, 241–83.

—— (1999). 'The Distribution of Subject Properties in Irish', MS, University of California, Santa Cruz.

—— and Hale, K. (1984). 'On the Syntax of Person–Number Inflection in Modern Irish', *Natural Language and Linguistic Theory* 1: 442–87.

McDonough, J. (2003). 'The Prosody of Interrogative and Focus Constructions in Navajo', in Carnie et al. (2003: 191–206).

Meier, R. P. (1990). 'Person Deixis in American Sign Language', in S. D. Fischer and P. Siple (eds.), *Theoretical Issues in Sign Language Research*, vol. 1: 175–90.

Meir, I. (1998). *Thematic Structure and Verb Agreement in Israeli Sign Language*. Ph.D. dissertation, Hebrew University of Jerusalem.

—— (2002). 'A Cross-Modality Perspective on Verb Agreement', *Natural Language and Linguistic Theory* 20: 413–50.

Milsark, G. (1974). *Existential Sentences in English*. Ph.D. dissertation, Cambridge, Mass.: MIT.

—— (1977). 'Toward an Explanation of Certain Peculiarities of the Existential Construction in English', *Linguistic Analysis* 3: 1–29.

Mithun, M. (1984). 'The Evolution of Noun Incorporation', *Language* 60: 847–93.

—— (1986). 'When Zero Isn't There', in *Proceedings of the 12th Annual Meeting of the Berkeley Linguistics Society*, Berkeley.

—— (1987). 'Is Basic Word Order Universal?', in R. Tomlin (ed.), *Coherence and Grounding in Discourse*. Amsterdam: Benjamins, 281–328.

Mohammad, M. (1990). 'The Problem of Subject–Verb Agreement in Arabic: Towards a Solution', in M. Eid (ed.), *Perspectives on Arabic Linguistics*, vol. 1. Amsterdam: Benjamins, 95–125.

Montler, T. (1991). *Saanich, North Straits Salish, Classified Word List*. Canadian Ethnology Series, Paper 119. Mercury Series. Chicago: Canadian Museum of Civilization / University of Chicago Press.

Moravcsik, E. (1978). 'Agreement', in J. Greenberg (ed.), *Universals of Human Language*, vol. 4. Stanford: Stanford University Press, 331–74.

Muller, C. (1984). 'L'inversion du sujet clitique en français et la syntaxe du sujet', *Linguisticæ Investigationes* 8(2): 9–47.

Munaro, N. (1999). *Sintagmi interrogativi nei dialetti italiani settentrionali*. Padua: Unipress.

Neeleman, A., and Van de Koot, H. (2002). 'The Configurational Matrix', *Linguistic Inquiry* 33: 529–74.

Neidle, C. J., Kegl, J. A., MacLaughlin, D., Bahan, B. J., and Lee, R. (2000). *The Syntax of American Sign Language: Functional Categories and Hierarchical Structure*. Cambridge, Mass.: MIT Press.

Nijhof, S., and Zwitserlood, I. (1999). 'Pluralization in Sign Language of the Netherlands (NGT)', in J. Don and T. Sanders (eds.), *OTS Yearbook, 1998–1999*. Utrecht: UiL OTS, 58–78.

Noguchi, T. (1992). 'A Note on Honorifics in Japanese', MS, University of Massachusetts, Amherst.

NSDSK (1999). *Nederlandse Gebarentaal op CD-ROM. Communiceren met dove kinderen thuis en op school, deel 3* [Sign Language of the Netherlands on CD-ROM. Communication with deaf children at home and at school, part 3]. Maarssen: The Bright Side of Life.

Oehrle, R. T. (1978). *The Grammatical Status of the English Dative Construction*. Ph.D. dissertation, MIT.

Ordóñez, F. (1997). *Word Order and Clause Structure in Spanish and other Romance Languages*. Ph.D. dissertation, City University of New York.

—— and Treviño, E. (1999). 'Left Dislocated Subjects and the Pro-Drop Parameter: A Case Study of Spanish', *Lingua* 107: 39–68.

Ouhalla, J. (1993). 'Subject Extraction, Negation and the Anti-Agreement Effect', *Natural Language and Linguistic Theory* 11: 477–518.

Oviedo, A. (1999). 'Versuch einer Beschreibung von Verben mit Klassifikatorhandformen in der Kolumbianischen Gebärdensprache', *Das Zeichen* 13: 420–31.

Paardekooper, P. (1948). 'U en UE', *De Nieuwe Taalgids* 41: 199–205.

Padden, C. (1988). *Interaction of Morphology and Syntax in American Sign Language*. New York: Garland.

Papanti, G. (1875). *I parlari italiani in Certaldo alla festa del 5. centenario di messer Giovanni Boccacci*. Livorno: Vigo.

Pesetsky, D. (1995). *Zero Syntax*. Cambridge, Mass.: MIT Press.

Pinto, M. (1997). *Licensing and Interpretation of Inverted Subjects in Italian*. Ph.D. dissertation, Utrecht University.

Pizzuto, E., Giuranna, E., and Gambino, G. (1990). 'Manual and Nonmanual Morphology in Italian Sign Language: Grammatical Constraints and Discourse Processes', in C. Lucas (ed.), *Sign Language Research: Theoretical Issues*. Washington, DC: Gallaudet University Press, 83–102.

Platzack, C. (1987). 'The Scandinavian Languages and the Null Subject Parameter', *Natural Language and Linguistic Theory* 5: 377–401.

—— (forthcoming). 'Embedded Imperatives', in Van der Wurff (forthcoming).

Plunkett, B. (1993a). 'The Position of Subjects in Modern Standard Arabic', in M. Eid and C. Holes (eds.), *Perspectives on Arabic Linguistics*, vol. 5. Amsterdam: Benjamins, 231–60.

—— (1993b). *Subjects and Specifiers in English and Arabic*. Ph.D. dissertation, University of Massachusetts, Amherst.

Poletto, C. (1995). 'The Diachronic Development of Subject Clitics in North Italian Dialects', in A. Battye and I. Roberts (eds.), *Clause Structure and Language Change*. Oxford: Oxford University Press, 295–324.

—— (1996). 'Three Types of Subject Clitics and the Theory of Pro', in A. Belletti and L. Rizzi (eds.), *Parameters and Functional Heads*. Oxford: Oxford University Press, 269–300.

—— (2000). *The Higher Functional Field: Evidence from Northern Italian Dialects*. Oxford: Oxford University Press.

Pollock, J.-Y. (1989). 'Verb Movement, Universal Grammar and the Structure of IP', *Linguistic Inquiry* 20: 365–424.

Postal, P. (1969). 'On so-called "Pronouns" in English', in D. A. Reibel and S. A. Schane (ed.), *Modern Studies in English*. Upper Saddle River, N.J.: Prentice Hall, 201–24.

Potsdam, E. (1998). *Syntactic Issues in the English Imperative*. New York: Garland.

Progovac, L. (1993). 'Non-Augmented NPs in Kinande as Negative Polarity Items', in S. Mchombo (ed.), *Theoretical Aspects of Bantu Grammar*, vol. 1. Stanford, Calif.: CSLI, 257–70.

Radford, A. (1988). 'Small Children's Small Clauses', *Transactions of the Philological Society* 88: 1–43.

Raposo, E. (1986). 'On the Null Object in European Portuguese', in O. Jaeggli and C. Silva-Corvalán (eds.), *Studies in Romance Linguistics*, vol. 24. Dordrecht: Foris, 373–90.

Rathmann, C., and Mathur, G. (2003). 'Is Verb Agreement the Same Cross-Modally?', in R. P. Meier, K. A. Cormier, and D. G. Quinto (eds.), *Modality and Structure in Signed Language and Spoken Language*. Cambridge: Cambridge University Press, 370–404.

Reinhart, T., and Reuland, E. (1993). 'Reflexivity', *Linguistic Inquiry* 24: 657–720.

Renzi, L., and Vanelli L. (1983). 'I pronomi soggetto in alcune varietà romanze', in P. Benincà, M. Cortelazzo, A. Prosdocimi, L. Vanelli, and A. Zamboni (eds.), *Scritti linguistici in onore di Giovan Battista Pellegrini*. Pisa: Pacini, 121–45.

Ritter, E. (1995). 'On the Syntactic Category of Pronouns and Agreement', *Natural Language and Linguistic Theory* 13: 405–43.

Rivano Fischer, E. (1991). *Topology and Dynamics of Interactions*. Lund: Lund University Press.

Rivero, M. L. (1994). 'Verb Movement and the Structure of IP in the Languages of the Balkans', *Natural Language and Linguistic Theory* 12: 63–120.

Rizzi, L. (1982). *Issues in Italian Syntax*. Dordrecht: Foris.

Rizzi, L. (1986a). 'Null Objects in Italian and the Theory of Pro', *Linguistic Inquiry* 17: 501–57.

—— (1986b). 'On the Status of Subject Clitics in Romance', in O. Jaeggli and C. Silva-Corvalán (eds.), *Studies in Romance Linguistics*, vol. 24. Dordrecht: Foris, 391–420.

—— (1991). 'Residual Verb Second and the Wh-Criterion', Geneva Generative Papers 2. Repr. in A. Belletti and L. Rizzi (eds.), *Parameters and Functional Heads*, Oxford: Oxford University Press, 1996, 63–90.

—— (1997). 'The Fine Structure of the Left Periphery', in L. Haegeman (ed.), *Elements of Grammar*. Dordrecht: Kluwer, 281–337.

Roberge, Y. (1986). *The Syntactic Recoverability of Null Arguments*. Kingston, Ontario: McGill-Queen's University Press.

Roberts, C. (1985). 'On the Assignment of Indices and their Interpretation in Binding Theory', in S. Berman, J. W. Choe, and J. McDonough (eds.), *Proceedings of NELS* 15: 362–76.

Roberts, I. (1993). *Verbs and Diachronic Syntax: A Comparative History of English and French*. Dordrecht: Kluwer.

—— (2004). 'The C-system in Brythonic Celtic Languages, V2 and the EPP', in L. Rizzi (ed.), *The Structure of CP and IP*, vol. 2. Oxford: Oxford University Press, 297–328.

—— and Roussou, A. (2002). 'The Extended Projection Principle as a Condition on the Tense Dependency', in P. Svenonius (ed.), *Subjects, Expletives, and the EPP*. Oxford: Oxford University Press, 125–55.

—— —— (2003). *Syntactic Change: A Minimalist Approach to Grammaticalization*. Cambridge: Cambridge University Press.

Roeper, T., and Rohrbacher, B. (1993). 'Free Pro-Drop in Child English and the Principle of Economy of Projection', paper presented at Conference on Child Language, Berne.

—— —— (2000). 'Null Subjects in Early Child English and the Theory of Economy of Projection', in S. Powers and C. Hamann (eds.), *The Acquisition of Scrambling and Cliticization*. Dordrecht: Kluwer, 345–96.

—— and Williams, E. (eds.) (1987). *Parameter Setting*. Dordrecht: Reidel.

Rohrbacher, B. (1992). 'English AUX^NEG, Mainland Scandinavian NEG^AUX and the Theory of V to I Raising', in *Proceedings of the 22nd Western Conference on Linguistics* (WECOL92).

—— (1994). *The Germanic Languages and the Full Paradigm: A Theory of V to I Raising*. Ph.D. dissertation, University of Massachusetts, Amherst.

—— (1999). *Morphology-Driven Syntax: A Theory of V-to-I and Pro-Drop*. Amsterdam: Benjamins.

Rooryck, J., and Postma, G. (2001). 'On Participial Imperatives', MS, Leiden University.

Roussou, A., and Tsimpli, I. (2002). 'Postverbal Subjects and Microparametric Variation', paper presented at the 25th GLOW Colloquium in Amsterdam.

Rupp, L. M. (1999). *Aspects of the Syntax of English Imperatives*. Ph.D. dissertation, University of Essex.

Ruzzante (1967). *Teatro*. Turin: Einaudi.

Safir, K. (1985). 'Missing Subjects in German', in J. Toman (ed.), *Linguistic Theory and the Grammar of German*. Dordrecht: Foris, 193–229.

Salas, A. (1992). *El mapuche o araucano*. Madrid: MAPFRE.

Samek-Lodovici, V. (1996). *Constraints on Subjects: An Optimality Theoretic Analysis*. Ph.D. dissertation, Rutgers University.

Schmaling, C. (2000). *Maganar Hannu: Language of the Hands: A Descriptive Analysis of Hausa Sign Language*. Hamburg: Signum.

Shlonsky, U. (1990). 'Pro in Hebrew Subject Inversion', *Linguistic Inquiry* 21: 263–75.

—— (1997). *Clause Structure and Word Order in Hebrew and Arabic*. Oxford: Oxford University Press.

Sigurðsson, H. Á. (1989). *Verbal Syntax and Case in Icelandic*. Ph.D. dissertation, University of Lund.

—— (1990). 'V1 Declaratives and Verb Raising in Icelandic', in J. Maling and A. Zaenen (eds.), *Modern Icelandic Syntax: Syntax and Semantics*, vol. 24. New York: Academic Press, 41–69.

Smeets, I. (1989). *A Mapuche Grammar*. Leiden: University of Leiden.

Smith, W. H. (1989). *The Morphological Characteristics of Verbs in Taiwan Sign Language*. Ph.D. dissertation, Indiana University.

Speas, M. (1990). *Phrase Structure in Natural Language*. Dordrecht: Kluwer.

—— (1991). 'Functional Heads and Inflectional Morphemes', *Linguistic Review* 8: 389–417.

—— (1994). 'Null Arguments in a Theory of Economy of Projections', *University of Massachusetts Occasional Papers in Linguistics* 17: 179–208.

—— (1996). 'Null Objects in Functional Projections', in J. Rooryck and L. Zaring (eds.), *Phrase Structure and the Lexicon*. Dordrecht: Kluwer, 187–211.

Sprouse, R., and Vance, B. (1999). 'An Explanation for the Decline of Null Pronouns in Certain Germanic and Romance Languages', in M. deGraff (ed.), *Language Creation and Language Change*. Cambridge, Mass.: MIT Press, 257–84.

Stokoe, W. C. (1960). *Sign Language Structure: An Outline of the Visual Communication Systems of the American Deaf*. Buffalo: Dept. of Anthropology and Linguistics, University of Buffalo.

Suñer, M. (1983). 'Pro$_{arb}$', *Linguistic Inquiry* 14: 188–91.

—— (2002). 'The Lexical Preverbal Subject in a Null Subject Language: Where Art Thou?', MS, Cornell University.

Supalla, T. R. (1982). *Structure and Acquisition of Verbs of Motion and Location in American Sign Language*. Ph.D. dissertation, University of California, San Diego.

—— (1986). 'The Classifier System in American Sign Language', in C. Craig (ed.), *Noun Classes and Categorization*. Philadelphia: Benjamins, 181–214.

Sutton-Spence, R., and Woll, B. (1999). *The Linguistics of British Sign Language: An Introduction*. Cambridge: Cambridge University Press.

Svenonius, P. (ed.). (2000). *Subjects, Expletives, and the Extended Projection Principle.* Oxford: Oxford University Press.

Tait, M. E., and Cann, R. (1990). 'On Empty Subjects', in E. Engdahl et al. (eds.), *Parametric Variation in Germanic and Romance: Proceedings from a DYANA Workshop.* Centre for Cognitive Science, University of Edinburgh.

Talmy, L. (1985). 'Lexicalization Patterns', in T. Shopen (ed.), *Typology and Syntactic Description.* Chicago: Chicago University Press, 57–149.

Taraldsen, T. (1980). *On the Nominative Island Condition, Vacuous Application, and the That-Trace Filter.* Bloomington: Indiana University Linguistics Club.

Tateishi, K. (1989). 'Subjects, SPEC, and DP in Japanese', in J. McDonough and B. Plunkett (eds.), *Proceedings of NELS 17.* Amherst, Mass.: GLSA, 619–40.

—— (1991). *The Syntax of Subjects.* Ph.D. dissertation, University of Massachusetts, Amherst.

Tervoort, B. T. (1953). *Structurele Analyze van Visueel Taalgebruik binnen een Groep Dove Kinderen.* [Structural analysis of visual language use within a group of deaf children.] Ph.D. dissertation, University of Amsterdam.

Thompson, C. (1996). 'The History and Function of the *yi-/bi-* Alternation in Athabaskan', in E. Jelinek, S. Midgette, K. Rice, and L. Saxon (eds.), *Athabaskan Language Studies: Papers in Honor of Robert Young.* Albuquerque: University of New Mexico Press, 81–100.

Thompson, R. and Emmorey, K. (2003). 'The Relationship of Eyegaze and Agreement Morphology in ASL: An Eye-Tracking Study', paper presented at the Linguistic Society of America meeting, Atlanta, Ga.

Toivonen, I. (2000). 'The Morphosyntax of Finnish Possessives', *Natural Language and Linguistic Theory* 18: 579–609.

—— (2001). *The Phrase Structure of Non-Projecting Words.* Ph.D. dissertation, Stanford University.

Tomaselli, A. (1990). *La sintassi del verbo finito nelle lingue germaniche.* Padua: CLESP.

Tortora, C. (1997). *The Syntax and Semantics of the Weak Locative.* Ph.D. dissertation, University of Delaware.

Tóth, I. (2000). *Inflected Infinitives in Hungarian.* Ph.D. dissertation, Katholieke Universiteit Brabant, Tilburg.

—— (2001). 'Licensing and Interpretation of Phonologically Null Elements', MS, Pazmany Peter Catholic University, Budapest.

Travis, L. (1984). *Parameters and Effects of Word Order Variation.* Ph.D. dissertation, MIT.

Tsao, F. (1977). *A Functional Study of Topic in Chinese: The First Step toward Discourse Analysis.* Ph.D. dissertation, University of Southern California.

Ud Deen, K. (2003). 'On the Omission of Agreement: The EPP and Null Constants', paper presented at the Lisbon Workshop on Agreement, Universidade Nova de Lisboa.

Vainikka, A. (1989). *Deriving Syntactic Representations in Finnish.* PhD. dissertation, University of Massachusetts, Amherst.

—— and Levy, Y. (1999). 'Empty Subjects in Finnish and Hebrew', *Natural Language and Linguistic Theory* 17: 613–71.

Van der Wurff, W. (ed.) (forthcoming). *Imperative Clauses in Generative Grammar.* Amsterdam: Benjamins.

Van Hoek, K. (1996). 'Conceptual Locations for Reference in American Sign Language', in G. Fauconnier and E. Sweetser (eds.), *Spaces, Worlds, and Grammar.* Chicago: Chicago University Press, 334–50.

Vance, B. (1989). *Null Subjects and Syntactic Change in Medieval French.* Ph.D. dissertation, Cornell University.

—— (1995). 'On the Decline of Verb Movement to Comp in Old and Middle French', in I. Roberts and A. Battye (eds.), *Clause Structure and Language Change.* Oxford: Oxford University Press, 173–99.

—— (1999). *Syntactic Change in Medieval France.* Dordrecht: Kluwer.

Vanelli, L. (1987). 'I pronomi soggetto nei dialetti italiani settentrionali dal Medio Evo ad oggi', *Medioevo Romanzo* 13: 173–211.

—— Renzi, L., and Benincà, P. (1985). 'Typologies des pronoms sujets dans les langues romanes', *Quaderni patavini di linguistica* 5: 49–66.

Vasishta, M., Woodward, J., and DeSantis, S. (1985). *An Introduction to the Bangalore Variety of Indian Sign Language.* Washington, DC: Gallaudet University Press.

Vermeerbergen, M. (1996). *ROOD KOOL TIEN PERSOON IN* [RED CABBAGE TEN PERSON IN]. Ph.D. dissertation, Vrije Universiteit Brussel.

Vikner, S. (1995). *Verb Movement and Expletive Subjects in the Germanic Languages.* Oxford: Oxford University Press.

Vilkuna, M. (1989). *Free Word Order in Finnish: Its Syntax and Discourse Functions.* Helsinki: Suomalaisen Kirjallisuuden Seura.

—— (1995). 'Discourse Configurationality in Finnish', in K. E. Kiss (ed.), *Discourse Configurational Languages.* Oxford: Oxford University Press, 244–68.

Wallin, L. (1996). *Polysynthetic Signs in Swedish Sign Language.* Stockholm: University of Stockholm.

Weerman, F. (1989). *The V2 Conspiracy.* Dordrecht: Foris.

Williams, E. (1989). 'The Anaphoric Nature of Theta-Roles', *Linguistic Inquiry* 30: 425–56.

Willie, M. (1991). *Navajo Pronouns and Obviation.* Ph.D. dissertation, University of Arizona, Tucson.

—— and Jelinek, E. (2000). 'Navajo as a Discourse Configurational Language', in T. Fernald and P. Platero (eds.), *The Athabaskan Languages: Perspectives on a Native American Language Family.* Oxford: Oxford University Press, 252–87.

Wind, M. de (1995). *Inversion in French.* Ph.D. dissertation, Groningen University.

*WNT* (1984). *Woordenboek der Nederlandsche Taal.* Leiden: Nijhoff.

Wolf, H. (2003). 'Imperatieven in de verleden tijd', *Taal en Tongval* 55: 168–88.

Yoon, J. (1985). 'On the Treatment of Empty Categories in Topic Prominent Languages', MS, University of Illinois.

Young, R., and Morgan, W. (1976). *The Navajo Language*. Education Division, U. S. Indian Service. Salt Lake City: Deseret Book Company.

—— —— (1987). *The Navajo Language: A Grammar and Colloquial Dictionary*, rev. edn. Albuquerque: University of New Mexico Press.

Zribi-Hertz, A. (1994). 'La syntaxe des clitiques nominatifs en français', in G. Kleiber and G. Roques (eds.), *Travaux de linguistique et de philosophie*, vol. 32. Strasbourg–Nancy: Klincksieck, 133–47.

Zubizarreta, M.-L. (1994). 'Grammatical Representation of Topic and Focus: Implications for the Structure of the Clause', *Cuadernos de Lingüística del Instituto Universitario Ortega y Gasset* 2: 181–208.

—— (1998). *Prosody, Focus and Word Order*. Cambridge, Mass.: MIT Press.

—— (1999). 'Word Order in Spanish and the Nature of Nominative Case', in K. Johnson and I. Roberts (eds.), *Beyond Principles and Parameters*. Dordrecht: Kluwer, 223–50.

Zwart, J. W. (1993). *Dutch Syntax*. Groningen Dissertations in Linguistics 10. University of Groningen.

—— (2001). 'Syntactic and Phonological Verb Movement', *Syntax* 4: 34–62.

Zwitserlood, I. (2003a). 'Word Formation Below and Above Little x: Evidence from Sign Language of the Netherlands', in A. Dahl, K. Bentzen, and P. Svenonius (eds.), *Nordlyd Tromsø University Working Papers on Language and Linguistics. Proceedings of the 19th Scandinavian Conference of Linguistics*, vol. 30: 488–502.

—— (2003b). *Classifying Hand Configurations in Nederlandse Gebarentaal (Sign Language of the Netherlands)*. Ph.D. dissertation, Utrecht University.

# Index